# THE MYSTICAL POETS
# OF THE ENGLISH CHURCH

# THE MYSTICAL POETS

OF THE

# ENGLISH CHURCH

BY

## PERCY H. OSMOND

"Many are the wand-bearers but few the God-possessed."—PLATO.

"When anything is read or sung or prayed that is more exalted and
fervent than your heart is, if you make this an occasion of a further
sinking down in the spirit of the Publican, you will then be helped and
highly blessed by those prayers and praises which seem only to fit, and
belong to, a better heart than yours."—WILLIAM LAW.

LONDON
SOCIETY FOR PROMOTING
CHRISTIAN KNOWLEDGE
NEW YORK: THE MACMILLAN CO.
1919

# PREFACE

THE author was led to begin the studies which preceded the writing of this book by the words of Dr. Inge in the Preface to his Bampton Lectures on *Christian Mysticism*: " In verse the lofty idealism and strong religious bent of our race have produced a series of poet-mystics such as no other country can rival ; it has not been possible in these Lectures to do justice to George Herbert, Vaughan the Silurist, Quarles, Crawshaw, and others who have all drunk of the same well". It would be ludicrous for the present writer to hope to emulate, in the remotest degree, Dr. Inge's brilliant scholarship and philosophic insight. As a matter of fact, this book is little more than an Anthology compiled from the mystical poets of the English Church, with briefer extracts from some outside that communion. Wherever possible, the compiler has elucidated the extracts by quotations from the prose-writings of the respective poets themselves. This method obviates the danger, which is a very real one to-day, that the writings of the mystics themselves should be neglected in favour of what others say about them. When the present writer has added his own comments, he has aimed at being popular, in the best sense of the word, but he is well aware that he has not always escaped the danger of being superficial. A further danger which he has certainly endeavoured to escape, but possibly not altogether successfully, is that of unconscious plagiarism. In dealing with a subject which has been as widely discussed as mysticism has been during recent years, he could hardly fail to reproduce thoughts, and may possibly have reproduced even words, which have been suggested to his mind by other writers. Whenever he has consciously borrowed, he has, of course, acknowledged his obligation ; but here he would express, in general terms, his deep indebtedness to the following writers on mysticism : Dr. Inge, Miss Underhill, Baron von Hügel, Bishops Chandler and Mercer, and various contributors to *The Seeker : a Quarterly Magazine of Christian Mysticism.*

On another point he would put himself right with his readers : he hopes it will be clearly understood that he writes, not with authority, but as the scribes. His own spiritual life is being lived on levels far lower, alas ! than the heights from which the mystics speak, and few can be more keenly alive than he is to the danger of unreality in writing on experiences which are not contained in one's own spiritual life. But it is not unreal to strive to make our own what is best in the thoughts of other people. There are, no doubt, some who can dwell amongst eternal verities without external aid, but most of us need such assistance. William Law's words are pre-eminently true of the poets dealt with in this book : " It is a great unhappiness to be unacquainted with these writers ". Some of them are numbered among the prophets of our race ; and even the dullest of them can stimulate and refresh. Their messages are not always marked by loftiness of utterance, but none of us need rise up from reading them without finding ourselves better men and women.

The title of this book may be assailed from two points of view. On the one hand, purists in mysticism may challenge the right of some of the poets discussed to the epithet "mystical". The writer is not unaware of the difference between mysticism and vital religion, or idealism, or allegorism, and he has tried to bring out those differences ; but he has not thought it right to deny the term "mystical" to some who have, at any rate, a close affinity. to that denomination, even though they may never have known that maximum intensity of religious experience that the greatest mystics have achieved. On the other hand, the literary critic may object that the word "poet" is a misnomer as applied to more than one of the verse-writers included. Undoubtedly, some of them have written woeful verse, viewed purely as verse,—what Dr. Johnson called "metrical devotions" ; but the author's main object has not been literary edification, and he has not scrupled to include some whose muse has hardly been equal to the greatness of their theme. Finally—to disarm yet another possible criticism—he would explain that certain poets outside the Anglican communion have been briefly noticed, in the hope of making the book a little more comprehensive —poets whose importance would have demanded much fuller treatment, had the scope of the work been wider.

It is sincerely hoped and believed that no copyright has been infringed without permission. For leave to quote lengthy extracts most grateful acknowledgments are due, and are hereby made, to the following : For Emily Brontë, Mr. C. K. Shorter (Messrs. Hodder & Stoughton) ; for T. E. Brown, Messrs. Macmillan & Co.; for the Rev.

*b*

A. S. Cripps, Mr. B. H. Blackwell ; for Father Hollings,
the Rev. Father Bull, S.S.J.E. (Messrs. Longmans, Green
& Co.); for George MacDonald, Dr. Greville MacDonald
(Messrs. Chatto & Windus) ; for Frederick Myers,
Messrs. Longmans, Green & Co.; for Francis Thompson,
Messrs. Burns & Oates ; for Traherne, both Messrs.
Dobell, and also, for the poems edited by Mr. H. I. Bell,
the Clarendon Press ; and in the case of her own poems,
Miss Evelyn Underhill (Messrs. Dent & Sons).

It may not be amiss to state that the MS. of this
volume was (with the exception of a few slight interpola-
tions) ready for the press when the war broke out, and was
placed aside until the times became more propitious.

# CONTENTS

# CHAPTER I.

## PRE-REFORMATION POETS.

ENGLISH religion has been described as "Christian by profession, materialistic in practice, agnostic in creed". Though uttered by an enemy of our nation, the words may not be devoid of truth. Indeed, despite the countless individuals known to many of us as God-fearing and devout Christians, it is difficult for the truest lovers of our country to claim for the average Englishman more, in the way of religion, than a high code of honour, a certain kindliness of heart, and a vague reverence for the memory of Jesus Christ. But of late years there have been signs that men and women are beginning to suffer from spiritual hunger and to long for closer touch with the unseen world. This tendency has, naturally, been more marked in recent years; but some while before the Great European War broke out materialism had been on the wane, and Mysticism had been "having a vogue". It is true that a good deal of modern mysticism is non-Christian, undisciplined, and unhealthy in tendency; but this fact imposes on Christians the duty of emphasizing the mystical aspects of the Catholic Religion.

There is still a proneness to confound mysticism with mystification, and to use the word as a missile; while the epithet 'mystic' has proved so useful to hymnodists and others that the minds of the unlearned may well be utterly confused as to its meaning. And yet the definitions of the

word are countless, nor can any writer on the subject evade
the responsibility of supplying one.   Various definitions will
have to be noted *passim* in the course of this work ; but
here, in an attempt to be as comprehensive as possible, we
may take a Christian mystic to be one who *knows* the
mysteries of the Faith.   Mysteries are open secrets—secrets
which can be known, though not expressed perhaps, by
anyone who will take sufficient interest, and make sufficient
effort, to know them.   The mystic does not simply believe
in GOD : he knows GOD by personal intercourse ; he has
a vivid sense of His constant Presence ; he consciously aims
at a more and more complete union of the soul with Him.
The mystic knows, by practical experience, Eternal Life,
though it may be obscured by the shadows of the seen and
temporal.   He knows something, at any rate, of the divine
meaning which underlies all material phenomena and mundane experiences.   His soul, its needs and aspirations, are
as real to him and as clamant as his body.

The word ' mysticism ' is derived, as few readers need
be reminded, from the Greek mysteries, into which the mystic
was initiated : its literal derivation is not decisively clear,
but may be taken to refer to the closing of the outward
senses in order that the inward may be the more susceptible.
Writers on mysticism have usually agreed upon the importance of observing three stages in the mystic's development.
These stages, the Purgative, the Illuminative, and the
Unitive Ways, are not hard and fast divisions ; they overlap
at times or run parallel with one another, but they roughly
mark the progressive stages by which the mystic advances
towards that conscious union with GOD which is his constant
goal.   The three rungs in this Mystic Ladder will again
demand attention when the *Psyche* of Joseph Beaumont is

under consideration ; but here it may be claimed at once
that this series of spiritual states is no arbitrary, cut-and-
dried division.   The process of purgation—the work of
penitence and self-surrender—must have begun in earnest
before Light can penetrate into the soul ; and unless it is
illuminated by a sense of GOD'S unfailing nearness in Nature
and in Man, unless it concentrates its attention upon the
revealed Loveliness of His nature and continually waits
upon Him to recognize His guidance, the soul will not
know experimentally the deepest recesses of the spiritual
life where " spirit with spirit can meet ".

Must this union with GOD culminate in the special experience called, sometimes ecstasy ('a standing-out' of the
soul from the body), sometimes rapture ('a being snatched-
away' from earthly consciousness) ?   Must the illuminative
stage be accompanied by the seeing of visions and the hearing of voices ?   Certainly, many of the greatest Christian
mystics, beginning with St. Paul, have had visions and revelations, and have been " caught up into the third heaven " ;
and consequently there has been a tendency to make such
experiences the *criteria* of the mystical consciousness.   But
we are coming to see more and more clearly that " Annihilation, Extasis, Liquefaction, Transformation, the Kiss
of GOD, and Ingression into the Divine Shadow "—to quote
Sir Thomas Browne's list of mystical experiences—are not
really essential to mysticism.   The mystic must indeed be
aware of his union with GOD ; he must be convinced that
GOD is in him and he in GOD ; and at times that awareness and that conviction will flood him with an intense joy
and a supreme sense of power, which may be figuratively
described as ecstatic or rapturous ; but he need not attain
that transformation or abolition of the personality that the

greatest mystics have always declared of secondary importance to the spiritual well-being.

The English nature shrinks from the discussion of such
intimate and ineffable experiences ; it is inclined indeed to
mistrust them—not necessarily to bar them out as unreal or
illusory, but to discourage them as tending to emphasize the
importance of mere feelings.   It is certain that in the case
of many of those whose writings are considered in the
following pages, any experimental knowledge of such a
nature would never have been revealed ; a sense of reticence
as to one's own privileges, and of reverence as to GOD's
disclosures, would have sealed the lips.   Those English
mystics who, in Thomas Fuller's words, " do knock at the
door of blasphemy though not always with intent to enter
thereat," have, for the most part, either left or never belonged to the Anglican Church.   Of Anglican mystics it
may be claimed that as a general rule their most marked
characteristic has been sanity—a sanity which is nowhere
clearer than in the way in which they have sought to gratify
their mystical aspirations in due balance and combination
with the other two elements of religion.   Baron von Hügel,
in his *Mystical Element in Religion*, has brought out very
clearly the threefold nature of a complete religion : the institutional element which, recognizing historical organizations
and external authority, submits to disciplinary routine and
obeys ceremonial injunctions, the rationalistic element which
checks any tendency to blind obedience and unintelligent
submission by insisting upon the right of the intellect to
challenge traditions and to question dogmas, and the mystical
element in which spiritual insight and intuition claim a yet
higher function than reason, and the soul's deep need of
GOD Himself will not rest satisfied with the substitution of

Church, or ceremonialism, or surface-fervour. The mystics of the English Church have never lost touch with Holy Scripture ; they have not failed to ' try ' the leadings of the Inner Light by the test of that Word of God which has been given as "a lantern unto our feet and a light unto our paths ". They have not despised the Sacraments, but, believing them to be effectual signs, have regularly and humbly used the Holy Communion as GOD'S wise and gracious aid in sustaining the sense of His Presence and the assurance of His goodwill at those times, known to all mystics, when faith must needs be called to the help of the emotions. Anglican mystics have very rarely given way to that misology, or disparagement of reason and learning, which almost inevitably results in extravagances and aberrations—the one-sidedness for which the Germans have the useful name ' Mystizismus ' as distinct from ' Mystik '. The mystics of the English Church have, too, been saved from the danger of excessive individualism which necessarily threatens those who cultivate the Inner Life, by the almost undue stress which English public opinion has laid upon good works and philanthropic activity. The thorough development of the parochial system, and the freedom of the clergy to enjoy family life with its humanizing influences, have been further safeguards. On the other hand, it should be admitted that these conditions have sometimes proved adverse to the cultivation of the Inner Life.

It would be difficult to find an Englishman in whom the more emotional and transcendental side of religion has found clearer utterance than it has in Jeremy Taylor. More than once he speaks with warm approbation of the three stages of the Mystic Way ; but, in the *Ductor Dubitantium* he warns ' the scrupulous man ' against "books of mystical theology which have in them the most high, the most troublesome, and the most mysterious nothings in the world, and little better than the effluxes of a religious madness " ; and in his discourse ' Of Meditation,' in the *Life of our Blessed Lord*, we find a warning note that may be taken as thoroughly typical of the Anglican attitude towards the less sober aspects of mysticism : " There is a degree of Meditation so exalted that it changes the very name and is called Contemplation ; and it is in the unitive way of religion, that is, it consists in unions and adherences to GOD ; it is a prayer of quietness and silence, and a meditation extraordinary, a discourse without variety, a vision and intuition of divine excellences, an immediate entry into an orb of light, and a resolution of all our faculties into sweetnesses, affections, and starings upon the divine beauty ; and is carried on to ecstasies, raptures, suspensions, elevations, abstractions, and apprehensions beatifical. . . . But this is a thing not to be discoursed of but felt. . . . They that pretend to these heights [Taylor is thinking of the claims of the wilder sectaries of his own age and country] call them the secrets of the kingdom ; but they are such which no man can describe ; such as GOD hath not revealed in the publication of the gospel ; such for the acquiring of which there are no means prescribed, and to which no man is obliged, and which are not in any man's power to obtain ; nor such which it is lawful to pray for or desire ; nor concerning which we shall ever be called to an account. . . . If a man be more in love with GOD by such instruments, or more endeared to virtue, or made more severe and watchful in his repentance, it is an excellent gift and grace of GOD. . . . But if the person be made unquiet, inconstant, proud, pusillanimous, of high opinion, pertinacious and confident in uncertain judgments, or desperate, it is certain they are temptations and illusions". This is, of course, the criterion expressed in the homely saying, " The proof of the pudding is in the eating," and more recently promoted into philosophical circles as the method of Pragmatism.

It would be futile to devote many pages to the mystical poets of the English Church in its medieval period ; they were, for the most part, anonymous, and their archaic words and forms make them difficult reading. One of the earliest poems that may be quoted is entitled *The Sea-farer*, and is found in the Exeter Codex of the eleventh century. It illustrates one of the two main types of the mystical consciousness—the type that is painfully conscious that " here we have no continuing city," that " we are strangers and pilgrims on earth, looking for the city that hath foundations, whose builder and maker is GOD". Seldom has poet striven more earnestly with unwieldy language to describe this Mystic Quest for things eternal in the midst of things temporal—the curious reader may be interested to notice in Tennyson's *The Voyage* how a similar subject is treated by one who inherited a more musical tongue and a subtler metrical system. The medieval Columbus, after a description of an actual voyage, unburdens

> The soul of the sea-weary
> Hunger-assailed.
>
> I may sing of myself now
> A song that is true,
> Can tell of wide travel,
> The toil of hard days ;
> How oft through all seasons
> I suffer'd and strove,
> Abiding within my breast
> Bitterest care. . . .

Comes again to me yearning
With eager desire ;
Loud cries the lone-flier,
And stirs the mind's longing
To travel the way that is tractless,
The death-way over the flood.
For my will to my Master's pleasure
Is warmer than this dead life
That is lent us on land ;
I believe not that earth-blessings
Ever abide.[1]

And so the anonymous poet describes, in language that cannot be satisfactorily modernized, how this world's transient joys must be exchanged for the lonely watches, the bitter hardships, and the spiritual storms to be faced by one who seeks the peaceful haven in the Heart of GOD. This recalls the advice of Plotinus, the great heathen saint and mystic, to gain " the open sea " and " flee to the Fatherland whence we have come out and where the Father is ". And—what is still more to the point—no student of the Bible can fail, on reading this poem, to recall how Scriptural is this symbolic use of the sea. Both Psalmist and Prophet speak of GOD as the only stiller of the raging of the sea. Our Lord's Stilling of the Tempest was an active parable enforcing the lesson, among others, that the tumultuous passions of the soul will be subdued to " a great calm " as soon as faith in Christ is roused. Nor is the spiritual meaning obscure underlying St. John's account of how the disciples " went down unto the sea and entered into a ship . . . and it was dark and Jesus was not come unto them," but when, conquering their fears, they took Him aboard,

[1] From Henry Morley's modernized version in *English Writers* (ii).

"immediately the ship was at the land whither they went". And once more, there is the vision of the new heaven and the new earth in which "the sea is no more"—no more separation from GOD'S Home, no more spiritual unrest, no more fear of storm or wreck.

Some readers may expect here a discussion on the *Vision of Piers Ploughman*, which deals with a somewhat similar pilgrimage in quest of truth.   This is often called a mystical poem, but it is difficult to see how the word, even in the widest sense, can be justifiably applied to what is, in turns, an allegory, a satire, and a political pamphlet on evils in Church and State, expounded in a series of imaginary visions.

The other great type of the mystical consciousness is that of the soul which feels, or longs to feel, that " My Beloved is mine and I am His ".   Many minds instinctively recoil from the symbol of the " Marriage of the Soul," by which countless mystics have striven to express something of that " craving of the soul for its perfect mate ".   None of us, however, object to singing the familiar words,

> Jesu, Lover of my soul,
> Let me to Thy bosom fly.

or again,

> Jesus ! my Shepherd, Husband, Friend.

Nor does the mystic lack Scriptural encouragement in this use of the language of earthly love to symbolize the yearnings of the soul.   Not to mention the *Song of Songs*, which will fall under notice when the poems of Francis Quarles are reached, *Psalm* xlv. is obviously a marriage-song and has been very largely applied by commentators to the nuptials of Christ and His Bride, an application to which the Church has given sanction by the headings in the Authorized Version.   Quite early in the pages of the Bible, the relation

between Jehovah and Israel had been represented as that of
husband and wife (cf. *Exodus* xxxiv. 15).   In *Isaiah* liv.
5, GOD is represented as saying " Thy Maker is thine
Husband ".   Both Jeremiah and Ezekiel speak of GOD as
Israel's Husband, and the whole argument of the prophecy
of Hosea turns upon the reality of that relationship between
GOD and the Jewish nation.   Our LORD, too, repeatedly
applied to Himself the title ' Bridegroom ' ; and St. Paul,
in words which have been incorporated into our Marriage-
Service, speaks of the " mystical marriage betwixt Christ and
His Church," and again, in a somewhat involved passage
in the Epistle to the *Romans* (vii. 1-6), describes the second
marriage contracted by the redeemed soul with Christ after
the death of " the old man ".   And the Bible closes with
the Apocalyptic vision of the marriage of the Lamb and the
Bride.   It is true that in Bible-times the relationship between husband and wife had not reached that point of
equality to which the advance of civilization has now brought
it, and which makes the figure a much less appropriate one
of the soul's relation to GOD.   Moreover, probably in one
only of the above passages, is the bride represented as an
individual soul, but either as the Jewish nation or as the
Christian Church ; but the mystics have claimed that the
emblem of the Church holds good of the faithful soul, which
may aptly be typified as a bride betrothed to Christ, striving
to hold fast to Him, sometimes acutely conscious of unfaith-
fulness to Him, yet longing to be bound to Him with an
inseparable bond of unending union.   All this is worth
dwelling upon, for this analogy will be constantly recurring
in these pages.   It obviously has its dangers, which Christian
mystics have not always escaped ; but we can fairly claim
that very few of the mystics of the English Church have

been guilty of bad taste, or of offending our sense of reverence, by borrowing too freely the phraseology of earthly passion, or by arrogating to their own individual souls a relationship which can rightly apply only to the Holy Catholic Church.

Of this type of divine love-song a good example, though somewhat didactic, is to be found in the *Love-ron* of the learned Franciscan, THOMAS HALES, who flourished about the year 1250. It was written, not to relieve his own feelings, but to edify the ladies of the cloister. The opening lines may be adapted to our modern language in some such way as this :—

> A maid of Christ begged me earnestly
> That I would make her a love-song,
> From which she might best learn
> To take another true leman [sweetheart].

The poet shows her, by such examples as Paris and Helen, how " false and fickle and fleeting " is human love, whereas he has a message from the one true King who, although even king Henry III is His vassal, seeks the maid's " willing troth ".

> His sight is all joy and glee,
> He is Day without any night ;
> Were not that maiden full blest
> That might dwell with such a knight ?

Virginity is His gift, a treasure better than silver or gold, which must be carefully guarded. This rime should be learnt by heart and taught to others ; and the poet ends,

> When thou sittest in longing,
> Draw forth this same writing ;
> With sweet voice do thou sing it,
> And also do as it bids.

> To thee He sendeth a greeting.
> GOD Almighty thee be with,
> And bring thee to His bride-chamber,
> There in heaven where He sits.

We notice here at once how practical was the piety of the mystics of medieval England. Their aspirations to union with GOD did not hinder them from undertaking the edification of other souls ; from their religious houses and cells they poured forth tracts, and sermons, and devotional aids, and, above all, poems. Some of these were in Latin, such as the poems of Queen Eleanor's chaplain, JOHN HOVEDON, who died in 1275. His best known poem, *Philomela*, has been printed abroad, but others, such as his *Canticum Divini Amoris*, remain in manuscript, and are likely to do so. But RICHARD ROLLE (*d.* 1349), while not altogether discarding the Latin tongue, wrote freely in the vernacular. He occupies, therefore, a most important place in the annals of English literature, while of English mystics he ranks amongst the very highest. The more important of his writings are in prose—a prose, however, even more essentially poetic than his verse. We learn much of his life and experiences from his own writings : he studied at Oxford and was deeply influenced by the writings of St. Bernard (whose *Jesu dulcis memoria* is a popular hymn in the English translation, " How sweet the name of Jesus sounds ") and of St. Bonaventura, whose influence upon Richard Rolle was so great that he has been called ' the English Bonaventura ' and seems, indeed, almost more than his master to deserve the title ' Doctor Seraphicus,' his heart being lit with a glow of divine love not unlike that attributed to the seraphim.

At the age of twenty, Richard fled from his home, became a hermit, and after three years spent in the purgative and illuminative ways, entered upon his more transcendental experiences. First, he felt a Heat, which seems to have been a physical sensation ; along with this, he tasted an ineffable sweetness ; and finally he heard a Song. Henceforth his heart was aflame ; no adverse circumstances could sour his intercourse with GOD, and his life was a melody, not merely in a metaphorical sense, for his days were spent in singing love-songs to Christ. But, dearly as he loved his solitude with its joys and raptures, he felt that he must help others to attain like joys. He became an itinerary missioner, and, after many physical sufferings and mental vexations, intermingled with wondrous holy consolations, he settled in the village with which his name is always associated, Hampole, in Yorkshire, and occupied his last years in literary labours and in ministering to a nunnery. We can best learn the light in which he regarded his life-work from the following apostrophe : " Come, youths and maidens, learn from me, a wonderful lover, how to love. Forsake the impure love of one another and embrace eternal love. O maidens, do not hanker after men ; do not adorn yourselves for men ; lo ! Christ, lovely of shape before the sons of men, the King of Heaven, wants your beauty and woos your love ".

Besides the poems in English and Latin known to be by Richard Rolle, a great number of anonymous pieces are believed, with something like certainty, to have been written or at least adapted by him. They are often beautiful little lyrics, rich in mystical fervour ; but there is a considerable sameness about them, and many do not lend themselves to transcription to modern literary form. Several have been skilfully modernized by the late Monsignor R. H. Benson in *A Book of the Love of Jesus*, a most valuable little

volume, from which the following extracts are quoted.   In
one piece, after recalling the love of Jesus in the Passion, the
poet breaks into what elsewhere he calls " a song of love-
longing " :—

> Jesu, my Lord, mine own sweeting,
> Hold me ever in Thy keeping ;
> Make of me Thine own darling,
> That I love Thee above all thing.
>
> .    .    .    .    .    .    .
>
> Jesu, if Thou from me dost go,
> Mine heart is full of pain and woe ;
> What may I say but ' Well-a-woe ! '
> When Thou, my Sweet, art gone me fro' ?
>
> Jesu, my Life, my Lord, my King !
> To thee my soul hath great longing ;
> Thou has wedded it with Thy ring ;
> When Thy will is, to Thee it bring !

This passionate devotion to the Person and Name of
JESUS is somewhat alien to twentieth-century ears, but
modern devotion would be none the worse for a little more
—perhaps there is more than some of us suspect—of the
glowing intimacy which Richard Rolle longed to teach other
souls.  " When a soul," he says, " offers herself to Jesus
truly, and meekly puts all her trust and desire in Him, and
busily keeps Him in her mind, our Lord Jesus, when he
wills, purges the affection of the soul, and fills it and feeds
it with sweetness of Himself, and makes His name in the
feeling of the soul as honey, and as song, and as anything
that is delightable ".   And again : " This Name, Jesus,
fasten it so in thy heart that it never come out of thy thought ;
and when thou speakest to Him and sayest ' Jesus,' through
custom, it shall be in thine ears joy, and in thy mouth honey,

and in thy heart melody ". Here is part of a lyric which expresses this delight felt by Rolle in the thought of Jesus and in the utterance of His Name :—

> Jesu, my joy and my loving !
> Jesu, my comfort clear !
> Jesu, my GOD ! Jesu, my King !
> Jesu, withouten peer !
>
> Jesu, my dear and my one joy !
> Delight Thou art to sing !
> Jesu, my mirth and my melody !
> Into Thy love me bring.

The mystical nature has not always responded to the love of GOD as readily as Richard Rolle did. Saul of Tarsus learnt how hard it is to kick against the goads, before he yielded himself to " that Tremendous Lover " of Whom a modern poet has sung so thrillingly. This thought of GOD'S Love-chase is the subject of an anonymous poem of the fifteenth century with a refrain, *Quia amore langueo*, borrowed from *Canticles* ii. 5, where, however, it is the soul, and not the Heavenly Bridegroom, which " faints with love ". The poem is printed in its original form in the 1866-7 volume of the Early English Text Society, but it is here quoted in the Rev. C. J. Abbey's modernized rendering, in *Religious Thought in Old English Verse* :—

> In a valley of this restless mind
>  I sought in mountain and in mead,
> Trusting a true love for to find.
>  Upon a hill then took I heed ;
>  A voice I heard—and near I yede [went]—
>   In great dolour complaining tho [then] :
>  " See, dear soul, how my sides bleed,
>   *Quia amore langueo.*

. . . . . . .

" I am true Love that false was never ;
 Mine own—man's soul—I loved her thus.
Because we would nowise dissever,
 I left My Kingdom glorious.
 I purvey'd her a palace full precious ;
  She fled, I follow'd, I lov'd her so,
 That I suffer'd this pain piteous,
  *Quia amore langueo.*

  .  .  .  .  .  .  .  .

" Long and love thou never so high,
 My love is more than thine may be.
Thou gladdest, thou weepest, I sit thee by :
 Yet wouldst thou once, love, look at Me !
 Should I always feedé thee
  With children's meat ? My love, not so.
 I will prove thy love with adversity,
  *Quia amore langueo.*"

The truth that GOD not only created us in love and
redeemed us in love, but also longs for us to return His love,
is one for which we may be grateful to be reminded. His
infinite need of us is a more appealing thought than our infinite need of Him, and in a generous heart it must strike a
responsive chord that a more selfish motive might fail to
touch. God stands at the door of our hearts and knocks ;
all the day long He stretches out His hands to us ; and
yet with many of us religion means no more than a perfunc-
tory attendance at services which are readily dropped if we
are " not getting good out of them ". The mystics insist,
on the one hand, that *our* love for GOD must be disinterested,
and, on the other hand, that *God* has a loving interest in
our souls.

# CHAPTER II.

EDMUND SPENSER ; GILES AND PHINEAS FLETCHER.

AMONG the mystical poets of the English Church place must be found for EDMUND SPENSER, not as the writer of *The Faerie Queene*, but as the hymnodist of Heavenly Love and Beauty. *The Faerie Queene* is an allegory, which we read for the noble ethical qualities there personified with an unfailing opulence of music and colour. But allegory and personification are not mysticism : they are not, strictly speaking, Platonism, and it is as a Platonic idealist that Spenser must be considered here. The Renaissance had, as its most important result, the re-introduction of Plato to the intellectual world, and Spenser was the first of our poets to expound that philosopher's views on Love and Beauty.[1] Platonic Idealism, though not in a strict sense mysticism, is closely akin to it ; indeed, Dr. Inge has told us that Plato is " the father of European mysticism ". Platonism may be described briefly as the love of the invisible and eternal inspired, sustained, and heightened by contemplating the beauty of the visible and the temporal. The *locus classicus* of the doctrine of Platonic love is the passage in the *Symposium* (203A, *seq.*), in which the Mantinean prophetess is represented as explaining the origin and meaning of Love. It is there urged that " the right procedure in the matter of Love is to begin with earthly beauties

[1] Some of the sonnets of Sir Philip Sidney's *Astrophel and Stella* must not be forgotten, however.

and to ascend towards that which is Beauty itself, using the former as steps, and from the love of one form to go on to that of two, from two to all beautiful forms, from beautiful forms to beautiful practices, from beautiful practices to beautiful notions, until from beautiful notions the notion of Absolute Beauty is reached, in the knowledge and contemplation of which final satisfaction may be found ".

From this passage, which is the fountain-head of much of the mystical doctrine expounded in subsequent extracts, it will be seen at once that ' Platonic Love ' is not in the least what it is popularly supposed to be.  As used in ordinary conversation or in periodical literature, a platonic lover means, apparently, one who does not proceed to the fruition of the object, but loves at a distance—one, in fact, whose ' intentions ' are strictly honourable but entirely remote.  But this is not in the least Plato's ideal lover : he is one who from love of a single person learns to recognize beauty as a quality intellectual and spiritual rather than physical, and by degrees ascends to the contemplation and worship of the Divine under one of its eternal attributes.

A similar doctrine is expounded by Plato in the dialogue *Phraedrus* (246, *seq.*), where we find the famous myth, in which the soul is compared to a charioteer with two winged steeds—the charioteer symbolizing the reason, the steeds the higher and the lower impulses.  Man's soul-chariot, in a previous existence, has journeyed round the universe in the train of the gods and has caught a glimpse of absolute justice, temperance, and knowledge, as they exist in the Ideal World.  Ever after it strives to regain the vision, but the carnal steed drags the soul earthward ; its wings are lost, and it is imprisoned in a human body. Thousands of years may pass before the higher state is

regained by a series of transmigrations, but the soul of the
' philosopher,' after the animal desires have been tamed and
a period of retribution has passed, will regain the sight of
that which truly *is*, the Divine Beauty, Truth, and Goodness in pure essence.

It is as an expositor of this contemplation of the beautiful and the good, and of the duty of using the divine gift of
Love as a means of uniting the soul to GOD, that Spenser
takes rank among poets who, though not actually mystics,
were certainly mystical in tendency. In the *Hymn in
Honour of Love*, references to these Platonic doctrines can
easily be traced, intermingled with conventional appeals to
Venus and Cupid. The *Hymn in Honour of Beauty* is
also pagan in tone, but the Idealism is there more clearly
expressed, as in such lines as these :—

> What time this world's great Workmaster did cast
> To make all things such as we now behold,
> It seems that He before His eyes had plac'd
> A goodly Pattern, to whose perfect mould
> He fashion'd them as comely as He could,
> That now so fair and seemly they appear,
> As nought may be amended anywhere.
>
> That wondrous Pattern, wheresoe'er it be,
> Whether in earth laid up in secret store,
> Or else in heaven, that no man may it see
> With sinful eyes, for fear it to deflore,
> Is perfect Beauty, which all men adore ;
> Whose face and feature doth so much excel
> All mortal sense, that none the same may tell.
>
> Thereof as every earthly thing partakes
> Or more or less, by influence divine,

So it more fair accordingly it makes,
And the gross matter of this earthly mine,
Which closeth it thereafter, doth refine,
Doing away the dross which dims the light
Of that fair beam which therein is empight [placed].

Spenser goes on to deny that beauty is " an outward
show of things that only seem " : earthly beauty may fade ;

But that fair lamp, from whose celestial ray
That light proceeds, which kindleth lover's fire,
Shall never be extinguish'd nor decay ;
But when the vital spirits do expire,
Unto her native planet shall retire,
For it is heavenly born and cannot die,
Being a parcel of the purest sky.

And so we reach the lines on the supremacy of the soul,
which vividly recall Plato's teaching, hinted at in connexion
with the myth referred to above, but more fully developed
elsewhere, as in the *Phaedo* (80, *seq.*), where it is argued
that the soul, as the immortal part of man's nature, must
rule the mortal body, and that the souls, not of the good,
but of the wicked, in the next life will be united to animals
having the same habits or natures as those which they themselves have acquired in their present life, the self-indulgent
assuming the form of asses and brutes of that kind, the unjust
and tyrannous that of wolves or hawks, the more civilized
and peaceful that of bees or ants or even that of man again.
Spenser, without adopting the theory of the transmigration
of souls, agrees that the nature of the body depends upon
the nature of the soul. His words state a fact which all
must have observed, and a truth which may have an important bearing on the resurrection body.

> So every spirit, as it is most pure,
> And hath in it the more of heavenly light,
> So it the fairer body doth procure
> To habit in, and it more fairly dight
> With cheerful grace and amiable sight :
> For of the soul the body form doth take ;
> And soul is form, and doth the body make.

Charles Kingsley made " a grand new discovery, which is as old as the Greeks, that souls secrete their bodies as a snail secretes its shell " ; and all of us know at least some men and women whose faces are outward and visible signs of inward and spiritual grace, and others, alas, whose facial expressions do not succeed in masking the pride or mean-ness or self-indulgence which are the main characteristics of their souls.    And it may be so not only in this life : if our Lord's words in *St. Mark* ix. 43 ff. are to be given their natural meaning, and if any argument may be rested on the analogy of our Lord's Resurrection Body with its glorious scars, we may humbly believe that some will enter life maimed in the struggle with bodily lusts, while others will have a spiritual body enhanced in beauty by the cultivation of consecrated thoughts and habits while on earth.

In the *Hymn of Heavenly Love*, Spenser sings the Triune Love, first emanating in the Angels " in their trinal triplicities " (a subject that will have to be considered when Heywood's *Celestial Hierarchy* is under notice), next breathing the breath of life into man, and, after man's fall, descending to his rescue in the Person of Jesus Christ, Whose self-sacrificing love must rouse in man an answering love :—

> Thenceforth all world's desire will in thee die,
> And all earth's glory, on which men do gaze,

Seem dirt and dross in thy pure-sighted eye,
Compar'd to that celestial Beauty's blaze,
With admiration of their passing light,
Blinding the eyes and lumining the spright.

Then shall thy ravish'd soul inspired be
With heavenly thoughts, far above human skill,
And thy bright radiant eyes shall plainly see
Th' Idea of His pure glory present still
Before thy face, that all thy spirits shall fill
With sweet enragement of celestial love,
Kindled through sight of those fair things above.

It is almost sacrilegious to present in mutilated form the
*Hymn on Heavenly Beauty*, in which Spenser soars to
supreme heights of exultant aspiration, with a majesty of
diction that matches the intensity of his fervour.   He touches
on the beauty of earth, sea, air, and sky, " the Heaven
where happy souls have place," that " where those Ideas on
high enranged be which Plato so admired," that " in which
do reign the sovereign Powers and mighty Potentates," until
he reaches " that highest far beyond all telling ".

But we, frail wights ! whose sight cannot sustain
The sun's bright beams when he on us doth shine,
But that their points rebutted back again
Are dull'd, how can we see with feeble eyne
The glory of that Majesty divine,
In sight of Whom both sun and moon are dark,
Compared to His least resplendent spark ?

The means, therefore, which unto us is lent
Him to behold, is on His works to look,
Which He hath made in beauty excellent,

And in the same, as in a brazen book,
To read enregister'd in every nook
His goodness, which His beauty doth declare ;
For all that's good is beautiful and fair.

Thence gathering plumes of perfect speculation
To imp the wings of thy high-flying mind,
Mount up aloft, through heavenly contemplation,
From this dark world, whose damps the soul do blind,
And, like the native brood of eagle's kind,
On that bright Sun of glory fix thine eyes,
Clear'd from gross mists of frail infirmities.

The poet describes GOD'S Throne as " built on eternity,"
His sceptre as " the rod of Righteousness," His seat as
Truth " that all about Him sheddeth glorious Light ".   In
His bosom sits Sapience, " the sovereign dearling of the
Deity," upon whose " goodly face " the poet admits his own
unworthiness to gaze.

But whoso may, thrice happy man him hold
Of all on earth whom GOD so much doth grace
And lets His own Beloved to behold ;
For in the view of her celestial face
All joy, all bliss, all happiness have place ;
Ne ought on earth can want unto the sight
Who of herself can win the wishful sight.

For she, out of her secret treasury,
Plenty of riches forth on him will pour,
Even heavenly riches, which there hidden lie
Within the closet of her chastest bower,
The eternal portion of her precious dower,
Which mighty GOD hath given to her free,
And to all those which thereof worthy be.

None thereof worthy be but those whom she
Vouchsafeth to her presence to receive,
And letteth them her lovely face to see,
Whereof such wondrous pleasures they conceive,
And sweet contentment, that it doth bereave
Their soul of sense, through infinite delight,
And them transport from flesh into the spright.

In which they see such admirable things
As carries them into an ecstasy,
And hear such heavenly notes and carollings
Of GOD'S high praise, that fills the brazen sky ;
And feel such joy and pleasure inwardly
That maketh them all worldly cares forget,
And only think on that before them set.

     .    .    .    .    .    .    .    .

     Ah, then, my hungry soul ! which long hast fed
On idle fancies of thy foolish thought,
And, with false beauties' flattering bait misled,
Hast after vain deceitful shadows sought,
Which all are fled, and now have left thee nought
But late repentance through thy folly's prief [proof] ;
Ah ! cease to gaze on matter of thy grief :

And look at last up to that sovereign Light,
From Whose pure beams all perfect beauty springs,
That kindleth love in every godly spright,
Even the love of GOD ; which loathing brings
Of this vile world and these gay-seeming things ;
With whose sweet pleasures being so possest,
Thy straying thoughts henceforth for ever rest.

This poem will be seen to be steeped in Platonic idealism,
which, after all, does not essentially differ from the teaching
of St. Paul and St. John.   St. Paul might well have had

in his mind the two steeds of the soul-charioteer, when, for instance, he told the Romans that " the mind of the flesh is death, but the mind of the spirit is life and peace ".    And Plato's doctrine of Love reappears in less fanciful guise in the teaching of St. John's 1st Epistle, as it culminates in the words, " Beloved, let us love one another : for love is of GOD ; and every one that loveth is begotten of GOD and knoweth GOD : he that loveth not knoweth not GOD, for GOD is Love ".    Only in the last few lines of his hymn does Spenser misinterpret his master, Plato, or perhaps, deliberately forsake him under the influence of a Puritanic environment.    It is not Platonism, but Neo-Platonism—a very different thing—that brands GOD'S world as loathsome and vile ; and it is but a pseudo-spirituality that leads one to suppose that GOD, Who is Love and of Whom comes love, could have placed men in a world of loveliness, unless He wished them to love it and Him in it.    To adapt St. John's words—if a man love not the earth and sea and sky, with all their beauties of form and colour which he hath seen, how can he love GOD Whom he hath not seen ?

Many poets have been fecundated by Spenser, but two have been, as it were, bewitched, taking as their model every accident of his style, and slavishly reproducing his phraseology.    The brothers FLETCHER, GILES and PHINEAS, were born to poetry, being the sons of a poet and cousins of the well-known dramatist.    Both took holy orders, held for a time fellowships at Cambridge, and ended their lives as parish priests in East Anglia.    After enjoying considerable contemporary fame, they sank into almost complete oblivion, but their merit has latterly received a qualified recognition, and their literary importance has been acknowledged as the link between Spenser and Milton, the debt of the latter to both being unmistakable.

Giles Fletcher, although the younger, came before the public as a poet before his brother, whom he predeceased by some twenty-seven years. Fuller tells us in the *Worthies* that he was "one equally beloved of the Muses and the Graces, having a sanctified wit, witness his worthy poem entitled *Christ's Victory*, made by him being but Bachelor of Arts, discovering the piety of a saint and divinity of a doctor. He afterwards applied himself to school-divinity (cross to the grain of his genius, as some conceive), and attained to good skill therein. When he preached at St. Mary's, his prayer before his sermon usually consisted of one entire allegory, not driven but led on, most proper in all particulars". Fuller adds that the unkindness of his parishioners and the inclement climate of the East Coast brought him to a premature grave about the year 1623. He could not have been more than twenty-one years of age when he wrote *Christ's Victory and Triumph*—a fact which may well plead extenuation for the undeniable faults of taste which mar many even of the finest passages. The verse, which is always melodious, rises at times to real majesty and power ; but the affections of style and the exaggeration of the imagery—the result of his homage to Spenser—seem utterly incongruous in a religious poem, which yet, somehow, rings absolutely true.

The first canto, entitled "Christ's Victory in Heaven," describes how Mercy and Justice, personified as women but spoken of as Ideas in the Platonic sense (i.e. eternal natures), plead before GOD concerning the fate of fallen man. Mercy is, of course, the successful pleader ; but the victory is not altogether satisfactory from an ethical point of view, the

poet having failed to show how the Atonement reconciles
the claims both of mercy and justice.

In the second canto, "Christ's Victory on Earth," we
have the Temptation in the wilderness described with quite
unwarrantable circumstance.   The devil is represented as having appeared in the disguise of "a good old hermit," while
the Christ is depicted in imagery borrowed very largely from
*The Song of Songs*, and in this connexion the poet says,

> One of ten thousand souls I am, and more,
> That of His eyes and their sweet wounds complain—
> Sweet are the wounds of love, never so sore—
> Ah, might He often slay me so again !
> He never lives that thus is never slain.

A very Spenserian passage is the elaborate description—
too elaborate and luscious in its detail—of the garden of
Vain-glory, to which "our first destroyer led our Saviour,"
and in which that sorceress sang Him a most delightful lyric,
too secular for quotation here.

Canto III, dealing with "Christ's Triumph over Death,"
is a very genuine outburst of loving devotion, in spite of its
over-elaboration and excess of antithesis, with its inevitable
suggestion of artificiality.

> See where the author of all life is dying :
> O fearful day !   He dead, what hope of living ?
> See where the hopes of all our lives are buying :
> O cheerful day ! they bought, what fear of grieving ?
> Love love for hate, and death for life, is giving :
> > Lo, how His arms are stretched abroad to grace thee,
> > And, as they open stand, call to embrace thee ;
> Why stayest thou then, my soul ?   Oh !   Fly, fly thither, haste
> > thee.

.    .    .    .    .    .    .    .    .    .

> The life, the which I once did love, I leave ;
> The love, in which I once did live, I loathe ;
> I hate the light that did my Light bereave ;
> Both love and life, I do despise you both,
> Oh that one grave might both our ashes clothe !
>     A Love, a Life, a Light, I now obtain,
>     Able to make my age grow young again,
> Able to save the sick, and to revive the slain.

Canto IV opens with a beautiful description of Nature's homage—as evidenced in the outburst of spring—to " Christ's Triumph after Death ".　And here the thought of Christ's hard-won peace in Heaven leads to congratulations on the peace enjoyed by Britain ; for Spenser flattered Eliza in his verse, therefore the disciple must flatter James, " picture of peace or breathing image rather ".　But the poet feels the incongruity, and offers an apology that he should " with his Stewart dare his Lord compare ".　After this aberration, however, the poem gets back to a much higher level, and, from the thought of the beauty of man's present dwelling, passes, in its closing stanzas, to describe the yet higher joys of Heaven with its Beatific Vision—the happy-making sight—of GOD.

> How can such joy as this want words to speak ?
> And yet what words can speak such joy as this ?
> Far from the world that might their quiet break,
> Here the glad souls the face of Beauty kiss,
> Pour'd out in pleasure, on their beds of bliss.
>     And drunk with nectar torrents, ever hold
>     Their eyes on Him, Whose graces manifold
> The more they do behold the more they would behold.
>
> Their sight drinks lovely fires in at their eyes ;
> Their brain sweet incense with fine breath accloys,

That on GOD'S sweating altar burning lies;
Their hungry ears [1] feed on their heavenly noise,
That angels sing, to tell their untold joys;
  Their understanding naked Truth, their wills
  The all- and self-sufficient Goodness fills,
That nothing here is wanting, but the want of ills.

 .  .  .  .  .  .  .  .  .

In the midst of this City Celestial,
Where the eternal Temple should have rose,
Lighten'd the Idea Beatifical:
End and Beginning of each thing that grows,
Whose self no end, nor yet beginning knows,
  That hath no eyes to see nor ears to hear,
  Yet sees and hears and is all-eye, all-ear,
That nowhere is contained and yet is everywhere.

Changer of all things, yet immutable,
Before and after all, the first and last,
That, moving all, is yet immovable,
Great without quantity, in Whose forecast
Things past are present, things to come are past,
  Swift without motion, to Whose open eye
  The hearts of wicked men unbreasted lie,
At once absent and present to them, far and nigh.

It is no flaming lustre made of light,
No sweet concent or well-tim'd harmony,
Ambrosia for to feast the appetite,
Or flowery odour mix'd with spicery,
No soft embrace or pleasure bodily,
  And yet it is a kind of inward feast,
  A harmony that sounds within the breast,
An odour, light, embrace, in which the soul doth rest.

---

[1] The 1st edition seems to have "cares," but the sense seems to demand "ears".

A heavenly feast no hunger can consume,
A light unseen, yet shines in every place,
A sound no time can steal, a sweet perfume
No winds can scatter, an entire embrace
That no satiety can e'er unlace,
 Engrac'd into so high a favour there
 The Saints, with their beau-peers, whole worlds outwear,
And things unseen do see, and things unheard do hear.

In Phineas Fletcher we find precisely the same faults of
bad taste, literary affectation, and riotous luxuriance of description, as are noticeable in his brother ; we find, too, the
same power to convey, in spite of everything, a conviction of
deep-seated reverence and piety. He was called by
Quarles "the Spenser of this age" ; and, like his master,
he was pre-occupied with the passion of love, sacred and
profane. He published a good deal more than his brother,
writing in a considerable variety of styles and metres ; and
he was even more of an anomaly, passing with no apparent
sense of contradiction from exquisite heights of purity and
tenderness to dwell on depths of fleshly imagery and description with something very like zest, and yet with an air
of unconscious innocence.

His earlier poems need not detain us. The earliest, *The
Locusts or Apollyonists*, written half in Latin, half in
English, deals—vigorously—with the Papal See, the Jesuits,
and the Gunpowder Plotters. It is a thoroughly characteristic seventeenth century polemic, which gains distinction
from Milton's debt to it. *Britain's Ida*, published in
1628 under Spenser's name, has been very confidently, but
one hopes erroneously, ascribed to the elder Fletcher. The
*Sicelides* was "a Piscatory as it hath been acted in King's
College in Cambridge," and it was soon followed by a

volume of *Piscatory Eclogues and other Poetical Miscellanies*, containing a number of the complimentary pieces so popular at Cambridge at the time.    In the same year, 1633, was published (with an intimation that it had been a long while in manuscript) the best known of Phineas Fletcher's works, *The Purple Island*.    This is a long poem of great audacity and beauty, which, in accordance with the fashionable ' cant ' of the age, is supposed to be sung, a canto a day, by the shepherd Thersil to his pastoral neighbours. As most readers will know, the Purple Island is Man, and the allegory is a most ingenious elaboration of Spenser's description in the *Faerie Queene* (II, ix) of Alma's Castle.

In the opening lines the poet complains that men will travel willingly to the remotest lands in search of material wealth,

> Yet this fair Isle, sited so nearly near
> That from our sides nor place nor time may sever ;
> Though to yourselves yourselves are not more dear,
> Yet with strange carelessness you travel never.

The thought is not particularly original, and may well have been due to a reading of the words in the famous passage on the memory in St. Augustine's *Confessions :* " Men travel to gaze upon mountain-heights and the waves of the sea, broad-flowing rivers and the expanse of the ocean and the courses of the stars, and pass by themselves, the crowning wonder ".

A description of the creation of the universe naturally culminates in the framing of the Island with " purple dust taken from the newborn earth," and its peopling

> With subjects apt to please
> So wise a Prince, made able to defend it
> Against all outward force or inward spite.

Yet it was allured from its peaceful moorings by Satan's
wiles ; and before describing how Christ repaired that disaster, the author devotes four cantos to the anatomical topo-
graphy of the Island, displaying so extraordinary an ingenuity
that he is forced to supply a very full marginal glossary, lest
the reader should fail to detect the references to bones,
cartileges, nerves, arteries, etc.

In the sixth canto we reach the Island's Prince, Intellect,
with his councillors, the five Senses, and with Common-sense,
Fancy, and Memory as the " pillars of the state ".  The
whole passage suggests that Fletcher may possibly have been
familiar with the Flemish mystic, Ruysbroeck's similar,
though not identical, allegory of the Kingdom of the Soul,
in which Free Will is the king, having Justice as his judge
in the Court of Conscience, and as his councillors, Knowledge and Discretion, dwelling in Reason.  In Fletcher's
allegory the Will (Voletta) is queen, and Conscience is her
maid-in-waiting.  After contrasting their present darkness
with the celestial light enjoyed by Intellect and Will when
first they wed " with melting happiness," he invokes the
Incarnate Christ, " Who the Deity enfleshed and man's
flesh deified " : —

> Receive, which we can only back return,
> (Yet that we may return, Thou first must give)
> A heart, which fain would smoke, which fain would burn
> In praise ; for Thee, to Thee would only live :
>     And Thou, Who sat'st in night to give us day,
>     Light and inflame us with Thy glorious ray,
> That we may back reflect, and borrow'd light repay.
>
> So we, beholding with immortal eye
> The glorious picture of Thy heavenly face

In his first beauty and true majesty,
May shake from our dull souls these fetters base ;
   And, mounting up to that bright crystal sphere
   Whence Thou strik'st all the world with shuddering fear,
May not be held by earth, nor hold vile earth so dear.

The scene in canto vii. opens in Heaven, GOD'S " standing-court," whence " down were flung those pure and living flames," who " disdained His royal service ". And the rest of this, and the whole of the next, canto are taken up with an account of Satan's enmity to man, and the co-operation of the World and the Flesh with " the enraged Dragon and his serpents bold ". All this gives the poet full scope for his noble gift of personification, as do also cantos ix. and x. in which we are told of Knowledge, Humility, Faith, Hope, Love, etc., the issue of the marriage between Spirit and Heaven. The two last cantos describe how Eclecta, daughter of the Intellect and Will, speeds her knights, the previously personified virtues and graces, to the Civil War. The battle rages with varying fortunes, until Eclecta breathes the following prayer :—

Ah, dearest Lord, my heart's sole sovereign,
Who sitt'st high-mounted on Thy burning throne,
Hark from Thy heavens, where Thou dost safely reign,
Cloth'd with the golden sun and silver moon :
   Cast down awhile Thy sweet and gracious eye,
   And low avail that flaming majesty,
Deigning Thy gentle sight on our sad misery.

To Thee, dear Lord, I lift this watery eye,
This eye which Thou so oft in love hast praised ; (*Cant.* i. 15).
This eye with which Thou wounded oft wouldst die ; (*Cant.* iv. 9).
To Thee, dear Lord, these suppliant hands are rais'd :

These be the lilies Thou hast often told me,
    Which if but once again may ever hold Thee,
Will never let Thee loose, will never more unfold Thee.

Seest how Thy foes despiteful trophies rear,
Too confident in Thy prolong'd delays ?
Come then, oh quickly come, my dearest dear :
When shall I see Thee crown'd with conquering bays,
    And all Thy foes trod down and spread as clay ?
    When shall I see Thy face and glory's rays ?
Too long Thou stay'st my Love ; come Love, no longer stay.

At this point the reader is positively staggered by a
piece of bathos, which not even the courtierly euphuism of
that age can acquit of blasphemy.   The immediate answer
to Eclecta's prayer is a clap of thunder and the appearance
of " an angel full of heavenly might," which a marginal
gloss explains to represent " our late most learned sovereign
in his Remonstrance and Comment on the Apocalypse ".
Many readers must be tempted here to lay down the poem
either in a fit of convulsive merriment or in a mood of
nauseated disgust.   But the poet quickly recovers himself :
in majestic lines he describes the entrance of Christ upon
the fight, His overthrow of the Dragon, and His reunion
with Eclecta, with the relation of whose crowning joys the
poem reaches its close :—

At length when joys had left her closer heart,
To seat themselves upon her thankful tongue,
First in her eyes they sudden flashes dart,
Then forth in the music of her voice they throng :
    " My Hope, my Love, my Joy, my Life, my Bliss,
    (Whom to enjoy is heaven, but hell to miss)
What are the world's false joys, what heaven's true joys to this ?

" Ah, dearest Lord ! does my rapt soul behold Thee ?
Am I awake ? and sure I do not dream ?
Do these thrice-blessed arms again enfold Thee ?
Too much delight makes true things feigned seem.
    Thee, Thee I see ; Thou, Thou thus folded art :
    For deep Thy stamp is printed in my heart,
And thousand ne'er-felt joys stream in each melting part."

Thus with glad sorrow did she sweetly plain her,
Upon His neck a welcome load depending ;
While He with equal joy did entertain her,
Herself, her Champions, highly all commending :
    So all in triumph to His palace went,
    Whose work in narrow words may not be pent ;
For boundless thought is less than is that glorious tent.

There sweet delights, which know no end nor measure ;
No chance is there, nor eating times succeeding :
No wasteful spending can impair their treasure ;
Pleasure full grown, yet ever freshly breeding :
    Fulness of sweets excludes not more receiving :
    The soul still big of joy, yet still conceiving ;
Beyond slow tongue's report, beyond quick thought's perceiving.

There are they gone, there will they ever bide ;
Swimming in waves of joys and heavenly loving :
He still a Bridegroom, she a gladsome Bride,
Their hearts in love, like spheres still constant moving :
    No change, no grief, no age can them befall :
    Their bridal bed is in that heavenly hall,
Where all days are but one, and only one is all.

Twenty years after the death of Phineas Fletcher there
was published a volume entitled *A Father's Testament*,
which, according to the publisher, had been written by that

(*Jeremiah* xxv. 4, xxxii. 33).   A lover breaks his sleeps to
wait at the door of his love : and 'is not His head filled with
the dew and His locks wet with the drops of the night ?'
(*Cant.* v. 2).   A lover will not break off for every denial,
nor will he be discouraged with many refusals : and doth
not our Lord ' wait to be gracious unto us ' (*Is.* xxx. 18),
even after we ' have wearied Him with our unkindness'
(*Is.* xliii. 24) ?   Some lovers have ventured : He hath
given His life for His beloved (*St. John* xv. 13).   Seeing,
therefore, such a lover so lovely thus woos such wretches,
so loathsome, let us thus answer His suit :—

> Me Lord ? canst Thou misspend
>   One word, misplace one look on me ?
>     Call'st me Thy love, Thy friend ?
>   Can this poor soul the object be
> Of these love-glances, those life-kindling eyes ?
> What ?   I the centre of Thy arms' embraces ?
>   Of all Thy labour I the prize ?
>   Love never mocks, Truth never lies.
> Oh, how I quake !   Hope fear, fear hope displaces.
> I would but cannot hope : such wondrous love amazes.

>   See, I am black as night,
>   See, I am darkness : dark as hell.
>     Lord, Thou more fair than light :
>   Heaven's sun Thy shadow.   Can suns dwell
> With shades ? 'twixt light and darkness what commerce ?
> *True, thou art darkness, I thy light : My ray*
>   *Thy mists and hellish fogs shall pierce.*
>   *With Me, black soul, with Me converse.*
> *I make the foul December flowery May :*
> *Turn thou thy thoughts to Me, I'll turn thy night to day.*

See, Lord, see I am dead,
  Tomb'd in myself, myself my grave :
    A drudge, so born, so bred—
  Myself even to myself a slave.
Thou Freedom, Life : can Life and Liberty
Love bondage, death ?    *Thy Freedom I, I tied*
  *To loose thy bonds : be bound to Me.*
  *My yoke shall ease, My bonds shall free.*
*Dead soul, thy spring of life My dying side :*
*There die, with Me to live : to live in thee I died."*

Carrying on the analogy of Christ the Lover, Fletcher speaks of the written Gospel as His love-letters, and the preached Gospel as His wooing ; " our hand, whereby we receive Him, is only our faith, by which the understanding assents and the will consents. . . . The Father of Lights, by the light of His Word, discovers unto us the Person of the Lord Jesus—in His Nature, GOD and Man : in His offices, King, Priest, and Prophet ; in His relation to us, Husband, Head, and Saviour ; in His Love and actions of love, Incarnation, Humiliation, Exaltation. This light He so effectually brings home to us by the work of His Spirit that, whereas heretofore we saw no beauty in Him that we should desire Him, now we see no beauty but in Him. . . . But is there nothing else demanded but the heart and will in this spiritual match and union with Christ ? Nothing more to make the match ; but after the marriage those conjugal duties are required, which will soon make us feel and confess how happy we are in such an espousal. Hearken then willingly to His suit, and thus in your hearts cheerfully answer Him :—

# CHAPTER III.

## DAVIES, DONNE, AND HEYWOOD.

Was Sir John Davies a mystical poet? There is very little that suggests the mystic in the quarrelsomeness of his earlier years, or in his later public career, which culminated in his appointment to the Chief Justiceship as a reward for a sycophantic decision, or again in his earlier poems, although the *Orchestra* is not uninfluenced by Plotinus's views on the ritual dance and chorus of the universe. But his third poem, the *Nosce teipsum*, published in 1599, demands treatment here, as dealing with a subject which engaged the attention of many mystics, and as containing passages, at least, subsidiary to mysticism.

The poem is, for the most part, dialectical in form and didactic in tone, a fine example of clear reasoning in verse which often rises to eloquence, if not to melody. It might, perhaps, be argued that its subject would have been better expressed in prose; but the author is manifestly moved by the intensity of feeling which we demand in poetry, and he has shown real skill in moulding his thoughts to the conditions of metrical expression. It may justly be called the first of the great line of philosophical poems which distinguish our literature.[1]

[1] Almost contemporaneous, though published later, are the poems of Fulke Greville, first Lord Brooke, which, if the pages of this volume could be unlimited, might well receive fuller treatment than mere mention in a footnote. His verse is, on the whole, far less successful than that of Davies; but his thought is deeper, and

The title is, of course, the Latin version of the celebrated utterance of the Delphic oracle, γνῶθι σεαυτόν, which Juvenal quotes as a maxim of worldly wisdom : know yourself and your limitations if you want to make your way in the world. But Clement of Alexandria refers to it as a spiritual motto : " it is the greatest of all lessons to know oneself ; for if a man knows himself, he will know GOD ". Our author, too, believes that autology is a necessary step to theology, relying, no doubt, on such texts as our Lord's saying, " The kingdom of GOD is within you ". A more mystical sense was then given to these words than is now conceded by New Testament scholars ; but there can be no doubt about the sense of the expanded form in the *New Saying*, discovered only in this century at Oxyrhynchus : " The kingdom of heaven is within you ; and whosoever shall know himself shall find it. Strive therefore to know yourselves and ye shall be aware that ye are the sons of the Almighty Father ". We are to seek, in fact, a reflection of the Divine Attributes in our own higher faculties, and we are to recognize our supreme dignity as being in a mutually loving relationship to GOD. But this carries us rather beyond the scope of Sir John Davies' poem, in which he claims, on his title-page, to expound the famous oracle " in two elegies, the first, of Human Knowledge, the second, of the Soul of man and the Immortality thereof," meaning by ' immortality ' the spiritual nature of the soul, as well as its continuity of existence both before and after this life.

The passages in which Davies refutes erroneous views as to the origin and nature of the soul need not detain us, nor

almost as mystical in tendency, especially in *A Treatise of Religion*, as witness this couplet :—

> Without, in power, we see Him everywhere ;
> Within, we rest not, till we find Him there.

> O ignorant poor man ! what dost thou bear
> Lock'd up within the casket of thy breast !
> What jewels and what riches hast thou there !
> What heavenly treasure in so weak a chest ! . . .

The supreme importance of self-knowledge is insisted upon more than once in the poems of JOHN DONNE, the famous Dean of St. Paul's :—

> But we know ourselves least ; mere outward shows
> Our minds so store,
> That our souls no more than our eyes disclose
> But form and colour.   Only he who knows
> Himself, knows more.

We are so often told, by those who ought to know, that Donne was a mystical poet, that there must be some truth in the assertion ; and yet it does not seem easy to vindicate the accuracy of the designation.   In his earlier poems, this elusive genius appears as a characteristic product of the Renaissance, with its curious amalgam of licence and seriousness : in some pieces he is quite shameless, in others he dallies with a theoretic Platonism, which, however, hardly carries conviction.   In one mood he wallows in sensualism ; in the next he idealizes love, praising the spirit within and deprecating the appeal of sex :—

> But he who loveliness within
> Hath found, all outward loathes,
> For he who colour loves, and skin,
> Loves but their oldest clothes.

The same thought is emphasized in *The Ecstasy* and in *Negative Love ;* while in *A Valediction forbidding Mourning* and in the song, *Soul's Joy, now I am gone* [1]

---

[1] The 'Higher Criticism' of Donne's work now ascribes this song to the Earl of Pembroke (see the *Cambridge Hist. of Eng. Literature*, iv. 209), but not a few competent critics are unconvinced.

(which George Herbert so characteristically parodied), he insists that souls do not part merely because bodies do.

In the curiously misnamed *Progress of the Soul*, the Platonic (or rather Pythagorean) doctrine of the transmigration of souls is utilized, in the savagely satiric vein of Swift, apparently to vent the author's spleen against Protestantism ; and its fragmentary nature may be due to a loss of courage on the part of Donne who was as yet unconvinced of the errors of Rome.

The *Anatomy of the World* introduces us to Donne's second phase, reached after a transition period in which he says that his Muse enjoyed " a chaste fallowness ". The reader will probably not need to be told that this poem is an encomium of Elizabeth Drury, a paragon of virtue who died, at the age of fifteen, in 1610. At her father's suggestion, Donne undertook to celebrate her in verse on each successive anniversary of her death ; but he got no further than the Second Anniversary, deterred presumably by the adverse criticism to which his *Letters* refer. Ben Jonson, in spite of his intense admiration of Donne's poetry, thought this piece " profane and full of blasphemies," and told the author that " if it had been written of the Virgin Mary it had been something " ; to which Donne replied that he intended to describe " the Idea of a Woman and not as she was ". The *First Anniversary* treats of " the frailty and the decay of this world " ; it has all the faults, and few of the merits of the *Second Anniversary*. The latter poem (also called, and more justly than that noted above, *The Progress of the Soul*) is, perhaps, the greatest of all Donne's poems ; and as his claim to the epithet ' mystical ' is based very largely upon it, lengthy extracts must be given here, omitting, however, the first eighty lines :—

She, she is gone; she's gone; when thou know'st this,
What fragmentary rubbish this world is
Thou know'st, and that it is not worth a thought;
He honours it too much that thinks it nought.
Think, then, my soul, that death is but a groom,
Which brings a taper to the outward room,
Whence thou spiest first a little glimmering light,
And after brings it nearer to thy sight;
For such approaches doth heaven make in death.
Think thyself labouring now with broken breath,
And think those broken and soft notes to be
Division, and thy happiest harmony.
Think thee laid on thy death-bed, loose and slack,
And think that but unbinding of a pack,
To take one precious thing, thy soul, from thence.
Think thyself parch'd with fever's violence;
Anger thine ague more by calling it
Thy physic; chide the slackness of the fit.
Think that thou hear'st thy knell, and think no more,
But that, as bells call'd thee to Church before,
So this to the Triumphant Church calls thee.
Think Satan's sergeants round about thee be,
And think that but for legacies they thrust;
Give one thy pride, to another give thy lust;
Give them those sins which they gave thee before,
And trust the immaculate Blood to wash thy score.
Think thy friends weeping round, and think that they
Weep but because they go not yet thy way.
Think that they close thine eyes, and think in this,
That they confess much in the world amiss,
Who do not trust a dead man's eye with that
Which they from GOD and angels cover not.
Think that they shroud thee up, and think from thence
They reinvest thee in white innocence.

Think that thy body rots, and—if so low
(Thy soul exalted so) thy thoughts can go—
Think thee a prince, who of themselves create
Worms, which insensibly devour their state.
Think that they bury thee, and think that rite
Lays thee to sleep but a Saint Lucy's night.[1]

After a long section on the ignominious and limited
circumstances of " us slow-pac'd snails who crawl upon our
prison's prison," and cannot " shake off this pedantry of
being taught by sense and phantasy," Donne calls on his
" drowsy soul " to contemplate the angelic songs and the
sight of " the Blessed Mother-Maid " and all the company
of heaven, whose bliss had been enhanced by the com-
panionship of his heroine.   A disquisition follows on Joys
accidental and essential, culminating thus :—

So much mankind true happiness mistakes ;
No joys enjoys that man, that many makes.
Then, soul, to thy first pitch work up again ;
Know that all lines which circles do contain,
For once that they the centre touch, do touch
Twice the circumference ; and be thou such :
Double on heaven thy thoughts on earth employ'd.
All will not serve ; only who have enjoy'd
The sight of GOD in fulness can think it ;
For it is both the object and the wit.
This is essential joy, where neither He
Can suffer diminution, nor we ;
'Tis such a full, and such a filling good,
Had the angels once look'd on Him, they had stood.
To fill the place of one of them, or more,
She whom we celebrate is gone before ;

[1] St. Lucy's Day, December 13, was the shortest day in the year, according to
the Old Style.

She, who had here so much essential joy
As no chance could distract, much less destroy ;
Who with God's Presence was acquainted so—
Hearing and speaking to Him—as to know
His face in any natural stone or tree,
Better than when in images they be ;
Who kept, by diligent devotion,
GOD'S image in such reparation
Within her heart, that what decay was grown
Was her first parents' fault, and not her own ;
Who, being sollicited to any act,
Still heard God pleading His safe pre-contract ;
Who by a faithful confidence was here
Betroth'd to GOD, and now is married there ;
Whose twilights were more clear than our mid-day ;
Who dreamt devoutlier than most use to pray ;
Who being here fill'd with grace, yet strove to be
Both where more grace and more capacity
At once is given ; she to heaven is gone,.
Who made this world in some proportion
A heaven, and here became unto us all
Joy—as our joys admit—essential.

With another sixty lines of far-fetched analogy and
hyperbolic flattery, the poem drags laboriously to its close.

In reading this rhapsody, we first need to digest the
surfeit of tortured ingenuity, which led Dr. Johnson to attack Donne as the leader of the " race of writers that may
be termed metaphysical poets ". Coleridge, who has better
claims to be heard on the subject of metaphysics, assures
us that " Donne was a poor metaphysician " ; but Dr.
Johnson had his own definition of metaphysics. " The
metaphysical poets," he says in his famous essay, " were
men of learning, and to show their learning was their whole

endeavour. . . . Their thoughts are often new, but seldom
natural ; they are not obvious, yet neither are they just ;
and the reader, far from wondering that he missed them,
wonders more frequently by what perverseness of industry
they were ever found."

When we have penetrated the layer of over-subtle
thought which so seldom reaches real profundity, and of
emotionalism which so rarely rings true, we find that the
dominant notion in Donne is that of the Transcendence of
the Infinite, conceived of as altogether external to, and even
alien from this present life.  But that is not the true mystical
note, which emphasizes rather the Immanence of the Infinite
in this world as a Presence within the finite.  The mystic
worships a GOD Who certainly transcends all nature, but
is a Power, not merely above and behind Nature, but in
Nature ; not least is He in man, whose body even is no
object of contempt or derision, and whose soul can even
now enjoy immediate contact with the Divine.  Donne, of
course, praises most extravagantly his heroine's body, but
only, as he says himself, as " the Idea of a woman ".  He
would, too, admit without hesitation that man can hold
communion with GOD and recognize His Presence in
Nature ; and, indeed, he attributes this faculty to the lady
in question.  But this is not the basis of his habitual thought,
as it would be if the attitude of his mind were essentially
mystical.

Similarly, in his more directly religious poems, in spite
of an absolutely genuine conversion after a period of disgust
with himself and with the world, the mystical note seems
never struck clearly.  He says of himself, very aptly, that
he must do

As giddy travellers do,
Which stray or sleep all day, and having lost
Light and strength, dark and tired must then ride post.

The reader gets the impression of an abject penitence
and a faltering faith, struggling—with very imperfect success—to burst through its clouds to the light of GOD's Love.
The well-known *Hymn to God the Father*, beginning
" Wilt Thou forgive that sin where I begun "—quite the
most melodious of Donne's poems—illustrates this clearly,
as does also the less familiar *Hymn to Christ, at the
author's last going into Germany* :—

In what torn ship so ever I embark,
That ship shall be my emblem of Thy ark ;
What sea soever swallow me, that flood
Shall be to me an emblem of Thy blood ;
Though Thou with clouds of anger do disguise
Thy face, yet through that mask I know those eyes,
Which, though they turn away sometimes,
They never will despise.

I sacrifice this island unto Thee,
And all whom I love there and who love me ;
When I have put our seas ' twixt them and me,
Put Thou Thy seas betwixt my sins and Thee.
As the tree's sap doth seek the root below
In winter, in my winter now I go,
Where none but Thee, the eternal root
Of true love, I may know.

Nor Thou nor Thy religion dost control
The amorousness of an harmonious soul ;
But Thou would'st have that love Thyself ; as Thou
Art jealous, Lord, so I am jealous now ;

Thou lovest not, till from loving more Thou free
My soul ; whoever gives, takes liberty ;
　　Oh, if Thou carest not whom I love,
　　　　Alas ! Thou lovest not me.

Seal then this bill of my divorce to all,
On whom those fainter beams of love did fall ;
Marry those loves, which in youth scattered be
On fame, wit, hopes—false mistresses—to Thee.
Churches are best for prayer that have least light ;
To see GOD only, I go out of sight ;
　　And to escape stormy days, I choose
　　　　An everlasting night.

Isaac Walton, in the *Life of Donne*, says that " his
book of *Devotions* may not unfittingly be called a sacred
picture of spiritual ecstasies " ; but the description is not at
all an apt one, for there is very little that is ecstatic, in the
true sense of the word, in the book. Even when allowance
is made for the fact that it was written in convalescence, the
general tone is morbid rather than ecstatic, illustrating the
lines written at the same sickness :—

　　I have a sin of fear, that when I have spun
　　　My last thread, I shall perish on the shore.

There is, for instance, the prayer : " As Thou hast given
me a repentance not to be repented of, so give me, O Lord,
a fear of which I may not be afraid ". And again, " I
need Thy thunder, O my GOD ; Thy music will not serve
me ". Throughout the *Devotions*, there is a constant
dwelling on the thought of sin and the less hopeful aspects
of the spiritual life. So it is in the *Divine Poems*. The
words found in the first of the *Holy Sonnets*, " Despair
behind and Death before," might serve as a motto for the

whole collection. The deprecations of his *Litany* are magnificent in their self-disclosing candour ; but the soul which they disclose is not mystical, even in the loosest sense of that loosely used word.

It is true that in his famous sermon on George Herbert's mother, Donne claims to be " of that quorum that can say, Come what scorns can come, come what terrors can come, *in Christo omnia possumus*, though we can do nothing of ourselves, yet as we are in Christ we can do all things, because we are fixed in Him, *secundum promissa* ". But yet he contemplates the possibility of Christ's return " in my night of ignorance, or wantonness, or inordinate and sinful melancholy and suspicion of His mercy," and he dwells on the terror of " standing in judgment under the guiltiness of some sins not buried in the wounds, not drowned in the blood of my Saviour ". If such words—and many more might be cited—were but the outcome of a passing reflexion, we might attribute them to the well-known mystical mood of reaction called 'the dark night of the soul'; but they mark the habitual trend of Donne's thoughts. And, in lieu of the mystic's claim that GOD may be known in this life and that eternal life may be a present possession, Donne tells us that " GOD is a future GOD, to man especially He is so ; man's consideration of GOD is specially for the future ".

This contention that Donne's cast of mind was essentially unmystical has, perhaps, been urged at undue length ; but, although in these pages the line round the mystical pale has not been drawn at all rigidly, the tendency to confuse mere theoretic Platonism and a tone of other-worldliness with mysticism is one against which it seems important to make a stand.

To some it may come as a surprise that THOMAS HEY-
WOOD should unhesitatingly be granted the epithet 'mystical,'
denied to Donne.  It is not, of course, as a playwright
that he is so classed, but as the author of the *Hierarchie*.
Heywood seems to have been born about the year 1575,
and to have lived into the 'Commonwealth'.  As a Fellow
of Peterhouse, Cambridge, he acquired some classical
learning, with which he made considerable play in his *Four
Ages* and elsewhere ; but, like his fellow-dramatist of
Stratford, he drifted on to the stage, and became one of the
most prolific of play-writers.  He claims to have had "an
entire hand or at least a main finger" in 220 plays, of
which, however, only about a score have survived.  Most
of them display nothing more than an unadorned pathos
and a somewhat crude humour, but two stand out as
masterpieces : *A Woman killed with Kindness* and *The
English Traveller*.  Both give us sublime pictures of a true
Christian gentleman, and lines redolent (as Swinburne has
said) of "English love and homely sense of home".
Charles Lamb's criticism is often quoted, but usually in too
abbreviated a form to do justice either to Lamb or to Heywood.  "Heywood is a sort of *prose* Shakespeare.  His
scenes are to the full as natural and affecting.  But we miss
the *poet*, that which in Shakespeare always appears out
and above the surface of *the nature*.  Heywood's characters in this play, for instance [*A Woman killed with
Kindness*], his country gentlemen, etc., are exactly what we
see, but of the best kind of what we see, in life.  Shakespeare makes us believe, while we are among his lovely
creations, that they are nothing but what we are familiar
with, as in dreams new things seem old ; but we awake and
sigh for the difference. . . . If I were to be consulted as to

a reprint of our old English dramatists, I should advise, to begin with, the collected plays of Heywood. He was a fellow-actor and fellow-dramatist with Shakespeare. He possessed not the imagination of the latter ; but in all those qualities which gained for Shakespeare the attribute of 'gentle,' he was not inferior to him. Generosity, courtesy, temperance in the depth of passion ; sweetness, in a word, and gentleness ; Christianism, and true hearty Anglicism of feelings, shaping that Christianism ; shine throughout his beautiful writings in a manner more conspicuous than in those of Shakespeare, but only more conspicuous inasmuch as in Heywood these qualities are primary, in the other subordinate to poetry. I love them both equally, but Shakespeare has most of my wonder. Heywood should be known to his countrymen, as he deserves."

In spite of his prodigious output of plays, Heywood found time for a good deal of miscellaneous writing. His masque, *Love's Mistress*, was a great favourite at Court ; he wrote in vindication of the Stage, and was an industrious biographer ; but what especially concerns us now is his *Hierarchie of the Blessed Angels, their Names, Orders, and Offices*. This is a work of genuinely mystical the-ology, a book being devoted to each of the nine choirs of angels, and each book containing " theological, philosophical, moral, poetical, historical, apothegmatical, hieroglyphical, and emblematical observations ". The hieroglyphics and emblems are highly entertaining, and the other ' observations ' give evidence of wide reading and deep thought ; whilst the pieces quoted below will prove his earnestness and piety, though hardly his possession of a musical ear.

The term ' Hierarchy,' and the whole basis of his scheme, Heywood borrowed from the Pseudo-Dionysius. This

writer, who, about the year 500, appropriated the name of
St. Paul's famous Athenian convert and in that guise won
the allegiance of Frenchmen as the patron-saint of Paris,
has usually been credited with the generation of modern
Christian mysticism.   But Miss Underhill has shown that
his Angelology had been, to some extent, anticipated by St.
Basil, from whose first *Homily on Faith* she quotes the
following passage : " Transcend in spirit all this universe,
take your flight above the skies, and, soaring at the sublime
heights, let the eyes of your soul rest upon the fairest of all
beings ; look upon the heavenly armies, the choirs of Angels,
consider the might of the Archangels, the glory of the
Dominations, the seats whereon the Thrones are established,
the Virtues, the Principalities, the Powers.   Then, transcending even all angelic natures, raising yourself in thought
beyond and above all creation, contemplate the Divine
Nature, steadfast and immovable, exempt from every vicis-
situde and every emotion, simple and indivisible, Inaccessible
Light, Ineffable Power, Limitless Splendour, Incomparable
Glory, the sovereign desirable Good, the Perfect Beauty
Which inflicts upon the enraptured soul an ineffable wound
of love, and of Which human language is powerless to tell
the Majesty."   But Dionysius had also encountered certain
views of the Gnostics, against whose teaching St. Paul, it
will be remembered, had aimed his Epistle to the *Colossians*.
Regarding all matter as inherently evil and, therefore, direct
fellowship with GOD as impossible for man, the Gnostics at
Colossae had worshipped a series of ' emanations ' believed
to exist between the soul and GOD, bridging an otherwise
impassible gulf.   Such views, in a purified form, had
reached Dionysius through the writings of the Neo-Platonist,
Proclus.   In his extant writings, Dionysius taught that man

cannot hope to rise to a knowledge of the Absolute, but may enjoy a fellowship with It. "It is impossible that the beams of the Divine Source can shine upon us unless they are shrouded in the manifold texture of sacred veils so as to prepare our powers for a fuller vision" (Westcott's translation). The keyword of his whole scheme is the word 'Hierarchy,' which he explains to mean "a sacred order, and science, and activity, assimilated as far as possible to the godlike, and elevated to the initiation of GOD proportionately to the Divine illumination conceded to it". GOD's Loveliness illumines angelic beings, who are as close to Him as creatures can be, and reflect it to others just below them, who, in their turn, act as mirrors, to receive and reflect these beams of primal light onwards to mankind ; each of the three angelic ranks falls into a further three-fold order and aims at the purification, illumination, and perfection of the rank below.

Anglicanism, as typified, for example, in Bishop Bull, has failed, perhaps, to appreciate the symbolic nature of Dionysius's scheme, and has taken exception to anyone speaking "so sublimely, so punctually, with so much assurance of the things above, as if he had himself surveyed the holy mansions and taken an exact inventory of all that is there". To-day it seems more necessary to deprecate the opposite extreme—the insensibility to their existence which marks the modern attitude towards angelic beings. Those who are content to exercise a reverent reserve, without insisting on positive definitions, may, with Sir Oliver Lodge—no unscientific ignoramus—accept the probability that the Deity carries on the universe through intermediary agents, and may adopt the view that "this is one of the many meanings of Immanence". "Nature," said Dr. Newman, "is not inanimate ; its daily toil is intelligent ; its works are duties." The laws and forces of Nature, climatic changes and the various forms of elemental action, are outward signs of the Presence of Him Who "maketh His angels winds and His ministers a flame of fire" : some such belief alone can give reality and intelligence to our singing of the earlier verses of the *Benedicite*.

Heywood does not follow Dionysius closely as regards the ranks and respective operations of the heavenly hierarchy, his treatment being modified by the study of St. Bernard and others. The thought of the Seraphim, who stand closest to the Absolute and are aglow with the fire of Divine Love, leads him to vindicate the Existence of GOD and to inquire into His nature, closing this first Book with the following meditation in verse, which has obviously been inspired by the magnificent passage in the tenth Book of St. Augustine's *Confessions*, beginning "I asked the earth" :—

> I sought Thee round about, O Thou my GOD!
>> To find Thy abode.
> I said unto the earth, 'Speak, art Thou He?'
>> She answered me,
> 'I am not.' I enquired of creatures all,
>> In general
> Contain'd therein : they with one voice proclaim
> That none amongst them challeng'd such a name.

Diligently he prosecutes his search through sea and sky, in peace and war, at Court, in city and in country. But all in vain ; and it is only in Introspection that he sees any hope of success. Self-scrutiny brings him, in the final stanzas of this meditation, at least to the stage in which he can say :—

And now, my GOD, by Thy illuminating grace,
　　　　Thy glorious face
(So far forth as it may discover'd be)
　　　　Methinks I see;
And though invisible and infinite
　　　　To human sight,
Thou in Thy mercy, justice, truth appearest,
In which to our frail senses Thou com'st nearest.

O make us apt to seek, and quick to find,
　　　　Thou GOD most kind!
Give us love, hope, and faith in Thee to trust,
　　　　Thou GOD most just!
Remit all our offences, we entreat,
　　　　Most good, most great!
Grant that our willing though unworthy quest
May, through Thy grace, admit us 'mongst the blest.

The name ' Cherubim ' means knowledge ; and to the
angelic choir so named (according to St. Bernard) the
Original Fount of Wisdom " deigns to reveal abundantly
the treasures of wisdom and knowledge which are hidden
in Him ".   In the Book devoted to the Cherubim, Heywood discusses the Names of God and shows His Nature
to be above the apprehension of man's reason or senses.
But, although infinitely above man, GOD is unspeakably
close to him ; and this conviction inspires the next meditation, almost ludicrously quaint in letter, but intrinsically
reverent in spirit.

I have wander'd like a sheep that's lost,
To find Thee out in every coast.
*Without* I have long seeking been,
Whilst Thou the while abid'st *within.*

Through every broad street and strait lane
Of this world's city, but in vain,
I have enquir'd.   The reason why?
I sought Thee ill; for how could I
Find Thee *abroad*, when Thou, mean space,
Had'st made *within* Thy dwelling-place?

I sent my messengers about
To try if they could find Thee out.
But all was to no purpose still,
Because, indeed, they sought Thee ill;
For how could they discover Thee
That saw not when Thou enteredst me?

Mine eyes could tell me?   If He were
Not colour'd, sure He came not there.
If not by sound, my ears could say
He doubtless did not pass my way.
My nose could nothing of Him tell,
Because my God He did not smell.
None such I relish'd, said my taste,
And therefore me He never pass'd.
My feeling told me that none such
There enter'd, for He did none touch.
Resolv'd by them how should I be,
Since none of all these are in Thee?

In Thee!   My GOD, Thou hast no hue
That man's frail optic sense can view;
No sound the ear hears; odour none
The smell attracts; all taste is gone
At Thy appearance; where doth fail
A body, how can touch prevail?
What even the brute beasts comprehend—
To think Thee such, I should offend

Yet when I seek my GOD, I enquire
For Light, than sun and moon much higher,
More clear and splendrous, 'bove all light,
Which eye receives not, 'tis so bright.
I seek a Voice beyond degree
Of all melodious harmony ;
The ear conceives it not : a Smell
Which doth all other scents excel ;
No flower so sweet, no myrrh, no nard
Or aloës, with it compar'd ;
Of which the brain not sensible is.
I seek a sweetness—such a bliss
As hath all other sweets surpass'd
And never palate yet could taste.
I seek That to contain and hold
No touch can feel, no embrace enfold.

So far this Light the rays extends
As that no place it comprehends.
So deep this Sound that, though it speak,
It cannot by a sense so weak
Be entertain'd.   A redolent grace
The air blows not from place to place.
A pleasant Taste, of that delight
It doth confound all appetite.
A strict embrace, not felt, yet leaves
That virtue, where it takes it cleaves.
This light, this sound, this savouring grace,
This tasteful sweet, this strict embrace,
No place contains, no eye can see,
My GOD is, and there's none but He.

Here, again, our poet has read St. Augustine to good
purpose : " What do I love when I love Thee ?   Not
bodily beauty, not transient glory, nor the light so pleasant

to our eyes ; not the harmonious melody of sweet songs,
nor the sweet scent of flowers, perfumes, and spices, not
manna and honey nor the joys of a carnal embrace.    It is
none of these that I love when I love my God ; and yet in
this love I find a light, a melody, a fragrance, a food, and
an embrace of the inward man : there, in the depths of my
soul, shines something not in space, sounds something uttered
not in time ; thence comes a fragrance no breeze can waft
away, and a flavour eating cannot lessen ; and an embrace
is there which no satiety can end : this I love when I love
my GOD." [1]

"Upon the Thrones GOD is seated," and they are
peculiarly open and responsive to every Divine impression.
This, accordingly, is Heywood's hymn in the Book named
after them :—

> As far as the East is distant from the West,
> Remove our sins from us ; in every breast
> Plant, in their stead, all goodness, GOD Immense,
> Whose smallest attribute passeth human sense,
> From Whom, in Whom, by Whom, all things subsist,
> Visible and unseen, Who, as Thou list,
> Thy works *about* doth compass, *within* fill,
> Cover *above*, *below* supportest still.
>
>         .      .      .      .      .      .      .
>
> So we with lips and hearts unfeign'd, O King,
> To Thee, for all Thy benefits, will sing
> This hymn : O Holy, Holy, Holy, Thee
> We do invoke, O Blessed Trinity,
> To enter us, Thy Temple ; make it a place
> Worthy Thy inning there, by Divine grace.

[1] Some readers will know the fine sonnet in which Archbishop Alexander (of
Armagh) in our own times paraphrased this passage from St. Augustine.  See too
the lines of Giles Fletcher on p. 29 above.

This, by the Father, of the Son we crave ;
This, by the Son, Good Father let us have ;
O Holy Spirit, that this may be done,
We entreat Thee, by the Father and the Son.

In Book IV, under the heading ' Dominations,' Heywood goes on to prove the existence of angels by the evidence of dreams and similar phenomena ; and then gives a detailed account (supported in his notes by references to Dionysius, St. Bernard, etc.) of the " three most blessed Hierarchies, each into three companies divided ". It is in this book that he indulges in the curiously inapposite parenthesis, complaining of the " curtailing " of the Christian names of contemporary poets—Will. Shakespeare, Ben. Jonson, etc. The complaint is but a serio-comic one ; and, to prove that it was not prompted by offended self-dignity, he adds, " I hold he loves me best that calls me Tom ".

In the section named after the Virtues, Heywood traces the reputed concordance between the concentric spheres of the Ptolemaic system of astronomy and the nine Angelic Choirs. It is worth recalling how each planet was once believed to be carried round the earth in a crystal sphere, and, as these spheres were made to revolve by the outermost *primum mobile*, they were supposed to produce the ' music of the spheres,' which only a very few highly privileged persons ever heard. Pythagoras heard it ; and from his account Plato evolved the Myth of Er, who, returning from the other world, described the great spindle of Necessity. This rested on the knees of Necessity and acted as an axis, the heavenly bodies revolving round it, each with a siren thereon, hymning a single note ; the Fates stood by to control the revolving whorls and added their voices to those of

the sirens.    Dante, in the *Paradiso*, had given sanction to
the theory that each concentric sphere was revolved by one
of the Angelic Choirs ; Spenser, Shakespeare, and Milton
(in *Arcades*) had referred to it with evident approval ; and
just about the time when Heywood was writing his lines—
they are hardly poetic enough to reprint—Galileo, under
the threat of torture, was solemnly abjuring the Copernican
system which was to undermine the whole theory, except as
a poetic figure of the harmony of Nature : this, as noted
above, may well be regarded as due to angelic agency.

The rest of Heywood's book may be rapidly summa-
rized.    In connexion with the Powers, he recounts the fall
of Lucifer and prays for true contrition of heart ; and under
the respective headings of Principats, Archangels, and
Angels, he discusses the nature of Demons (with a prayer
for defence against temptations), Genii and mythical creatures like fauns (with an Act of Submission to GOD'S Will
in view of man's limitations), and Fairies and Magic.    But,
though attracted by such notions, he insists that they are
utterly unreliable and must be tested by the light of Holy
Scripture.

In his final Meditation, he begs some measure of the
gifts and graces of the various angelic orders, after first re-
assuring himself, as it were, in the lines quoted below, that
the angels were not meant to shut men out from the Presence
of GOD, but that what we are told of them is intended to
bring within our mental grasp the reality and activity of that
Presence.

> Betimes awake thee,
> And unto sad and serious contemplation,
> Dull soul, betake thee ;
>        Thyself retire,

5

And after the great GOD of thy salvation
    With care enquire.
Withdraw thyself within thy heart's close centre,
Whither, save Him alone, let nothing enter.

Then let thine heart
Thus say : My GOD, let me behold Thy face ;
Show in what part,
        Or in what ground
Of the vast world, what corner or what place,
        Thou mayest be found.
How shall I find Thee, if Thou be'st not here ?
Or why not present, being everywhere ?

# CHAPTER IV.

## GEORGE HERBERT, HARVEY, AND QUARLES.

WHEN the Kalendar of our Prayer-Book is brought up to date, one of the very first names to be added to the Anglican hagiarchy must surely be that of 'holy GEORGE HERBERT'. Probably nine critics out of ten would, on mature reflection, name him as the foremost of the distinctively sacred poets of England ; and yet it is becoming increasingly difficult to find even Church-people who are really familiar with his verse. Of those, however, who have devoted time and thought to its perusal, few will fail to endorse Walton's verdict, that *The Temple* is "a book, by the frequent reading thereof, and the assistance of that Spirit that seemed to inspire the author, the reader may attain habits of peace and piety, and all the gifts of the Holy Ghost and Heaven". Of greater names, it will be enough to instance the comfort which it brought to Charles I in his captivity, the deep influence (spiritual as well as literary) which it exerted on Henry Vaughan, and, in a less degree, on Crashaw, and the avowal of Richard Baxter : "I must confess, after all, that next to the Scripture-poems there are none so savoury to me as Mr. George Herbert's. . . . Herbert speaks to GOD like a man that really believeth in GOD and whose business in the world is most with God ; heart-work and heaven-work make up his book". Cowper, too, while deprecating his "Gothic uncouthness," found in the tortures of dejection that Herbert " was the only author I had any delight in reading ; I pored over him all day long, and, though I found not there—what I might have found—a cure for my malady, yet it never seemed so much alleviated as when I was reading him ". And Coleridge, no unexacting critic, never loses an opportunity of praising Herbert, not only as " a Churchman and a Christian," but as an " exquisite master of this species of poetry, where the scholar and the poet supplies the material and the perfect well-bred gentleman the expressions and the arrangement ". But Coleridge also insisted that " to appreciate what Herbert wrote, it is not enough that the reader possess a cultivated judgment or even poetic sensibility, unless he be likewise a Christian, and both a zealous and an orthodox Christian ". This just observation disposes of a good deal of the disparagement that Herbert's reputation has to make head against in some critical quarters.

But to say all this is not to establish his title to a place in a gallery of mystical poets. He is sometimes written off as non-mystical, because his religion had a very strong vein of the institutional element. He was, indeed, zealous for the rites and ordinances of the Church ; but we have seen above that it is the chief merit of the mystical writers of the English Church that they have not developed the mystical at the expense of the other elements of religion. Herbert claims his place here, or rather, he would never claim it, but must be conceded it, as an exemplar of the mysticism which has been defined as the science of Divine love. From the beloved Apostle who learnt from his Master, " If a man love Me, he will keep My words, and My Father will love him, and we will come unto him and make our abode with him " ; and from St. Paul, who prayed that his converts,

" being rooted and grounded in love, might be able to comprehend what is the breadth and length and depth and
height, and to know the love of Christ which passeth knowledge, in order that they might be filled with all the fulness
of GOD "; through St. Augustine, who wrote his *Confessions* " for love of GOD's love," and St. Bernard, who
" loved GOD because he loved Him and that he might love
Him more "; through Ruysbroek, Suso, St. Catherine of
Siena, and St. John of the Cross, greatest of all mystical
poets ; through St. Francis de Sales with his motto, *Ou
mourir ou aimer*, and Fénelon, confident that " the soul
is united to GOD when its affections are given to Him because He is what He is "; right up to mystics of these
latter days, the student of mysticism can trace this " approach of the soul to GOD through the desire of love ".
Miss Underhill quotes as one of the best modern definitions
of mysticism, these words of M. Berger : " the concentra-
tion of all the forces of the soul upon a supernatural object,
conceived and loved as a living Person ".   And more recently still, M. Joly accepted the following as the best
definition he had ever come across : " Mysticism is the love
of GOD "; and he added that " every Christian, who is in
a state of grace, loves GOD and is more or less of a mystic,
but the mystic properly so called . . . is one who is
wrapped up in, and filled with, the love of God ".   By
this criterion George Herbert indisputably takes standing
among the mystics.

*The Parody* may be named, perhaps, as the key-poem
to the *Temple*.   A parody, Dr. Johnson tells us, is " a
kind of writing in which the words of an author or his
thoughts are taken and by a slight change adapted to some
new purpose ".   Usually this purpose is to burlesque the

original ; but it is quite in keeping with Herbert's temperament that his purpose is to idealize Donne's poem, which is
referred to on p. 47 above.   Herbert's version is given here
in full :—

> Soul's joy, when Thou art gone,
>     And I alone,
>     Which cannot be,
> Because Thou dost abide with me,
>     And I depend on Thee ;
>
> Yet when Thou dost suppress
>     The cheerfulness
>     Of Thy abode,
> And in my powers not stir abroad,
>     But leave me to my load—
>
> Oh, what a damp and shade
>     Doth me invade !
>     No stormy night
> Can so afflict, or so affright,
>     As Thy eclipsed light.
>
> Ah, Lord, do not withdraw,
>     Lest want of awe
>     Make sin appear,
> And when Thou dost but shine less clear,
>     Say that Thou art not here.
>
> And then what life I have,
>     While Sin doth rave,
>     And falsely boast,
> That I may seek but Thou art lost,
>     Thou and alone Thou know'st,

> Oh, what a deadly cold
>       Doth me enfold !
>       I half believe
> That Sin says true ; but, while I grieve,
> Thou com'st and dost relieve.

Here, at once, we are reminded that Herbert was, in a literary sense, the disciple of Donne, whose technical faults, in some measure, he reproduces.   But further, this poem introduces us to the two distinctive features of Herbert's spiritual experience : the determination to give sacred love that paramount place in verse which he felt to have been usurped by profane love, and the alternations of joy and grief which nearly all mystics have undergone according as the sense of GOD'S Presence has been accentuated or has grown dim. " I was borne up to Thee," says St. Augustine, " by Thy beauty, and then borne down from Thee by mine own weight."   Likewise the Psalmist : " Thou didst turn Thy face from me and I was troubled " ; but " Thou hast turned my heaviness into joy ".   These two features can be abundantly illustrated from George Herbert's poems.

When seventeen years of age, he sent his mother some sonnets, meaning in them, he said, " to declare my resolution that my poor abilities in poetry shall be all and ever consecrated to GOD'S glory ".   In the first of these he asks

> Why are not sonnets made of Thee ? and lays
> Upon Thine altar burnt ?   Cannot Thy love
> Heighten a spirit to sound out Thy praise
> As well as any she ?

We find the same thought again and again in *The Temple*, as, for instance, in the pair of sonnets entitled *Love*, and in the following lines named *Dulness* :—

Why do I languish thus, drooping and dull,
    As if I were all earth ?
Oh, give me quickness, that I may with mirth
    Praise Thee brimful.

The wanton lover in a curious strain
    Can praise his fairest fair,
And with quaint metaphors her curled hair
    Curl o'er again.

Thou art my loveliness, my life, my light,
    Beauty alone to me ;
Thy bloody death, and undeserv'd, makes Thee
    Pure red and white.

When all perfections as but one appear,
    That those Thy form doth show,
The very dust where Thou dost tread and go
    Makes beauties here.

Where are my lines, then ? my approaches, views ?
    Where are my window-songs ?
Lovers are still pretending, and even wrongs
    Sharpen their Muse.

But I am lost in flesh, whose sugar'd lies
    Still mock me, and grow bold ;
Sure Thou didst put a mind there, if I could
    Find where it lies.

Lord, clear Thy gift, that with a constant wit
    I may but look towards Thee :
Look only ; for to love Thee who can be,
    What angel fit ?

In spite, then, of a deep sense of unworthiness, Herbert was in very deed and truth, in love with GOD. The late Dr. Moberley, one of the most cautious and reverent of theologians, justified the use of such an expression on the ground that the phrase ' to love ' is inadequate, and has too often been perverted to degraded uses. " It is difficult," he adds, " for our imagination to emphasize too strongly what the meaning would be of ' being in love with ' Christ crucified and risen ; or to how much it would be the practical key in the way of the translation of the spirit of Calvary into the animating spirit of individual Christian life. What engrossing of faculties, what absorption of desire, what depth of thought, what wistfulness of kindness, what strength of will, what inspiration of power—to endeavour or to endure —would forthwith follow with spontaneous, silent, irresistible sequence, if once we were ' in love ' ! " [1]   And this was actually the case with George Herbert ; but his ' calf-love ' (if the expression is here permissible) had been severely tested. In the first of several pieces entitled *Affliction*, he says :—

> When first Thou didst entice me to Thy heart,
>     I thought the service brave :
> So many joys I writ down for my part,
>     Besides what I might have
> Out of my stock of natural delights,
> Augmented with Thy gracious benefits.
>
> .   .   .   .   .   .   .   .   .
>
> At first Thou gavest me milk and sweetnesses ;
>     I had my wish and way ;
> My days were strewed with flowers and happiness :
>     There was no month but May.
> But with my years sorrow did twist and grow,
> And made a party unawares for woe.

[1] *Atonement and Personality*, pp. 146 ff, 1901.

Ill-health came, the first premonitions of consumption, and, with restoration to health, the loss of friends—friends whose influence at Court had encouraged the hopes of worldly advancement. But this disappointment only heightened the allurements of secular learning and "academic praise," as Public Orator at Cambridge. Another period of ill-health was recognized and accepted as GOD'S leading. And the poem ends with the magnificent couplet,

> Ah, my dear GOD, though I am clean forgot,
> Let me not love Thee, if I love Thee not.

Noble as is the motto of St. Francis de Sales quoted above and the similar outcry of Gertrude More—"Oh, let me love, or not live!" how much sublimer is George Herbert's determination to love GOD in all circumstances, and his desire—if he should cease to love Him—not merely to die, but, far worse than that, to cease to love Him.

That the service of GOD was chosen with open eyes, let the poem which borrows its motive from our Lord's parable of *The Pearl* of great price bear witness. "I know the ways of learning," says the friend to whom Bacon dedicated his *Instauratio Scientiæ*, with acknowledgment of assistance rendered, "yet I love Thee." With yet greater assurance could this scion of a noble house, whose grace of diction and bearing had won the marked approval of royalty, claim to "know the ways of Honour, what maintains the quick returns of courtesy and wit". This rivalry of the World to GOD'S addresses was an outstanding feature of Herbert's younger years; but he tells us in this poem that the Flesh, too, advanced insistent claims. But yet he keeps his plighted troth :—

I know all these, and have them in my hand:
Therefore not sealed, but with open eyes
I fly to Thee.

Here we have one of the metaphors, in which Herbert's
verse abounds and of which such readers as are not con-
versant with seventeenth century pursuits are apt to complain. This is from hawking; elsewhere it is from the
bowling-green, or some obsolete game of cards. When
these images do not ' come off,' we are justified in condemning them as ' conceits '; and it must be admitted that George
Herbert's imagery does not invariably elucidate his meaning. This failure is the result, not always of the use of
obsolete phraseology, but sometimes of the abuse of analogy
and the strained ingenuity of wit, into which he was led by
his admiration of Donne. Here, however, the imagery,
once grasped, helps the imagination and heightens the effect
of the emotion which the poet is trying to express.

But, though his renunciation of Learning, Honour, and
Pleasure was complete and whole-hearted, there were inevitably moments when Herbert was tempted to regret his
choice. *Submission*, for all its playful tone, gives us a
touching insight into the persistent pressure of worldly dis-
tractions; *The Collar* depicts rather the attractions of the
flesh; while both these rivals figure in *The Quip*. The
title of this piece means, it is perhaps needless to say, the
repartee; and, with extraordinary delicacy of workmanship
—the joint-product of art and emotion—the impression is
given that the quick retort is checked again and again, and
the appeal for GOD's support substituted just, but only
just, in time: " But Thou shalt answer, Lord, for me ".

The ideals of his childhood, fostered by a saintly mother,
the frustrated purposes of his early manhood, and the in-

creasing intensity of his devotion to GOD, all pointed clearly
to the Priesthood as his vocation.   But, although he knew
in how low an estimation the ministry was very generally
held at the time, his own ideals were so lofty and his
humility so deep, that he long hesitated to advance from
the Diaconate to the higher Order.   *Aaron, The Priesthood*, and *The Windows* all express something of this
diffident irresolution.   But, at last, recognizing that his
sense of unworthiness was becoming a thwarting of GOD'S
will, he capitulated, confident that

> In Thee I will overcome
> The man who once against Thee fought.

And so began that wonderful, brief ministry which is
mirrored in *The Priest to the Temple*, and has hallowed
for all time the Church and Parish of Bemerton.   Henceforth, he vowed to think always, and speak, of Jesus as his
' Master ' ; and it was doubtless at the time when he
registered this vow that he penned the lovely poem headed
*The Odour*, opening with the lines,

> How sweetly doth ' My Master ' sound !   ' My Master ! '
> As ambergris leaves a rich scent
> Unto the taster,
> So do these words a sweet content,
> An Oriental fragrancy—' My Master ! '

Although the context shows that the relationship which
he had in his mind here was that of servant and master,
yet, when one recalls his resolve to consecrate to the praise
of GOD poetic gifts so often prostituted to the flattery of
frail flesh, it may not be fanciful to suspect that there lurked
at the back of his mind the thought of the relationship between a lover and his mistress.   At any rate, henceforth

no knightly lover of the Middle Ages was ever more punctilious in the fulfilment of his *devoirs*, or more sensitive to the frowns of his lady, than Herbert was in his chivalrous attachment to his Master and in his agonized awareness of any cloud between them.   Only one pleasure, outside the direct service of GOD, was retained—music, and that only because it " knows the way to Heaven's door " ; only one pursuit, outside his ministerial activities, was followed— verse-making, and that, as he tells GOD in *The Quiddity*, because

> It is that which, while I use,
> I am with Thee, and *most take all*—

implying by the proverbial allusion that in sacred verse he finds full recompense for the lack of secular interests.   And, in his verse-making, Love is the all-absorbing theme—Love and its antithesis, Sin.   The immensity of Sin and Love is the subject of *The Agony*, a poem in which wit, imagina- tiveness, and intensity are finely intermingled :—

> Philosophers have measured mountains,
> Fathom'd the depths of seas, of states, and kings,
> Walk'd with a staff to heaven, and traced fountains :
> But there are two vast spacious things,
> The which to measure it doth more behove ;
> Yet few there are that sound them—Sin and Love.

> Who would know Sin, let him repair
> Unto Mount Olivet ; there shall he see
> A Man so wrung with pains that all His hair,
> His skin, His garments bloody be.
> Sin is that press and vice, which forceth pain
> To hunt his cruel food through every vein.

Who knows not Love, let him assay
And taste that juice which, on the Cross, a pike
Did set again abroach; then let him say
If ever he did taste the like.
Love is that liquor, sweet, and most divine,
Which my GOD feels as Blood, but I as wine.

Especially noteworthy is the thought in the final couplet
—a thought repeated more than once in *The Temple*.   In
his sacramental doctrine, Herbert does not argue from the
sign to the grace, but conversely he merges the sign entirely
in the thing signified, as again, in *Divinity* :—

He doth bid us take His Blood for wine.

Here and there a mystic has been found who has claimed
such immediate and uninterrupted communion with GOD as
to be in the position to despise and neglect sacramental aids.
Not so Herbert, to whom the Holy Eucharist is a veritable
' love-feast,' the expression of love on both sides—Christ's
love to us, and our love to Christ.   It would be difficult to
convey this idea more blithely than he does in *The Banquet*,
with its opening lines,

Welcome, sweet and sacred cheer,
Welcome dear ;
With me, in me live and dwell ;
For Thy neatness passeth sight,
Thy delight
Passeth tongue to taste or tell.

The same jubilant welcome greets the " dear feast of
Lent ".   It was no conventional observance, no mere ecclesiastical custom.   The Church's rule offers " an occasion "
for fasting, of which " true Christians should be glad " to
take advantage, for " Christ has gone that way ".

> Perhaps my GOD, though He be far before,
> May turn and take me by the hand.

But, just as his sacramental communions were but incidents in a life of continuous communion with GOD, so Herbert's Lenten fast was but a phase in a life of constant detachment and mortification. His asceticism had in it no sourness, no hard scrupulousness; for it was the irrepressible outcome of his love. To quote Dr. Moberley again : " The daily unselfish-ness—more and more smiling and spontaneous—the quiet stringency and gladness of detailed self-discipline; do we not see how this, as the unconscious, or the conscious, imitation of the Cross, by one who is in love with the Crucified, may be just the natural homage, the relief which *will* not be denied, of a devoted love, welling up and bub-bling over in act ? "

George Herbert's attitude towards the Bible can be illustrated by his letter to Nicholas Ferrar, on returning the latter's translation of Valdesso's *Considerations*. Valdesso was a mystic of the type which extols the inner light at the expense of the Bible. Herbert, whose opinion had been sought, recommended the publication of Ferrar's translation, chiefly because of " the great honour and reverence which Valdesso everywhere bears towards our dear Master and Lord ". But, at the same time, he took exception to various passages in which the Holy Scriptures seemed disparaged. In the margin of one ' Consideration ' he notes, " I like none of it, for it slights the Scriptures too much. . . . All the Saints of GOD may be said in some sort of sense to have put confidence in Scripture ; but not as a naked word severed from GOD, but as the Word of GOD, and in so doing they do not sever their trust from GOD ; but by trusting in the Word of GOD, they trust in GOD." Again, " I much

mislike the comparison of images and Holy Scripture, as if
they were both but alphabets, and after a time to be left.
The Holy Scriptures have not only an elementary use, but
a use of perfection ; neither can they ever be exhausted."
This sort of "disparagement of Scripture" will, he fears,
"set up enthusiasms"—using a word which had not then
the nobler significance now attached to it, but, as will appear
again in these pages, denoted a bewildered fanaticism with
a reckless denial of moral obligations. To George Herbert
the Bible was a book of "infinite sweetness," of which
"each verse doth shine" and was to be "sucked by the
heart" : it was not only a guide-book ; it gave wings to
the affections. To the lover, like Herbert, absorbed in the
Beloved Who is always nigh, the Word, which comes from
Him, reveals love and attracts love :—

> Nay, I will read Thy book, and never move
> Till I have found therein Thy love,
> Thy art of love, which I'll turn back on Thee.

That mutual love is Herbert's first thought in the morning :—

> Teach me Thy love to know ;
> That this new light, which now I see,
> May both the work and workman show ;
> Then by a sunbeam I will climb to Thee.

It is his last thought at night :—

> My GOD, Thou art all love.
> Not one poor minute escapes Thy breast,
> But brings a favour from above ;
> And in this love, more than in bed, I rest.

And for the intervening hours, he begs for

> Such a heart whose pulse may be
>     Thy praise.

But he is well aware that, with all its good-will, his heart is fickle ; and so he cries, in *Frailty*,

> Oh, brook not this, lest if what even now
>     My foot did tread,
> Affront those joys, wherewith Thou didst endow
>     And long since wed
> My poor soul, e'en sick of love.

Here we have almost the only reference to be found in Herbert's poems, full as they are of Scriptural allusion, to the *Song of Songs* : it is a striking testimony to his reverent attitude towards GOD that, although *The Temple* is full of the most ardent love, here alone does it touch upon the symbol of the 'Marriage of the Soul'. In this connexion, however, it is necessary to recall a stanza in *Perseverance*, found in the Williams MS. :—

> For who can tell, though Thou hast died to win
> And wed my soul in glorious paradise,
> Whether my many crimes and use of sin
> May yet forbid the banns and bliss.

George Herbert has some striking passages on man's place in the universe. Although, in one mood, the sense of GOD's purity and perfection discovers his own pettiness, and almost convinces him that " man is but grass " and " cannot praise GOD's Name," yet he knows, with Hegel, that " in man Nature comes to self-consciousness," and therefore he must praise. This is the subject of *Providence*, where Man is declared " the world's high-priest," privileged and bound to offer sacrifice for those incapable

of such high action.   Nature, he goes on to show, is one
grand harmony :—

> If we could hear
> Thy skill and art, what music would it be !
>
> Thou art in small things great, not small in any ;
> Thy even praise can neither rise nor fall ;
> Thou art in all things one, in each thing many ;
> For Thou art infinite in one and all.

And so we note again the absorption of the lover in the
Beloved, Whose Name is whispered by the breeze, Whose
beauty is reflected in the flower.

The poem entitled *Man* must be printed in full, for
in the opinion of many it is Herbert's masterpiece.   It has,
indeed, a philosophic breadth lacking to most of his poems ;
but it is without the graceful intimacy that endears him to
his regular readers.   It states the doctrine, popularized by
Paracelsus and often emphasized by subsequent mystics,
that man is a microcosm—a little world in himself, a minia-
ture or quintessence of the universe—the macrocosm, every
part of which has its counterpart in him and pays its due to
him as the pinnacle of Nature.   Modern biology has thrown
unexpected light on this claim of man to " recapitulate the
whole gamut of creation ".   Astronomy, on the other hand,
has long exploded the geocentric theory of the universe,
endorsed by Herbert in this poem.   And yet that brilliant
scientist, Dr. A. R. Wallace, has shown that there is a
great deal to be said for the view that the universe was
created for the express purpose of providing a home for man,
the ultimate goal of the evolutionary process.

> My GOD, I heard this day
> That none doth build a stately habitation,

But he that means to dwell therein.
What house more stately hath there been,
Or can be, than is Man ? to whose creation
All things are in decay.

For man is everything,
And more : he is a tree, yet bears more fruit ;
A beast, yet is, or should be, more :
Reason and speech we only bring ;
Parrots may thank us, if they are not mute,
They go upon the score.

Man is all symmetry,
Full of proportions, one limb to another,
And all to all the world besides ;
Each part may call the farthest, brother,
For head with foot hath private amity,
And both with moons and tides.

Nothing hath got so far,
But Man hath caught and kept it as his prey ;
His eyes dismount the highest stars ;
He is in little all the sphere ;
Herbs gladly cure our flesh, because that they
Find their acquaintance there.

For us the winds do blow ;
The earth doth rest, heaven move, and fountain flow ;
Nothing we see but means our good,
As our delight or as our treasure ;
The whole is either our cupboard of food,
Or cabinet of pleasure.

The stars have us to bed;
Night draws the curtain, which the sun withdraws:
Music and light attend our head.
All things unto our flesh are kind
In their descent and being; to our mind
In their ascent and cause.

Each thing is full of duty:
Waters united are our navigation;
Distinguished, our habitation; [divided, to form land].
Below, our drink; above, our meat;
Both are our cleanliness.   Hath one such beauty?
Then how are all things neat!

More servants wait on Man
Than he'll take notice of: in every path
He treads down that which did befriend him
When sickness makes him pale and wan.   [medicinal
O mighty love!   Man is one world, and hath        herbs].
Another to attend him.

Since then, my GOD, Thou hast
So brave a palace built, O dwell in it,
That it may dwell with Thee at last!
Till then afford us so much wit,
That as the world serves us, we may serve Thee,
And both Thy servants be.

In *Man's Medley*, Herbert develops the complementary
truth, as old as the Book of Genesis, that man belongs to
two worlds, finite and infinite, leads two lives, mortal and
immortal, and has obligations to both.   The thought in
*The Pulley* is of man's wondrous blessings and endow-
ments, all rendered futile and unsatisfying, if "he rest in
Nature and not the GOD of Nature".   The poem was

probably suggested by St. Augustine's words : " Thou hast
made us for Thyself, and our hearts are restless till they
rest in Thee " ; but, no doubt, it reproduces his own experience, as hinted at in his message to Ferrar, that in *The
Temple* he would find " a picture of the many spiritual
conflicts that have passed between GOD and my soul before
I could subject mine to the will of Jesus my Master, in
Whose service I have now found perfect freedom ".

That " service " is the subject of *The Elixir.* The
lines are too familiar for quotation, but they have a close
bearing on George Herbert's mystical standing.  Like
Brother Lawrence, he had learnt that " the practice of the
Presence of GOD " was no visionary or unpractical aloof-
ness from commonplace pursuits ; that everyday duties,
however prosaic, were no hindrance to union with GOD.
His intense love for GOD was the Elixir, the Tincture, the
Philosopher's Stone, which, turning all baser metal into
gold, made every menial action " fine," and led him to ful-
fil each task, not out of self-respect (as one who consults a
looking-glass), but out of devotion to GOD (as one who
gazes at the heavens through a telescope).  Bishop
Chandler's latest book of mystical theology, *The Cult of
the Passing Moment*, from which the following passage is
borrowed, might almost be described as an expansion of
Herbert's poem : " The Saints have regarded the moment
*sub specie æternitatis ;* each moment has had for them
an infinite value, and an infinite significance, and an infinite
claim on their attention.  Each has made its claim upon
them in the name of GOD, and each particular ' claim has
been recognized and welcomed with the enthusiastic devotion which every one regards as due to the service of GOD
*in general.*  The Saints have differed from other Christians

in that this general devotion to GOD's service has been translated by them into a particular devotion to the several claims
which GOD makes in each moment as it comes.    And, as
these particular claims upon them are mostly concerned with
things which seem trivial and unimportant, it has been truly
said that the Saints are the people who do ordinary things
extraordinarily well."

Did George Herbert ever attain the specific experience
known as rapture or ecstasy ?   Who can say ?   He would
have been the last man to speak openly of such an experience.
But certainly, with or without ecstacies in the literal sense,
he lived the ecstatic life.   Moreover, in each of the poems
named *The Temper* (a word which in its original sense
implies a mixture of opposites), there is, perhaps, a hint at
the experimental knowledge of some such transcendent
emotions.   In one he asks,

> Where is that mighty joy
> Which just now took up all my heart ?

In the other he exclaims,

> How should I praise Thee, Lord ! how should my rhymes
> Gladly engrave Thy love in steel,
> If what my soul doth feel sometimes,
> My soul might ever feel.
>
> Although there were some forty heavens, or more,
> Sometimes I peer above them all ;
> Sometimes I hardly reach a score ;
> Sometimes to hell I fall.
>
> O, rack me not to such a vast extent ;
> Those distances belong to Thee ;
> The world's too little for Thy tent,
> A grave too big for me.

Wilt Thou meet arms with man, that Thou dost stretch
    A crumb of dust from Heaven to Hell ?
Will great GOD measure with a wretch ?
    Shall he Thy stature spell ?

Oh, let me, when Thy roof my soul hath hid,
    Oh, let me roost and nestle there ;
Then of a sinner Thou art rid,
    And I of hope and fear.

Yet, take Thy way ; for, sure Thy way is best :
    Stretch or contract me, Thy poor debtor ;
This is but tuning of my breast,
    To make the music better.

Whether I fly with angels, fall with dust,
    Thy hands made both, and I am there ;
Thy power and love, my love and trust,
    Make one place everywhere.

Here he seems to recognize that man's love needs to be purified, strengthened, uplifted by the withdrawal of sensible supports and delights : " It is expedient for you that I go away ".  There is the danger, of which Tauler speaks, that we should " desire such inward fervour and sweet peace more for their own sake than for the Giver Himself ; thus we fall into spiritual wantonness ".  So, too, in *The Flower*, one of the most exquisite of all his pieces, Herbert clearly sees GOD'S purpose of love in withdrawing the sense of His Presence :—

There are Thy wonders, Lord of Love,
    To make us see we are but flowers that glide ;
Which when we once can find and prove,
    Thou hast a garden for us where to bide.

Who would be more,
Swelling through store,
Forfeit their Paradise by their pride.

When he is aware that an actual fall from grace has
caused the sense of desolation he is quite inconsolable, as,
for instance, in *Sighs and Groans*.  But in *Praise*, and
in *An Offering*, his relief when GOD's smile is seen again,
bursts into joyous melody.  In *The Method*, though not
conscious of any deadly sin, he has an unhappy recollection
of having, perhaps, slighted GOD's love by careless prayer ;
while in *Complaining* he is simply depressed by the sense
of unworthiness that every true lover knows.  Only very
rarely, as in *The Cross*, does he seem to have any suspicion
that the sense of GOD's absence is not altogether unconnected with the physical lassitude of an invalid.

In not a few pieces George Herbert makes use of arti-
ficial tricks of rhyme and metre, which give a suggestion of
insincerity.  But it was part of his mystical nature that in
quite trivial outward signs he could perceive, and by them
tried to convey deep inward meanings.  And so we get the
lines built up, as it were, in the very shape of *The Altar*,
his reflections on Easter spreading themselves to simulate
*Wings*, and other almost childlike freaks and effects.  In
*Denial*, because " my heart was broken as was my verse,"
there is a failure in rhyme in the last line of each stanza except in the last of all ; and a similar device is adopted in
the closing lines of *Home*.  But in neither of these poems
is it possible to doubt the sincerity of the spiritual distress,
just as in the pieces to be referred to next, the poignancy of
dejection is unmistakable.  For sheer misery it would be
impossible to out-do the poem called *Longing*, which, as

perhaps the supreme expression of the sense of dereliction
in the English language, must be quoted at full length :—

> With sick and famish'd eyes,
> With doubling knees and weary bones,
> To Thee my cries,
> To Thee my groans,
> To Thee my sighs, my tears ascend ;
> No end ?
>
> My throat, my soul is hoarse ;
> My heart is wither'd like a ground
> Which Thou dost curse ;
> My thoughts turn round,
> And make me giddy : Lord, I fall,
> Yet call.
>
> From Thee all pity flows :
> Mothers are kind, because Thou art,
> And dost dispose
> To them a part :
> Their infants them, and they suck Thee,
> More free.
>
> Bowels of pity, hear ;
> Lord of my soul, love of my mind,
> Bow down Thy ear ;
> Let not the wind
> Scatter my words, and in the same
> Thy name.
>
> Look on my sorrows round ;
> Mark well my furnace. Oh, what flames,
> What heats abound !
> What griefs, what shames !
> Consider, Lord ; Lord, bow Thine ear,
> And hear !

Lord Jesu, Thou didst bow
Thy dying head upon the tree ;
        Oh, be not now
        More dead to me.
Lord, hear.   " Shall He that made the ear
                Not hear ? "


        Behold, Thy dust doth stir :
It moves, it creeps, it aims at Thee ;
        Wilt Thou defer
        To succour me,
Thy pile of dust, wherein each crumb
                Says, ' Come ' ?


        To Thee help appertains :
Hast Thou left all things to their course,
        And laid the reins
        Upon the horse ?
Is all lock'd ? hath a sinner's plea
                No key ?


        Indeed the world's Thy book,
Where all things have their leaf assign'd ;
        Yet a meek look
        Hath interlin'd.
Thy board is full, yet humble guests
                Find nests.


        Thou tarriest, while I die,
And fall to nothing ; Thou dost reign,
        And rule on high,
        While I remain
In bitter grief ; yet am I styl'd
                Thy child.

Lord, didst Thou leave Thy throne,
Not to relieve ?   How can it be
That Thou art grown
Thus hard to me ?
Were sin alive, good cause there were
To bear :

But now both sin is dead
And all Thy promises live and bide ;
That wants his head,
These speak and chide,
And in Thy bosom pour my tears
As theirs.

Lord Jesus, hear my heart,
Which hath been broken now so long,
That every part
Hath got a tongue :
Thy beggars grow ; rid them away
To-day.

My Love, My Sweetness, hear :
By these Thy feet, at which my heart
Lies all the year,
Pluck out Thy dart,
And heal my troubled breast, which cries,
Which dies.

In *Assurance*, too, we have a record of that very darkest night of the soul, when, in the midst of torturing doubts and fears, faith blindly clings to earlier certitudes ; while *The Search* expresses the agonizing sense of the immeasurable distance which seemed at times to separate him from GOD'S Presence, and yet in its last lines he ventures faintly to recall past intimacies :—

When Thou dost turn, and wilt be near,
What edge so keen,
What point so piercing can appear
To come between ?

For as Thy absence doth excel
All distance known,
So doth Thy nearness bear the bell,
Making two one.

All these pieces, and many more that might be adduced, illustrate most strikingly Ruysbroeck's account of the alternations of excitement and depression to which the fervid lover of GOD is liable : " No tongue can describe the many storms and agitations which arise from the two sides of love, for love makes a man now hot, now cold, now bold, now timid, now joyous, now sorrowful ; it brings him fear, hope, despair, tears, complaints, songs, praises, and such things without number. Such are the sufferings of those who live in the passion of love ; and yet this is the most spiritual and the most useful life that a man can live, each according to his own capacity. But where man's method fails and can reach no higher, then GOD'S method begins ; where man, by his sufferings, his love, and his unsatisfied desires, entwines himself with GOD, and cannot be united to HIM, then the Spirit of our Lord cometh as a fierce fire which burns, and consumes, and swallows up all things in itself, so that the man forgets his inward exercises, and forgets himself, and feels just as if he were one spirit and one love with GOD."

It is in one of his happier, calmer moods that we should wish to take leave of George Herbert ; and for this we might choose *The Call*, or better still, *Clasping of Hands*, with its elaborate phrasing of spontaneous gaiety, and the characteristic prayer in its closing couplet :—

> Oh, be mine still ; still make me Thine ;
> Or rather make no Thine and mine.

But, as a final extract from George Herbert's verse,
nothing could be more appropriate than *The Glance*, a poem
full of intimate allusiveness, in which he looks back over his
whole life to the time when the Eternal Love first, as it were,
caught his eye and brought to light his sinfulness. Seen
with hideous clearness from the propinquity to GOD he had
now attained, the unobtrusive vanity, the tinge of worldliness,
and the occasional hotness of temper, which were the only
faults ever laid to his charge, seemed a veritable " weltering
in sin ". Since then, in spite of the many clouds which had
dimmed the light of GOD'S countenance, he had never long
been cut off from the original Source of Light. And now
he was able to look forward with calm confidence to the
timeless time when he would see the Beloved with open
face, and would know even as also he was known.

> When first Thy sweet and gracious eye
> Vouchsafèd even in the midst of youth and night,
> To look upon me, who before did lie
>> Weltering in sin,
>> I felt a sugar'd strange delight,
> Passing all cordials made by any art,
> Bedew, embalm, and overrun my heart,
>> And take it in.

> Since that time many a bitter storm
> My soul hath felt, even able to destroy,
> Had the malicious and ill-meaning harm
>> His swing and sway ;
>> But still Thy sweet original joy
> Sprung from Thine eye, did work within my soul,
> And surging griefs, while they grew bold, control,
>> And got the day.

If Thy first glance so powerful be—
A mirth but open'd, and seal'd up again—
What wonders shall we feel when we shall see
Thy full-ey'd love !
When Thou shalt look us out of pain,
And one aspect of Thine spend in delight
More than a thousand suns disburse in light,
In Heaven above.

The 1640 edition of *The Temple* contained, as a sort of Appendix, an anonymous collection of poems entitled *The Synagogue*, and, until quite recently, it has been customary to issue the two collections together. Isaak Walton announced that the author of *The Synagogue* was CHRISTOPHER HARVEY, who, according to Anthony à Wood, was "a minister's son of Cheshire, was born in that county, became a battler of Brazen-nose College in 1613, aged sixteen years ; took the degree of Arts, that of Master being completed in 1620, Holy Orders, and at length was made Vicar of Clifton in Warwickshire". Walton, to whom he was personally known, seems to have valued his verses as highly as those of Herbert, coupling the two together as having power to

Raise sad thoughts above the earth
And fix them there,
Free from the world's anxieties and fear.

But Harvey was a sensible, as well as a devout man, and he had clearer views on his own standing as a poet ; his sub-title places his work fairly satisfactorily, explaining *The Synagogue* to be "the shadow of *The Temple*, sacred poems and private ejaculations in imitation of Mr. George Herbert ". The imitation is, indeed, too servile ; and at times the writer touches such depths of infelicity that, on

reading the earlier pieces, one almost wonders if the whole
affair be not an elaborate burlesque.   But the piety of the
man becomes more and more apparent, until in the latter
pages one clearly recognizes the workings of a truly mystical
soul.   The mysticism is closely akin to that of George Herbert, as will appear in the following piece, entitled *Resolution and Assurance*:—

> Lord, Thou wilt love me.   Wilt thou not ?
> Beshrew that ' not ' :
> It was my sin begot
> That question first : Yes, Lord, Thou wilt.
> Thy Blood was spilt
> To wash away my guilt.
>
> Lord, I will love Thee.   Shall I not ?
> Beshrew that ' not ' :
> 'Twas death's accursed plot
> To put that question : Yes, I will,
> Lord, love Thee still,
> In spite of all my ill.
>
> Then life and love continue still
> We shall, and will,
> My Lord and I, until,
> In his celestial hill
> We love our fill,
> When He hath purged all mine ill.

Among other poems which might be quoted if more
space were at command, are *Comfort in Extremity*, *In-
mates*, and *The Curb*, all very reminiscent of George
Herbert.   A pleasing trilogy consists of *The Loss*, *The
Search*, and *The Return*.   In *The Loss*, adopting his
favourite symbol of the Spiritual Marriage, Harvey re-

lates how "the match was made between my Love and me," but, having dismissed all sorrows and cares, as not befitting a honeymoon, "I found my Love was gone". In recording his Love's Return, he records also his own experience, that "Heavenly Joys on earth are bitter-sweets". Meanwhile, he had given himself unto prayer in these terms :—

Tell me, oh ! tell me (Thou alone canst tell),
Lord of my life, where Thou art gone to dwell :
For in Thy absence heaven itself is hell :
    Without Thee none is well.

Or, if Thou beest not gone, but only hid'st
Thy Presence in the place where Thou abid'st,
Teach me the sacred art, which Thou provid'st
    For all them whom Thou guid'st,

To seek and find Thee by.  Else here I'll lie
Until Thou find me.  If Thou let me die,
That only unto Thee for life do cry,
    Thou diest as well as I.

For if Thou live in me, and I in Thee,
Then either both alive, or dead, must be :
At least I'll lay my death on Thee, and see
    If Thou wilt not agree.

For, though Thou be the Judge Thyself, I have
Thy promise for it, which Thou canst not wave,
That who salvation at Thy hands do crave,
    Thou wilt not fail to save.

Oh ! seek, and find me then ; or else deny
Thy truth, Thyself.  O Thou that canst not lie,
Show Thyself constant to Thy word ; draw nigh ;
    Find me.  Lo, here I lie.

In 1647 Harvey published another volume of verse ; and it is characteristic of his diffidence that this, too, was issued anonymously and was derivative, just as *The Syna-gogue* had been ; the various poems of the *Schola Cordis* are based on the emblems and texts of the Dutchman, Haeften. The scope of the work is sufficiently indicated in the sub-title : " The Heart of itself gone away from GOD ; brought back again to Him ; and instructed by Him ; in forty-seven Emblems ". Although there is no formal digest of mystical theology, the poet, unconsciously perhaps, takes the reader very helpfully up the various rungs of the Mystic Ladder. The opening sections—on *The Infection of the Heart*, *The Vanity of the Heart*, *The Hardness of the Heart*, etc.—describe spiritual conditions inimical to fellowship with GOD. *The Division of the Heart*, and *The Insatiableness of the Heart*, treat of the two complementary truths on which the possibility of the mystical life is based—GOD'S need of man, and man's need of GOD. In the former poem Christ is represented as saying,

> Have I betroth'd thee to Myself, and shall
> The devil and the world intrude
> Upon my right
> E'en in My sight ?
> Think not thou canst Me so delude ;
> I will have none unless I may have all.

Here we recall the passage in the *Imitatio Christi* (iv. 8), where the Beloved says, " Give thyself wholly, . . . but if thou stand upon thyself and dost not offer thyself up freely unto My will, the oblation is not complete, neither will there be entire union between us ". While the poem on *The Heart's Insatiableness* is an amplification of St.

7

Augustine's words, to which reference has already been made in connexion with George Herbert's *Pulley : Fecisti nos ad Te, et inquietum est cor nostrum donec requiescat in Te.* Harvey had evidently felt that awful sense of futile emptiness which comes to one who begins to yield to the Divine attraction—an emptiness which nothing can satisfy but " the fulness of Him that filleth all in all ".

> Let him have all the wealth, all the renown
> And glory that the world can crown
> Her dearest darlings with ; yet his desire
> Will not rest there, but will aspire :
> Earth cannot hold him, nor the whole creation
> Contain his wishes or his expectation.

Man must direct his ambition heavenward ; for

> There a Triune GOD in glory sits,
> Who all grace-trusting hearts both fills and fits.

The next set of ' Odes ' deals with the Purgative Way, describing, among other similar processes, the Circumcision, Contrition, Softening, Cleansing, and Sacrificing of the Heart. While, among the sections dealing with the Il- luminative Way, we have *The Renewing of the Heart* and *The Enlightening of the Heart* with its character- istic finale :—

> There's healing in Thy wings ; Thy light is life ;
> My darkness death. To end all strife
> Be Thou my Husband ; let me be Thy wife ;
> Then both the light and life that's Thine,
> Though light and life divine,
> Will all be mine.

Three Odes on the Tilling, Seeding, and Watering of the Heart lead up to *The Flowering of the Heart*, which reproduces the imagery of the Song of Songs, where the Bridegroom describes His sister-spouse as " a garden enclosed," and the Bride calls on the Beloved to " come into His garden ".   To St. Theresa, it had always been a great delight to " think of my soul as a garden in which the Lord walks," and she had described four kinds of prayer under an allegory of four ways by which a garden may be watered, simple Mental Prayer being comparable to watering with a bucket from a well, the Prayer of Quiet to the action of a waterwheel, the Prayer of Union to irrigation by trenching, and the Prayer of Rapture to a shower direct from the heavens.   Harvey, too, took manifest delight in the thought that his heart was a garden, planted by our Lord with the seeds of His grace, which must be watered and cultivated with a view to His visits :—

> Those lilies I do consecrate to Thee,
> Beloved Spouse, which spring, as Thou mayest see,
> Out of the seed Thou sowest ; and the ground
> Is better'd by Thy flowers when they abound.

In *The Wounding of the Heart* he seems to introduce that phase of final, excruciating purification which so many mystics have had to undergo before achieving union with GOD.   In its closing stanzas he recognizes, and acquiesces in the purpose of love :—

> Lord, empty all Thy quivers ; let there be
> No corner of my spacious heart left free,
>     Till all be but one wound, wherein
>     No subtle, sight-abhorring sin
> May lurk in secret, unespied by Thee ;
>     Perfect Thy purchas'd victory,
>     That Thou may'st ride triumphantly,
> And leading captive all captivity,
> May'st put an end to enmity in me.

> Then, blessed Archer, in requital, I
> To shoot Thine arrows back again will try ;
> By prayers and praises, sighs and sobs,
> By vows and tears, by groans and throbs,
> I'll see if I can pierce and wound Thy heart,
> And vanquish Thee again by Thine own art ;
> Or, that we may at once provide
> For all mishaps that may betide,
> Shoot Thou Thyself, Thou polish'd Shaft, to me,
> And I will shoot my broken heart to Thee.

This owes something, perhaps, to George Herbert's *Artillery ;* in *The Flying of the Heart* his metrical prank noted above (p. 88) has been deliberately reproduced :—

> Oh, that it once were winged like the dove
> That in a moment mounts on high !
> Then should it soon remove
> Where it might lie
> In love :
> And lo,
> This one desire
> Methinks hath imp'd it so,
> That it already flies like fire,
> And e'en my verses into wings do grow.

And so we reach *The Union of the Heart*, where we are told that

> Many things meet and part, but Love's great cable
> Tying two hearts makes them inseparable.

And *The Rest of the Heart :*—

> My busy, stirring heart, that seeks the best,
> Can find no place on earth wherein to rest ;
> For GOD alone, the Author of its bliss,
> Its only Rest, its only Centre is.

But the poet does not stay here, for he knows only too well that the Heart needs constant *Bathing* in Christ's Blood, *Binding* with the band of love, *Propping* by the Everlasting Arms, *Scourging* with the rod of Fatherly correction, *Hedging* with thorns (cf. *Hosea* ii. 16), *Fastening* with the Fear of GOD, which he calls "the soul's sentinel," and sustaining with *The New Wine*, for (like his master, Herbert) Harvey is perfectly clear as to the value of the sacramental aids to the Unitive Life.

Until comparatively recent times, *The School of the Heart* was attributed to FRANCIS QUARLES, to whose work it bears a superficial resemblance. After a period spent at Christ's College, Cambridge, Quarles had become a member of Lincoln's Inn and Cup-bearer, or Steward, to Princess Elizabeth, the wife of the unfortunate Elector Palatine. Subsequently he served Archbishop Usher in Ireland as private secretary, and for a brief period he held the post, often bestowed on literary favourites, of Chronologer to the City of London. His earliest poem, on the Book of *Jonah*, entitled *The Feast of Worms*, was the precursor of a good deal of Biblical paraphrase, in which mystical leanings are clearly revealed. In *Sion's Sonnets* he versified the *Song of Songs*, a book with an obvious appeal to all who are helped by the symbol of the Spiritual Nuptials ; while in *Job Militant* we find passages emphasizing the Mystic Quest. Here is one of them :—

> Great Majesty, since Thou art everywhere,
> Oh, why should I misdoubt Thy Presence here?
> I long have sought Thee, but my ranging heart
> Ne'er quests, and cannot see Thee where Thou art:
> There's no defect in Thee, Thy light hath shin'd,
> Nor can be hid, Great GOD, but I am blind.

Oh, clear mine eyes, and with Thy holy fire
Inflame my breast, and edge my dull desire :
Wash me with hysop, cleanse my stained thoughts,
Renew my spirit, blur forth my secret faults ;
Thou tak'st no pleasure in a sinner's death,
For Thou art Life ; Thy mercy's not beneath
Thy sacred justice : Give Thy servant power
To seek aright, and, having sought, discover
Thy glorious Presence ; let my blemish'd eye
See my salvation yet before I die.

Later he published the *Emblems Divine and Moral*, which attained an immediate popularity, and have but recently lost their place on the shelf of household theology. Latterly, he devoted himself mainly to devotional works in prose ; but, having penned a most gallant defence of Charles I, he fell under Parliamentary displeasure, suffered the loss of his books and manuscripts, and died, it is said, of a broken heart, in 1644.

The popularity of the *Emblems* has always been largely dependent on the plates, which were borrowed originally from the *Pia Desideraria* of Herman Hugo. The Dutch plates were, more or less, copied by William Marshall, an artist of real merit ; but subsequent editions have contained plates of no artistic value, often grotesque, if not actually blasphemous in their vulgarity. The outstanding feature of the whole series is that the Deity is represented as a child— a fact worth remembering when the mind recoils, as it does sometimes, from the erotic expressions occasionally used in the poems. Isaac Williams, in *The Baptistery*, a work of a similar nature, to which reference will be made again in these pages, said that Quarles' *Emblems* made a special appeal to him, by depicting GOD as

> A child with more than angel's ken,
> Mixing among the things of men,
> With warning dread and sweet control,
> And more than manhood in Thy soul :
> With this huge world of sea and land
> A ball within Thine infant hand.

The literary scheme of each Emblem consists of a text from the Bible, the poem itself, two or more extracts (demonstrating a diligent study of mystical theology), and a four-lined epigram. The writer's standpoint could hardly be expressed better than in his own words, in the ' Entertainment ' of the Third Book :—

> All you, whose better thoughts are newly born,
> And—rebaptiz'd with holy fire—can scorn
> The world's base trash ; whose necks disdain to bear
> The imperious yoke of Satan ; whose chaste ear
> No wanton songs of sirens can surprise
> With false delight ; whose more than eagle eyes
> Can view the glorious flames of gold, and gaze
> On glittering beams of honour, and not daze ;
> Whose souls can spurn at pleasure, and deny
> The loose suggestions of the flesh, draw nigh.
>
>     And you, whose amorous, whose select desires,
> Would feel the warmth of those transcendent fires,
> Which, like the rising sun, put out the light
> Of Venus' star, and turn her day to night ;
> You that would love, and have your passions crown'd
> With greater happiness than can be found
> In your own wishes ; you that would affect
> Where neither scorn, nor guile, nor disrespect
> Shall wound your tortur'd souls ; that would enjoy
> Where neither want can pinch, nor fulness cloy,
> Nor double doubt afflicts, nor baser fear

Unflames your courage in pursuit; draw near,
Shake hands with earth, and let your soul respect
Her joys no further than her joys reflect
Upon her Maker's glory; if thou swim
In wealth, see Him in all; see all in Him:
Sink'st thou in want, and is thy small cruse spent?
See Him in want; enjoy Him in content:
Conceiv'st Him lodg'd in cross, or lost in pain?
In prayer and patience find Him out again:
Make Heaven thy mistress; let no change remove
Thy loyal heart—be fond, be sick of love:
What if He stop His ear, or knit His brow:
At length He'll be as fond, as sick as thou:
Dart up thy soul in groans; the secret groan
Shall pierce His ear, shall pierce His ear alone:
Dart up thy soul in vows; thy sacred vow
Shall find Him out, where Heaven alone shall know:
Dart up thy soul in sighs; thy whispering sigh
Shall rouse His ears, and fear no listener nigh:
There's none, there's none shall know but Heaven and thou.
Groans fresh'd with vows, and vows made salt with tears,
Unscale His eyes, and scale His conquer'd ears:
Shoot up the bosom-shafts of thy desire,
Feather'd with faith, and double-fork'd with fire;
And they will hit: fear not, where Heaven bids 'Come';
Heaven's never deaf but when man's heart is dumb.

These lines clearly demonstrate Quarles' position, not only as a mystic, but as a poet, too. He had an extraordinary technical facility, but his skill in rhyming and his metrical fluency were not sufficiently under the control of a sound and refined taste. His own references, found in various pieces, to "the rhetoric of my torments," "the sad tautology of lavish passion," "the frantic language of my foolish fear," are entirely to the point: gaudy rhetoric and

rhapsodical vulgarisms are all too frequent, and it is not easy
to distinguish literary hyperbole from genuine emotion. The
exposition of *Canticles* v. 8, exemplifies this difficulty :

You holy virgins, that so oft surround
    The city's sapphire walls ; whose snowy feet
Measure the pearly paths of sacred ground,
    And trace the New Jerusalem's jasper street :
Ah ! you whose care-forsaken hearts are crown'd
      With your best wishes ; that enjoy the sweet
        Of all your hopes ; if e'er you chance to spy
        My absent Love, O tell Hm that I lie
Deep-wounded with the flames that furnac'd from His eye.

I charge you, virgins, as you hope to hear
    The heavenly music of your Lover's voice ;
I charge you, by the solemn faith you bear
    To plighted vows, and to that loyal choice
Of your affections, or, if aught more dear
      You hold ; by Hymen, by your marriage joys ;
        I charge you, tell Him that a flaming dart,
        Shot from His eye, hath pierc'd my bleeding heart,
And I am sick of love, and languish in my smart.

Tell Him, O tell Him, how my panting breast
    Is scorch'd with flames, and how my soul is pin'd ;
Tell Him, O tell Him, how I lie oppress'd
    With the full torment of a troubled mind ;
O tell Him, tell Him, that He loves in jest,
      But I in earnest ; tell Him He's unkind :
        But if a discontented frown appears
        Upon His angry brow, accost His ears
With soft and fewer words, and act the rest in tears.

O tell Him, that His cruelties deprive
    My soul of peace, while peace in vain she seeks ;

Tell Him, those damask roses that did strive
    With white, both fade upon my sallow cheeks;
Tell Him, no token doth proclaim I live,
      But tears, and sighs, and sobs, and sudden shrieks;
          Thus if your piercing words should chance to bore
          His heark'ning ear, and move a sigh, give o'er
To speak; and tell Him, tell Him, that I could no more.

If your elegious breath should hap to rouse
    A happy tear, close harb'ring in His eye,
Then urge His plighted faith, the sacred vows,
    Which neither I can break, nor He deny;
Bewail the torment of His loyal spouse,
      That for His sake would make a sport to die:
          O blessed virgins, how my passion tires
          Beneath the burden of her fond desires!
Heaven never shot such flames, earth never felt such fires!

Here—apart from the appeal to our sense of the ridiculous in such lines as "if your piercing words should chance to bore," and the unintentional profanity of other lines—the triteness of the imagery and the falsetto quality of the general tone give an inevitable suggestion of insincerity. But the following prayer rings true, and seems to voice a heartfelt longing for Illumination and Union:—

Eternal GOD, O Thou that only art
    The sacred fountain of eternal light,
And blessed loadstone of my better part,
    O Thou my heart's desire, my soul's delight,
Reflect upon my soul, and touch my heart,
      And then my heart shall prize no good above Thee;
      And then my soul shall know Thee; knowing, love Thee;
And then my trembling thoughts shall never start
      From Thy commands, or swerve the least degree,
Or once presume to move, but as they move in Thee.

And, unless a wife's testimony is always suspect where a departed husband is concerned, the sincerity of Quarles' devotion was touchingly vindicated by Ursula, his wife, who affirmed that "he preferred GOD and religion to the first place in his thoughts. . . . As for GOD, he was frequent in his devotions and prayers to Him, and almost constant in reading or meditating on His Word. . . . As for his religion, he was a true son of the Church of England, an even Protestant, not in the least degree biased to this hand of superstition or that of schism, though both those factions were ready to cry him down for his inclination to the contrary. . . . When he was at home, his exhortations to us to continue in virtue and godly life, were so pious and frequent, his admonitions so grave and piercing, his reprehensions so mild and gentle, and, above all, his own example in every religious and moral duty so constant and manifest, that his equal may be desired, but can hardly be met withal. . . . The blessed end of my dear husband was every way answerable to his godly life, or rather, indeed, surpassed it ; for, as gold is purified in the fire, so were all his Christian virtues more refined and remarkable during the time of his sickness. . . . He thanked GOD that, whereas he might have justly expected that his conscience should have looked him in the face like a lion, it rather looked upon him like a lamb ; and that GOD had forgiven him his sins and, that night, sealed him his pardon. . . . The rest of his time he spent in contemplation of GOD and meditating upon His Word, especially upon Christ's sufferings, and what a benefit those have that, by faith, could lay hold on Him, and what virtue there was in the least drop of His Precious Blood : intermingling here and there many devout prayers and ejaculations, which continued

with him as long as his speech, and after, as we could perceive by some imperfect expressions. . . ."

Almost beyond controversy, the high-water mark of
Quarles' achievement, both as mystic and as poet, was
reached in the lovely exegesis of *Canticles* ii. 16. Here
we feel that, despite the unreality of the classical allusion,
we have a record of a truly experiential union of the soul
with GOD.

> E'en like two little bank-dividing brooks,
>     That wash the pebbles with their wanton streams,
> And having rang'd and search'd a thousand nooks,
>     Meet both at length in silver-breasted Thames,
>         Where in a greater current they conjoin :
> So I my Best-beloved's am ; so He is mine.
>
> E'en so we met ; and, after long pursuit,
>     E'en so we join'd, we both became entire ;
> No need for either to renew a suit,
>     For I was flax, and He was flames of fire.
>         Our firm united souls did more than twine :
> So I my Best-beloved's am ; so He is mine.
>
> If all those glittering monarchs that command
>     The servile quarters of this earthly ball,
> Should tender in exchange their shares of land,
>     I would not change my fortunes for them all :
>         Their wealth is but a counter to my coin ;
> The world's but theirs : but my Beloved's mine.
>
> Nay, more ; if the fair Thespian ladies all
>     Should heap together their diviner treasures,
> That treasure should be deem'd a price too small
>     To buy a minute's lease of half my pleasure ;
>         Tis not the sacred wealth of all the Nine
> Can buy my heart from Him, or His from mine.

Nor time, nor place, nor chance, nor death can bow
My least desires unto the least remove :
He's firmly mine, by oath ; I His, by vow :
He's mine by faith ; and I am His by love :
He's mine, by water ; I am His, by wine :
Thus I my Best-beloved's am ; thus He is mine.

He is mine altar ; I His holy place :
I am His guest ; and He my living food :
I'm His by penitence ; He mine by grace :
I'm His by purchase ; He is mine by blood :
He's my supporting elm ; and I His vine :
Thus I my Best-beloved's am ; thus He is mine.

He gives me wealth ; I give Him all my vows :
I give Him songs ; He gives me length of days :
With wreaths of grace He crowns my conquering brows ;
And I His temples with a crown of praise,
Which He accepts : an everlasting sign
That I my Best-beloved's am ; that He is mine.

Scarcely inferior to this, either in poetic merit or in
fervour, is the expansion of the Psalmist's cry, " Whom
have I in Heaven but Thee, and there is none upon earth
that I desire in comparison with Thee," culminating in
the lines :—

Without Thy Presence, earth gives no refection ;
Without Thy Presence, sea affords no treasure ;
Without Thy Presence, air's a rank infection ;
Without Thy Presence, Heaven itself's no pleasure :
If not possess'd, if not enjoy'd in Thee,
What's earth, or sea, or air, or Heaven, to me ?

Nothing would be gained by quoting the passages in
which Quarles has expressed himself with a voluptuousness

more akin to Persian Sufism than to Christianity.   But by
tacking his more amorous transports on to the words of the
*Song of Songs*, he has tacitly pleaded Scriptural justification for this use of metaphors borrowed from earthly passion
to express the most intimate relations of the soul to GOD.
In view of the Appendix D to Dr. Inge's lectures on *Christian Mysticism*, there is no need here to enter fully into the
question of the mystical interpretation of the *Canticles*.
The reader may be reminded, however, that the chapter-
headings in the Authorized Version of the Bible give sanction
to the exegesis which finds two main characters in the
Drama, Solomon and the Shulamite maiden.   But this
traditional interpretation could only by very strained methods
explain the text.   The modern interpretation overcomes
most of the difficulties by finding, not two, but three main
characters : the Shulamite, her shepherd-lover, and King
Solomon, besides the subsidiary groups of the Shulamite's
brothers and the ladies of Solomon's Court.   But even those
who reject the extreme allegorical method and insist that the
book was originally a sort of masque portraying human love,
can justify the inclusion of such ardent dialogues, such passionate aspirations, and such voluptuous descriptions in the
pages of Holy Writ, only by admitting a certain amount of
allegory.   The constancy and devotion of the Shulamite to
her true love, in spite of Solomon's advances, may, at any
rate, be ' applied,' we are told, to the relations between
Christ, the Church, and the World.   If so, it is but a short
step further to apply it to the devotion and constancy of the
individual soul to Christ in the face of the counter-attractions
of the world.   And, although in some cases the method has
led to a lack of restraint which makes painful reading, in
surer hands it has proved a fruitful help to devotion.   St.

Bernard, who preached eighty-six sermons on the first two chapters of the Book, warned his hearers that "the heart is unworthy to read this sacred Song unless the flesh has been subjected to the spirit by discipline, and unless the burdensome pomp of the world has been rejected as insupportable". On the other hand, he insisted that "the spirit of love is needed by anyone who wishes to gain a true knowledge of the things read therein . . . a cold heart can neither understand nor appreciate its words of ardent emotion" (Eales' translation). In more modern times, Dr. Neale, who followed the traditional interpretation and did not always escape a tendency to over-allegorize, published a volume of *Sermons on the Song of Songs*, which may be recommended to anyone wishing to see what rich spiritual sustenance the Book can be made to yield. He was not far short of the truth (although he overlooked the *Gospel according to St. John*) when he claimed that the *Canticles*, "next to the *Psalms*, have been the greatest support and comfort of GOD's Saints from the beginning of the Church—perhaps to some of His Saints even more than the *Psalms*".

# CHAPTER V.

## CRASHAW AND BEAUMONT.

AT Peterhouse, Cambridge, in 1637, under the congenial Mastership of John Cosin, subsequently Bishop of Durham, two senior members of the foundation were encouraging one another in verse-making and in the study of mystical theology. For some half-dozen years they would be together, anxiously watching the gathering clouds ; and then, when the storm burst, their paths would separate : one would remain within the fold of the persecuted Church of England until she should weather the storm, and would spend the rest of a long life in her service, reaping the ample fruits of his loyalty ; the other would seek food and shelter elsewhere, and, having accomplished much in a short space, would lay down this mortal life in middle age.

RICHARD CRASHAW can be claimed as a mystical poet of the English Church only as concerns the years previous to 1646, the formative years, no doubt, of his genius, but not those in which the greater number of his most ardent lines were penned. Son of a Puritan and bigotedly anti-Roman father (who, however, edited some mystical devotions of Roman origin), he had graduated at Pembroke Hall, and, while there, had come under the influence of the Ferrar household at Little Gidding, within a ride from Cambridge. There he learnt that " almost Lessian temperance " of which the editor of his poems speaks, and which he him-

(112)

self recommended so warmly in one of his pieces. There, too, he found a perfect exemplification of the *Religious House and Condition of Life*, which he expanded from a portion of Barclay's Latin Poem, *Argenis*. Of no other household in England at that time could it have been said more justly that—

> Reverent discipline, and religious fear,
> And soft obedience, find sweet biding here;
> Silence and sacred rest; peace and pure joys;
> Kind loves keep house, lie close, and make no noise;
> And room enough for monarchs,[1] while none swells
> Beyond the kingdoms of contentful cells.
> The self-remembering soul sweetly recovers
> Her kindred with the stars; not basely hovers
> Below: but meditates her immortal way
> Home to the original Source of Light and intellectual Day.

And there, again, at Little Gidding, Crashaw would have heard much of George Herbert, and would probably have seen *The Temple* in manuscript. He openly avowed his discipleship to the Saint of Bemerton in his lines *On Mr. George Herbert's Book*, and by allowing his first volume of poems to be entitled *Steps to the Temple*.

In the lines on Shelford's *Treatise of Charity*, his revolt against the paternal theology finds pointed utterance :—

> Be it enacted then
> By the fair laws of thy firm-pointed pen,
> GOD'S services no longer shall put on
> A sluttishness for pure religion:
> No longer shall our churches' frighted stones
> Lie scatter'd like the burnt and martyr'd bones
> Of dead Devotion.

[1] Charles I had paid a visit to " the Arminian Nunnery " early in 1642.

And, no doubt, it was the comeliness of ceremonial and the devotional warmth to be found at Peterhouse, under Cosin's *régime*, that induced Crashaw to transfer his quarters thither. Of his life there, the anonymous editor of the *Steps to the Temple* gives us a delightful glimpse : " In the Temple of GOD, under His wing, he lead his life in St. Mary's Church, near St. Peter's College ; there he lodged under Tertullian's roof of angels ; there he made his nest more gladly than David's swallow near the House of GOD, where, like a primitive saint, he offered more prayers in the night than others usually offer in the day ; there he penned these poems, ' Steps ' for happy souls to climb Heaven by ". There seems some confusion here between the Church of Little St. Mary, easily accessible by covered way from Peterhouse but with no decorative angels, and Peterhouse Chapel, famous for its wealth of angelic decoration ; both, probably, were frequented by this devoutest of poets.

His editor tells us, further, of " his skill in poetry, music, drawing, limning, graving . . . his subservient recreations for vacant hours," his mastery of " the richest treasures of the best Greek and Latin poets," and his proficiency " in five languages (besides his mother-tongue), viz., Hebrew, Greek, Latin, Italian, Spanish ". It is certain that he had thoroughly studied the great Spanish mystics, making a special cult of St. Theresa. But only one side of that Saint's nature seems to have appealed to Crashaw, who leaves unnoted her level-headedness, her sense of humour, and her practical genius for organisation. The first half of his *Hymn to the Name and Honour of the Admirable St. Theresa* is taken up with her futile attempt, at the age of seven, to win the crown of martyrdom at the hands of the Moors. And then he exclaims—

Thou art Love's victim ; and must die
A death more mystical and high ;
Into Love's arms thou shalt let fall
A still surviving funeral.
His is the dart must make the death
Whose stroke shall taste thy hallow'd breath ;
A dart thrice dipp'd in that rich flame
Which writes thy Spouse's radiant name
Upon the roof of Heaven, where aye
It shines ; and with a sovereign ray
Beats bright upon the burning faces
Of souls which in that Name's sweet graces
Find everlasting smiles : so rare,
So spiritual, pure, and fair
Must be the immortal instrument
Upon whose choice point shall be sent
A life so lov'd : and that there be
Fit executioners for thee,
The fairest and first-born sons of fire,
Blest seraphim, shall leave their quire,
And turn Love's soldiers upon thee
To exercise their archery.
　　Oh, how oft shalt thou complain
Of a sweet and subtle pain :
Of intolerable joys :
Of a death, in which who dies
Loves his death, and dies again,
And would for ever be so slain.
And lives, and dies ; and knows not why
To live, but that he thus may never leave to die.
　　How kindly will thy gentle heart
Kiss the sweetly-killing dart,
And close in his embraces keep
Those delicious wounds, that weep

Balsam to heal themselves with ; thus
When these thy deaths, so numerous,
Shall all at last die into one,
And melt thy soul's sweet mansion ;
Like a soft lump of incense, hasted
By too hot a fire, and wasted
Into perfuming clouds, so fast
Shall Thou exhale to Heaven at last.

. . . . . . . .

Thou shalt look round about, and see
Thousands of crown'd souls throng to be
Themselves thy crown : sons of thy vows,
The virgin-births with which thy sovereign Spouse
Made fruitful thy fair soul.   Go now
And, with them all about thee, bow
To Him.   " Put on (He'll say) put on,
My rosy love, that thy rich zone
Sparkling with the sacred flames
Of thousand souls, whose happy names
Heaven keep upon thy score : thy bright
Life brought them first to kiss the light,
That kindleth them to stars."   And so
Thou with the Lamb, thy Lord, shalt go,
And wheresoe'er He sets His white
Steps, walk with Him those ways of light,
Which who in death would live to see,
Must learn in life to die like thee.

This was written as an Anglican (for which due apology
was subsequently made) ; as was also the greater part of
*The Flaming Heart*, to which, however, the magnificent
peroration was added by Crashaw in his Roman days.
Some readers will remember how deep an impression was
made on John Inglesant, in the well-known romance, by

the Life of St. Theresa so-named. The character of Inglesant himself is not unlike that of Crashaw, who assuredly "followed with an eager sympathy the sublime but mysterious way of devotion pointed out in it," but, unlike Inglesant, was probably not "repelled by the exaggeration of the duty of self-denial, the grotesque humility, the self-denunciation for the most trifling faults". The greater part of Crashaw's poem is devoted to a tasteless criticism of the frontispiece of the book ; the last sixteen lines alone are worth quoting :—

> O thou undaunted daughter of desires !
> By all thy dower of lights and fires ;
> By all the eagle in thee, all the dove ;
> By all thy lives and deaths of love ;
> By thy large draughts of intellectual day,
> And by thy thirsts of love more large than they ;
> By thy brim-filled bowls of fierce desire ;
> By thy last morning's draught of liquid fire ;
> By the full kingdom of that final kiss
> That seized thy parting soul, and seal'd thee His ;
> By all the heavens thou hast in Him,
> Fair sister of the seraphim ;
> By all of Him we have in thee ;
> Leave nothing of myself in me.
> Let me so read thy life, that I
> Unto all life of mine may die.

The longing expressed here, to be clean rid of self, was a tendency to extreme Quietism imbibed from St. Theresa and her compatriot, St. John of the Cross. St. Theresa inculcated a passivity as thorough as ever Molinos did : understanding, memory, and will are to be swallowed up in GOD, if one is to reach that Prayer of Rapture in which all the faculties and senses are absolutely useless. And Dr.

Inge quotes as sayings of St. John of the Cross—" Empty thy spirit of all created things and thou wilt walk in the Divine Light " ; " The soul must lose entirely its human knowledge and human feelings in order to receive Divine knowledge and Divine feelings " ; it must lie " as it were, outside itself ".   It is the desire for passive absorption into the Absolute—" an extinguishing of all particularity," (as Eucken expresses it), " a voluntary abdication of the me " (in Récéjac's phrase)—that constitutes for some the essence of mysticism.   The psychologist quoted last tells us that " in order to approach the Absolute, mystics must withdraw from everything, even themselves ".   But this, in its bald sense, cannot win the assent of the Christian mystic, who knows, indeed, that union with GOD is irreconcilable with self-love, self-will, or self-satisfaction, but denies that it demands self-effacement.   It was not, at any rate, in his Anglican days that Crashaw thought it inconsistent to have many interests and to cultivate a many-sided personality.

Before leaving this poem, it is worth noticing that the very title, *The Flaming Heart*, would make a special appeal to Crashaw, for whom the symbols, Blood and Fire, had as strong an attraction as they have for our modern Salvationists.   Just as Light is the key-word to Henry Vaughan's thought, so these two words constantly recur in Crashaw's verse.   It is not necessary to multiply examples, but his epigram to the poem on St. Mary Magdalene may be taken as an instance of the way in which he harps upon these two aspects of spiritual zeal :—

Lo, where a wounded heart with bleeding eyes conspire !
Is she a flaming fountain, or a weeping fire ?

Another favourite simile is that of spiritual intoxication.

This occurs, for instance, in the *Pathetical Descant upon the Devout Plainsong of Stabat Mater Dolorosa* :—

> Oh, let me suck the wine
> So long of this chaste Vine,
> Till, drunk of the dear wounds, I be
> A lost thing to the world, as it to me.

Elsewhere we find this aspiration :—

> Some drink from men to beasts ; Oh then
> Drink we till we prove more, not less than men,
> And turn not beasts, but angels.   Let the King
> Me ever in these His cellars bring,
> Where flows such wine as we can have of none
> But Him Who trod the wine-press all alone.

In the *Anima Christi* of St. Ignatius, the petition, " Blood of Christ, inebriate me," has repelled many to whom the rest of that beautiful devotion makes a strong appeal, and who experience no sense of unreality in appropriating the Psalmist's words, " My soul is athirst for GOD ".   But a longing to slake one's spiritual thirst is a most wholesome appetite compared with Crashaw's repeated longings for " a sweet inebriated ecstasy ".   These remind us of the late Prof. James's contention, in his *Varieties of Religious Experience*, that " the drunken consciousness is one bit of the mystic consciousness " : " Drunkenness brings its votary from the chill periphery of things to the radiant core ".   In the lines just quoted, the poet possibly had in mind St. Paul's appeal to the Ephesians : " Be not drunk with wine, wherein is excess, but be filled with the Spirit ".   This, however, is a most guarded exhortation and bears very little relation to some of Crashaw's spiritual drinking-songs, which find a more exact counterpart in the bacchanalian lays of Mohammedan

mysticism.   It is not uncharitable to suggest that to Crashaw, as to many another, the main attraction of Rome
lay, perhaps, in the sensuous splendour of her ceremonial,
which not infrequently induces an emotional intoxication.

In the *Ode prefixed to a little Prayer-Book given to
a young gentlewoman*, the same metaphor is passingly introduced, but the stress here is on the metaphor of the
spiritual nuptials :—

> Dear soul, be strong !
> Mercy will come ere long,
> And bring his bosom fraught with blessings,
> Flowers of never-fading graces,
> To make immortal dressings
> For worthy souls, whose wise embraces
> Store up themselves for Him, Who is alone
> The Spouse of virgins, and the Virgin's Son.
> But if the noble Bridegroom when He come,
> Shall find the loitering heart from home,
>
> .    .    .    .    .    .    .
>
> Doubtless some other heart
>     Will get the start
> Meanwhile, and stepping in before,
> Will take possession of that secret store
> Of hidden sweets and holy joys ;
> Words that are not heard with ears
> (Those tumultuous shops of noise),
> Effectual whispers, whose still voice
> The soul itself more feels than hears ;
> Amorous languishments, luminous trances ;
> Sights which are not seen with eyes ;
> Spiritual and soul-piercing glances,
> Whose pure and subtle lightning flies
> Home to the heart, and sets the house on fire

And melts it down in sweet desire :
>     Yet does not stay
To ask the window's leave to pass that way ;
Delicious deaths, soft exhalations
Of soul ; dear and divine annihilations ;
>     A thousand unknown rites
Of joys and rarified delights ;
An hundred thousand goods, glories, and graces ;
And many a mystic thing which the divine embraces
Of the dear Spouse of spirits, with them bring ;
>     For which it is no shame
That dull mortality must not know a name.

.     .     .     .     .     .     .     .

Happy indeed who never misses
To improve that precious hour,
>     And every day
>     Seize her sweet prey,
All fresh and fragrant as He rises,
Dropping with a balmy shower
A precious dew of spices ;
Oh, let the blissful heart hold fast
Her heavenly armful ; she shall taste
At once ten thousand paradises ;
>     She shall have power
>     To rifle and deflower
The rich and roseal spring of those rare sweets,
Which with a swelling bosom there she meets :
>     Boundless and infinite—
>     Bottomless treasures
Of pure inebriating pleasures.
Happy proof ! she shall discover
>     What joy, what bliss,
How many heavens at once it is
To have her GOD become her Lover.

It would hardly be possible for an Englishman to go further in the expression of sensuousness ; but then Crashaw was by no means typically English. His piety, his whole cast of mind was essentially Latin : it had none of the frigid decorum of Anglicanism ; it palpitated with the warmth of more Southern natures.

The ode *To the Same Party concerning her Choice* is very similar in motive to the mediæval *Love Ron* quoted on page 11 above :—

> Dear, Heaven-designed soul !
>> Amongst the rest
> Of suitors that besiege your maiden breast,
>> Why may not I
>> My fortune try
> And venture to speak one good word,
> Not for myself, alas, but for my dearer Lord ?
>
> .  .  .  .  .  .  .
>
> 'Tis time you listen to a braver love,
>> Which from above
>> Calls you up higher
>> And bids you come
>> And choose your room
> Among his own fair sons of fire.
>
> .  .  .  .  .  .  .
>
> Let not my Lord, the mighty Lover
> Of souls, disdain that I discover
>> The hidden art
> Of His high stratagem to win your heart :
>> It was His heavenly art
>> Kindly to cross you
>> In your mistaken love ;
>> That, at the next remove

Thence, He might toss you
And strike your troubled heart
Home to Himself, to hide it in His breast,
The bright ambrosial nest
Of love, of life, and everlasting rest.

Two shorter pieces dealing with this aspect of mystic
love may be quoted.   The first speaks of the ineffability of
the experience, a mark of the mystical consciousness which
Crashaw, and others, might well have borne in mind more
constantly :—

Eternal Love ! what 'tis to love Thee well,
None but himself who feels it, none can tell ;
But oh ! what to be lov'd of Thee as well,
None, not himself who feels it, none can tell.

The other is a most charming *Song*, in which, without
one word that jars, there is an unmistakable glow of passionate sincerity :—

Lord, when the sense of Thy sweet grace
Sends up my soul to seek Thy face,
Thy blessed eyes breed such desire,
I die in Love's delicious fire.
        O Love, I am Thy sacrifice !
Be still triumphant, blessed eyes !
Still shine on me, fair suns, that I
Still may behold, though still I die.

Though still I die, I live again ;
Still longing so to be still slain ;
So gainful is such loss of breath ;
I die even in desire of death.
        Still live in me this loving strife
Of living death and dying life ;
For, while Thou sweetly slayest me,
Dead to myself, I live in Thee.

The first volume of Crashaw's poems, *The Steps to the Temple with other Delights of the Muses* (the latter being secular pieces), was published in 1646, about the time when, having been ejected from his fellowship for refusing to adopt Presbyterianism, he had joined the Roman communion. His second volume, *Carmen Deo Nostro*, he prepared, without himself seeing it through the press, at Paris, whither he had naturally gravitated ; for there Henrietta Maria was doing her utmost to ruin the English Church by the partial distribution of her favours amongst the English exiles. Crashaw not only secured the pecuniary assistance of which he was in sore need, but, by the Queen-mother's influence, he obtained a post in the suite of Cardinal Palotta at Rome. But, Rome being at that time no place for a Saint, his patron soon preferred him to a stall at Loreto, where, within a few months, he passed to the open vision of Christ for which he had so ardently longed. It is a pleasing reflexion that he should have spent his last days in tending that Holy House, our Lady's cottage, which angels are reported to have rescued from infidel hands, and to have borne for safe keeping to the Italian laurel-grove. In this connexion, it is impossible to refrain from giving Cowley's words :—

> How well, blest Swan, did Fate contrive thy death,
> And made thee render up thy tuneful breath
> In thy great mistress' arms ! thou most divine
> And richest offering of Loreto's shrine !
> Where like some holy sacrifice to expire,
> A fever burns thee, and love lights the fire.
> Angels, they say, brought the fam'd chapel there,
> And bore the sacred load in triumph through the air,—
> 'Tis surer much they brought thee there, and they
> And thou, their charge, went singing all the way.

The poetry of Crashaw is peculiarly open to adverse criticism : the ' utterness ' of his sentiment, the intensity of his emotion, the cheap glitter of his diction, at times almost provoke the reader into flippant comment.    He accepted wholeheartedly Cowley's conception of poetry as

> Figures, conceits, raptures, and sentences
> In a well-worded dress ;

and it would be possible to extract from his lines a lengthy list of intolerable conceits, with their consequent suggestion of insincerity.    It would be easy to pile up epithets descriptive of his metricious emotionalism, his convulsive hysteria, his limitless hyperbole.    And yet, at his best, his verse has supreme merit, and has had an extraordinary influence upon modern poets, such as Coleridge (not obviously, perhaps, but on his own admission), Shelley, Swinburne, Coventry Patmore, and Francis Thompson.    And, in spite of all the faults of style that, on a hasty reading, give an impression of superficialty, the more one reads him, the more surely the conviction grows that we have in his sacred verse the utterance of a pure and unfeigned sanctity.    Cowley's [1] tribute of praise is so happy and unsolicited that the excerpt begun above may well be carried further :—

> Pardon, my Mother Church, if I consent
> That angels led him when from thee he went ;
> For even in error, sure, no danger is
> When join'd with so much piety as his.
> Ah ! mighty COD, with shame I speak it, and grief ;
> Ah ! that our greatest faults were in belief !
> His faith, perhaps, in some nice tenets might
> Be wrong ; his life, I'm sure, was in the right.

[1] Cowley has one or two pieces (e.g. *The Ecstasy*), which throw light on his interest in mystical theology.

JOSEPH BEAUMONT, the second of our Peterhouse mystics, would certainly not have been so complaisant concerning Crashaw's defection to Rome. He was of the unbending school of Anglicanism which had strong views as to the infallibility of the English Church, but, at the same time, knew how seriously she was threatened by the Papacy. It was not possible then to regard Popery in England as an extinct volcano ; and, therefore, every one who became reconciled to Rome was to the keen Anglican, not merely a fool, but a dangerous fool.

In his Anglican days, Crashaw had exercised a potent influence over Beaumont, whom he had guided into the paths of mystical theology and had taught the trick of the concettists. Some of Beaumont's earlier pieces are thoroughly Crashavian, notably *Jesu inter Ubera Mariae, St. Mary Magdalene's Ointment*, and *The True Love-knot.* When he began his *chef-d'œuvre, Psyche or Love's Mystery*, he expressed his keen desire for Crashaw's help and revision. But, on their expulsion from Peterhouse, their paths diverged, never again to meet on this side of the grave. Beaumont was more fortunate than most of his brother-clergy. He was allowed to live in tranquillity at Hadleigh ; and by the generosity of Robert Quarles, who had been intruded into his fellowship, he continued to enjoy the full stipend of that office. His great deprivation was in the matter of the interdicted Offices of the Church, especially the Blessed Sacrament. In the *Psyche* he complains that, though at one time

> I once a week at least
> Could at this Board of Wonders be a guest,

it was then fourteen months since he had received Communion,

> Which yet I then was fain to steal, and so
> A thief that day to Paradise did go.

Another spiritual difficulty was also pressing hard ; we can follow it in his minor poems with a sympathetic interest, not unmingled with amusement.   It was his custom on each anniversary of his birthday to take his spiritual bearings and to register afresh, in verse, his self-dedication to Christ. Like George Herbert (to whom he pays a graceful tribute in one of his pieces), he had resolved to dedicate his rhyming faculty entirely to the Divine Lover ; but, unlike Herbert, he seems to have made a definite vow of celibacy. He had, however, miscalculated his strength of will, or, it may be, misunderstood GOD'S will ; and, in his poems, we can follow the conflict between what he imagines to be his higher and his lower wills.   At first, he appears to have a clear conviction that Jesus could not be the Bridegroom of his soul if another were the bride of his body.   He thought of GOD, apparently, as "a Jealous GOD" in a sordidly literal sense : One Who would resent an earthly attachment as the erection of an idol in the sanctuary.   It followed that no beauty, charm, or virtue could be worthy to be put, for one moment, in competition with His claims.   But at times he dimly discerns that there need be no question of conflicting claims ; that earthly love need not come between the soul and GOD, but may raise the soul to GOD.   In one or two passages he anticipates somewhat the tenets of Coventry Patmore, and is able to comfort himself with the reflexion,

> So now my vows shall stand, though I
>           Still magnify
>        That gentle, precious soul,
>     Letting my meditations roll

In that dear sphere where Thou Thyself, Great Love,
With such enamouring grace art pleas'd to move.

But many a pang of remorse was suffered before he reached the full conviction that he was called, not to the single, but to the married life. " He that is able to receive it," said our Lord, " let him receive it " ; but it must be " for the kingdom of heaven's sake ". GOD's rule, whether it be in the individual heart or in society, may be more truly advanced by matrimony and family life, with its ceaseless opportunities for the exercise of unselfishness and mutual forbearance. Each individual has to decide the question, not under the influence of the appearance of things or the pleasure they may afford, but in view of their ultimate effect in leading to or diverting from GOD ; and Beaumont was well aware that, in reaching that decision, there is the amplest room for self-deception. But he can be acquitted, at least, of acting on impulse or of neglecting to probe his conscience. After a hesitation of six years, he took the decisive step and married, being now in his thirty-fifth year. Later he incorporated in his *Psyche* a touching elegy, in which he extolled the lady's virtues, and bewailed her loss : she had, he claimed, supplied him with the copy which he needed in portraying the ideal beauty of his Psyche.

His marriage brought Beaumont not only " the mutual society, help, and comfort," which the English Church permits to her clergy, if she does not positively encourage it ; his wife was the step-daughter of Bishop Wren, who, though at the time of the wedding he seemed most unlikely to be of any help as a patron, at the Restoration became a power both in the Realm and in the University of Cambridge. Beaumont was appointed a royal chaplain, and, in quick succession, Master of Jesus College, Cambridge, and of his old college, Peterhouse.   Here he exercised a somewhat dictatorial discipline, and adorned the Chapel with his own artistic productions, which have not entirely satisfied modern tastes.   From childhood he had been a lover of learning, and the suspension of professional activities during the Interregnum had given him an opportunity, of which he had made excellent use, to read, if not widely, at least thoroughly ; his reward came in 1674, when he was appointed Regius Professor of Divinity, an office which he held until his death in 1699.

Before considering the *Psyche* in detail, some more of Beaumont's minor pieces may be noticed.   In them he is generally more spontaneous and inspired than in his more sustained effort.   The *Morning Hymn* and the *Evening Hymn* are both delightful sacred lyrics, and have often been reprinted in anthologies.   *Home* deserves quotation here as a forcible statement of one of the great aspects of mystical truth—the truth that man is essentially a spiritual being, whose true home is not amid the distracting perils and unsatisfying pleasures of the world, but in the inward sphere where the indwelling Presence of GOD gives that " peace which the world cannot give ".

> What is House and what is Home,
> Where with freedom thou hast room,
> And may'st to all tyrants say
> This thou canst not take away ?
>
> .    .    .    .    .    .    .
>
> Seek no more abroad, say I,
> House and Home, but turn thine eye
> Inward and observe thy breast ;
> There alone dwells solid rest.
> That's a sole immured tower

9

Which can mock all hostile power.
To thyself a tenant be,
And inhabit safe and free.
Say not that this House is small,
Girt up in a narrow wall :
In a cleanly, sober mind
Heaven itself full room doth find.
The Infinite Creator can
Dwell in it ; and may not man ?
Here content make thy abode
With thyself and with thy GOD.
Here in this sweet privacy
May'st thou with thyself agree,
And keep House in peace, though all
The universe's fabric fall.
No disaster can distress thee,
Nor no Fury dispossess thee :
Let all war and plunder come,
Still may'st thou dwell safe at Home.

Home is everywhere to thee,
Who can'st thine own dwelling be ;
Yea, though ruthless Death assail thee,
Still thy lodging will not fail thee ;
Still thy soul's thine own ; and she
To an House remov'd shall be,—
An eternal House above,
Wall'd, and roof'd, and pav'd with Love.
There shall these mud walls of thine,
Gallantly repair'd, outshine
Mortal stars ;—No stars shall be
In that Heaven but such as thee.

Beaumont explains his motive in undertaking the composition of the *Psyche :* " The turbulence of these times

having deprived me of my wonted accommodations of study,
I deliberated, for the avoiding of mere idleness, what task
I might safeliest presume upon without the society of books,
and concluded upon composing this poem, in which I endeavour to represent a soul led by Divine grace and her
guardian angel through the different temptations and assaults
of lust, pride, heresy, persecution, and spiritual dereliction,
to a holy and happy departure from temporal life to heavenly
felicity ". The result was a poem, believed to be the long-
est in the English language, presenting for the most part a
rather dull and conventional study of mystical theology.
It is, in fact, as the name implies, a psychological treatise.

Certain scientists have usurped the name of Psychology
and applied it to a dismal science which seems at times to
have but the remotest connection with the ψυχή. Even in
Beaumont's lifetime, Locke laid the foundations of a so-
called Introspective Psychology, by investigating his own
mind as a " thinking-thing " and trying to explain the nature
of knowledge altogether apart from Idealism. And now
Locke's Psychology has given place to a psychological
science based on physiology, which repudiates any interest
in the soul. In a luminous book, recently published, which
claims to be a manual of ' practical psychology,' the writer
says quite definitely, " I have not hitherto mentioned the
soul, simply and solely because the subject appears to me
to be altogether outside the scope of a work on psychology ".[1]
Latterly, this physio-psychology has especially set itself to
explain religious phenomena by reducing them to physical
phenomena ; and so zealously has this aim been prosecuted

---

[1] *Know Your Own Mind*, by Wm. Glover, Cambridge, 1914, p. 197. The
author goes on, of course, to support his contention, but not very convincingly, as it
seems to the present writer.

that the highest experiences of the soul have been altogether explained away as pathological—hysterical states, nerve-storms, etc.[1]  But experiments in psycho-physiology, how-ever interesting, cannot be exhaustive enough to have much true value : the observations made cannot be sufficiently close and exact.  Moreover, this Psychologism (as it has been aptly called) stands condemned as a science, by the fact that it demolishes the phenomena which it professes to investigate : religion which is scientifically explained loses its religious character.  True psychology should deal, surely, with the relationship that exists between spirit and spirit, the human spirit and the Divine.  It should take account, certainly, of Intellect, Will, and Feeling, but only as under the control and guidance of the soul, the Psyche.  It must make it clear that the soul may be ' lost ' for the sake of the ' world,' but, on the other hand, can be sublimated to a state of intense vitality.  It must insist that those who would know its secrets must go to spiritual experts and not to physicists, since those secrets transcend all material experi-ence.  This is the Psychology that Beaumont expounded, possibly without full experimental knowledge, but, at any rate, along the lines laid down by those who have spoken from actual experience.

The 1st Canto introduces Psyche's unseen friend and unseen enemy—Phylax, her guardian angel, and Satan, who sneers at the " tricks, charms, promises, and mystic arts," by which Christ strives " to woo these silly hearts ". Canto II describes the struggle between Lust and Charis in the heart of Psyche, who, in the next canto, receives from her Spouse, by the instrumentality of Phylax, a ' Token '—

---

[1] Henry Vaughan knew what a temptation it is to a medical man to adopt such views ; see p. 145 below.

a belt, rich in gems and embroidery.  On putting on this girdle, Psyche suffers sudden agonies,

> Whilst from her labouring breast she breaking sees
> A shapeless lump of foul deformities,

Abortive embryos, unformed lust,
Pin-feather'd fancies, and half-shap'd desires,
Dim dawns of fondness, doubtful seeds of rust,
Glimmering embers of corruptive fires,
> Scarce something, and yet more than nothing was
> That mystic chaos, that dead living mass.

Oh, how tormenting is the parturition
Of tender souls, when they unload themselves
Of their blind, night-conceiv'd brats of Perdition !
Oh, how the peevish and reluctant elves,
> Mad with their own birth, viperously contend
> The worried bowels of the heart to rend !

Here we have that Arousing and Disillusionment of the soul which must precede the beginning of the Purgative process.  But Psyche, having recognized the danger from sensuality, has to subdue the other main cause of separation from GOD—pride.  Under the instigation of Pride, the three great faculties, the Passions, the Reason, and the Will, rise in rebellion—the Passions especially protesting against the austerities by which Psyche had striven to win Detachment.  For her encouragement Phylax expounds (in eleven cantos) the scheme of Redemption, from the Fall of man to the outpouring of the Holy Spirit at Pentecost. But the thought of the Holy Spirit calls to mind the blasphemous vagaries which were flourishing in England at that time under the pretence of the Spirit's inspiration, and strong rebuke is administered to ' enthusiasts ' in the account

of the Heresy into which Psyche falls.  When she is re-
claimed from her aberrations by Ecclesia, she enters zealously upon a course of Mortification.

The soul has thus persevered in both parts of Purgation ;
and now, having been detached from all that hinders union
with GOD, she may hope to win a closer attachment to
Him.  Having "through the Spirit mortified the deeds of
the body," she may look forward to that enhanced vitality
which mystical writers call Illumination.  In the twenty-first
canto we reach what Beaumont calls 'The Sublimation '.

> Rare souls are they, who still forgetting what
> Behind them conquered lies, with restless heat
> Reach at new laurels, and adventure at
> Whate'er inviteth gallantry to sweat ;
>> Who, like our Psyche, scorn their course to stop
>> Till they have doubled fair Perfection's top.
>
> For as the generous spark is not content
> With having climb'd the air's first stage, since by
> The spurring fervour of its natural bent
> Above the third it aims, and needs must die
>> Unless it may its high design achieve,
>> And in fire's elemental bosom live :
>
> So Psyche, who to excellence's sphere
> Steer'd her brave course, now for a second flight
> Her wings and resolution did prepare,
> Knowing a third remained still, which might
>> Her former venture frustrate if in this
>> She coward turn'd and bow'd to weariness.

To enlighten and strengthen her aspirations, she enters
on a course of meditation on Holy Writ, especially on
"David's blessed well," on the Song of Songs, and on the

Gospel-story. But she has to learn the difficult lesson
taught by Thomas à Kempis in the *Imitatio* (Bk. II, c.
6) : " That good and sweet affection which thou sometimes
feelest, is the effect of grace present and a sort of foretaste
of thy heavenly home ; but hereon thou must not lean too
much, for it cometh and passeth away again.   But to strive
against evil motions of the mind which may befall thee,
and to reject with scorn the suggestions of the devil, is a
notable sign of virtue and shall have great reward.   Let
no strange fancies, therefore, trouble thee, which on any
subject whatever may crowd into thy mind.   Keep to thy
purpose with courage and an upright intention towards
GOD.   Neither is it an illusion that sometimes thou art
suddenly rapt on high, and presently returnest again unto
the accustomed vanities of thy mind.   For these thou dost
unwillingly suffer rather than commit ; and so long as they
displease thee and thou strivest against them, it is a matter
of reward and no loss."

Of this Psyche has yet to be convinced.   At present
she complains very sadly,

> Oh, now I am a thousand things a day !
> But were I once to Thee entirely join'd
> No objects should Thy Psyche steal away,
> Nor into their vain selves transform my mind :
>> Thyself and mine I should behold in thee,
>> And all things else I could desire to see.

> So I no longer should this moment be
> All hope, and nothing else but fear the next :
> So by no checker of pure clarity
> And gloomy doubting should I still be vex'd :
>> So to itself my life no more shall give
>> The lie, nor I be dying while I live.

And now, the passions having been subdued by Detachment and Mortification, and the reason having been convinced by Meditation on GOD'S Word, the will has to be offered up in entire Self-surrender. Accordingly, to the will, Thelema, Psyche addresses herself, striving to win its consent by a recital of the glorious prospect before it :—

> Jesus, the Sovereign Lord of thee and me,
> Will give thee leave to make Himself thy prey :
> Reach then thine arms of noble love, that He,
> Imprison'd in thy embraces, may
> > For ever make thee free, and with the best
> > Of Heaven fill up and deify thy breast.

The doctrine of Deification has been treated historically by Dr. Inge in an appendix to his Bampton Lectures. It is obviously liable to extravagant statement, and we know that, during the 'Commonwealth,' it was stated by 'enthusiasts' in the crudest terms. But with such 'enthusiam' Beaumont had no sympathy. If challenged, he would, no doubt, have explained that his notion of deification was based on St. Peter's words concerning the prospect of becoming "partakers of the Divine nature, having escaped the corruption which is in the world through lust". His goal would be the closest possible union with the Divine Nature, short of that identification of personality, in the possibility and actuality of which some mystics have deluded themselves into believing.

Having won the Will's consent, Psyche offers it up as a whole burnt-sacrifice on the altar of her heart. It is accepted, in union with the Will of Christ, and the soul experiences ineffable joys.

Canto xxii was discreetly suppressed until 'the saints'

of the Parliamentary army were no longer in supreme power in England : it describes the trials of the soul under Persecution, and, except for its topical interest, scarcely deserves the space allotted to it in the psychological scheme. But the next Canto is of very special interest : it is an account of the great Dereliction undergone by so many mystics before the final consummation of their love, an experience analogous to that of our Lord upon the Cross. Beaumont insists that it is sent in love, to save the soul from the danger of over-confidence and spiritual pride. This is precisely the line taken by Tauler : " GOD leads the soul through these exercises and operations of His hand as through fire and water by turns, until the works of self-sufficiency are driven out from all the secret corners of the spirit ; and the man henceforth is so utterly ashamed of himself and so casts himself off that he can never more ascribe any greatness to himself, but thoroughly perceives all his own weakness, in which he now is and always has been. . . . He who has arrived at this point is not far from the threshold of great mercies, by which he shall enter into the bride-chamber of Christ. Then when the day of his death shall come, he shall be brought in by the Bridegroom with great rejoicings." Beaumont describes Psyche as being engulfed in clouds and as feeling in her heart " a leaden dumbness,"

Since Charis here forebore her spritely part :
    When blacker than the rest one heavy cloud
    Down to the ground before her face did crowd.

Out of this cloud a hand held to her a cup filled with terrors, and a voice bade her drink,  She obeyed, saying,

    I would not fear the most appalling face
    Of any sorrow, which did not forbid

The sight of Thine.   But now thine eyes, alas,
In strange Aversion's angry cloud are hid :
  How shall I steer through this vast deep, who may
  Not see the stars which are to guide my way !

Despair comes with counsels of suicide ; but Psyche stands
firm, and, having learnt at last that we are " not sufficient
of ourselves to think anything as of ourselves but our sufficiency is of GOD," she is restored to the light of Grace
and is " ravished by visions of beatitude ".   In unmeasured
terms she expresses her longing for death :—

In sweetness why art Thou so infinite ?
Or why must that Infinitude appear
To any soul to fire her with delight,
If to the Fount she may not come and there
  Quench her impatient thirst ?   O Jesu, be
  Still what Thou art ; but then, be so to me !

Be so to me, and oh, be so with speed !
Death is not death compared with delay :
This teacheth every moment to exceed
All those long years I till this cruel day
  Have tediously measured ; and now
  I older by an age each minute grow.

Receiving, at length, the longed for summons " to her
royal Spouse's marriage-bed," with an end of earthly existence not unlike that of St. Theresa, Psyche " with three
deep sighs cried out, ' O love,' and died ".

It is open to any one to argue that such mystical Psychology as Beaumont gives us in this poem would have been
better expounded in unadorned prose ; but, apart from the
fact that he belonged to a family of poets, the reading
public in those days (unlike that of our own age) found

keen pleasure in poetry, and especially in allegorical poetry.[1] To reach a wider circle of readers, Beaumont adopted a mode of expression which involved a good deal of florid writing, constant appeals to the more emotional suscepti- bilities of men, and a neglect of those qualifications which should accompany any dissertation on the Mystic Ladder. Christianity was not designed to be a complex system of rules and devices for fostering spiritual moods, with a con- sequent self-vexing introspection and scrupulosity. Never- theless, the Christian's aim must be to train himself for union with GOD, if not here, at any rate hereafter ; and few will succeed in this training unless it is systematic. And, what- ever we prefer to call it, Purgation must be the foundation of the spiritual edifice—a foundation constantly to be in- spected and renewed, else our animal tendencies will under- mine and ruin the entire structure. It is the lack of this solid foundation that makes the mysticism of Shelley and some of our modern poets so thin, and so disastrous in its results. The rapturous worship of Beauty, the communion with Nature, ends in sensual pollution and insolent revolt ; for there has been no stern attempt to cleanse the soul and to keep it clean, no effort to practise the nonconformity of

[1] But for exigences of space, some account should be given of a very similar poem by the much-abused Benlowes, whose *Theophila* (1652) deals with the same phase of mysticism, but is marred by wilful eccentricities. Perhaps the most successful part of the poem is Theophila's Love-Song, which does not lend itself, however, to brief extraction. The following lines from the Canto on 'Admiration' may be given as furnishing an epitome of the poem :—

> Love darts all thoughts to its Belov'd ; doth place
>   All bliss in waiting on His grace ;
> It languisheth with hope to view Him face to face,
>
> And ushers in that Beatific Love,
>   Which so divinely flames above,
> And doth to vision, union, and fruition move.

St. Paul : " Be not conformed to this world, but be ye transformed by the renewing of your mind ".  On the other hand, Purgation is not the whole of the spiritual life, as some religionists would seem to suppose, who practise self-renunciation but fail to wait upon GOD in meditation and contemplation, and so have never been illuminated, have never passed " out of darkness into His marvellous light ". Or—to adopt the symbol especially dear to Beaumont— they may have passed the threshold of the guest-chamber, but they have not the wedding-garment, without which they may not take part in the marriage-supper of the Lamb, as Bride to the Heavenly Bridegroom.

# CHAPTER VI.

## HENRY AND THOMAS VAUGHAN ; JOHN AND SAMUEL PORDAGE.

IT is with a certain sense of relief, not unlike that felt in passing from a hot-house into the fresh air, that we turn from the perfervid, sensuous mysticism of Quarles, Crashaw, and Beaumont to the more restful, but no less intense, mysticism of HENRY VAUGHAN,—the Silurist, to give him the title which he chose for himself, as marking his Welsh origin.

Although Vaughan acknowledged an incalculable spiritual debt to George Herbert, and ' fetched ' a large number of figures and phrases from Herbert's poems, the two represent entirely different aspects of mysticism. Herbert sought union with the GOD Who is Love, in the depths of his own heart ; Vaughan sought union with the GOD Who is Light, mainly in His manifestations in Nature. Herbert, again, was the tortured victim of constant fluctuations of feeling ; Vaughan aimed, with considerable success, at a life of unruffled serenity.

The son of a Welsh squire, Henry Vaughan was at first destined for the Law, but subsequently took up Medicine. Poetry, however, had always been his main interest, and he early began to write verse of distinction, in which the influence both of Ben Jonson and of Donne is evident. At the outbreak of the Civil War he joined

(141)

the Royalist forces, not as a combatant, apparently, but as a physician. He was present at the battle of Rowton Heath where he lost a very dear friend ; and he was one of the besieged garrison of Beeston Castle, which fell in November, 1645. The privations of the siege, and a subsequent imprisonment (dimly hinted at in his poems), induced a serious illness, which lingered on for some years. This, and the loss of friends, turned his thoughts to deeper themes than amatory verse and "this juggling fate of soldiery". Moreover, about this time, when perhaps in his twenty-seventh year, he fell in with a copy of *The Temple*, the reading of which marked his Awakening as a mystic. Henceforth Herbert is the

> Dear friend ! whose holy, ever-living lines
> Have done much good
> To many, and have check'd my blood,
> My fierce, wild blood, that still heaves, and inclines,
> But is still tam'd
> By those bright fires which thee inflam'd.

And the rest of a life, which ended only in 1695, was spent in ministering to the bodily ailments of his Welsh neighbours, and in meditative walks and communings with the GOD of Nature, the Lord of Light and Peace.

Pascal has told us of " the wholly fresh point of view from which a soul sees itself and everything else when GOD first vouchsafes to visit it. The new light causes a strange fearfulness and troubles the satisfaction hitherto found in those things which were its delight. . . . The man begins to wonder at the blindness of his past life, and, reflecting upon the length he has gone on without perceiving these things, and how certain it is that the soul, being immortal, can find no rest in perishable things, he is filled with devout

amazement and a most healthful wonder. . . . This up-
lifting is so mighty and transcendent that it does not pause
at Heaven : unsatisfied with the angels or the spirits made
perfect, the soul passes on throughout creation to the Throne
of GOD where it finds rest." No one who has studied
Vaughan's writings, in prose and verse, can fail to note how
apposite these words are to his spiritual history. His own
account of his Awakening may be read in *The Garland*,
where he makes confession of his carelessness in youth, and
acknowledges again his debt to the rousing influence of
Herbert, referring especially to the poem entitled *Life*, the
lesson of which Vaughan summarizes here.

In the Dedication of the first volume of his sacred verse,
*Silex Scintillans*,[1] he speaks gratefully of GOD's mercy
in forgiving his " sinful youth," and " every publish'd
vanity " ; and in the Preface he says, " Blessed be GOD
for it, I have by His saving assistance suppressed my greatest
follies, and those which escaped from me, are, I think, as
innoxious as most of that vein used to be ; besides, they
are interlined with many virtuous, and some pious mixtures.
What I speak of them is truth, but let no man mistake it
for an extenuation of faults as if I intend an apology for
them, or myself, who am conscious of so much guilt in both,
as can never be expiated without special sorrows, and that
cleansing and precious effusion of my Almighty Redeemer."

---

[1] This title, the Spark-giving Flint, does not seem to describe quite aptly the
contents of the volume. The original edition had an emblematic frontispiece, more
or less illustrative of the title, and explained by some Latin verses headed *Authoris
de se Emblema*. The metaphor occurs, too, in a poem called *The Tempest*, in
which he prays, since

> Flints will give no fire
> Without a steel, oh, let Thy power clear
> Thy gift once more, and grind this flint to dust.

The poem entitled *Mount of Olives* contains a description of the early transports experienced when his Awakening was followed by his first Illumination :—

> When first I saw True Beauty, and Thy joys,
> Active as light and calm without all noise,
> Shin'd on my soul, I felt through all my powers
> Such a rich air of sweets, as evening showers
> Fann'd by a gentle gale convey, and breathe
> On some parch'd bank . . .

It may be well to draw special attention at once to the description here of GOD's joys as being " active as light and calm without all noise ". These two aspects of Vaughan's mysticism will require full consideration later ; but here it may be noticed, in passing, that he wrote scarcely one single piece in which he did not make mention of the symbol of light and of the quality of calmness.

Vaughan, as will have been made clear already, knew well that unremitting Purgation must precede full Illumination, and, if space could be spared, many a fervent prayer for perseverance in this stage of his mystical progress could be quoted from his poems. The piece entitled *Misery* may be taken as evidence that his self-conquest was not accomplished without difficulty. It describes, with much dramatic power, how he is at times tempted to rebel against his self-appointed seclusion, but is soon aware of the void caused by the consequent exclusion of GOD ; in answer, however, to the appeal of penitence, GOD returns and " fills all the place ".

> I sit with Thee by this new light,
> And for that hour Thou'rt my delight ;
> No man can more the world despise,
> Or Thy great mercies better prize :

I school my eyes, and strictly dwell
Within the circle of my cell ;
That calm and silence are my joys,
Which to Thy peace are but mere noise.
At length I feel my head to ache,
My fingers itch and burn to take
Some new employment ; I begin
To swell and foam and fret within.

. . . . . . .

I storm at Thee, calling my peace
A lethargy, and mere disease ;
Nay, those bright beams shot from Thy eyes
To calm me in these mutinies,
I style mere tempers, which take place
At some set times, but are Thy grace.
Such is man's life, and such is mine,
The worst of men, and yet still Thine.

But, in spite of backslidings, he pursued a course of detached meditation, both on the printed Word and on the
Book of Nature. *The Search*, which begins with one of
Vaughan's beautiful descriptions of the sunrise, suggests that
he practised—not with entire satisfaction, to judge from the
closing lines—the exercise recommended by St. Ignatius
Loyola as a help in the Illuminative Way, of vividly picturing the scenes of the Gospel-story, and imagining oneself
actually present, taking part in the incidents. Of his communings with Nature—a subject to be treated later at some
length—we read in *Vanity of Spirit* :—

Quite spent with thoughts, I left my cell, and lay
Where a shrill spring tun'd to the early day.
I begg'd her long, and groan'd to know
Who gave the clouds so brave a bow,

10

Who bent the spheres, and circled in
Corruption with this glorious ring ;
What is His name, and how I might
Descry some part of His great light.

I summon'd Nature ; pierc'd through all her store ;
Broke up some seals, which none had touch'd before ;
Her womb, her bosom, and her head,
Where all her secrets lay abed,
I rifled quite ; and having pass'd
Through all the creatures, came at last
To search myself, where I did find
Traces and sounds of a strange kind.

The result of all this persevering Purgation and Meditation was a glorious Illumination in the form of the well-
known vision of Eternity, so finely set forth in *The World :—*

I saw Eternity the other night,
Like a great ring of pure and endless light,
    All calm, as it was bright ;
And round beneath it, Time in hours, days, years,
        Driv'n by the spheres
Like a vast shadow mov'd ; in which the world
    And all her train were hurl'd.
The doting lover in his quaintest strain
        Did there complain ;
Near him, his lute, his fancy, and his flights,
        Wit's sour delights ;
With gloves, and knots, the silly snares of pleasure,
        Yet his dear treasure,
All scatter'd lay, while he his eyes did pour
        Upon a flow'r.

The darksome statesman, hung with weights and woe,
Like a thick midnight-fog, mov'd there so slow,

He did not stay, nor go ;
Condemning thoughts—like sad eclipses—scowl
            Upon his soul,
And clouds of crying witnesses without
        Pursued him with one shout.
Yet digg'd the mole, and lest his ways be found,
            Work'd underground,
Where he did clutch his prey ; but one did see
            That policy :
Churches and altars fed him ; perjuries
            Were gnats and flies ;
It rain'd about him blood and tears, but he
            Drank them as free.

The fearful miser on a heap of rust
Sate pining all his life there, did scarce trust
        His own hands with the dust,
Yet would not place one piece above, but lives
            In fear of thieves.
Thousands there were as frantic as himself,
        And hugg'd each one his pelf ;
The downright epicure plac'd heaven in sense,
            And scorn'd pretence ;
While others, slipp'd into a wide excess,
            Said little less ;
The weaker sort slight, trivial wares enslave,
            Who think them brave ;
And poor, despised Truth sate counting by
            Their victory.

Yet some, who all this while did weep and sing,
And sing, and weep, soar'd up into the ring ;
        But most would use no wing.
O fools (said I) thus to prefer dark night
            Before true light !

> To live in grots and caves, and hate the day
>> Because it shows the way ;
> The way, which from this dead and dark abode
>> Leads up to God ;
> A way where you might tread the sun, and be
>> More bright than he !
> But as I did their madness so discuss,
>> One whisper'd thus,
> " This ring the Bridegroom did for none provide,
>> But for His bride ".

Here Vaughan seems to be using something more than a mere poetic figure of speech, and to be describing a definite image seen in some sort of trance, not unlike the visions of Ezekiel. But, just as the symbolic details of the Prophet's vision were influenced by his recollection of the furniture of the Temple, the composite creatures of Babylonian sculpture, and possibly by some passages in the Psalms, so the form in which the truth was bodied forth to the mind of Vaughan was apparently influenced by his previous thought on the subject. A circle has always been a favourite symbol of Eternity ; and Vaughan was a good enough Platonist to know the passage in the *Timaeus* which speaks of " a moving image of eternity," and " the forms of time, days and nights and months, revolving according to a law of number in imitation of eternity " ; but it is not so certain that he would have read the writings of the German mystic, Suso, in which the bestowal by GOD of the ring of eternity on His followers is spoken of, exactly as in the last lines of this poem. There can be very little doubt that the figure of " the darksome statesman " was suggested by Oliver Cromwell, with whose statecraft the poet's mind would be much preoccupied. While both Light and Calm, as noted

above, had from his Awakening made a very special appeal
to him, and are strongly insisted upon in this vision.

Light is of such outstanding importance in Vaughan's
mysticism that a rapid *resumé* of the use of that symbol in
mystical writings must be attempted. " Mysticism," says
Emerson, " finds in Plato all its texts " ; and in the poem
last quoted there is a pointed allusion to the famous allegory
in the seventh book of the *Republic*, in which this world
of sight is represented as a cave or den : in it nothing is
seen but shadows cast on a wall by a fire ; and those who,
having ascended into the light of day and having, in spite
of the dazzling tortures at first experienced, learnt something
of the truth and reality of things, on their return are mocked
as unpractical visionaries. But the Christian writer need
not go to Plato for texts on the subject of Enlightenment.
On the first page of his Bible, he finds Creation described
as the descent of Light upon a dark, chaotic void.   In the
Psalms and Prophetical Books he finds countless sayings in
which GOD is represented as the eternal Source of life-giv-
ing and joy-dispensing Light—sayings fully understood only
when " the Word was made flesh and dwelt among us, full
of grace and truth," claiming to be " the Light of the world "
and proffering " the light of life ".   St. John, both in the
Prologue to his Gospel and in his 1st Epistle, insists that
the very nature of GOD is Light—intellectual, moral, and
spiritual Light.   To St. Peter, usually classed as non-
mystical, conversion is a " calling out of darkness into GOD'S
marvellous light ".   Nor is St. Paul backward in pressing
the doctrine of illumination : in his first extant letter Christians are called " sons of light " ; the Ephesian Christians
are exhorted to " walk as children of light " ; those at
Rome, to " put on the armour of light ".

That Vaughan was steeped in these and other similar texts is proved by the prayers given in his beautiful prose-manual of devotion, *The Mount of Olives*. " We must prevent the sun," he says, in recommending the following prayer for use, " When thou dost awake " :—

" O GOD the Father, Who saidst in the beginning, Let there be light, and it was so ; enlighten my eyes that I never sleep in death, lest at any time my enemy should say, I have prevailed against him.

" O GOD the Son, Light of light, the most true and perfect Light, from Whom this light of the sun and the day had their beginning ; Thou that art the Light shining in darkness, enlightening every one that cometh into this world, expel from me all clouds of ignorance and give me true understanding, that in Thee and by Thee I may know the Father, Whom to know is to live and to serve is to reign.

" O GOD the Holy Ghost, the Fire that enlightens and warms our hearts, shed into me Thy most sacred light, that I may know the true joys of Heaven, and see to escape the illusions of this world. Ray Thyself into my soul that I may see what an exceeding weight of glory my enemy would bereave me of for the mere shadows and painting of this world. . . ."

And again, " at the setting of the sun " he suggests this " Elevation of the soul to the True Light " :—

" The path of the just, O my GOD, is as the shining light that shineth more and more unto a perfect day of eternity. But the wicked neither know nor understand ; they walk in darkness, and from the inward darkness their minds pass at last into the outward, eternal darkness. O most miserable and undone soul ! to whom Thy sun is set, that everlasting Sun, which on Thy holy elect never setteth but is always at

the height, full of brightness and consolation.  A heavy
night sits in the noon-day upon those souls that have forsaken Thee ; they look for light and behold darkness, for
brightness and they walk in obscurity.  They grope for the
wall like the blind, as if they had no eyes ; they stumble at
noon-day as in the night ; they are in desolate places as
dead men.  But on those that walk with Thee an everlasting day shines.  This sun of the firmament hath his course ;
it riseth, setteth, comes up again, and again goes down.
But Thou, Lord, knowest no vicissitudes, Thou art the
Ancient of Days ; Thou art the Rock of Ages from everlasting to everlasting.  O Thou the same to-day and
yesterday and for evermore, Thou bright and morning star
springing from on high, illuminate me who am now sitting
in darkness and in the shadow of death.  O Light of light,
the brightness of Thy Father's glory, enlighten all inward
obscurities in me, that after this life I may never be cast into
the outward darkness.  O most blessed, most merciful and
Almighty Jesus, abide, I beseech Thee, with me ; for it is
towards evening and the day is far spent.  As long as Thou
art present with me, I am in the light ; but when Thou art
gone, I am in the shadows of death and amongst the stones
of emptiness.  When Thou art present, all is brightness, all
is sweetness ; I am in my GOD'S bosom ; I discourse with
Him, watch with Him, walk with Him, live with Him, lie
down with Him.  All these most dear and unmeasurable
blessings I have with Thee, and want them without Thee.
Abide then with me, O Thou Whom my soul loveth !
Thou Sun of Righteousness with healing under Thy wings,
arise in my heart ; refine, quicken, and cherish it ; make
Thy light there to shine in darkness, and a perfect day in
the dead of night."

Christian mystics have, no doubt, borrowed much of their phraseology from the Greek mysteries, Clement of Alexandria and Origen especially having set themselves to incorporate into Christianity what was best in heathenism ; and in this connexion it is noteworthy that the former speaks of Christ as the True Photagogos, Who sheds light upon the convert and brings him near to GOD, filling him with a hallowed gladness, just as the priestly light-bringer was supposed to do in the Greek mysteries. Furthermore, few Christian mystics would repudiate all debt to the Neo-Platonic writings of Plotinus, in which the analogy between physical and spiritual light is constantly developed—the purity, bountifulness, and ubiquity of light, as it comes from its source, laying upon man the duty and privilege of reflecting it back thither and illuminating all around him. Certainly, St. Augustine was led by his sympathy with Neo-Platonism to use very freely the imagery of light : the *Confessions* are full of it, but the passage most strikingly to our purpose here is that in which he describes how, with GOD'S guidance, he entered into his inmost self (vii. 10) : " I entered and beheld with the eye of my soul (such as it was), above the same eye of my soul and above my mind, the Light Unchangeable—not this common light, which shines for all flesh ; nor as it were a greater of the same kind, as though the brightness of this should shine out more and more brightly and with its greatness take up all space. Not such was this light, but different, yea far different from all these. Nor was it above my soul as oil is above water, nor yet as the sky is above the earth ; but it was above me because it made me, and I was below it because I was made by it. He that knoweth the Truth, knoweth that Light ; and he that knoweth it, knoweth Eternity." It was, how-

ever, Dionysius the pseudo-Areopagite, who definitely
formulated the doctrine of Illumination as the cardinal process of Christian mysticism.    This has been already spoken
of, on p. 58 above, when Heywood's poetry was under
consideration.    Dionysius taught that the beams of primal
light are received and reflected onwards by each successive
rank in the hierarchies, celestial and ecclesiastical, and in
each there is a process of purification, illumination, and perfection.

Whether or no Vaughan knew the climax of the *Paradiso*, where Dante describes his gaze into "the ray
authentical of sovereign Light," it would be impossible to
decide ; but he would almost certainly be familiar with
the great illumination of Jacob Boehme, who became suddenly surrounded by divine light, and, with unutterable joy,
looked for seven days into the secrets of GOD'S Kingdom.
The brother of Thomas Vaughan, 'the alchemist,' could
not fail to know something of Boehme's teaching ; and he
would study with special appreciation his doctrine of Christ
as the coming forth of Light from the abysmal Fire of the
GODHEAD, and his teaching on enlightenment in such works
as the *Dialogue concerning the Supersensual Life* and
the *Discourse between Two Souls*.    The last lines of
*The World* may conceivably have been influenced by
Boehme's statement that when GOD'S Love, the primal
light, is first rayed into a soul, it is espoused to the Divine
Sophia and " the seal-ring of Christ's victory impressed into
its essence ".

Whatever the source of his constant use of the mystical
symbol of light, Vaughan ranks as one of the great illumina-
tives and might well have appropriated the motto of the
University of Oxford : *Dominus Illuminatio mea*.    Take

his definition, in *Quickness*, of true life, as opposed to the false :—

> Life is a fix'd, discerning light,
> > A knowing joy ;
> No chance or fit ; but ever bright,
> And calm, and full, yet doth not cloy.

> 'Tis such a blissful thing, that still
> > Doth vivify,
> And shine and smile, and hath the skill
> To please without eternity.

> *Thou* art a toilsome mole, or less,
> > A moving mist.
> But life is, what none can express,
> A quickness, which my GOD hath kiss'd.

Whereas to George Herbert Jesus is " My Master," Vaughan prefers to call Him " My dear, bright Lord, my Morning Star ! "  He thinks almost entirely in terms of light.  The Fall of Man was a sullying of brightness and a withdrawal of light, a thought expressed in the *Ascension Hymn*, and in the lines to the Inward Light :—

> Fair and young Light ! my guide to holy
> Grief and soul-curing melancholy ;
>
> .    .    .    .    .    .
>
> How blest had men been, had their sire
> Liv'd still in league with Thy chaste fire !

Childhood, to Vaughan, was a time of light ; and in *The Retreat* (which is known to have inspired Wordsworth's glorious *Immortality Ode*) he looks back to his own infancy, with its " bright shoots of everlastingness," and expresses his longing to win his way back to that state of innocence.  The poet seems here to accept the Platonic doctrine of Reminiscence : Plato had taught, in his allegorical way, that the souls of men, before their earthly lives, have followed in the train of the gods and seen the glorious vision of Ideal Truth, Goodness, and Beauty ; life on earth must be an effort to regain the lost vision, and, with it, eternal life. With this Platonism Vaughan combines very beautifully our Lord's teaching that " Except ye convert and become as little children, ye shall not enter into the kingdom of heaven ".

> Oh, how I long to travel back,
> And tread again that ancient track !
> That I might once more reach that plain
> Where first I left my glorious train ;
> From whence the enlighten'd spirit sees
> That shady City of palm-trees.
> But ah ! my soul with too much stay
> Is drunk, and staggers in the way !
> Some men a forward motion love ;
> But I by backward steps would move,
> And where this dust falls to the urn,
> In that state I came, return.

Less known, and not quite so successful artistically, are the similar pieces, *Looking back* (published in his later volume, *Thalia Rediviva*) and *Childhood*, the latter beginning

> I cannot reach it ; and my striving eye
> Dazzles at it, as at eternity ;

and ending

> An age of mysteries ! which he
> Must live twice that would GOD'S face see ;
> Which angels guard, and with it play,
> Angels ! which foul men drive away.

How do I study now and scan
Thee, more than e'er I studied man,
And only see through a long night
Thy edges and thy bordering light !
Oh, for thy centre and mid-day !
For sure that is the narrow way !

In some prefatory lines to the second edition of the *Silex Scintillans*, Vaughan appeals to the 'wits' of his age to

Shun not holy fire,
But with true tears wash off your mire.
Tears and these flames will soon grow kind,
And mix an eye-salve for the blind.
Tears cleanse and supple without fail,
And fire will purge your callous veil.
Then comes the light ! which when you spy,
And see your nakedness thereby,
Praise Him Who dealt His gifts so free,
In tears to you, in fire to me.

Quite conceivably the reference in this last line is to an actual appearance of fire in his first illumination, such as Pascal and other *illuminés* experienced ; but more probably he means the fire of affliction—sickness and loss of friends.　He envies the lot of these departed friends, since " they are all gone into the world of Light," and it is his constant prayer that he may himself soon be permitted to enter that world.　He likes to think of " GOD's Saints " as " shining lights " who " all night " (meaning by that the term of earthly existence),

Like candles, shed
Their beams, and light
Us into bed.

For, after all, the grave is a

> Calm and sacred bed, where lies
> In death's dark mysteries
> A beauty far more bright
> Than the noon's cloudless light.

Naturally, the thought of light colours his view of the Day of Judgment :—

> O Day of life, of light, of love!
> The only day dealt from above!
> A day so fresh, so bright, so brave,
> 'Twill show us each forgotten grave,
> And make the dead, like flowers, arise
> Youthful and fair to see new skies.
> All other days compar'd to thee
> Are but Light's weak minority.

And the Envoy to the *Silex Scintillans* is a vivid description of the subsequent joys of the blest, when " the new world's new-quickening Sun " shall " pierce and pass " through His creatures, now become " cloudless glass, transparent as the purest day ".

Perhaps the finest passage in the whole of Vaughan's poetry is that in which he touches on the doctrine of the Divine Darkness :—

> There is in GOD, some say,
> A deep but dazzling darkness ; as men here
> Say it is late and dusky, because they
> See not all clear.
> Oh for that Night! where I in Him
> Might live invisible and dim!

Plato had spoken of the sight being darkened by excess of light, and Plotinus had taught that, in the perfect light of

God's Presence, man could see as little as in complete darkness. Dionysius, combining such teaching with the Psalmist's account of God as "making darkness His secret place," and with St. Paul's description of Him as "dwelling in light unapproachable," maintained that union with God is possible only to those "who have left behind all divine lights and sounds and heavenly discourses, and have passed into that darkness where He really is". This doctrine of "the super-essential radiance of the divine darkness" was accepted wholeheartedly by many later mystics, notably by Ruysbroeck, and it is interesting to find John Keble (in his *Miscellaneous Poems*) speaking of

> Heaven's eternal fountain, where enshrin'd
> God hides Himself in brightness.[1]

An intense appreciation of the beauty and significance of the dawn of day is only what we should expect of Vaughan, who has written some of the most striking lines in English Literature on that natural phenomenon and its spiritual suggestiveness. "Mornings are mysteries," he says; and it is clear, from his prose devotions as well as from his verse, that he was ever up betimes, to lose nothing of the revelations and loveliness of daybreak. Recalling how the cock "watches for the morning hue," he asks,

> Shall Thine own image think it much
> To watch for Thine appearing hour?
>
> .    .    .    .    .    .
>
> If joys, and hopes, and earnest throes,
> And hearts whose pulse beats still for light,

[1] The reader may also be referred to the angelic hymn to God the Father, in *Paradise Lost*, III, 372 ff.

> Are given to birds ; who, but Thee, knows
> A love-sick soul's exalted flight ?
>> Can souls be track'd by any eye
>> But His Who gave them wings to fly ?

But a far more appealing thought arises from the recollection that Christ, " rising up a great while before day, went out and departed into a solitary place, and there prayed " :—

> If this calm season pleas'd my Prince,
> Whose fulness no need could evince,
> Why should not I, poor silly sheep,
> His hours, as well as practice, keep ?
> Not that His hands are tied to these,
> From Whom Time holds his transient lease ;
> But mornings new creations are,
> When men, all night sav'd by His care,
> Are still reviv'd ; and well He may
> Expect them grateful with the day.

*The Morning-Watch* is another ecstatic hymn evoked by the approaching sun-rise, with " the great chime and symphony of Nature ".   But Vaughan's supreme utterance in this connexion is *The Dawning*, in which the reflection that Christ's Second Coming would most appropriately occur at that hour, leads on, through a magnificent description of Nature's expectant alertness at the day-spring, to a prayer that he, too, may be found ready by " the Day-spring from on high ".   The poem demands quotation in its entirety :—

> Ah ! what time wilt Thou come ? when shall that cry
> " The Bridegroom's coming ! " fill the sky ?
> Shall it in the evening run
> When our words and works are done ?

Or will Thy all-surprizing light
    Break at midnight,
When either sleep, or some dark pleasure
Possesseth mad man without measure?
Or shall these early, fragrant hours
    Unlock Thy bowers?
And with their blush of light descry
Thy locks crown'd with eternity?
Indeed, it is the only time
That with Thy glory doth best chime;
All now are stirring, every field
    Full hymns doth yield;
The whole creation shakes off night,
And for Thy shadow looks—the light;
Stars now vanish without number,
Sleepy planets set and slumber,
The pursy clouds disband and scatter,
All expect some sudden matter,
Not one beam triumphs, but from far
    That morning-star.
Oh, at what time soever Thou,
Unknown to us, the heavens wilt bow,
And with Thy angels in the van,
Descend to judge poor careless man,
Grant I may not like puddle lie
In a corrupt security,
Where, if a traveller water crave,
He finds it dead and in a grave;
But at this restless, vocal spring
All day and night doth run and sing,
And though here born, yet is acquainted
Elsewhere, and flowing keeps untainted;
So let me all my busy age
In Thy free services engage;

And though—while here—of force I must
Have commerce sometimes with poor dust,
And in my flesh, though vile and low,
As this doth in her channel flow,
Yet let my course, my aim, my love,
And chief acquaintance be above ;
So when that day and hour shall come,
In which Thyself shall be the sun,
Thou'lt find me dress'd and on my way,
Watching the break of Thy great day.

Before leaving the subject of Light, Vaughan's fondness
for the epithet ' white ' should be noticed.   Its frequent use
is not simply due to the exigences of a weak rhyming faculty,
for it is often used independently of rhyme.   It is partly to
be explained by the close affinity of whiteness to lightness ;
but it has further reference to the meaning of the Welsh
word for ' white ' : it has been pointed out by Welsh
scholars that *gwyn*, a word doubtless familiar to Vaughan,
contains the meaning ' holy ' as well as ' white '.   Learning
this, one feels at once how aptly he speaks of the purpose
of the Incarnation as being " to make stain'd man more
white than snow," of the holy dead as " white pilgrims," of
childhood as being filled with " white celestial thoughts "
and " white designs," and of the patriarchal age as " those
white days that durst no impious mirth expose ".   And one
knows instinctively that, in spite of the conscientiousness
which often leads him to bitter self-accusation, he himself
spent the " white days " and " calm golden evenings " which,
in another poem, he attributes to the patriarchs.

Calmness has already been mentioned as a quality dear
to Vaughan.   He tells us, more than once, that he was by
nature ' fierce,' and we can well believe it of so thorough a

11

Celt ; moreover, he lived in times when Churchmen were exposed to much exasperating persecution, and that he was tempted to the exasperation thus roused is evident enough. But he recognized that, just as fellowship with Him Who is Light is an impossibility if we are walking in darkness, so He Who is our Peace cannot dwell where noise and disturbance reign unchecked. He knew well how easy it is to be secularized by failure in recollection or by loss of self-control, and how quickly spiritual energy is dissipated by fussy introspection or by tumultuous remorse. He would wholeheartedly have endorsed Plotinus's insistence on being " collected into calm " as an indispensable condition to being " filled with light ". Accordingly, he set himself to cultivate interior self-possession, and to listen in awed silence to the voice of GOD in his own heart and in Nature. In many of the foregoing extracts, and in others for which space cannot be found, he constantly recurs to the words ' calm,' ' without all noise,' etc. *Distraction*, *Retirement*, and *Peace*, are all to the point here, the last-named especially illustrating M. Récéjac's dictum : " The mystic consciousness loves nothing so much as Peace ; its supreme vision is a perfectly organic Society living in Order and Love ". Elsewhere Vaughan speaks of " a sweet self-privacy " ; he says that if only he could keep his days " calm and unhaunted," he would be " in heaven all the year long ". In the poem named *The Men of War*, in which his resentment against the Parliamentary troops is not quite successfully stifled, he yet prays for " a sweet, revengeless, quiet mind " ; and in the lines on Charles Walbeoffe's heart, he described the standard at which he himself evidently aimed :—

No outward tumults reach'd this inward place :
'Twas holy ground, where peace, and love, and grace

> Kept house, where the immortal restless life,
> In a most dutiful and pious strife,
> Like a fix'd watch, mov'd all in order still;
> The will serv'd GOD, and every sense the will.

And when the Church, but not, alas ! religion, had come to her own again in England, he rejoiced that he was able to "hive" in a

> Happy, harmless solitude,
> Our sanctuary from the rude
> And scornful world; the calm recess
> Of faith, and hope, and holiness.

It is fatally easy to find fault with one's own age, and to give oneself airs of superiority to contemporary foibles ; but no thoughtful observer can fail to note to-day the lack of recollection, the absence of mental peace or interior silence. The war-spirit, with its childish faith in ' getting things done ' and with its disregard of the value of prayer, has but accentuated a trait sufficiently marked before. The age seems convinced that happiness is to be found, not in repose, but in racket. Rest means intolerable boredom ; to be thrown on oneself spells depression. *Ennui* must be driven away by incessant diversion and novelty ; thought must be stifled by chatter and slang. Even spirituality must be expressed in terms of organisation and multiplied addresses. But, at least, we have begun lately to see that, even in our public services, we need to learn from the Quakers to keep silence before GOD as well as to pray to Him ;[1] and it may be hoped that the widespread interest in mysticism, with its stress on meditation and contemplation, on the importance of waiting upon GOD and practising interior recollection,

---

[1] The hearty thanks of the Church are due to Canon Hepher, of Winchester, for his efforts in this direction. Note, *inter alia*, his *Fellowship of Silence*.

will lead more and more of us to lay to heart GOD'S word
spoken by the Psalmist, " Be still and know that I am GOD,"
to listen to the whispers of the "still small voice," and,
whenever we can do so without undue singularity, to seek,
like Vaughan, " a resolved retreat" from the world's follies,
so as to be more ' at home' to GOD.

In a little poem on the words, " Rabbi, where dwellest
Thou ?" Vaughan reveals, with a beautiful gush of feeling,
his awareness of the Indwelling Presence of GOD :—

> My dear, dear GOD !   I do not know
> What lodg'd Thee then, nor where, nor how ;
> But I am sure Thou dost now come
> Oft to a narrow, homely room,
> Where Thou too hast but the least part ;
> My GOD, I mean my sinful heart.

But he further sought GOD'S Presence, in a way not
common at the time, in Nature.[1]   He had bitterly mourned
over the loss of that intimate intercourse between heavenly
and earthly beings which seems so marked a feature of
patriarchal days : "Oh," he sighs, in *Religion*, "how
familiar then was heaven !"   And, in *Corruption*, he
attributes that early familiarity to the still lingering traces of
Paradisaical felicity before the Fall :—

> Man in those early days
> Was not all stone and earth ;
> He shin'd a little, and by those weak rays
> Had some glimpse of his birth.
>
> .    .    .    .    .    .    .    .
>
> Nor was heaven cold to him ; for each day
> The valley or the mountain

[1] Andrew Marvell must not be forgotten ; but, deeply religious as he was, his
Nature-mysticism was not, in the narrower sense, religious.

Afforded visits, and still Paradise lay
    In some green shade or fountain.
Angels lay lieger here ; each bush, and cell,
    Each oak, and highway knew them ;
Walk at the fields, or sit down at some well,
    And he was sure to view them.
Almighty Love ! where art Thou now ? . . .

But by cultivating detachment and interior recollection,
by adopting the practice (which he applauds in Isaac) of
evening meditation in the fields, by midnight vigils spent in
contemplation of the stars (of which several of his poems
give evidence), and by walks abroad at daybreak, he himself became clear-eyed. We can be confident that he
carried out his own recommendation in *Rules and
Lessons :—*

Walk with thy fellow-creatures ; note the hush
    And whispers amongst them.   There's not a spring
Or leaf but hath his morning-hymn.   Each bush
    And oak doth know I AM.

Like the " righteous man," of whom he wrote that he
loves

    Heaven's sweet solitude, those fair abodes
    Where turtles build and careless sparrows move,

who " never meddleth pitch," Vaughan came to " see
invisibles," and at times even " into glory peeped ".

It is an open question whether or no we are to understand literally this latter claim, found in the lines beginning,
" They are all gone into the world of light ".   In issuing
his devotional manual, *The Mount of Olives*, Vaughan
felt it necessary to parry any sneers at ready-made prayers.
" I envy not," he says, " their frequent ecstasies and raptures
in the third heaven ; I only wish them real, and that their

actions did not tell the world, they are rapt into some other place. Nor should they who assume to themselves the glorious style of 'Saints,' be uncharitably aroused, if we that are yet in the body and carry our treasures in earthly vessels, have need of these helps." This passage is sometimes appealed to as testifying his contempt for rapture. But, taking the context into consideration, and bearing in mind the extravagance and hypocrisy of a good deal of the 'enthusiasm' of those times, it is hardly fair to conclude that he would have spoken contemptuously of a well-authenticated rapture. But, although he speaks of having "strange thoughts transcending wonted themes," and of "peeping into glory," it is at least possible that, in his desire to preserve an unruffled calmness of soul, he would not encourage himself in transports, just as he did not give way to vehement grief when he had to bewail the sense of GOD'S absence : his more habitual approach to spiritual joys was expressed, probably, in *The Favour :*—

> O Thy bright looks! Thy glance of love
> Shown, and but shown me from above!
> Rare looks! that can dispense such joy
> As without wooing wins the coy,
> And makes him mourn, and pine, and die,
> Like a starv'd eaglet, for Thine eye.
> Some kind herbs here, though low and far,
> Watch for and know their loving star.
> Oh, let no star compare with Thee!
> Nor any herb out-duty me!
> So shall my nights and mornings be
> Thy time to shine, and mine to see.

Vaughan's main importance in English Literature rests upon his influence on Wordsworth, whom he encouraged

to recognize the Divine in external Nature—and, through
Wordsworth, on modern poetry in general.   Beginning with
a clear knowledge of his own sinfulness seen in the light of
GOD's holiness, Vaughan had passed through mortification,
detachment, and meditation, to a state of inward calm and
lucidity ; and while this process was maturing inwardly, he
had outwardly set himself to search and study Nature.   It
is noteworthy that even his Biblical meditations had led him
to consider especially Scriptural views of Nature.   Of the
three Psalms which he paraphrased, two are great Nature
Psalms : the 104th, the author of which has been called
" the Wordsworth of the ancients," and the 65th, in which
GOD's dealings with men through natural processes are
glowingly celebrated.   In that most original poem in which
he looks back to the origin of the paper and binding of
*The Book* in his hand, he claims that he has loved GOD's
works because " in them he lov'd and sought GOD's face ".
To Vaughan, in fact, Nature is a great Sacrament in which
spiritual truths and emotions are conveyed to us by outward
means ; the visible is a revelation of the invisible ; natural
phenomena are signs, means, and pledges.   He has learnt to
" heighten his devotions " by " observing GOD in His works ".
    It would be difficult to find a better exemplar than
Vaughan of that mysticism of which Bishop Chandler
writes in his *Faith and Experience,* as being " a curious
blend of optimism and pessimism.   The world, considered
as a possible satisfaction of man's nature, is declared to be
hopelessly inadequate ; being fragmentary, evanescent, and
ineffective, it cannot satisfy a demand for unity, eternity, and
perfection. . . . On the other hand, the visible order is
transfigured for him with gleams of glory from another
world ; it is charged with a meaning and a purpose not its

own ; it whispers a spiritual secret, hints at a divine origin ; it presents itself, with all its confusions and failures, as a medium through which the spiritual world flashes its signals to our souls ; it justifies itself as being just a shadow or reflection in the water, of ' a city that hath foundations whose builder and maker is GOD '. . . . In so far as it is a shadow, it is an object of contempt and derision. . . . But because it is a shadow of that which is perfect, of that Being of Whom the desire is planted in man's heart, it is invested with an inexhaustible significance and a beauty of infinite suggestiveness ". " Each tree, herb, flower," says Vaughan, " are shadows of His wisdom and His power ".

It was a genuine grief to him that man would not rise above materialism : " Oh, that man would do so ! " he cries in *The Tempest*,

> That he would hear
> The world read to him ! all that vast expense
> In the creation shed, and slav'd to sense,
> Makes up but lectures for his eye and ear.

> Sure, Mighty Love, foreseeing the descent
> Of this poor creature, by a gracious art
> Hid in these low things snares to gain his heart,
> And laid surprises in each element.

He, at least, would strive to show man that he " can have a lesson played him by a wind or wave " ; and poem after poem draws out, sometimes as its whole motive, sometimes merely as an aside, the parables of Nature. The mist rising from the bosom of the lake, to fall again later in a shower, recalls misty prayers followed by tears of contrition, which in due course bring " sunshine after rain ". To bring out the value of *Affliction*, he asks,

> Did not He, Who ordain'd the day,
>     Ordain night, too ?
> And in the greater world display
> What in the lesser He would do ?
> All flesh is clay, thou know'st ; and but that GOD
>     Doth use His rod,
> And by a fruitful change of frosts and showers
>     Cherish, and bind thy powers,
> Thou wouldst to weeds and thistles quite disperse.

He compares *Religion* to a spring, sweet and health-giving at its source, but, before it wells forth, tainted by " seizing on veins of sulphur underground ". He dwells on the metamorphosis of the " drowsy silkworm," and the preservation of a root underground through winter, as types of the Resurrection ; on the song of birds, undaunted by darkness and storms, as an encouragement to praise GOD in all circumstances ; on the silent obedience and order of the planets, as enforcing the lesson of dutifulness. His soliloquy on *The Waterfall* must not be ruined by any curtailment :—

> With what deep murmurs, through Time's silent stealth,
> Doth thy transparent, cool, and watery wealth,
>     Here flowing fall,
>     And chide and call,
> As if his liquid, loose retinue stay'd
> Ling'ring, and were of this steep place afraid,
>     The common pass,
>     Where clear as glass,
>     All must descend
>     Not to an end,
> But quick'ned by this deep and rocky grave,
> Rise to a longer course more bright and brave.

Dear stream ! dear bank ! where often I
Have sat and pleas'd my pensive eye ;
Why, since each drop of thy quick store
Runs thither whence it flow'd before,
Should poor souls fear a shade or night,
Who came—sure—from a sea of light ?
Or, since those drops are all sent back
So sure to thee that none doth lack,
Why should frail flesh doubt any more
That what GOD takes He'll not restore ?
O useful element and clear !
My sacred wash and cleanser here ;
My first consigner unto those
Fountains of life, where the Lamb goes !
What sublime truths and wholesome themes
Lodge in thy mystical, deep streams !
Such as dull man can never find,
Unless that Spirit lead his mind,
Which first upon thy face did move
And hatch'd all with His quick'ning love.
As this loud brook's incessant fall
In streaming rings restagnates all,
Which reach by course the bank, and then
Are no more seen : just so pass men.
O my invisible estate,
My glorious liberty, still late !
Thou art the channel my soul seeks,
Not this with cataracts and creeks.

Perhaps the most original of all Vaughan's poems is that
entitled *The Timber*.   It tails off in a disappointing way,
as so many of his pieces do, but it contains a striking reference to the curious theory of Resentience, according to which
the corpse of a murdered man retains

Some secret sense which make the dead blood run
        At his approach that did the body kill.

In like manner, says Vaughan, a dead tree, on the approach
of high winds, will show a resentment against " those who
broke in life its peace ".    And so he draws the moral :—

And is there any murtherer worse than sin ?
        Or any storms more foul than a lewd life ?
Or what resentient can work more within
        Than true remorse, when with past sins at strife ?

He that hath left life's vain joys and vain care,
        And truly hates to be detain'd on earth,
Hath got an house where many mansions are,
        And keeps his soul unto eternal mirth.

But though thus dead unto the world, and, ceas'd
        From sin, he walks a narrow, private way,
Yet grief and old wounds make him sore displeas'd
        And all his life a rainy, weeping day.

It is interesting to note, in passing, that in the poem called
*Dressing*, he applies this theory of Resentience very beautifully to the flowing of Christ's Blood as we, His murderers,
approach His Body at the Holy Communion.

Those were the days before Bacon's teaching had taken
root, and before the Royal Society had persuaded scientists
to test theories by experiment and demonstration.   Vaughan,
apparently, not only practised the purely herbal medicine of
his forefathers, but accepted such crude astrological notions
as the magnetic attraction of stars for their subject herbs.
Readers of *John Inglesant* will remember the Italian
physician who recommended " thyme which is under
Saturn " as being " therefore very fitted for melancholy

men," and had " no faith in the new doctrine of chemical
compositions and receipts," pronouncing them, not only dear,
but dangerous expedients.   In *The Favour*, quoted above,
Vaughan drew his lesson from this theory of astral influence.
We also find references in his verse to the astrological terms
' houses ' and ' schemes,' to the elixir (already noticed
under George Herbert), and to such doctrines as that of
signatures which was so important a feature of Boehme's
philosophy.   All this, however, was not of the essence of
Henry Vaughan's thought, but was absorbed from the researches of his twin-brother.

THOMAS VAUGHAN published but few poems, and
those of no very great value ; but he gains importance, not
only as throwing light on some of his brother's thought, but
also as giving an interesting glimpse into a fresh variety of
mysticism, a combination of theosophy, in which a supernatural knowledge of Nature is sought, and, apparently, of
theurgy, in which the power to hold converse with the
world of spirits is claimed.

The Silurist seems to have had a very genuine affection
for his brother, whose death he mourned in the elegiac
eclogue, *Daphnis*, and for whose efforts to penetrate the
secrets of Nature he seemingly claims success in the following lines :—

> Ah, happy Daphnis ! who, while yet the streams
> Ran clear and warm, though but with setting beams,
> Got through, and saw by that declining light
> His toil's and journey's end before the night.

After winning a fellowship at Jesus College, Oxford,
Thomas Vaughan accepted the family living of Newton
St. Bridget, whence he was ejected by Parliamentarians on

the usual charges of " drunkenness, immorality, and bearing arms for the King," charges which are now known to have seldom conveyed any moral stigma.    After a short stay at Oxford, he settled in London and worked at chemistry with Sir Robert Moray, one of the founders of the Royal Society, whose patronage was no mean testimonial to Vaughan's worth.    Burnet speaks of Moray as " the most universally beloved and esteemed by all men of both sides and sorts of any man I have ever known in all my life.    He was a pious man, and in the midst of armies and courts he spent many hours a day in a devotion which was of a most elevating strain.    He had gone through the easy parts of mathematics and knew the history of Nature beyond any man I ever yet knew."    Both the great diarists of the period, Evelyn and Pepys, spoke of him in a similar strain.    With such a patron, Thomas Vaughan might well claim to be " a philosopher of nature and no mere student of alchemy " ; and Anthony Wood assures us that he was " a great chemist, a noted son of the fire, an experimental philosopher, a zealous brother of the Rosicrucian fraternity ".    This latter denomination Vaughan himself disclaimed ; but his disavowal may have been part of the secretiveness which was typical of that elusive brotherhood.

It is not necessary here to make any attempt to decide the question whether Rosicrucianism was founded early in the fifteenth century by an actual Christian Rosenkreuz as a philanthropic society of students of occult lore, as stated in the *Fama* and *Confessio Fraternitatis Rosae Crucis ;* or whether those writings were the work of Valentine Andrea, who, early in the seventeenth century, attempted to popularize his hopes of social reform under a veil of fiction, but was taken too seriously by the credulous and exploited

by the unscrupulous.[1]  Vaughan, at any rate, while rejecting
the claims of various charlatans, who without warrant called
themselves Rosicrucians and made extravagant pretensions
to alchemical nostrums, wholeheartedly believed the Brothers
of the Rosy Cross to have inherited most valuable *arcana*
of supra-normal processes from earlier adepts ; and he issued
an English translation of the *Fama* and of the *Confessio*
as a genuine account of Rosicrucianism.

At the Restoration he does not seem to have resumed
the pastoral office ; he continued his chemical researches in
the neighbourhood of London, removing to Oxford at the
outbreak of the Plague, and finally to Albury, near that city,
where he died in 1666, apparently as the consequence of
inexperienced handling of mercury, in the parsonage-house
of Dr. Kem, a notorious Parliamentary spy and Restoration
turn-coat.

Thomas Vaughan's books were written in prose (with a
few poems interspersed), usually under the pseudonym
Eugenius Philalethes.[2]  In 1650 he published *Anthroposophia Theomagica, Anima Magica Abscondita*, and
*Magia Adamica*.  In the first-named, besides a pleasing
little poem entitled *A Stone and the Stony Heart*, we
find some lines addressed *To God*, that might well have
been written by his brother Henry :—

> My GOD, my life !  Whose essence man
> Is no way fit to know or scan ;
> But should approach Thy Court a guest
> In thoughts more low than his request.

---

[1] Andrea so claimed in an autiobiography, and not a few investigators have accepted his version of the origin of Rosicrucianism.  See R. A. Vaughan : *Hours
with the Mystics*, II. 100 ff.—a very prejudiced critic.

[2] It is, perhaps, worth noting that 'Rosicrucians' nearly always assumed a
*nom de plume*.

> When I consider how I stray,
> Methinks 'tis pride in me to pray ;
> How dare I speak to Heaven, nor fear
> In all my sins to court Thy ear ?
> But as I look on moles that lurk
> In blind entrenchments and their work,
> Their own dark prisons to repair,
> Heaving the earth to take in air :
> So view my fetter'd soul, that must
> Struggle with this her load of dust ;
> Meet her address, and add one ray
> To this mew'd parcel of her day ;
> She would, though here imprison'd, see,
> Through all her dirt, Thy Throne and Thee.
> Lord, guide her out of this sad night,
> And say once more, Let there be light.

These writings led to a controversy with Dr. Henry
More, the Cambridge Platonist, to whom much space must
be devoted later. It was Vaughan's attacks on Aristotle,
Galen, and Descartes, that especially angered the Doctor,
who complained, too, that Vaughan had " more desire to
be thought a conjurer than a Christian," and " Conceited
every heaving up by a hypochondriacal flatulency to be a
rapture of the soul ". But he admits here and there a
*lucida intervalla :* " What you have delivered in these
pages, bating a few hyperboles, might become a man of
more settled brain than Anthroposophus. But while you
oppose so impetuously what may with reason be admitted,
and propound so magisterially what is not sense, I must tell
you, Anthroposophus, that you betray to scorn and derision
even those things that are sober in the way that you affect,
and hazard the soiling of the highest and most delicate truths

by your rude and unskilful handling of them." In *Anima abscondita* it was the sexual imagery that offended More : " a mere Morris-dance and May-game of words, that signify nothing but that you are very young and very sportful " ; but here, too, " there are some good things that fall from you in your own style and many cited out of considerable authors, but you do so soil and besmear all with your juvenile immoralities and phantastries that you lose as much in the one as you get in the other ". We can understand the Silurist's complaint that his brother has had to deal with some who " inwardly are true black Moors indeed " ; and subsequently More regretted his share in this controversy, declining to republish his *Lash of Alazonamastix* and *Mastix : his Letter to a Private Friend*, further extracts from which will be given when the Doctor's own mystical experiences, there most eloquently described, are under consideration.

Later, Thomas Vaughan published *Aula Lucis*, *Euphrates*, and *Nollius's Chymist's Key*. In the last-named he paraphrases some lines from Augurellius, which merit quotation as illustrating the high ideals that prompted his own researches :—

> The greedy cheat with impure hands may not
> Attempt this art, nor is it ever got
> By the unlearn'd and rude : the vicious mind
> To lust and softness given, it strikes stark blind.
>
> .    .    .    .    .    .    .    .
>
> But the sage, pious man who still adores
> And loves his Maker, and His love implores,
> Who ever joys to search the secret cause
> And series of His works, their love and laws,
> Let him draw near; and, joining will with strength,
> Study this art in all her depth and length.

But Thomas Vaughan's most important work (according to Mr. A. E. Waite, our chief authority on this type of mysticism, who has recently edited a new edition of it) was a tract entitled *Lumen de Lumine*.   In this, as in all his writings, he was mainly influenced by Reuchlin, who had so brilliantly championed the Jewish mysticism of the Cabbala ; by Paracelsus, whose erratic temperament obscured the value of his contribution to medical research ; and, above all, by Cornelius Agrippa, on whose *De Occulta Philosophia* he wrote an Enconium with these opening lines :—

> Nature's Apostle and her choice high-priest,
> Her mystical and bright Evangelist,
>
> .    .    .    .    .    .    .
>
> I am unbody'd by thy books, and thee,
> And in thy papers find my ecstasy.

The *Lumen de Lumine*, in spite of Mr. Waite's admirable Introduction and Notes, is far from easy reading. Vaughan follows his masters in adopting the occult terminology, of which Ben Jonson complained in *The Alchemist* that it was deliberately contrived to cheat the public :—

> What else are all your terms,
> Whereon no one of your writers 'grees with other ?
> Of your elixir, your *lac virginis*,
> Your stone, your medicine, and your chrysosperme,
> Your sal, your sulphur, and your mercury . . .

Those who wish to learn the rudiments of the alchemical *patois* may be recommended to consult Miss Underhill's *Mysticism*, Pt. I, c. vi, § 3, where they will find the essential outlines clearly sketched with an avoidance of distracting detail.   Vaughan meets Jonson's charge in this particular tract by urging, in the first place, that it is " very

12

unreasonable if you expect that language from men which GOD has not given them " : how can human language cope with Divine facts ? Moreover, the alchemist is dealing with " a very great secret, neither is it lawful to publish it expressly " ; but he insists that " it is to be seen, and I have been an eye-witness of it myself ".

In his Preface he declares that he will take no further part in controversy. " I have referred my quarrel to the GOD of Nature ; it is involved in the concernments of His truth. I am satisfied with the peace and rest of a good conscience ; I have written nothing but what GOD hath verified before my eyes in particular and is able to justify before the world in general. I have known His secret light ; His candle is my schoolmaster ; I testify those things which I have seen under His very beams, in the bright cir- cumference of His glory. When I first put my thoughts to paper, GOD can bear me witness, it was not for any private ends. I was drawn and forced to it by a strong admiration of the mystery and majesty of Nature. It was my design to glorify the truth, and in some measure to serve the age, had they been capable of it. But the bar- barous insults I have met withal, and without any deserts of mine, have forced my charity to keep at home. Truly, had I not been robbed of my peace, I had imparted some things which, I am confident, this generation will not receive from another pen. But the times, in this respect, fall not in with Providence, for the years of discovery are not yet come."

The tract itself, which he declares to contain the key to all his writings, begins with a few lines of verse describing the dawn, such as the Silurist himself might have penned. Then follows, in prose, a symbolic account of a visit to the innermost regions of the universe, where he was vouchsafed an interview with *Thalia*,[1] the Spirit of Nature, who, in reward for his disinterested devotion, gave him the key to her secrets with an admonition not to divulge them too openly. She also expounded to him certain doctrines (which she had obviously learnt from Cornelius˙Agrippa) concerning the three parts of magic : elemental, containing the secrets of physic, celestial, containing those of astrology, and spiritual, those of divinity—three branches of one science, and to be successfully studied only as an integral whole.

Having apostrophized in verse the spot on which Thalia had rested, Vaughan translates a letter, which she had left behind her, from the Brothers of the Rosy Cross. In Mr. Waite's words, it "describes, under the allegory of a mountain, a certain profound state of introspection," leading to " the deep secret of a meeting in the spirit ". It would be impossible here to follow Vaughan through all his occult account of the various mysteries revealed by Thalia ; but a few passages should be quoted, and first, one that throws some light on the Silurist's *The Night*, mentioned on p. 157 above :—

" When I seriously consider the system or fabric of this world, I find it to be a certain series, a link or chain, which is extended from unconditioned to unconditioned, from that which is beneath all apprehension to that which is above all apprehension. That which is *beneath* all degrees of sense is a certain horrible, inexpressible darkness. The magicians call it active darkness, and the effect of it in Nature is cold, etc. For darkness is the countenance of

---

[1] *Thalia* was in classical literature the Muse of idyllic poetry ; cf. the title of Henry Vaughan's last volume of verse—*Thalia Rediviva : the Pastimes and Diversions of a Country Muse.*

cold, the complexion, body, and matrix of cold, as light is the face, principle, and fountain of heat. That which is *above* all degree of intelligence is a certain infinite, inaccessible fire or light. Dionysius calls it Divine Obscurity, because it is invisible and incomprehensible. The Jew styles it *Ain*—that is, *nihil*, or nothing—but in a relative sense, or, as the schoolmen express it, *Quo ad nos*—with respect to us. In plain terms, it is pure Deity, having no veil. The middle substance or chain between these two is that which we commonly call Nature."

The kernel of Vaughan's book is the section on the Prester or primal fire, described as the " throne of the Quintessential Light from whence He dilates Himself to generation ". " He that hath once passed the Aquaster," says Vaughan, meaning by that term external phenomena or symbols, " enters the fire-world and sees what is both invisible and incredible to the common man. He shall discover to the eye the miraculous conspiracy that is between the Prester and the sun ; he shall know the secret love of heaven and earth, and the sense of that deep Kabalism : ' There is not a herb here below but he hath a star in heaven above, and the star strikes him with her beam and says to him, Grow'. He shall know how the fire-spirit hath his root in the spiritual fire-earth and receives from it a secret influx, upon which he feeds, as herbs feed on that juice and liquor which they receive at their roots from this common earth. This is it which our Saviour tells us : ' Man does not live by bread alone, but by every word that comes out of the mouth of GOD '. He meant not by ink and paper, or the dead letter ; it is a mystery, and St. Paul hath partly expounded it. He tells the Athenians that ' GOD made man to the end that he should seek the Lord,

if haply he might feel after Him and find Him '.   Here is
a strange expression, you will say—that a man should feel
after GOD, or seek Him with his hands ; but he goes on
and tells you where you shall find Him : ' He is not far,'
saith he, ' from every one of us ; for in Him we live and
move and have our being '."   The bearing of all this on
Henry Vaughan's philosophy and verse is sufficiently
obvious.

In the *Characters* of Samuel Butler, the satirist of spiritual vagaries, Thomas Vaughan is not at all obscurely, nor
very kindly, delineated as ' An Hermetic Philosopher '.
The passage is too long for reproduction here ; but some of
the lines descriptive of Ralph in his *Hudibras*, an equally
unfriendly portrait, may be quoted :—

> He had First Matter seen undress'd ;
> He took her naked, all alone,
> Before one rag of form was on.
> The Chaos, too, he had descried,
> And seen quite through—or else he lied.

Vaughan may have been deluded, but he did not consciously lie.   To quote Mr. Waite again, he was " a man
of transparent sincerity, . . . he never claimed final attainment in respect of the mystery which absorbed him on the
outward plane ; so also he arrogated nothing to himself in
the grades of mystical achievement, but he had reached
after some manner the degree of certitude ".

All readers may not be aware that certain writings produced in Egypt, probably, over a period of several centuries,
are attributed to Hermes Trismegistus, who has sometimes
been identified with the Egyptian god, Thot, the mythical
inventor of writing and the first physician    His philosophy

is found in such sayings as this : " Thou sayest GOD is invisible ; but be advised, for who is more manifest than He ? for therefore hath He made all things that thou by all things mayest see Him ".[1]  Sir Thomas Browne says in the *Religio Medici,* " The severe schools shall never laugh me out of the philosophy of Hermes, that this visible world is but a picture of the invisible, wherein, as in a portrait, things are not truly, but in equivocal shapes, and as they counterfeit some more real substance in that invisible fabric ".  Both the Vaughans would have subscribed to these words : it is by Hermetic principles that the cryptic utterances of Thomas Vaughan can alone be interpreted, and it was probably by the study of those principles that his brother Henry attained that Sacramental view of Nature which gives his poems their special distinction.

In the year 1661, there was published a long poem entitled *Mundorum Explicatio,* or the Explanation of an Hieroglyphical Figure . . . being a Sacred Poem written by *S. P. Armig.*  In the Preface, the author explains that he was led to write the poem by studying the Figure, which was the work of another hand ; and in the poem itself, while insisting that Heaven can be attained by those still on earth, he admits that he himself had not been accounted worthy to attain that bliss, but he claims to know some who have been so privileged.  There is good reason to believe [2] that this poem was the work of SAMUEL PORDAGE, whose father, John Pordage, probably drew the hieroglyphical figure and recounted the experiences described.

---

[1] Quoted from *The Mind to Hermes,* published in pamphlet form by Mr. J. R. Watkins, who has also issued a large work in three volumes, by G. R. S. Mead, on *Thrice-Greatest Hermes.*

[2] *Vide* British Museum Catalogue.

Samuel is known as the writer of a volume of amatory poems, a few plays, and some satires aimed at Dryden, who in the second part of *Absalom and Ahitophel* treats him as beneath notice, referring to him, in passing, as "lame Mephibosheth, the wizard's son ". The 'wizard,' John Pordage, had been Rector of Bradfield, Berks, and had won fame (or notoriety) as a student of Jacob Boehme. After surviving several charges of Pantheism and of holding intercourse with evil spirits, he was ejected for alleged ignorance and incapacity, and practised as a physician. He wrote mystical books which have won greater recognition on the Continent than in England, and claimed to have had the truth of Boehme's theosophy supernaturally revealed to him. With Jane Leade, he formed the Philadelphian Society, " a coterie of some twenty ghost-seers " ; and, despite much ridicule and misrepresentation, he retained to the last a name for genuine devoutness and unblemished purity of life. His more important tenets are expounded in this poem, which may fairly be described as an attempt to systematize and popularize the more practical part of Boehme's philosophy. As such, in spite of its very slight poetic merit, it must be passed under review.

The author's aim is to elucidate the mysteries of ' the three worlds,' beginning with the External World, and in it, first Man, concerning whom we have the characteristic views that he is a microcosm of the great outward world, and is differentiated from beast by

> Reason and an immortal spark
> Which hides itself within his hollow ark.

This doctrine, that " the spirit of man contains a spark from the power and light of God," Boehme learnt from

Valentine Weigel, who, in turn, had inherited it from the great group of German mystics, Eckhart, Suso, and Tauler. Eckhart, especially, had emphasized the existence of " a divine spark at the apex of the mind," by means of which man can know GOD and hold intercourse with Him.

In a glowing passage on earth's beauty, marred though it be as a result of the Fall, the poet describes the hidden treasures underground, the flora and fauna on the surface, and the stars with their ' influence ' on man and on nature. And here he introduces the distinction between the fallen Adamical state, which may be called Babylon, and the regenerate state, Jerusalem or, if you like, Paradise. But where is Paradise now ?

> As day dwells in the shadows of the night,
> As darkness doth involve the splendid light,
> As the bright flame lies hidden in the coal,
> So lurking lies the holy place in all
> The universe : so lies Jerusalem
> And Sion, clouded o'er with Babylon.
> But yet the gulf 'twixt them's as great, I say,
> As betwixt light and darkness, night and day ;
> For though in one another hid they be,
> They yet together cannot stand, you see ;
> For when the darkness spreads its wings, the light
> Flies : so bright day doth chase away the night.
> When night comes, she involves the shining day :
> When day comes, it hides night within its ray.
> Thus dwell the Principles in one another ;
> Thus hell and heaven blended are together ;
> Thus is the good part of the earth hid in
> The evil part, the spacious realm of sin.

Soon we reach a passage which reminds us that John

Pordage was " an inveterate spirit-seer " and receiver of
revelations.  The world's great Spirit, we are told, was
created pure, but the devil imitates its magic.  To this
Mundane Soul " there belong of spirits an innumerable
throng," which must be clearly distinguished from Satan's
" black spirits ".  There are astral spirits, fire spirits, air
spirits, earth spirits, water spirits, and subterranean spirits ;
and

> By these *arcana's* deep are oft made known
> To men, and secrets of this world are shown.

As to magic, it is threefold : this world's natural magic,
the light world's sacred magic, and the dark world's dia-
bolic magic.  The last it is unlawful to investigate ; while
man should rise above this world's magic, " which clothed
Adam in his fleshly garb " ; but he is free to study sacred
magic,

> For Christ, our Saviour, hath thrown down the wall
> Which wrath erected had through Adam's Fall,
> Which barr'd us from the secrets of that place
> Illuminated by our Saviour's face,
> And gives free leave unto the holy-wise
> Adam's lost magic now to re-agnize :
> Through which true man may able be to know
> The internal world's, and this world's secrets too.

There are, the poet insists, numberless spirits from the
dark and the light internal worlds, to be seen by the internal eye, and sometimes even by the external eye ; for
they can assume outward form as good angels or as evil
demons.  Satan sends forth dark spirits to lure men to
evil passions ; while Christ sends forth the spirits of the
Light-world, charging them to protect men and endow them
with virtues.  Man's free-will may reject the aid of the

latter ; and the deliberate choice of evil must inevitably end in hell, with regard to which all notion of physical torment must be rejected.

The second part of the poem introduces an allegory (which it is almost impossible to read without recognizing Bunyan's debt to S. P.) of "the true progress of a soul from the court of Babylon to the city of Jerusalem". A pilgrim, overcoming the pleasures and passions with which Satan strews his path, passes through Contrition to Longing for Union with Christ. He receives a picture, the Life of our Lord, for his imitation, and is encouraged in the devout reception of the Holy Communion ; for the poet, despite his mystical flights, will countenance no disparagement of the Blessed Sacrament. By the practice of Detachment he is "diswedded from the world," and is then espoused to Sophia, by whose beauty he is "drawn into an ecstasy". And now "his inner senses' fivefold gate" is opened : he *sees* the angels in the world of light, *hears* the angelic choir, *smells* "Paradisaical odours," *tastes* "heavenly manna," and feels "the heavenly *touch* of Love, the tincture which doth from Christ's Body flow". But soon he is "rapt into a heavenly lethargy," which seems to be the State of Silence so eloquently described by Hugo of St. Victor : "When the soul is completely withdrawn into its inner kingdom, the lips are mute ; thought, not able to comprehend in any way the ineffable joy it receives, can say nothing ; and reason, too, is condemned to silence ; for when the sanctuary of thought is inundated with divine unction, human reason has no longer anything to do. Intoxicated with this perfume, it is overcome with the sleep of celestial felicity and sinks into rest, melting under the kissses of the supreme light." Here is Pordage's account :—

This is the silent passive state in which
GOD with His finger souls doth often touch :
This is the sleep of Jacob, this the trance
Of Paul, when he did to the heavens advance :
This is the state in which the soul's blest eye
Sees GOD (beyond thought) intellectually :
This is the state in which Sophia will
Souls, emptied thus, with her blest Spirit fill.
Then is the soul made fit to receive
Those bounties which Heaven's blessed hand doth give.
For whilst thoughts do her empty vessel fill,
Receive she can't Heaven's higher bounties well.

Flying beyond reason to intuition, the soul catches glimpses
of Eternity, and gains clear demonstration of the supremacy
of Love. At this point, accordingly, the poet introduces
the distinctive tenets of the Philadelphian Society, founded
by John Pordage and Jane Leade : all individual men are
truly lovable, as bearing the Father's image, and Mankind as
a whole may be likened to an edifice built up of diverse stones.

Some there are nearer knit than others, thus
John unto Christ the most beloved was.
Here spirits signatur'd alike conjoin,
And in a mystic union combine :
Here spirits be espous'd, and here they see
That they meet helps unto each other be.
Some can't receive from every vessel though,
Their thirsty souls drink what from others flow.
One gives, another receives, and he
Gives to another, here's the harmony.
Saints thus combin'd are like a tower that
Unshaken stands against the devil's shot.
He fears such unions; therefore all his art
And cunning he still uses them to thwart.

> O blessed union ! whom GOD thus doth join
> Let no man venture for to discombine.
> This doth produce a love implete with bliss,
> Which far above natural affection is.
> No man but he that has it the virtue knows
> Of this love which from pure union flows.

Such doctrine has, even within the memory of many living to-day, led to the direst moral disaster.   Nothing of the sort, though, could be laid to the charge of Pordage ; and in the poem, it is earnestly maintained that such spiritual union must be based on self-sacrifice, sympathy, and " love devoid of lust ".

Returning to the allegory, the devil poisons the pilgrim so that he feels too much complacency in his visions, and voices, and spiritual unions.   But an angel having convicted him of spiritual pride, he sacrifices " all Heaven's gifts divine " on the altar of True Resignation.   It was the misuse of reason, the poet suggests, that misled the pilgrim ; not that reason is to be banished,

> But that our reason should its weakness own,
> Confess that Heaven's *arcana's* are unknown
> To her ; that her weak eyes can't gaze upon
> The glorious splendour of bright Wisdom's Sun ;
> And not to dare with a proud scrutiny
> To search Heaven's secrets with her purblind eye.

Some may here ejaculate ' Misologist ! ' but Pordage's rejoinder would no doubt be our Lord's gratulation : " I thank Thee, O Father, Lord of heaven and earth, that Thou hast hid these things from the wise and understanding, and hast revealed them unto babes ".   Having reached the childlike state requisite to true illumination, the pilgrim mounts a chariot and is driven to the summit of a hill, whence he sees the four worlds : the outward world which he had just left, the devil's dark internal world, the Light-world or Paradise, and the Eternal world.   Here the poet undertakes the almost impossible task of moulding Boehme's theosophy to the conditions of rhyme and metre.

> The Triune GOD hath generated from
> Eternity, in His eternal womb,
> Two Principles (so called because they be
> The outspoken word of the great Deity ;
> So their *principium* is—else they have none—
> Their breathing out or manifestation) :
> The Dark and Light.   That we call First, and this
> The holy Light world and the Second is.
> GOD in the first is known a Judge severe,
> Angry and jealous, wrathful and austere.
> But in the Second He doth solely move
> In light,—in meekness, gentleness, and love.
> The First gives being to the Dark World, and
> The Light doth in the Second's essence stand.
> Nor can that be called evil : harmonize
> The Second with it, and it makes Paradise.

And so on, through all the jargon of ' Sulphur, Salt, and Mercury,' which Boehme inherited from Paracelsus.   As to Hell, GOD willed it not, nor did He make anyone in the First Principle, or Wrathful State ; but Lucifer scorned the Second, or Love Principle, and, accordingly, by the operation of automatic law, he passed into the First.   Adam, who was created in Lucifer's stead, was seduced into the same inevitable consequence of wrong choice.   Hence the necessity of the Incarnation of Christ, Who, triumphing over Hell and Death, regained what Adam lost, and will come again in glory to convert the Earth into a Paradise.   A description of Paradise follows, in which it is explained that the Ideas of all things in this world are to be found in their purity in Paradise : flowers, trees, scents, etc. ; and there, too, are the fruits and gifts of the Tree of Life : gifts of tongues, wisdom, healing, etc.   Magic was " a name of glory once," but has become discredited because it has been sought with unworthy motives.   Men study Plato, Trismegistus, Plotinus, and Agrippa ; they expend endless labour in search of the Philosopher's Stone, but all in vain. For they lack the " holy Key " of Prayer ; they slight the sacred Scriptures ; and " selfish aims close in their hearts do lie ".   Success in this quest is impossible, unless one is first truly dead and then regenerated.

> He then who pure is and regenerate,
> And blessed so that he may freely eat
> Of this beatifying fruit, he then
> Becomes Heaven's Sophus, or Magician.
> O those bless'd bonds which fast together tie
> GOD and the soul, man and the Deity !
> Nothing's impossible for him to do,
> Who this bless'd state and pitch attain'd has to ;
> For if to him, to GOD it must be so :
> His will is GOD'S—they are no longer two ;
> He willeth nothing but by Heaven's will.
> Then what shall dare not his command fulfil ?
> He now is sovereign over all the world, and all
> Things that therein are, shall obey his call.
> For by this art of Divine Magic he
> May shroud himself in invisibility,
> Walk on clouds, stand in a flame of fire,
> And through the walls—if doors be shut—retire,
> May walk upon the surliest seas, while they
> Smoothing their rugged fronts his feet obey.

To him diseases bow their eager heads,
And at his touch they leave their nasty beds
And fly to Hell, from whence they came; for by
His touch and word restor'd is Purity.

It is this particular feature of the Philadelphians' creed that especially exasperated R. A. Vaughan in his *Hours with the Mystics*. Pordage's demonology gave ample scope for his characteristic *persiflage*. Of Jane Leade all that he deigned to say was, that " the magical power of faith is her one idea. . . . Some of the German Romanticists have revived this idea—never, perhaps, wholly dead. . . . Such a doctrine is but one among the many retrogressions of the mediæval school." Here we have the crude Protestant conviction that miracles do not happen except in the pages of the Bible, a conviction to which even Anglicanism succumbed, making, however, a somewhat shamefaced exception in the case of monarchs, for whose magical touch a special service was provided. Had Vaughan lived into our own days, he would have learnt that the English Church is being recalled by the heterodox to sounder Scriptural views, and that even the vested interests of the medical profession, and its instinctive promptitude to detect quackery, are beginning to yield to the conviction that there is a great deal to be said for Spiritual Healing. Our poet, at any rate, adduces plentiful Scriptural proof of the power over spirits, diseases, and elements, exerted by GOD-united men.

All this while the allegory has been sustained only by the expedient of putting this expository section into the mouth of the Angel, who now called upon the pilgrim to drink " the sacred wine of Love ". He obeyed, and " without sin drank into drunkenness ". And it severely tests our gravity to find that, as so often happens in similar sublunary circumstances, he broke into song and dance : a choric dance with the Theological Virtues, and a Hymn of Love. Then, amid " fierce flames and happy heat," he sees a ravishing vision of the glorified Humanity of Christ ; and here Part II (and with it the allegory) ends.

In the 3rd Part, which deals with the Eternal World (as the 1st had dealt with the External, and the 2nd with the Internal Worlds), the poet sets himself, in the first place, to show that Heaven may be attained on earth :—

> For nothing is more near than Heaven to thee,
> Wert thou not blind, hadst thou but eyes to see.
> The deeper into thyself dost go,
> The more thou Heaven approachest to.
> For what's indeed a soul's departure hence
> But motion from this Circumference
> Unto the Centre, let it centre where
> It will, or in the light or darker sphere ?

After speaking of the Divine Nature, he explains how

> The Father with a strong desire
> Thirsts for the Son, from whence springs up a Fire,
> Which Fire, not reaching GOD'S most sacred Heart,
> Is full of anguish, bitterness, and tart.
> This is the Fire that enkindleth Hell,
> Where all the damned and the devils dwell.
> But the same Fire, when that sacred Love,
> Or Heart of GOD, itself to it doth move,
> Straight blazeth forth into a meek and bright
> Joy and desire of Eternal Light :
> This is the light of Heaven and pleasant joy,
> In which all bliss is, not the least annoy.
> And thus, O reader, if thou art not blind,
> Heaven's bliss and joy, Hell's pain and torment, find

> Thou wilt to come from one deep root, and even
> Perceive the true cause both of Hell and Heaven ;
> And thus thou seest how they together dwell,
> Hell hid in Heaven, Heaven in the midst of Hell.

All this, of course, is derived from Boehme,[1] as is also the description that follows of Man as an epitome of all three worlds, the External World being represented in his Flesh, the Internal Worlds spread about his Heart, the Eternal manifested in his Head.   In the Eternal sphere three mansions may be distinguished, an outer, an inner, and an inmost. These are (not very satisfactorily) appropriated respectively to the Father, the Son, and the Holy Spirit.   Of the outer, Light is the main feature ; of the innermost, Love ; while the intermediate mansion, which is the angels' dwelling-place and throbs with their activities and songs of praise, is the focus of Life.

At this point the allegory is, for a moment only, re-introduced, and the pilgrim's union with GOD is touched upon, with becoming reticence ; for the poet has now reached the plumbless depths of his theme.   In the Abyss of the Godhead lies " The Cloudy Glory,"

> That represents GOD past the reach of creature,
> Beyond the forms of the Eternal nature :
> GOD in Himself : GOD in the abstract : where
> We may say what He is not, but we dare
> Not say here what He is.   For neither He
> Can good or evil, light or darkness be,
> Nor this nor that, here in this place; nor can
> Nor ought to be search'd into by man.

---

[1] For a valuable exposition, sympathetic and yet critical, of this doctrine, the reader may be referred to an article by the late Rev. G. W. Allen, in *The Seeker*, August, 1916.

> Here as a Nothing He to us doth seem,
> Nor can man further knowledge have of Him.

This is a limitation upon which all the profounder mystics, from Plotinus onwards, have insisted, a difficulty which justifies us in defining the better sort of Agnosticism as " a mysticism which is afraid of lowering GOD by setting Him within our reach " (Boutroux).   But our poet is unwilling to leave us a prey to such Agnosticism, however noble. He agrees with Dr. Caird in representing GOD as " the One in Whom all is lost and yet the One in Whom all is found " ; and his farewell message is this :—

> GOD will not here be known ; but yet He is,
> And will be, known upon the Throne of Bliss.
> He will be known in Nature increate ;
> His wonders there man ought to meditate,
> Where he the *Arcana's* of Heaven's majesty,
> With eyes of Truth, and with true eyes, may see.
> O Reader, therefore, to the Orb of Love
> Your eyes and meditations now remove,
> Where thou by constant prayer mayst obtain
> A sight of what here under clouds remain,
> And with clear eyes must see those things of worth,
> Which by my pen are darkly shadow'd forth.

# CHAPTER VII.

## H. MORE, NORRIS, AND TRAHERNE.

A MODERN writer on mysticism speaks in a somewhat disparaging tone of " the tepid speculations of the Cambridge Platonists ". However justly that expression may be applied to the group as a whole, there was nothing tepid about HENRY MORE, its most prominent member. Materially, More lived in Fellows' Buildings, Christ's College, Cambridge ; but spiritually, he lived in the land of Beulah, where the sun shineth night and day. Although in his latter days subject to moods of depression—a weakness of the flesh entirely thrown off on his death-bed—the evidence of his friends leaves clear conviction that habitually he knew the " joy unspeakable and full of glory ". The reproof which he addressed to Thomas Vaughan has been quoted on p. 175 above ; but this is the proper context for the passages, there omitted, in which he attempts to describe his own mystical exaltations.

He claims to have " sat and sung " under a direct light from God, a " true chemical fire that has purged my soul and purified it, and has crystallized it into a bright throne and shining habitation of the divine majesty. This free light is that which, having held my soul in itself for a time, taught me in a very sensible manner that vast difference between the truth and freedom of the spirit and anxious impostures of this dark personality and earthly bondage of the body.

This is my oracle, my counsellor, my faithful instructor and
guide, my Life, my Strength, my Glory, my Joy, my com-
municated GOD. . . . He that is come hither, GOD hath
taken him to His own familiar friend ; and though he speaks
to others aloof off in outward religions and parables, yet He
leads this man by the hand, teaching him intelligible docu-
ments upon all the objects of His Providence ; speaks to
him plainly in His own language ; sweetly insinuates Himself
and possesses all his faculties—understanding, reason, and
memory. This is the Darling of God, and a Prince among
men, far above the dispensation of either miracle or prophecy.
For him the deep searchers and anxious solicitors of Nature
drudge and toil, contenting themselves with the pitiful wages
of vainglory or a little wealth. Poor Gibeonites ! that hew
wood and draw water for the Temple. This is the Temple
of GOD ; this is the Son of God whom He hath made
' heir of all things,' the right Emmanuel, the holy mystery
of the living members of Christ. Hallelujah ! From this
principle which I have here expressed, have all those poems
I have wrote had their original : and as many as are moved
with them aright, they carry them to this Principle from
whence they came. But to those whose ignorance makes
them contemn them, I will only say to them what our
Saviour said to Nicodemus : ' The wind bloweth whither
it listeth, and thou hearest the sound thereof, but knowest
not from whence it comes nor whither it goes '."

There follows a warm defence of the philosophy of Descartes, whom, however, More came gradually to distrust.
Even here he insists that Cartesianism bears no proportion
to " that Principle I told you of. I say that a free univer-
salized spirit is worth all. How lovely, how magnificent a
state is the soul of man in, when the life of GOD inactuating

her, shoots her along with Himself through heaven and
earth, makes her unite with, and, after a sort, feel herself
animate the whole world, as if she had become GOD and
all things. . . . This is to become Deiform, to be thus suspended (not by imagination but by union of life κέντρον
κέντρῳ συνάψαντα, joining centres with GOD) and by a
sensible touch to be held up from the clotty dark personality
of this compacted body.   Here is love ; here is freedom ;
here is justice and equity in the super-essential causes of
them.   He that is here looks upon all things as one, and on
himself, if he can then mind himself, as a part of the whole ".

Here, in another parenthesis, More attempts to rebut the
charge of enthusiasm ; but he is soon back to his original
subject.   " GOD hath permitted to me all these things, and
I have it under the broad seal of Heaven.   Who dare
charge me ?   GOD doth acquit me.   For He hath made
me full Lord of the four elements, and hath constituted me
Emperor of the world.   I am in the *fire of choler* and am
not burned ; in the *water of phlegm* and am not drowned ;
in the *airy sanguine* and yet not blown away with every
vain blast of transient pleasure or false doctrines of men ; I
descend also into the sad *earthly melancholy* and yet am
not buried from the sight of my GOD.   I am, Philalethes
(though I dare say thou takest me for no bird of Paradise),
*Incola coeli in terra*, an inhabitant of Paradise and Heaven
upon earth. . . . I still the raging of the sea.   I clear up
the lowering heavens and with my breath blow away the
clouds.   I sport with the beasts of the earth ; the lion licks
my hand like a spaniel, and the serpent sleeps upon my hand
and stings me not.   I play with the fowls of heaven, and
the birds of the air sit singing on my fist.   All the Creation
is before me, and I call every one of them by their proper

names. This is the true Adam, O Philalethes : this is
Paradise, Heaven, and Christ. All these things are true
in a sober sense. . . . Where is my reason inconsequent
with the attributes of GOD, the common notions of men, the
phenomena of Nature, or with itself ? But for the bottom
of all these things, that, I confess, you cannot reach to nor
judge of ; that is Divine sense, the *white stone* in which
there is a name written but none can read but he that hath
it. But for the guidance of my reason and imagination, they
have so safe a steersman, viz. that Divine touch of my soul
with GOD, and the impregnation of my understanding from
the Most High, that judgment and caution have so warily
built the outward fabric of words and fancy, that I challenge
any man to discover any ineptitude in them, or incoherency."

This very lengthy quotation (if, in view of its interest and
eloquence, it needs apology) will conclusively clear More of
the charge of tepidity ; and it will be appealed to later,
when it is claimed that Dr. Bucke should have included
him in the list of those who reached that higher plane of
existence called Cosmic Consciousness. But it can hardly
be denied that it exposes him to the charge of being " inflated
with egotism " (Isaac D'Israeli). It was not, however, the
egotism that repels by its pompous self-conceit, but rather
an innocuous vanity, an almost childlike delight in his own
exploits, which he makes no attempt to conceal, and the
openness of which only endears him to us the more deeply.
It is to this egotistic loquacity that we owe our intimate
knowledge of his spiritual progress and achievement.

The *Prefatio* to the Latin edition of his *Works* contains
a delightful autobiographical disclosure, beginning at his
emancipation from inherited Calvinism and growing sense of
the Divine Presence during his three years at Eton, and his

thirst for knowledge as an undergraduate at Cambridge, which resulted in an attitude of morbid scepticism. More recorded this in a Greek epigram which he called 'Απορία (lit. Difficulty or Straits) and himself translated :—

Know I

Nor whence, nor who I am, poor wretch !
Nor yet—Oh, madness !—whither I must go.
But in Grief's crooked claws fast held I lie,
And live, I think, by force tugg'd to and fro—
Asleep or wake all one.   O father Jove,
'Tis brave, we mortals live in clouds like Thee.
Lies, night-dreams, empty toys, fear, fatal love,
This is my life : I nothing else do see.

But a study of Neo-Platonic philosophers, of whom he especially names Marsilio Ficino and Plotinus, (reminding us of Coleridge's contention that his school would more accurately be called the Cambridge Plotinists), led him, after taking his degree, to doubt the supreme importance of mere knowledge and to give thought to the Mystic Ladder of purgation, illumination, and union.    Above all he was helped, he says, by " that truly golden book," the *Theologia Germanica.*

It is little short of a calamity not to know this noble book, one of the sanest and most practical of devotional helps, written by a member of the society called " Friends of GOD," but introduced to Protestantism by Luther, who ranked it " next to the Bible and St. Augustine ".    Its great lesson is the importance of self-renunciation, the supreme necessity of surrendering that I-hood which is at the root of all sin. " The more the Self, the I, the Me, the Mine, that is self-seeking and selfishness, abate in a man, the more doth GOD'S ' I,' that is GOD Himself, increase in him."    " Where a man cometh out of himself and his own things, there GOD entereth in with His own, that is with Himself." Meditating on such passages as these, suddenly (" as in a moment or the twinkling of an eye ") More awoke to the fact that he was self-centred, futilely revolving round himself as the centre of his universe. At once he accepted the theocentric system of the spiritual life, and, unappalled by the inevitable difficulties, began his purgation.

> GOD'S Spirit is no private empty shade,
> But that great Ghost that fills both earth and sky,
> And through the boundless universe doth lie,
> Shining through purged hearts and simple minds,
> When doubling clouds of thick hypocrisy
> Be blown away with strongly brushing winds.
> Who first this tempest feels, the Sun he after finds.

So he wrote subsequently in his great poem ; but meanwhile the stern struggle had been fought out between the Divine Will and the self-will, which More calls " the *Punctum saliens* or first motions of the New Life ". Writing long afterwards to his disciple, John Norris, he insists that we must aim at " a perfect exinanition of ourselves, that we may be filled with the sense of GOD, Who worketh all in all, and feelingly acknowledge whatever good is in us to be from Him, and so be no more elated for it than if we had none of it, nor were conscious to ourselves we had any such thing. And to be thus self-dead and self-annihilated is the only sure passage into eternal life, peace and glory, and is the most safe and lovely condition of the soul that possibly can be attained to. . . . This mystical death or spiritual annihilation, whereby all self-wishing is destroyed, is the peculiar transcendency of the Christian state above that of the noblest heathen philosophers that ever were.    And whosoever feels it will find it so."

But by all this More did not intend to uphold the unsocial ideal of the *Via Negativa*.    In the last of his *Divine Dialogues*, he strongly reproved the desire to be " free of secular occasions," and in the *Conjectura Cabbalistica*, he condemned " those that endeavour after so still, so silent and demure a condition of mind that they would have the sense of nothing there but peace and rest, striving to make their whole nature desolate of all Animal Figurations whatsoever. . . . The true Divine Life would destroy nothing that is in nature, but only regulate things and order them for the more full and sincere enjoyments of man, reproaching nothing but sinfulness and enormity." What he sought by self-suppression was spiritual expansion, as he suggests in his paraphrase of Boreel's Hymn :—

> So that at last, I being quite releas'd
> From this strait-lac'd egoity,
> My soul will vastly be increas'd
>           Into that All
>           Which One we call,
> And One in itself doth all imply.

And this aim he achieved.    " There shone in upon me daily," he says, " a greater assurance than ever I could have expected, even of those things which before I had the greatest desire to know.    Insomuch that within a few years I was got into a most joyous and lucid state of mind, and such plainly as was ineffable ; though, according to my custom, I have endeavoured to express it, to my power, in another stanza of eight verses, both in sense and title answering in a way of direct opposition unto the former : which is

called (as that 'Απορία, Imperviousness and Emptiness, so
this) 'Ευπορία, Fulness and Perviousness." This is his
translation :—

> I come from Heaven, am an immortal ray
> Of GOD—Oh, joy!—and back to GOD shall go.
> And here sweet Love on His wings me up doth stay.
> I live, I am sure, and joy this life to know.
> Night and vain dreams be gone.   Father of Lights,
> We live, as Thou, clad with eternal Day.
> Faith, wisdom, love, fix'd joy, free-winged might,
> This is true life ;  all else death and decay.

This brief ' epigram,' however, did not satisfy his longing
for self-expression.   He attempted a fuller record of his experiences and speculations in " a pretty full poem called
*Psychozoia*, or the Life of the Soul, stirred up to it, I believe, by some heavenly impulse of mind ".   This poem,
which was written in 1640, when More was twenty-six
years of age, was not intended for publication, and was deliberately made obscure.   He added to it from time to time ;
but, when discovered by friends, he at first purposed to destroy the manuscript.   Yielding, however, to their advice,
he published the whole collection in 1642, under the title
*Psychozoia Platonica or a Platonical Song of the Soul
consisting of four several Poems*.   Five years later, he
reissued this collection, with the addition of some shorter
pieces, under the title *Philosophical Poems*.

In this more prosaic age, we are inclined to consider More
ill-advised in attempting to expound his philosophy in verse.
Certainly he was misguided in adopting the Spenserian
stanza and the archaic language, for which paternal readings
from the *Faerie Queen* had given him a predilection.   As,
later, he expressed his more important views in lucid and

virile prose, his verse was not taken very seriously, even in his own life-time ; subsequently it dropped almost entirely out of sight.   But Southey studied it ; and, though admitting it to be " strange and sometimes unreadably uncouth," found " lines and passages of the highest feeling and most exquisite beauty ".   To Campbell it was " a grotto whose gloomy labyrinth we might be curious to explore for the strange and mystic associations they excite ".   To Palgrave, soundest of modern critics, it suggested the passionate power and imaginative fury of Lucretius, " working in a larger and happier ether," and he found it " impossible to glance at More's poems without an impression of strange imaginative force, of singular and delightful depth of mystical conviction ". Professor Tulloch's estimate (as that of the most important student of More's position) must be quoted at length, from the second volume of his *Rational Theology in England in the Seventeenth Century ;* he regards his poems as " in some respects the most singular attempt in literature to turn metaphysics into poetry.   Apart from the ' notes ' and ' interpretation general,' which he has himself happily furnished, they are barely intelligible.   Even with such assistance they are a most intricate and perplexing study.   Not only the strain of thought and complexities of Neo-Platonic allusion, but the involutions and phantasies of the verse itself, contribute to this.   Yet there are here and there not a few genuine gleams both of poetic and spiritual insight ; and the mental picture which the poems present is altogether so curious as to reward the patience of a congenial student."

It is only fair to say that the poet warns the reader to expect " no light wanton Lesbian vein," and that, if he is out of sympathy with the theme, he will only find " dark numerous nothings ".   Indeed, with a certain truculence, he compares some of his readers to chalky cliffs and empty groves, heedless of a lyre's charms and incapable of praise or blame.   He was, however, far from being satisfied with the ability of his Muse to expound his theme ; and in the curious mixture of self-depreciation and self-defence which he entitled *Ad Paronem*, he complained,

> A rude confused heap of ashes dead
>> My verses seem, when that celestial flame,
> That sacred spirit of life 's extinguished
>> In my cold breast.   Then 'gin I rashly blame
>> My rugged lines : This word is obsolete ;
>> That badly coin'd ; a third too oft doth beat
> Mine humorous ears.

After this piece of self-criticism it is hardly necessary to insist that More's pre-occupation with his matter spoils his lyric flow, and leads him constantly to emit the harshest phrases and most awkward words ; that his ideas struggle through his poems like flies in treacle ; and that he has absolutely no gift for personification.   And yet, in spite of intentional obscurity and a wayward diction, there can never be any doubt about the vigour and earnestness of the poet's mind, which, in the longer poems, expresses itself at times in language of real dignity, and in the shorter pieces, composed for the most part to be sung to his favourite instrument, the theorbo, often finds graceful and almost limpid utterance.

We are told quite definitely by the author that the purpose of the *Song of the Soul* is to " give some fair glimpse of Plato's hid philosophy," as modified, however, by other philosophic systems, including the Jewish Cabbala.

> So if what's consonant to Plato's school
> (Which well agrees with learned Pythagore,
> Egyptian Trismegist, and the antique roll

Of Chaldee wisdom, all which time hath tore,
But Plato and deep Plotin do restore),
Which is my scope, I sing out lustily.
If any twitten me for such strange lore,
And me, all blameless, brand with infamy,
GOD purge that man from fault of foul malignity.

The earlier sections deal, very cumbrously, with " the famous Platonical Trinity," which the poet strives to adapt to the Christian doctrine of the Blessed Trinity, one of his favourite theories being the dependence of Plato on Moses. Setting out from the saying of Numenius, " What is Plato but Moses speaking in the language of Athens ? " and relying on a reading, which substitutes Moses for Moschus, in a statement by Iamblichus, More takes it as an established fact that " Platonists and Pythagoreans got their philosophy from Moses ".[1]

Anyone who has read Plato's hesitant speculations in the *Timaeus* is free to say, as Aubrey Moore did say in *Lux Mundi*, that " a truth revealed by GOD is never out of relation to previous thought," and that " there was an intellectual preparation for the doctrine of the Trinity ". But it seems impossible to claim that Henry More satisfactorily adapts to the theological system of the Catholic Church the ontological system of Plotinus, wherein $\nu o\hat{v}s$, i.e. Pure Intelligence, and $\psi v\chi\acute{\eta}$, or the World-spirit, emanate from $\tau\grave{o}$ $\ddot{\epsilon}\nu$, the Absolute. Especially difficult is it to find any common term between the Holy Spirit and the World-spirit, which More conceives as an unconscious, incorporeal substance " pervading the whole of the universe and exercising a plastical power therein," not itself GOD, but an

---

[1] See his *Conjectura Cabbalistica*, pp. 3, 43, 73, 100 ff., and *The Mystery of Godliness*, p. 68.

instrument by whose means GOD is saved from the derogatory and none too successful manipulation of matter.[1]

It would be profitless to follow in detail the terribly involved account of " the deep Centre and First Root of all things " (called indifferently Ahad and Atove, or Atuvus), whose Son, Aeon (spoken of as Eternal Life, the Idea, the Intellectual World, and the Logos) marries Psyche (whose garment is " all this visible world "). The lines often bristle with proper names which suggest the horrific monsters of antediluvian times and are only very partially elucidated in the glossary : the easiest, perhaps, are Hyle (the First Matter of Neo-Platonism and the Chaos of the Biblical Cosmogony) and Haphe (the principle of sensuous apperception). The section dealing with the two lands, Aptery (whose inhabitants are wingless) and Pteroessa (the land of winged souls who rise above mere worldly aspirations) is fairly intelligible. Here and there we reach a patch of light : in the following stanza, for instance, an important mystical truth gradually emerges when we know that by an ' Autæsthesian ' is meant one who indulges self, that ' On ' is the Greek for the being, and that the author has just been speaking of ' Autoparnes ' (by which he means self-denial) and of Hypomene (or patience) :—

> So both their lives do vanish into mine
> And mine into Atuvus' life doth melt,
> Which fading flux of time doth not define,
> Nor is by any Autaesthesian felt.
> This life to On the good Atuvus dealt ;
> In it's all joy, truth, knowledge, love, and force :

[1] See especially his prose treatise on *The Immortality of the Soul*, Bk. III, chaps. XII., XVI.

> Such force, no weight created can repel it.
> All strength and livelihood is from this source ;
> All lives to this first spring have circular recourse.

In dealing with the rest of this stupendous work, it will probably be most helpful to make a few short extracts illustrating some of the more outstanding points of More's philosophy. Of these, the first may well be the Pre-existence of the Soul, a doctrine on which he laid very special emphasis and to which modern thinkers are by no means hostile.[1] Here is his answer to the question, " Tell what we mortals are, tell what of old we were " :—

> A spark or ray of the divinity,
> Clouded in earthly fogs, yclad in clay :
> A precious drop sunk from Eternity,
> Spilt on the ground, or rather slunk away.
>
> . . . . . . . .
>
> We after fell into low phantasy,
> And after that into corporeal sense.
>
> . . . . . . . .
>
> Thus groping after our own centre's near
> And proper substance, we grew dark, contract,
> Swallow'd up of earthly life.

Omitting his views on the three vehicles of spiritual being, ethereal, aerial, and terrestrial, we note his insistence that the Divine spark, however dimmed, is never wholly extinguished. GOD

> Can rear the soul into her pristine state.
> He can them so enlarge and elevate
> And spreaden out, that they can compass all,
> When they no longer be incarcerate
> In this dark dungeon, this foul fleshly wall,
> Nor be no longer wedg'd in things corporeal.

[1] See, e.g. Sir O. Lodge's *Reason and Belief*, chaps. ii. and iii.

But this presupposes the resolute purgation of all blinding passions :—

> Fear, anger, hope, fierce vengeance, and swoln hate,
> Tumultuous joy, envy, and discontent,
> Self-love, vainglory, strife, and fell debate,
> Unsatiate covetise, desire impotent,
> Low-sinking grief, pleasure, lust violent,
> Fond emulation—all these dim the mind
> That with foul filth the inward eye yblent,
> That light that is so near it cannot find.
> So shines the sun unseen on a tree's rugged rind.

> But the clear soul by virtue purified,
> Collecting her own self from the foul steam
> Of earthly life, is often dignified
> With that pure pleasure that from GOD doth stream,
> Often is enlighten'd by that radiant beam
> That issues forth from His Divinity.
> Then feelingly immortal she doth deem
> Herself, conjoin'd by so near unity
> With GOD, and nothing doubts of her eternity.

As an illustration of his doctrine of illumination, perhaps the best passage will be one in which he borrows and adapts an allegory from Cornelius Agrippa :—

> Like to a light fast-lock'd in lanthorn dark,
> Whereby, by night, our weary steps we guide
> In slabby streets, and dirty channels mark ;
> Some weaker rays through the black top do glide,
> And flusher streams, perhaps, from horny side.
> But when we've pass'd the peril of the way,
> Arriv'd at home, and laid that case aside,
> The naked light how clearly it doth ray,
> And spread its joyful beams as bright as summer's day.

E'en so the soul in this contracted state,
Confin'd to these strait instruments of sense,
More dull and narrowly doth operate.
At this hole hears; the sight must ray from thence;
Here tastes; here smells. But when she's gone from hence,
Like naked lamp she is one shining sphere,
And round about has perfect cognoscence
Whate'er in her horizon doth appear.
She is one orb of sense, all eye, all airy ear.

It should be noted that the reference here is not, as might
be supposed, to the condition of the soul after its departure
from this life, but to its condition in moments of ecstasy or
' standing-out ' from the body.

On the Unitive way, the following passage is, probably, as
good as any other, and is notable for its sacramental allusion :—

But they whose soul's deiform summity
Is waken'd in this life, and so to GOD
Are nearly join'd in a firm unity
(This outward body is but earthly clod
Digested, having life transfus'd abroad,
The world's life and our lower vitality
Unite in one), their souls have their abode
In Christ's own Body, and are eternally
One with our GOD by true and strong community.

When we are clothed with this outward world,
Feel the soft air, behold the glorious sun,
All this we have from meat that is daily hurl'd
Into these mouths. But first of all we won
This priviledge by our first union
With this world's body and diffused spright.
In the higher world there's such communion.
Christ is the Sun that by His cheering might
Awakes our higher rays to join with His pure might.

14

And when He hath that life elicited,
He gives His own dear Body and His Blood
To drink and eat.   Thus daily we are fed
Unto eternal life.   Thus do we bud,
True heavenly plants, suck in our lasting food
From the first spring of life, incorporate
Into the higher world (as erst I show'd
Our lower rays the soul to subjugate
To this low world), we fearless sit above all fate,

Safely that kingdom's glory contemplate,
O'erflow with joy by a full sympathy
With that world's Sprite, and bless our own estate,
Praising the fount of all felicity
The lovely light of the blest Deity.
Vain mortals, think on this, and raise your minds
Above the body's life ; strike through the sky
With piercing throbs and sighs, that you may find
His face.   Base fleshly fumes your drowsy eyes thus blind.

Passing to the shorter pieces, some of these are found in
the *Divine Dialogues*, published in 1668 ; but space cannot be spared even for *Resolution*, the best of these, with
its magnificent witness to More's attitude of fearless faith in
GOD's Providence.   Of the shorter *Philosophical Poems*,
extracts must be made from *Cupid's Conflict ;* it is his
highest flight in verse, and his delightful but unsystematic
biographer, Richard Ward, tells us (in the second, unpublished part of the *Life*) that it is an autobiographical record
of a struggle between higher and lower aspirations :—

Who seek for pleasure in this mortal life
     By diving deep into the body base
Shall lose true pleasure.   But who gainly strive
     Their sinking souls above this bulk to place,

> Enlarg'd delights they certainly shall find,
> Unbounded joys to fill their boundless minds.

When I myself from mine own self do quit
  And all things else, then an all-spreading Love
To the vast universe my soul doth fit,
  Makes me half-equal to All-seeing Jove.
    My mighty wings high-stretch'd, then clapping light
    I brush the stars, and make them shine more bright.

Then all the works of GOD with close embrace
  I dearly hug in my enlarged arms.
All the hid paths of heavenly Love I trace,
  And boldly listen to His secret charms.
    Then clearly view I where true Light doth rise
    And where eternal Night low-pressed lies.

  .    .    .    .    .    .    .    .

Thrice happy he whose name is writ above,
  And doeth good, though gaining infamy ;
Requiteth evil turns with hearty love,
  And recks not what befalls him outwardly ;
    Whose worth is in himself, and only bliss
    In his pure conscience that doth naught amiss ;

Who placeth pleasure in his purged soul,
  And virtuous life his treasure doth esteem ;
Who can his passions master and control,
  And that true lordly manliness doth deem ;
    Who from this world himself doth clearly quit,
    Counts nought his own but what dwells in his spirit.

So when his sprite from this vain world shall flit,
  It bears all with it whatsoe'er was dear
Unto itself, passing in easy fit,
  As kindly ripen'd corn comes out of the ear.
    Thus mindless of what idle men will say,
    He takes his own and stilly goes his way.

The little piece entitled *Devotion* proves that More could claim no immunity from that mood of mystical reaction called the Dark Night of the Soul.   It has, moreover, a special interest of its own, as showing the only signs in More's writings of the influence of George Herbert ; it is strikingly reminiscent of the latter, both in matter and form :—

Good GOD, when Thou Thy inward grace doth shower
>    Into my breast,
>  How full of light and lively power
>    Is then my soul !
>    How am I blest !
How can I then all difficulties devour !
>    Thy might,
>    Thy Sprite,
With ease my cumbrous enemy control.

If Thou once turn away Thy face and hide
>    Thy cheerful look,
>  My feeble flesh may not abide
>    That dreadful stound [blow].
>    I cannot brook
Thy absence.   My heart, with care and grief then gride [pierced],
>    Doth fail,
>    Doth quail.
My life steals from me at that hidden wound.

My fancy 's then a burden to my mind.
>    Mine anxious thought
>  Betrays my reason, makes me blind.
>    Near fears drad [dreaded]
>    Make me distraught.
Surpris'd with fear my senses all I find.
>    In hell
>    I dwell,
Oppress'd with horror, pain, and sorrow sad.

My former resolutions all are fled—
    Slipp'd o'er my tongue.
My faith, my hope, my joy are dead.
    Assist my heart,
    Rather than my song.
My GOD, my Saviour, when I am ill-bested,
    Stand by,
    And I
Shall bear with courage undeserved smart.

As a final extract, we may take the opening lines of
*Charity and Humility*, which must be recognized as a
colloquy. Its lesson, that humility is the home of charity,
was one that the spiritual pride and uncharitableness of
the 'enthusiasts' of the mid-seventeenth century sorely
needed :—

Far have I clambered in my mind,
But nought so great as Love I find :
Deep-searching wit, mount-moving might,
Are nought compar'd with that good sprite.
Life of delight and soul of bliss !
Sure source of lasting happiness !
Higher than heaven !   Lower than hell !
What is Thy tent ?   Where mayest Thou dwell ?
    " My mansion hight [is called] Humility,
    Heaven's vastest capability.
    The further it doth downward tend,
    The higher up it doth ascend.
    If it go down to utmost nought,
    It shall return with that it sought."
Lord, stretch Thy tent in my strait breast ;
Enlarge it downward, that sure rest
May there be pight [pitched] for that pure fire,
Wherewith Thou wontest to inspire
All self-dead souls. . . .

More's attitude towards enthusiasm (in its technical sense) is not quite consistent. Besides countless references *passim*, he devoted a whole treatise to the subject, in which he seems to beg the question from the very outset, by defining enthusiasm as " a full but false persuasion in a man that he is inspired ". What he had in mind was, of course, the disorderly psychic phenomena which make the religious history of ' Commonwealth' days such painful reading, with its record of self-deception and misology, of anti-nomianism and blasphemy. Against such aberrations More waged ceaseless and effective warfare ; but he protested (as well he might) that " to such enthusiasm as is but the triumph of the soul of man inebriated, as it were, with the delicious sense of the Divine life, that blessed root and original of all holy wisdom and virtue, I am as much a friend as I am to the vulgar fanatical enthusiasm a professed enemy ".

Earlier quotations, both in prose and verse, have recorded his own claims to rapture and ecstasy ; and much more to the same effect might be adduced from his biography, and from his writings ; such as the passage on Divine Madness in the second of the *Divine Dialogues*. It is clear that he enjoyed at times that consciousness of the cosmos, with its intellectual enlightenment, its sense of elation and conviction of immortality, which has been experienced in our own times by Walt Whitman and Richard Jeffries (amongst others), and has been carefully studied by the Canadian psychologist, Dr. Bucke. This ' dispensation' More seems to have reached by the age of twenty-five ; he could enter it, apparently, at will ; and, whether or not he was in danger at one time of losing it, he was in the full enjoyment of it on his death-bed.

But he imposed on himself and urged upon others a three-fold guard against self-delusion or loss of balance : reason, morality, and Church authority.   In all sorts of ways, and on every sort of occasion, he insisted that reason must command the mystical consciousness : no being " blown above reason," no " Light within that loves darkness," found any place in his system.   In urging, too, that an enlightened conscience can claim no release from the rules of Christian morality, he was able to demonstrate that " lurking fumes of lust had tainted the fancies of those pretenders to inspiration ".   And thirdly, only " sullen self-sufficiency " will " undervalue the helps without, which the grace of GOD has provided for His Church ".

Among his contemporaries Henry More enjoyed a brilliant reputation, and very few in his lifetime would have predicted the complete neglect which has befallen his writings.   But it is not difficult to account for his failure. He had, in an exaggerated degree, the faults of his age. He wrote too much and too fast.   He was incapable of reducing his philosophy to a system.   He was a 'crank,' dominated by extravagant notions—a victim of Predictionism and credulity.   He was a pedant, deficient in the critical faculty and in the historical sense.   He was academic in the fullest sense of the word, an almost slavish adherent of Plato, without really understanding his master's teaching. He welcomed new light, but too often he failed to absorb it.   He was a recluse, living in a library, and bereft of the wholesome irritants which a parochial charge and family life would have provided.

And yet, after all, did he fail ?   Can such a word be applied to one whose character and spiritual ideas, whose benign and gracious presence—in a word, whose personality

was an inspiration to old and young ?  In the Common
Room of Christ's College they found him " one of the
merriest Greeks they were acquainted with," and yet (or,
should it be said rather ?—and therefore) they spoke of him
as " the holiest person upon the face of the earth " ; moreover, they turned to him " whenever there was any more
than ordinary occasion for the exercise of prudence ".  In
a grasping, worldly age of bigotry and fierce controversy, it
was an achievement very unlike failure to set an example
of disinterestedness that could decline two deaneries and
two bishoprics, of a toleration upheld consistently as " the
flower of all Christian graces," whether Puritan or Anglican
was uppermost, and of a courtesy in controversy which his
opponents could explain only on the assumption of hypo-
critical acumen.

As for posthumous success, it is no unenviable fate to have
had one's works recommended by Dr. Johnson as a con-
firmation of the hopes of immortality, and extolled by Coleridge as containing " more original, enlarged, and elevating
views of the Christian dispensation than I have met with in
any other single volume ".  It is true that Coleridge has to
admit More's shortcomings, more or less as touched on
above ; but he pronounces him to have " both the philosophic and the poetic genius, supported by immense erudition " ; and he believes that " there are few writers whose
works could be so easily defecated as More's : mere omission
would suffice ; and perhaps one half (an unusually large
proportion) would come forth from the furnace pure gold ;
and if but a fourth, how great a gain ! "

More handed on the task of reconciling Platonism with
Christianity, and of upholding the torch of Reason in re-

ligious matters, to one who understood better the teaching of
Plato, and had a clearer sense of what was repugnant to
reason—JOHN NORRIS, a member of the sister-University,
who had definitely ranged himself among the more devoted
of More's disciples. He had carried on an open correspondence with the Cambridge philosopher in a spirit of
genuine deference, had addressed to him an Ode which
lacked nothing of the hyperbole expected in poetic enconiums,
and in his numerous prose treatises lost few opportunities
of " naming him with particular honour and reverence ".

Norris had won an All Souls' fellowship from Winchester
and Exeter College, and by 1687, when his *Miscellanies*
appeared, had already gained a considerable reputation as
a preacher and as a poet. His sermons on *The Beatitudes*
were popular, in both senses of the word, passing through
fifteen editions in forty years. As a poet, he was a follower
of Cowley, and in the opinion of his contemporaries reached
his highwater-mark of achievement with so-called Pindaric
Odes on *The Passion of Our Blessed Saviour* and on
*The Consummation*. In the Preface to his *Poems* (published 1684, *æt.* 27), he appears in an ambitious and far
from diffident light, deploring that " poetry is of late mightily
fallen from the beauty of its idea and from its ancient majesty
and grandeur, as well as credit and reputation ". His own
design is " to restore the declining genius of poetry to its
primitive and genuine greatness, to wind up the string of
the Muse's lyre, and to show that sense and gracefulness
are as consistent in these as in any other compositions ".
The reading public seems to have taken him at something
approaching his own valuation, for the collection reached a
tenth edition in 1730.

Perhaps the most persistent note of these poems is the

longing (despite the allurements of Fame) for the retirement
always so dear to the mystical temperament.   More than
once we are reminded of Thoreau, who would, at least,
have endorsed the piece entitled *My Estate*, a stanza of
which may be given, though not essentially mystical :—

> While you a spot of earth possess with care,
> Below the notice of the geographer,
>   I by the freedom of my soul
>   Possess, nay more, enjoy the whole ;
>   To the universe a claim I lay.
>   Your writings shew—perhaps you will say—
> That is your dull way ; my title runs more high,
> 'Tis by the charter of Philosophy.

Several poems bear witness to poignant grief at the loss
of a little niece ;  and, although he drew up in prose a *Con-
solatio philosophica* to mollify the wound, the result was an
intensified conviction of the " vanity of all sublunary bliss ".
But in *The Retraction* this is modified in favour of music
and friendship.   He evidently had to parry charges of inconsistency in these two respects, and in his letters made
elaborate and, of course, successful apologies for his attitude
towards these indulgences.   The friendship, however, proves
to be something closer than bachelor *camaraderie ;* for
soon we find him resigning his fellowship, marrying a wife,
and retiring to the living of Newton St. Loe in Somerset.
While there, he addressed to Lady Masham, daughter of
the Cambridge Platonist, Cudworth, an open letter on *The
Conduct of Human Life*, in which he makes an interesting
self-disclosure : " I have spent about thirteen years in the
most celebrated university in the world, and, according to
the ordinary measures, perhaps not amiss, having accomplished myself in a competent degree both with such learning

as the academical standard requires and with whatever else
my own private genius inclined me too.   But truly I cannot
say that I have ordered my studies in that theatre of learning
so much to my own satisfaction as to my reputation with
others.   To be free with you, I must declare that, when I
reflect upon my past intellectual conduct, I am as little satisfied with it as I am with my morals, and that I think I have
nigh as much to answer for the former as I have for the
latter, being very conscious that the greatest part of it has
been employed in unconcerning curiosities, such as derive no
moral influence upon the soul that contemplates them.   But
I have now, if I sufficiently understand myself, a very different taste and apprehension of things, and intend to spend
my uncertain remainder of time in studying only such things
as make for the moral improvement of my mind, and the
regulation of my life, not being able to give an account upon
any rational and consistent principles why I should study
anything else.   More particularly, I think, I shall apply myself to the reading of such works as are rather persuasive
than instructive, such as are sapid, pathetic, and divinely
ravishing, such as warm, kindle, and enlarge the interior,
and awaken the divine sense of the soul, as considering with
myself that I have now, after so much reading and speculation, more need of heat than light.   Though, if I were for
more light still, I think this would prove the best method of
illumination, and that, when all is done, the love of GOD is
the best Light of the soul. . . . Perhaps you will say I am
already countrified since I left the university.   How far that
*metamorphosis* may seize upon me, I can't yet tell.   If
solitude and retirement be enough to bring it, I am, I confess,
in great danger, being now got into a little corner of the
world, where I must be more company to myself than I have

been ever yet.　But the best on it is, I have not been so great a stranger to my own company all along as to fear any great alteration by it now."

It could hardly have been disgust for its seclusion that led Norris, in 1691, to exchange the benefice of St. Loe for that of Bemerton.　The deprivation of a well-loved Diocesan as a Non-juror may have been a contributing factor to his decision ; but the main attraction to Bemerton is more likely to have been the associations, still comparatively fresh, with George Herbert.　The exchange was not, however, entirely satisfactory ; and from his letters (preserved in the Bodleian) it is evident that, after the cordial relations which he had enjoyed with Bishop Ken, a kindred spirit both ecclesiastically and poetically, he found the broad but shallow Churchmanship, and the bustling, mundane nature of Burnet an episcopal trial.　Here, nevertheless, he settled for the remaining twenty years of his life—*bene latuit*, as the tablet to his memory on the chancel-wall of the little church so happily puts it.　His pastoral ideals, eloquently expressed in a Visitation sermon preached for Bishop Ken, were worthy of Herbert's successor ; and there is ample evidence that he did not fall far below them in practice.　He found time, too, for a quite surprising amount of literary output, aiming more especially (as he says in that delightful blend of Platonic philosophy, cold logic, and ardent devotion, *Reason and Religion*) at the edification of " the learned reader who perhaps needs as much to be assisted in his devotion as the more ignorant, and whose heart may want as much to be inflamed as the other's head does to be instructed ".

But, in spite of pastoral and literary activity, Norris seems to have made Contemplation his chief concern.　" Happy," he wrote while at Bemerton, " the contemplative man,

The world envies him not, but rather pities him as a melancholy forlorn creature, because he partakes not in their joys nor relishes their pleasures ; but he has Meat to eat that they know not of, even that Meat upon which angels feed, the solid and substantial Bread of Truth. . . . When we are alone, then we ' come to ourselves ' ; and then, if we seek for truth with due care and attention, we find it because it is in ourselves. Noise disturbs, company amuses, and business distracts ; but in a state of solitude and retreat all impediments are removed from the soul, except that inseparable one of the body ; and so she may put forth her faculties to the utmost stretch, and employ them within the whole sphere of their present activity." He reverts continually in his writings to the joys of Contemplation ; and in his best known essay, on *Happiness*, after defining it as " an habitual, attentive, steady application or conversion of the spirit to GOD and His divine perfections," he glances at the various gradations propounded by " the masters of mystic theology ". He declines, however, to express any approval of these refinements of classification, but is prepared to " affirm in general that the soul may be wound up to a most strange degree of abstraction by a silent and steady contemplation of GOD. . . . Certain it is, that there are exceeding great measures of abstraction in Contemplation ; so great that sometimes whether a man be in the body or out of the body he himself can hardly tell."

But there was nothing of Plato's ' shell-fish ' about this life of retirement and meditation. Far from being indifferent to human interests, Norris, in urging a similar course on others, always added qualifying clauses in favour of " the discharge of the common offices of humanity " or " the

prosecution of the public good ".   And in *The Return*
he versifies to the same effect :—

> Dear Contemplation, my divinest joy,
>     When I thy sacred mount ascend,
>     What heavenly sweets my soul employ !
> Why can't I there my days for ever spend ?
> When I have conquer'd thy steep heights with pain,
> What pity 'tis that I must down again !
>
> And yet I must ;  my passions would rebel,
>     Should I too long continue here.
>     No ;  here I must not think to dwell,
> But mind the duties of my proper sphere.
> So angels, though they heaven's glories know,
> Forget not to attend their charge below.

All Norris's verse, with the exception of a very few pieces
incorporated in his *Theory of the Ideal World* (1701-4),
belongs to his Oxford days ;  but the whole collection was
subjected to drastic revision in later life, the author " leaving
out what was incorrigible and making improvements up and
down as occasion offered ".

His Platonism is revealed in many a poem, notably in
companion-pieces on *Beauty* and *Love*, while the germs of
his idealistic philosophy appear in *A Divine Hymn on
the Creation ;* but in view of more important extracts
awaiting quotation, none of these requires more than a passing
reference.

The practical doctrine on which Norris laid the greatest
stress was the duty of the entire love of GOD.   One of his
earliest publications had been on the subject ;  and he had
to follow this up by printing a consequent correspondence
with Mary Astell, one of the devoutest women in an age
of devout women, who, but for a skilful engineering of the

forces of bigotry, would have revived in England ' the religious life ' for women 150 years before the Tractarians
succeeded in doing so.   In the Preface to these *Letters
concerning the Love of God*, Norris wrote, " Men may
wrangle for ever about abstruse theories and sooner dispute
themselves out of charity than into truth ; but our wills have
at present a larger capacity than our understandings, and
our love to GOD may be very flaming and seraphic when,
after the greatest elevation and soar of thought, our conceptions of Him are but faint and shadowy. . . . Other
gifts and graces, whether intellectual or moral, come indeed
from Heaven ; but they often leave us upon earth.   Love
only elevates us up thither, and is able to unite us to GOD.
'Tis this indeed that gives us the strictest union with Him
in this life : by faith we live upon GOD, by obedience we
live to Him, but 'tis by love alone that we live in Him."
In the correspondence itself he argues that to make GOD
the only direct and primary object of love is perfectly consistent with the love of our neighbours, the apparent contradiction being " because of the equivocation of the word
' Love,' which when applied to GOD in the First Command-
ment signifies desiring Him as a good, and when applied
to men in the Second signifies, not desiring them as a good,
but desiring good to them ".   In the already quoted essay
on *Happiness*, he breaks out with indignation, " 'Tis not the
sophistry of cold logicians that shall work me out of the belief of what I feel and know, and rob me of the sweetest
entertainment of life, the passionate love of GOD.   Whatever some men may pretend who are strangers to all the
affectionate heats of religion, and therefore make philosophy
a plea for their indevotion, and extinguish all holy ardours
with a syllogism ; yet I am firmly persuaded that our love

of GOD may be not only passionate, but even wonderfully
so, and passing the love of women."   He goes on to quote
Bellarmine's computation of the degrees in the love of GOD,
one of which he prefers to call ' seraphic love ' and identifies
with " the unitive way of religion, which is so-called because
it unites us to GOD in the most excellent manner that we
are capable of in this life. . . . Here the happy soul reposes
herself and says, ' It is good to be here '.   Here she dies,
and here she lives.   Here she loses, and here she finds herself. . . . And here I place the greatest happiness attainable
by man in this life, as being the nearest approach to the
state of the blessed above, the outer court of Heaven."
After this, the following stanzas from his poem on *Seraphic
Love* may seem a sheer drop into prose :—

> Through Contemplation's optics I have seen
> Him Who is fairer than the sons of men,
> The source of good, the Light archetypal,
>> Beauty in the original.
>> The fairest of ten thousand, He,
>> Proportion all and harmony.
>> All mortal beauty is but a ray
>> Of his bright ever-shining day,
>> A little feeble twinkling star,
> Which, now the Sun's in place, must disappear :
> There is but One that's good, there is but One that's fair.
>
> To Thee, Thou only fair, my soul aspires,
> With holy breathings, languishing desires.
> To Thee my enamour'd, panting heart does move,
>> By efforts of ecstatic love.
>> How do Thy glorious streams of light
>> Refresh my intellectual sight !
>> Though broken, and strained through a screen

> Of envious flesh, that stands between !
> When shall my imprison'd soul be free,
> That she Thy native uncorrected light may see,
> And gaze upon Thy beatific face to all eternity ?

Perhaps the greatest of Norris's mystical poems is that which he entitled *The Elevation*, and himself carefully annotated. It may be given in full, with the more apposite comments. He explains that the general design of the poem is " to represent the gradual ascent of the soul by contemplation to the supreme good, together with its firm adherency to it, and its full acquiescence in it. All of which is done figuratively under the allegory of a local elevation from the feculent regions of this lower world." The purpose of the fourth stanza is " to insinuate the great facility and pleasure of the divine life to one that is arrived to an habit of it ; for, as the magnetic influence of the earth can have no force upon him that is placed in the upper regions beyond the sphere of its activity, so (which is the counterpart of the allegory) the inclinations of the animal nature have little or no power over him who has advanced to the heights of habitual contemplation ". The line, " Drawn by the bent of ethereal tide," is interpreted by an allusion to the Cartesian hypothesis of *vortices*. As regards the fifth stanza, the poet, without actually accepting the doctrine of the pre-existence of souls, claims that it has weighty supporters and may, at least, be advanced as an hypothesis. And for "the compendious description of GOD " by the symbol of light, in the closing lines, he educes " authority both human and divine," i.e. both Platonic and Johanine.

> Take wing, my soul, and upwards bend thy flight
> To thy originary fields of light.
> Here is nothing, nothing here below

15

That can deserve thy longer stay;
A secret whisper bids thee go
To purer air and beams of native day.
The ambition of the towering lark out-vy,
And, like him, sing as thou dost upward fly.

How all things lessen which my soul before
Did with the grovelling multitude adore!
    Those pageant glories disappear,
    Which charm and dazzle mortals' eyes:
    How do I in this higher sphere,
How do I mortals with their joys despise!
Pure, uncorrupted element I breathe,
And pity their gross atmosphere beneath.

How vile, how sordid here those trifles show
That please the tenants of that ball below!
    But ah! I've lost the little sight;
    The scene's remov'd, and all I see
    Is one confus'd dark mass of night:
What nothing was, now nothing seems to be.
How calm this region, how serene, how clear:
Sure, I some strains of heavenly music hear.

On, on! The task is easy now and light;
No steams of earth can here retard thy flight.
    Thou needst not now thy strokes renew;
    'Tis but to spread thy pinions wide
    And thou with ease thy seat wilt view,
Drawn by the bent of the ethereal tide.
'Tis so, I find; how sweetly on I move,
Not let by things below, and help'd by those above!

But see! To what new region am I come?
I know it well: it is my native home.

Here led I once a life divine,
Which did all good, no evil know.
Ah !   Who would such sweet bliss resign
For those vain shows which fools admire below ?
'Tis true ;  but don't of folly past complain,
But joy to see these blest abodes again.

A good retrieve—but lo !  while thus I speak,
With piercing rays the eternal day doth break ;
The beauties of the Face divine
Strike strongly on my feeble sight.
With what bright glories does it shine !
'Tis one immense and ever-flowing Light.
Stop here, my soul ;  thou canst not bear more bliss ;
Nor can thy now rais'd palate ever relish less.

In this poem Norris's Platonism is somewhat distorted by
the influence of Plotinus, who identified the Good with an
unintelligibility only to be approached by abstraction.   It is
not the only occasion on which Norris takes this line ;  but
when he does so it is in surrender to a rhetorical current,
and, so far as the present writer is aware, he never seriously
upholds the Neo-Platonic insistence on emptying the mind
of all positive contents : the annihilation of thought and
consciousness is entirely alien to his teaching.   Nor does he
anywhere accept the full Dionysian doctrine of the Divine
Darkness as inaccessible, super-luminous light.   Lines here
and there in his poems speak of our inability to win any
clear vision of GOD in this life ;  but such lines merely borrow
the Pauline phrase of " seeing through a glass darkly," and
bring with it, almost as a corollary, the Apostolic addition,
" but then face to face ".   Certainly the *Hymn to Darkness*, an almost irresistible opportunity for a propagandist of

Dionysius's views, has no relation to the teaching of the
pseudo-Areopagite.

In his prose writings Norris sometimes dwells on the importance of meditating upon Death. Many will be repelled
by his disparagement of the ordinary pursuits of this world,
and would challenge his contention that " the consideration
of Death is the most compendious way of making a man
wise ". But at least he practised what he preached, and
two or three of his poems are devoted to " that amazing
curiosity ". *The Meditation*, though possibly a better piece
of work technically, is more morbid and low-toned than
*The Prospect*, which sounds a brooding, wistful note in
these opening lines :—

> What a strange moment that will be,
> My soul, how full of curiosity,
> When wing'd, and ready for thy eternal flight,
> On the utmost edges of thy tottering clay,
> Hovering and wishing longer stay,
> Thou shalt advance, and have eternity in sight !
> When just about to try that unknown sea,
> What a strange moment that will be.

In *The Aspiration* he modulates into another key. It
is still a minor key, so poignant is the longing for unhampered
union with GOD, but a note of certitude carries it at times
into the major. The frequency with which this piece finds
its way into anthologies of sacred verse suggests that modern
criticism gives it the highest place in Norris's poetic achievement :—

> How long, great GOD, how long must I
> Immur'd in this dark prison lie !
> Where at the grates and avenues of sense
> My soul must watch to have intelligence ;

Where but faint gleams of Thee salute my sight,
Like doubtful moonshine in a cloudy night.
        When shall I leave this magic sphere,
        And be all mind, all eye, all ear !

        How cold this clime !   And yet my sense
        Perceives even here Thy influence.
Even here Thy strong magnetic charms I feel,
And pant and tremble like the amorous steel.
To lower good and beauties less divine
Sometimes my erroneous needle does decline ;
        But yet—so strong the sympathy—
        It turns, and points again to Thee.

        I long to see this excellence
        Which at such distance strikes my sense.
My impatient soul struggles to disengage
Her wings from the confinement of her cage.
Would'st Thou, great Love, this prisoner once set free,
How would she hasten to be link'd to Thee !
        She'd for no angel's conduct stay,
        But fly and love on all the way.

Norris has been unfairly neglected by historians of English
philosophy, and it is, therefore, the more pleasing to find the
appreciative notice given in the *Cambridge History of
English Literature* to his mystical modification of Cartesianism.   Professor Sorley speaks of him, in the 8th volume
of that monumental work (p. 348), as the most important
of the English followers of Malebranche, but " no mere
follower : he had thought out—one may even say, he had
lived—the theory for himself ".   While still at Oxford,
Norris wrote : " That we see and know all things in GOD
is a notion which I very early lighted upon, by the natural
parturiency of my own mind, before I had consulted with

any authors that might imbue me with it. But afterwards I met with some that confirmed me in it. For it is a notion very frequently touched upon by Platonists, . . . but by none that I know of so copiously, so purposely, and so dexterously managed as by the incomparable M. Malebranche, who, I think, has established the truth of it beyond all cavil or exception." He proceeded to give " a summary account of what that excellent person has meditated upon " and to add further considerations of his own which had led him to a clear conviction that " man sees and knows all things in the Divine *Logos*, or Ideal World, which is that true *Light within* him so much talked of by enthusiasts, who by a kind of blind parturiency of mind have confusedly glanced at what we have here more distinctly explained : that all our Light and Illumination proceeds wholly from Him Who at first said, ' Let there be light,' that we see so much of truth as we see of GOD, that the Ideas which are in GOD are the very Ideas which we see, and that the Divine *Logos* is our wisdom, as well as ' the Wisdom of the Father '." All this is in the *Reason and Religion* of 1689 (pp. 185-227) ; but he continued to work out the implications of his theory until, in 1701, he felt justified in issuing the work which he called *An Essay towards the Theory of the Ideal or Intellectual World*, and supplemented, in 1704, with a second part, dealing with the Ideal World considered in its relation to human understanding. He complains that " the Ideal World which is within us (if we may not rather be said to be in it) and to which we ourselves are intimately united, . . . this great and capacious world of Light and Truth, of essential Order, Beauty and Proportion, is yet in a manner unthought of and forgotten by us ". He defines it as being " intelligibly that which this world is sensibly, the

eternal model and exemplar of all created essence, distinctly
exhibitive of all that is or ever can be, and so the measure
and standard, not only of what actually is, but of the whole
possibility of being ". Here and there he expresses himself
in terms beneath which the critical philosopher may detect
Pantheistic dangers ; but those to whom this frequent charge
against mystics is but a wire-drawn bugbear, will find many
a passage of real eloquence and deep devotional ardour,
which occasionally finds vent in verse, as in the following
lines :—

> Lay down, proud heart, thy rebel arms,
> And own thy Conqueror divine ;
> In vain thou dost resist such charms,
> In vain the arrows of His Love decline.
>
> There is no dealing with this potent Fair :
> I must, my GOD, I must love Thee.
> Thy charms but too victorious are :
> They leave me not my native liberty.
>
> A holy force spreads through my soul
> And ravishes my heart away.
> The world its motion does control
> In vain ; the happy captive will not stay.
>
> No more does she her wonted freedom boast,
> More proud of Thy celestial chain ;
> Free-will itself were better lost
> Than ever to revolt from Thee again.
>
> Sun of my soul, what shall I do
> Thy beauties to resist, or bear ?
> They bless, and yet they pain me too :
> I feel Thy heat too strong, Thy light too clear.

I faint, I languish, I almost expire ;
My panting heart dissolving lies.
Thou must shine less, or I retire :
Shade Thou Thy light ; I cannot turn my eyes.

Anything like a full examination of Norris's *magnum
opus* is beyond the scope of this volume ; but reference
should be made to the characteristic line of thought pursued
in the concluding section of his treatise. He urges on
Christians the duty of thinking rather than of reading, not
exclusively, but to a very much greater extent than obtained
at the time ; " for since," he argues, " according to the
principles of this theory, Ideas and Ideal Truths (the true
subject of our studies) are within ourselves, by reason of
that union which we naturally have with the Divine Word
or Wisdom, the universal Reason of all spirits, it follows
that the most direct and natural way for the discovery of
truth is, instead of going abroad for intelligence, to retire
into ourselves and there with humble and silent attention,
both to consult and receive the answers of interior Truth,
even of that divine Master which teaches in the school of
the breast ".

No doubt Norris exaggerated the capacity of ordinary
mortals to evolve truths out of their inner consciousness ;
and at times he approached that depreciation of learning
which, in the opinion of many, puts certain mystics out
of court. He had a conviction that " knowledge and devotion often go asunder," and that learning was often no more
than " a culpable curiosity and an accountable vanity,
and only a laborious way of being idle and impertinent ".
He approved of well-read men, " if it were meant by that
those who have cleared and improved their understanding
by reading, but not those who have read a great deal and

merely confounded their notions by doing so ".   So far we
can all follow him ; but it is hardly possible to give the
answer which he so obviously expects, when he imagines
the case of a prisoner wasting on trifles a brief opportunity
to prepare for trial, and asks if that is " more absurd than
to have a man who has so great a concern upon his hands
as the preparing for eternity, all busy and taken up with
quadrants and telescopes, furnaces, syphons, and air-pumps ".

We must bear in mind, however, that his strongest dia-
tribes against learning were addressed to a blue-stocking of
the school of Locke, living in an age of arid controversy,
and perhaps in special need of the message, " Væ sapienti ;
this is not a place to be wise in ".   To Lady Masham he
expressed at great length and in eloquent prose the argument which he sang in doggerel verse :—

> 'Tis not that knowledge I despise ;
> No, you misconstrue my design ;
> Or that to enthusiasm I incline
> And hope by inspiration to be wise.
>
> .    .    .    .    .    .    .    .
>
> Thought I, for anything I know,
> What we have stamp'd for science here
> Does only the appearance of it wear,
> And will not pass above, though current here below.
>
> .    .    .    .    .    .    .    .
>
> Or, grant some knowledge dwells below,
> 'Tis but for some few years to stay
> Till I'm let loose from this dark house of clay,
> And in an instant I shall all things know.

Nor is this the only poem in which Norris takes this line :
we have another instance in the piece called *Curiosity*,

while that which he definitely entitled *Against Knowledge*
reaches this uncompromising conclusion :—

> Happy and wise, two blessings are
> Which meet not in this mortal sphere.
> Let me be ignorant below,
> And when I've solid good, then let me know.

But this extract must not be left as his last word, without
being qualified by another in prose, wherein he begs his
contemporaries to seek knowledge less by reading and arguing than by meditation (i.e. " by sheer dint of thinking "),
by prayer (the method, he points out, which is recommended
by St. James), and by purification of heart, " that heavenly
lure which invites not only the Holy Spirit, but also the
Divine *Logos*, to come and dwell in the soul with His Ideal
Communications. This we may be assured of from His
own mouth : ' If a man love Me, My Father will love him,
and We will come unto him and make our abode with him '.
The pure, chaste, and good soul shall not only be loved by
the Divine *Logos*, but be also of His council and privacy.
For this is the Spouse of the Word Eternal, Who first assumed innocent nature, and then assumes innocent persons,
the first by a natural, the second by a mystic union. This
is the ' beloved disciple ' who has the privilege to lean upon
the bosom of his Lord and to be admitted to His more secret
communications. And therefore says the Psalmist, ' The
secret of the Lord is with them that fear him, and He will
show them His covenant '. And says our Lord Himself,
' Blessed are the pure in heart, for they shall see GOD '."

Earlier chronologically than Norris, but not so close a
follower of Henry More, comes THOMAS TRAHERNE, a
mystical writer of the very highest rank, whose discovery

by the late Mr. Bertram Dobell has been the most thrilling bibliographical event of the twentieth century.  " We need," said Ruskin in *Unto This Last*, "examples of people who, leaving Heaven to decide whether they are to rise in the world, decide for themselves that they will be happy in it, and have resolved to seek, not greater wealth, but simpler pleasure ; not higher fortune, but deeper felicity ; making the first of possessions, self-possession ".  No more striking example of such a person could be named than Traherne, who not only sought and found happiness for himself, but resolutely set himself to teach it to others ; to show them in what it consists, and how it may be attained.  Here is his own statement addressed ' To the Critical Peruser,' of his motive and method :—

> The naked truth in many faces shown,
> Whose inward beauties very few have known,
> A simple light, transparent words, a strain
> That lowly creeps, yet maketh mountains plain,
> Brings down the highest mysteries to sense
> And keeps them there ; that is our excellence :
> At that we aim ; to the end thy soul might see
> With open eyes thy great *Felicity*,
> Its objects view, and trace the glorious way
> Whereby thou may'st thy highest bliss enjoy.

As ' Light ' is to Henry Vaughan, so is ' Felicity ' to Traherne : it is the key-word to his mysticism.  He is wholly preoccupied with " the true mysterious depths of blessedness," of which he supplies the following schedule :—

1. A manifestation of GOD'S infinite love.
2. The possession of infinite treasures.
3. A return of infinite thanksgivings.
4. A fulness of joy which nothing can exceed.

5. An infinite beauty and greatness in the soul.

6. An infinite beauty in GOD's kingdom.

7. An infinite union between GOD and the soul (as well in extent as in fervour).

8. An exact fitness between the powers of the soul and its objects, neither being desolate, because neither exceedeth the other.

9. An infinite glory in the Communion of Saints, every one being a treasure to all the residue and enjoying the residue, and in the residue all the glory of all the worlds.

10. A perfect indwelling of the soul in GOD, and GOD in the soul ; so that, as the fulness of the Godhead dwelleth in our Saviour, it shall dwell in us ; and the Church shall be the fulness of Him that filleth all in all.

It is, perhaps, an open question whether he was well-advised in choosing the word, ' Felicity,' which, like the word ' Happiness,' contains the idea of chance, an idea which Traherne would most emphatically exclude. ' Beatitude ' might be a more appropriate choice, suggesting to our minds, as it does, a joy independent of circumstances, and recalling those conditions of blessedness revealed by our Lord in the Sermon on the Mount. These the world would reject as unmitigated misery, but Traherne accepted whole-heartedly, and in accepting verified : in poverty he sought and found the kingdom of heaven ; cultivating meekness, he inherited the earth ; having purified his heart, he won the clear vision of GOD.

Of his outward life very little is known, and that little was uneventful. Born, perhaps, in the year 1634, the son, it is supposed, of a Hereford cobbler, he graduated at Brasenose College, Oxford, and took Holy Orders. After ministering for some years at Credenhill, near his native city,

he became chaplain to Sir Orlando Bridgeman, Lord Keeper
of the Seals, perhaps also serving the parish of Teddington,
in which his patron lived.    Bridgeman was a man of learning and piety, who attempted a scheme of comprehension
and toleration in Church matters, and lost his office in circumstances entirely honourable to himself.    He retained
Traherne's services until his death in 1674, the latter dying
a few months later, ' worth ' about £12 by cash computation, exclusive of books and clothes.

Shortly before his death, Traherne, who had already
published an able, and perchance timely, exposure of *Roman
Forgeries*, prepared for the press a work of outstanding
merit on *Christian Ethics*, of which the age was not
worthy apparently.    Twenty-five years after his death, Dr.
Hickes, the non-juring ' Bishop of Thetford,' published " at
the request of a friend of the author " a volume which he
called *A Serious and Pathetical Contemplation of the
Mercies of God in several most Devout and Sublime
Thanksgivings for the Same*.    The author's name is nowhere mentioned ; but he is described as " Chaplain to the
late Lord Keeper Bridgeman," and internal evidence conclusively proves it to be the production of Traherne, whose
affinity in this work to both the matter and form of Walt
Whitman's writings is most remarkable.    Certain of his
writings remained in manuscript, to find an appreciative
public in the twentieth century.    The *Poetical Works*
were edited and published in 1906 by Mr. Dobell, who
two years later issued the *Centuries of Meditation*, an
unfinished work in prose.    Subsequently, Mr. H. I. Bell
discovered in the British Museum, and edited for publication by the Oxford Press, a manuscript containing most of
the poems in Mr. Dobell's volume and several others not

included there, with the title *Poems of Felicity containing Divine Reflexions on the Native Objects of an Infant Eye*, by Thomas Traherne, B.D., author of the *Roman Forgeries* and *Christian Ethics*.

Traherne's prose has seldom been surpassed for sustained force and eloquence, rising at times to passages of gorgeous word-painting. It is steeped in poetry and earns him the title of poet more justly than his verse does, the latter being for the most part weak in lyrical quality and suffering from constant repetition of the same rhymes. He was, in fact, no singer, though indisputably a poet of extraordinarily imaginative fertility. It should perhaps be pointed out in his defence that the persistent recurrence of the words ' pleasures ' and ' treasures,' which mars so many of his pieces is due, not to a failure in rhyming aptitude, but to his mental engrossment in the connotation of those terms, which occur incessantly in his prose also.

Of his inner life it is comparatively easy to form a picture. His character and demeanour are sketched for us by the anonymous friend to whom we owe the posthumous *Contemplation :* he describes him as being " of a very comprehensive soul and very acute parts, so fully bent upon the honourable function in which he was engaged, and so wonderfully transported with the Love of GOD to mankind, with the excellency of those divine laws which are prescribed to us, and with those inexpressible felicities to which we are entitled by being created in and redeemed to the divine image, that he dwelt continually amongst these thoughts with great delight and satisfaction, spending most of his time when at home in digesting his notions of these things into writing, and was so full of them when abroad that those who would converse with him were forced to endure some discourse

upon these subjects, whether they had any sense of religion
or not ".    Further details as to his devout Churchmanship,
his cheerful disposition, and his charitable habits, mitigate
the impression conveyed that to some of his less heavenly-
minded contemporaries he must have been an intolerable
bore.

The steps by which Traherne became beatified (if it is
permissible to use thus an expression which has been nar-
rowed down in its ordinary significance) are recounted in
the third century of his *Meditations*, and also, but less im-
pressively, in several of his poetical pieces.    It was originally
a birthright, and he could recall the vivid apprehensions of
his infancy, each child being born—so he was convinced—
an Adam in Eden.    This is, of course, akin to Vaughan's
thought, and to Wordsworth's doctrine that " Heaven lies
about us in our infancy " ; [1] but Traherne lays much greater
stress upon it than any one else, making it the foundation
stone of his philosophic system that we must rewin " an
infant-eye," or, better still, never lose it.    Quite a number
of poems deal with this, of which *Wonder* and *The Pre-
parative* are, perhaps, the most successful, but none can vie
with the prose version in the *Centuries of Meditation*.
Presumably, all of us can recall the wonder of infancy ;
but, being without Traherne's enthusiastic vitality, it was
probably a stolid sense of ruminating awe, rather than the
exuberant delight which he describes.    Most of us would
be inclined to say, with Coleridge, that this is " the wonder
of ignorance," and is " worn away by custom and familiarity ".    But Traherne knows it to be more than that : it
is the babe's innate sense of the greatness of his heritage,
and the spontaneous seeking of his source in GOD ; and he

[1] Cf. too the lines quoted from Keble, p. 356 below.

insists that parents are sadly at fault in not fostering this innate sense and discouraging all grasping notions of *meum* and *tuum ;* for private ownership (or, as he calls it, " proprieties ") is really at the root of the world's evil, leading to " envy, avarice, and fraud " and dulling the soul's appreciation of common blessings.  Very bitterly does he regret, in *Apostasy* and elsewhere, that his own parents permitted his infant-eye to be blinded and his felicity to be eclipsed, first with gaudy toys, and then with the esteem of riches.  Thus he lost his intuitive appraisement of the true " riches of Nature " and his enjoyment of " the whole world " in common with his fellows.  But

> First impressions are immortal all,
> And let mine enemies whoop, cry, roar, or call,
> Yet these still whisper, if I will but hear,
> And penetrate the heart, if not the ear.

In minute detail he recounts, in his *Meditations*, usually with duplicates in verse, how, at various lucid intervals throughout his boyhood dissatisfaction with the world's vanities convinced him that he had missed truth and reality. Betaking himself earnestly to Bible-study, he received a first instalment, at least, of the illumination which he was seeking :—

> There I was told
> That I the Son of GOD am made,
> His Image.  Oh, Divine !  And that fine gold,
> With all the joys which here do fade,
> Are but a toy, compared to the bliss
> Which heavenly, Godlike, and eternal is ;
>
> That we on earth are kings ;
> And, though we are cloth'd with mortal skin,

Are inward cherubim, have angels' wings :
Affections, thoughts, and minds within
Can soar through all the coasts of heaven and earth,
And shall be sated with celestial mirth.

He was now at the University, entering with zest into the prescribed subjects for his degree, and, as a *parergon*, studying what used to be called ' natural philosophy '. But, alas ! " there was never a tutor that did professly teach Felicity, though that be the mistress of all other sciences " ; nor to this day has such a Chair been endowed, and who, save Traherne himself, could ever have adequately filled it ?

Anthony Wood, in his brief notice of Traherne, says that he left Oxford for a time ; and this may be the period to which Traherne himself refers in his account of the dedication of his life and powers to the search for Felicity ; " in which," he adds, " I was so resolute that I chose rather to live upon £10 a year, and to go in leather clothes, and feed upon bread and water, so that I might have all my time clearly to myself, . . . and GOD was so pleased to accept of that desire that, from that time to this, I have had all things plentifully provided for me without any care at all, my very study of Felicity making me more to prosper than all the care in the whole world ; so that through His blessing I live a free and kingly life, as if the world were turned again into Eden, or much more, as it is at this day ". It was now, probably, that he wrote the poem called *The Approach*, the three central stanzas of which are here extracted :—

O Lord, I wonder at Thy love
Which did my infancy so early move,
But more, at that which did forbear
And move so long, though slighted many a year,

16

But most of all, O GOD, that Thou
Shouldst me at last convert, I scarce know how.

Thy gracious motions oft in vain
Assaulted me : I sent my God away,
Much griev'd that He could not impart His joy.
　　I careless was, nor did regard
The end for which He all these thoughts prepar'd.

But now with new and open eyes
I see beneath as if above the skies ;
　　When I on what is past reflect,
His thoughts and mine I plainly recollect.
　　He did approach me, nay, did woo ;
I wonder that my GOD so much would do.

He had become again as a little child. How Ruskin,
who complained that people seem to be made wretched by
conversion, would have rejoiced in Traherne, who fulfilled
exactly the advice given in *The Crown of Wild Olives*
to backslide into the cradle and regain a childlike Humility,
Faith, Charity, and Cheerfulness. It was by those virtues
that Traherne was " led to the study of the most obvious
and common things, . . . Air, Light, Heaven and Earth,
Water, the Sun, Trees, Men and Women, etc., and others
as common, but invisible : the Laws of GOD, the Soul of
Man, Jesus Christ and His Passion, with the Ways of God
in all ages. . . . To my unspeakable wonder, they brought
me to all the things in Heaven and earth, in Time and
Eternity, possible and impossible, great and little, common
and scarce ; and discovered them all to be infinite treasures ".
Where else could we find a more signal exemplar of the
mysticism that " divines and moves towards the spiritual in
the common things of life " ?

The corner-stone of Traherne's system is that man has
been "created in and redeemed to the Divine Image".
The implications of this truth are reiterated with such re-
dundance of exposition, both in prose and verse, that it is
but a lame and meagre statement to say that, by ' the Image
of GOD,' he means the power to understand GOD's works
and to enter into His loving joy in them.   He maintains
that to have full joy in GOD's works you must take them
home, as it were, to your very self :—

> For me the world created was by Love ;
> For me the stars, the seas, the sun, do move ;
> The earth for me doth stable stand ;
> For me each fruitful land ;
> For me the very angels GOD made His
> And my companions in bliss.

And, to drive this home, Traherne is lavish in the use of
the first person singular, a device which on a careless reader
may leave an impression of monstrous conceit ;  but it should
be noted that, in a section where the self-revelation becomes
especially intimate, he adopts the third person : " he from
whom I received these things," etc.   It is in this section, too,
that he acknowledges himself to have been " ten years studying before he could  satisfy his  self-love ".   But he submits
that " self-love is the basis of all love ;  but when we do
love ourselves, and self-love is satisfied infinitely in all its
desires and possible demands, then it is easily led to regard
the Benefactor more than itself, and for His sake overflows
abundantly to all others ".   In Traherne's case, this overflow gushes forth in many a poem, of which *Love, Goodness*, and *Meekness* may be particularized.

Another point on which he insists most urgently is the
necessity to be insatiable in desire.   GOD has given man a

heart of infinite capacity, and has made many worlds full
of infinite and eternal treasures ; therefore

> 'Tis mean ambition to desire
> A single world :
> To many I aspire,
> Though one upon another hurl'd :
> Nor will they all, if they be all confin'd,
> Delight my mind.

In his vocabulary, a want is a " sacred occasion and
means of Felicity " ; accordingly we get this characteristic
thanksgiving :—

> For giving me desire,
> An eager thirst, a burning ardent fire,
> A virgin infant flame,
> A love with which into the world I came,
> An inward hidden heavenly love,
> Which in my soul did work and move,
> And ever me inflame
> With restless longing, heavenly avarice
> That never could be satisfied,
> That did incessantly a Paradise
> Unknown suggest, and something undescried
> Discern, and bear me to it ; be
> Thy Name for ever prais'd by me.

Needless to say, he has no patience with the Other-
worldliness which places happiness in another life.  There
is no doubt whatever about his parsing of Eternity : it is in
the present tense, infinitive mood, and active voice.  He
called on every man

> To act as if his soul did see
> The very brightness of Eternity.

His map of the Universe contains a Heaven where

blessings are both had and prized, an Earth where blessings are had without being prized, and a Hell where blessings are prized without being had. One of the four pieces entitled *Thoughts* expresses his views on Heaven :—

GOD'S glory endless is and doth surround
And fill all worlds without or end or bound.
What hinders, then, but we in Heaven may be
Even here on earth, did we but rightly see ?
As mountains, chariots, horsemen all on fire,
To guard Elisha did of old conspire,
Which yet his servant could not see, being blind,
Ourselves environ'd with His joys we find.
Eternity itself is that true light
That doth enclose us being infinite.

.     .     .     .     .     .     .

Oh, give me grace to see Thy face, and be
A constant mirror of Eternity.
Let my pure soul, transformed to a thought,
Attend upon Thy throne, and, as it ought,
Spend all its time in feeding on Thy love,
And never from Thy sacred Presence move.
So shall my conversation ever be
In Heaven, and I, O Lord my GOD, with Thee.

His doctrine of the Godhead contains some very daring features. Starting from the premise that the very act of creation proves GOD to have felt a need, he reaches the conclusion that " want is the fountain of all His fullness " ; and, as a converse, he argues that by failing in appreciation of His gifts we mar His Felicity.

Our blessedness to see
Is even to the Deity
A Beatific Vision !   He attains
His ends while we enjoy.   In us He reigns.

So Traherne sings in *The Recovery*, the whole of which should be studied, as also *The Anticipation*, *The Demonstration*, and *Amendment*, the last-named opening thus :—

That all things should be mine,
This makes His bounty most divine ;
But that they all more rich should be,
And far more brightly shine,
As used by me :
It ravisheth my soul to see the end
To which this work so wonderful doth tend.

That we should make the skies
More glorious far before Thine eyes
Than Thou didst make them, and even Thee
Far more Thy works to prize,
As used they be
Than as they're made, is a stupendous work,
Wherein Thy wisdom mightily doth lurk.

Limits of space make it impossible to deal with his solution of the problem of evil (with which he grapples quite boldly, even if to some readers he may seem far from solving it), or with his belief in the Communion of Saints (in which, indeed, he consciously and unceasingly lived), or with the outpourings of his loving devotion to the Redeemer (in Whose Cross he finds " the throne of delights, the centre of Eternity, the Tree of Life in the midst of the Paradise of GOD "). But special attention must be drawn to the success with which, in an age when it was particularly difficult to do so, he co-ordinated the ideals of Hellenism and Hebraism. He followed the τὸ καλόν of Hellenism with the " clean hands and pure heart " of Hebraism, taking the keenest pleasure in the beautiful without any consciousness of sensual entanglement. He was in perfect agreement with St. Paul's contention, that any sort of fanatical asceti-

cism is a sign of weakness, while true strength lies in rising
superior to all notions of clean and unclean. He was
singularly free from that fear of things, especially of oneself,
in which R. L. Nettleship traced the source of "half the
troubles of life". This clear-sight and self-harmony were
his, because he had learnt the secret—so difficult, but so
desirable to learn—of the true as opposed to the false asceticism. There is to be no giving up for the sake of giving
up, no narrowing of the field of consciousness, no stunting
of human vitality, no sharp dividing-line between sacred and
secular. But, decidedly, there is to be discipline, the discipline of self-control and of obedience to Christ, which in
itself is a thing of joy and beauty. Traherne's was the
" wise and noble, warm because ever love-impelled asceticism," of which Baron von Hügel speaks in his *Eternal
Life*, " the instrument, concomitant, and guardian, though
never the first motive or the last end, of the entire life ".
He had mastered self ; he had broken free from the world ;
his " soul had escaped as a bird out of the snare of the
fowler " ; he had his foot upon every impulse which would
divert his aim ; but that aim was not a negative, but a positive aim, nothing less than self-realization in union with GOD,
" Who giveth us all things richly to enjoy ". GOD, the
Ego, and the World being harmoniously related, he set
himself fearlessly to develop every faculty and aptitude
which GOD had given him, and to tap every source of pure
joy. Learning, which Norris felt to be a hindrance and
danger, could and, so far as Traherne was concerned, should
" lead to all contentments, joys, and satisfactions, to all
praise, triumphs, and thanksgivings, to all virtues, beauties,
adorations, and graces, to all dominion, exaltation, wisdom,
and glory, to all holiness, union, and communication with

GOD, to all patience, and courage, and blessedness ".   He
declined to regard the Christian vocation as a call to any
sort of separation from human interests and activities, although a clear call from human sin, especially the fatal sin
of avarice.   He felt no loss of touch with heavenly things,
no deprivation of GOD'S Presence in social intercourse.
On the contrary, his soul " hated solitude ".   Not that he
could ever be desolate ; for, at times of enforced solitude,
by the workings of a sanctified imagination, " all the joys
and all the treasures, all the counsels and all the perfections,
all the angels and all the saints of GOD were with him ".
In his enthusiasm of humanity, he speaks of the miserable
poverty of " loving one person with a private love " : a
great part of his Felicity is " loving all cities and all kingdoms, all kings and all peasants, and every person in all
worlds with a natural, intimate, and familiar love ".   And
in the *Serious and Pathetical Contemplation*, one of the
special blessings for which he recognizes his thanks as due
to GOD is a sociable disposition.

The sense of beauty he prized as a special treasure, to be
trained to the uttermost.   The world was transfigured for him
by GOD'S Immanence.   " Can you take too much joy in your
Father's works ? " he asks ; " He is Himself in everything ".
Beauty is the token of the Presence of GOD, the Invisible
Loveliness, Who thus impresses one of His attributes on the
world.   To meet with a beautiful sight is to pass consciously
into that Presence, a Presence radiating love and evoking
the response of loving praise.   This is true, however, only for
those who think ; and in the poem called *Walking*, Traherne
gives us a fresh version of the story of Eyes and No-eyes :—

> To walk abroad is not with eyes,
> But thoughts, the fields to see and prize ;

> Else may the silent feet,
> Like logs of wood,
> Move up and down, and see no good,
> Nor joy nor glory meet.

But Traherne's emotions were stirred and his praises stimulated not only by beauty of sky, and sea, and sunlight, and scenery ; he took a frank delight in the human body, a delight springing partly from interest in its perfect mechanism, and partly from admiration of the nude. His faith in the Incarnation enabled him to perceive the " new meaning," brought out so finely by Dr. Illingworth in *Lux Mundi* (1891, pp. 211 ff.), which finds the human body " at once earth's fairest flower and most marvellous machine ". In *The Person* and other poems, as also in the *Meditations* and in the *Contemplation* (where there is a splendid thanksgiving on the subject), Traherne sings the praises of the human body ; but he makes it clear that it is, above all, as the organ of a soul that he esteems it : " My body without my soul is a carcase, so is my soul without Thy Spirit a chaos ". " Christianity," says Dr. Illingworth (*ut supra*), " is the only religion which does equal justice to this truth, while precluding its illegitimate perversion. It includes the truth by the essential importance which it assigns to the human body, and therefore to the whole material order with which that body is so intimately one ; while it excludes its perversion by showing the cause of that importance to lie in its connexion, communion, union with the Spirit, and consequent capacity for endless degrees of glory." This is precisely Traherne's position ; and his message is this, or something very like it : Earthly things are divine, love them wholeheartedly ; the present is eternity, live in it intensely ; thus will you find GOD, one of Whose Names is Felicity.

# CHAPTER VIII.

## BYROM, BROOKE, AND BLAKE.

FOR "an age destitute of depth or earnestness," whose "very merits were of the earth, earthy," the earlier half of the eighteenth century could have shown a surprisingly large number of persons interested in mysticism. One or two of these were poets, or at least, rhymesters.

JOHN BYROM—best known to modern Churchmen by his fine Christmas hymn, "Christians, awake, salute the happy morn,"—was the son of a prosperous Manchester linen-draper, and, while at Cambridge, won literary repute by several contributions to the 8th volume of *The Spectator*, the best volume, according to Dr. Johnson. Two of these were essays on the subject of dreams (Nos. 586 and 593), and show a seriousness of thought combined with a lightness of touch very characteristic of the man. A third (No. 603) was a pastoral poem of pleasing grace and vigour, which, according to rumour, was composed as a compliment to the daughter of Dr. Bentley, Master of Trinity College. If, as insinuated at the time, Byrom's motive was to secure the great Master's interest in an approaching election to a fellowship, the stratagem succeeded, and he was duly elected fellow of Trinity in 1714. But this post, which could be held only by a clerk in holy orders, he soon resigned, finding it impossible to reconcile his conscience with the oath abjuring the Stuarts which was obligatory on the clergy. It may be

mentioned here that, although he did not secede from the
Established Church, he lived in the closest intimacy with
the Non-jurors, especially with Dr. Deacon, the Non-juring
Bishop at Manchester.

Being a younger son, it was necessary for Byrom to adopt
some profession, and, with a view to practising medicine,
he made a stay at Montpelier, the famous school of medicine
in South France. It is interesting to recall a similar stay at
the same town by another mystically-minded student of
medicine, Sir Thomas Browne ; and we can well believe
that the latter's attitude of sympathetic reverence towards
the devotional practices witnessed there would have been
adopted by Byrom also. It was at Montpelier that Byrom
was first drawn to the study of the mystics, whom he de-
cribes in a letter as " the most impregnable body of friends
to piety that life and letters can unite and exhibit " : his
interest in Madame Bourignon began here, while a rhymed
letter to a friend bore witness to his enthusiasm for Malebranche.

Although henceforth known as Dr. Byrom, he does not
appear to have taken a degree in medicine, nor did he ever
make any serious attempt to practise as a physician. But
his entrance into the estate of matrimony made some immediately remunerative work imperative, and he now turned
to good account his ingenuity in shorthand, in which ac-
complishment he secured a large *clientèle* of influential pupils
in the three centres of London, Cambridge, and Manchester.
A competent judge has pronounced his stenographic system
to be " the most scientific and, in fact, the parent of all
other sound systems ". His election as Fellow of the Royal
Society was a signal tribute to his intellectual attainment
and also, perhaps, to his social charm. In 1740, by the

death of his elder brother, he inherited the family estate, and lived in domestic retirement until his death in 1763.

From his Cambridge days Byrom kept a diary, which has been published by the Chetham Society, and is one of the most delightful productions of the eighteenth century. In its self-restrained candour we can trace his spiritual development, and cannot fail to admire a self-portrait, quite unconsciously drawn, of a pure-hearted, reverent-minded Christian, fond of social intercourse and with a keen sense of humour (but shrinking instinctively from all that was coarse), humble, unselfish, and warm-hearted, conscientious but strikingly free from censoriousness, admirable in all domestic relations, capable of wholehearted hero-worship, above all, ardently devout.

Many an entry records his intercourse with mystically-minded friends and the study of mystical writings, such as Loyola's *Exercises*, Albert the Great's *Paradise of the Soul*, Thomas à Kempis, Fénelon, Norris of Bemerton, and Thomas Vaughan, whose book he cannot understand. In certain anti-mystical circles he wins a most unmerited notoriety for unbelief in evangelical truth, a charge of which he easily clears himself, while pleading guilty to ignorance and sinfulness. Special interest attaches to his relations with the Wesleys, whose hostility to mysticism pains him as being due to prejudice and culpable misunderstanding. In later times they aroused his just resentment by their uncharitable attitude towards William Law, whose disciple Byrom was proud to call himself.

It is as an exponent in verse of Law's prose that Byrom gains importance in the annals of English mysticism. William Law, widely known as the author of the *Serious Call*, is still insufficiently appreciated as a mystical writer.

His doctrine is a clarified version of Boehme's theosophy, and is presented in writings of lucid forcefulness and of devotional fervour. Byrom had been attracted by the *Serious Call* (though that was not, of course, a mystical work), and had versified the parable of *The Pond*. In March, 1729, he ventured, with great trepidation, to call on Law, then living as chaplain-tutor to the Gibbons family at Putney. They discussed the philosophy of Malebranche, and Byrom repeated his verses about *The Pond* : " Mr. Law said he must have a copy of them, and desired I would not put the whole book into verse, for then it would not sell in prose— so the good man can joke ".

This was the beginning of a close intimacy between the two men, whose relations were not unlike those of Johnson and Boswell. Law could be rude and dictatorial, while Byrom accepted all his snubs with deep humility, submitting, for the most part, to the views of the divine and following his guidance in the matter of reading. Law set himself to wean Byrom from his admiration for Mesdames Bourignon and Guyon, many of whose views and practices he denounced as extravagant, and turned his attention to Tauler, Suso, Ruysbroek, and, above all, Boehme. To read the last-named, Byrom learnt the German language ; but, like many another, he found him far from easy to understand. In his usual way of versifying his thoughts, he wrote some epigrammatic lines on *The Reply of Socrates* :—

> When Socrates had read, as authors note,
> A certain book that Heraclitus wrote,
> Deep in its matter and obscure besides,—
> Asked his opinion of it, he replied :
> " All that I understand is good and true,
> And what I don't, is, I believe, so too ".

All the haranguing, therefore, on the theme
Of deep obscurity in Jacob Boehme,
Is but itself obscure ; for he might see
Farther, 'tis possible, than you or me.
Meanwhile, the goodness of his plainer page
Demands the answer of the Grecian sage.

When Law settled at King's Cliffe, Byrom could manage but an occasional visit to him ; but their friendship remained intact, and Law came to see more and more clearly the beauty of his disciple's character and the depth of his piety. A slight rift in the intimacy was ended by a letter from Law, worth quoting for the light which it throws on their relationship :—

" My dear Laureate, whom I love and esteem with all the truth of Christian fellowship. Nothing but such goodness as I know possesses your heart could overlook so much neglect as I have shown to one of my most valued friends, who all this time of disrespectful silence has had every affection of esteem that I can possibly have to those with whom I am in the truest Christian love united. If you ask how all this has come to pass, one who knows neither you nor me can tell you as much as I can. You must place it amongst those wonders of infatuation which have only been hurtful to myself. . . . Dear doctor, forgive, and renew your usual correspondence with one who sincerely believes he cannot esteem you enough. . . ."

The title ' Laureate ' refers, of course, to the poems which Byrom had written in paraphrase of Law's writings, at the special request of the latter, first made in 1749. Byrom had good-naturedly acceded to the request, but delayed fulfilment of his promise until Law wrote a sharp expostulation. To this Byrom replied that the delay was due, not to any disinclination (for " labours of this kind afford the most agreeable occupation to me "), but to diffidence induced by " the depth and moment of the matters, and the fear of mistaking or treating them unworthily ".   In judging these metrical paraphrases, then, it is only fair to remember that they were undertaken with genuine reluctance, to please a " dear Master," and in the hope of extending his beneficial influence.   The poet offered, both in prose and verse, ample apologies for his temerity.

The first attempt Byrom made to versify Law's tenets was in the *Epistle to a Gentleman of the Temple*, in which he contrasted Bishop Sherlock's doctrine of the Fall with that of Law in *The Spirit of Prayer*.   It is a long piece of argumentative verse which, in spite of considerable technical skill, must be admitted to be but a prosy production.   In opposition to the Bishop's statement that Adam, though guilty of eating the forbidden fruit, " did not die, the sentence being requited," Law had insisted that " no sooner had he got this knowledge of good and evil by the opening of the bestial life and sensibility within him, but in that day, nay, in that instant, he died ; that is, his heavenly spirit, with its heavenly body, were both extinguished in him. . . . Our fall is nothing else but the falling of our soul from this celestial body and spirit, into a bestial body and spirit of this world.   Our rising out of our fallen state, or Redemption, is nothing else but the regaining our first angelic spirit and body, which in Scripture is called our inward, or new man, created in Christ Jesus ".   So Byrom :—

> The Life, which Adam was created in,
> Was lost the day, the instant of his sin.
> Just as the rebel angels, when they fell,
> Were dead to Heaven, though alive to Hell ;

So man, no longer breathing heavenly breath,
Fell to this life, and died the Scripture Death.

Very closely, paragraph by paragraph, Byrom follows
Law's contention that Adam had been created to supply
the place of Lucifer, whose fall produced the Chaos ; that
Adam's failure had been retrieved by Christ, Who has
secured us the power of a New Birth, " a real birth of the
Son and the Spirit of GOD in the soul," not " something or
other, this or that which the critics say may be called a new
birth by a certain figure of speech ". And Law's claim
that his doctrine gets rid of " a load of difficulties that have
been raised about the fall of man and original sin," is thus
paraphrased by Byrom, with great felicity :—

> If by the first man's sin we understand
> Only some breach of absolute command,
> Half-punish'd, half-remitted, by a grace
> Like that which takes in human acts a place :
> The more we write, the more we still expose
> The Christian doctrine to its reasoning foes.
> But once convinc'd that Adam, by his crime,
> Fell from Eternal Life to that of Time,
> Stood on the brink of death eternal too,
> Unless created unto Life anew,—
> Then every reason teaches us to see
> How all the truths of Sacred Writ agree ;
> How life restor'd arises from the grave ;
> How man could perish, and how Christ could save.

This doctrine of the Fall is repeatedly enunciated by
Byrom in his metrical essays, of which another constant
theme is the meaning of the expression, the Wrath of GOD.
Perhaps the piece which (apart from its painfully undigni-

fied metre) deals best with this, is that in which he sets
himself to show (with Law) that

> No wrath in the Giver had Christ to atone,
> But to save a poor perishing world from its own.
>
> . . . . . . . . .
>
> All wrath is the product of creaturely sin ;
> In immutable love it could never begin ;
> Nor, indeed, in a creature, till opposite will
> To the love of its GOD had brought forth such an ill ;
> To the love that was pleas'd to communicate bliss
> In such endless degrees, through all nature's abyss ;
> Nor could wrath have been known, had not man left the state
> In which nature's GOD was pleas'd man to create.

So far it is fairly easy to yield 'assent : often enough, the
belief in GOD'S anger is the reflexion of man's own sulkiness
or despondency.   But another stanza is much more difficult
to accept in all its implications :—

> There is nothing that justice and righteousness hath
> More opposite to it than anger and wrath ;
> As repugnant to all that is equal and right,
> As falsehood to truth, or as darkness to light.
> Of GOD, in Himself, what the Scripture affirms
> Is Truth, Light, and Love—plain, significant terms.
> In His Deity, therefore, there cannot befal
> Any falsehood, or darkness, or hatred at all.

Many will feel that Boehme and his school [1] ignore, or
reject, large tracts of Scriptural expression, not merely in
the way of isolated texts, but in the accounts, for instance, of
Holy Week.   Just at the time when Christ's love was being

---

[1] Their tenets have more recently found an able champion in Ritschl : " The
notion of the affection of wrath in God has no religious worth for Christians, but is
an unfixed and formless *theologoumenon* ".   Sir Oliver Lodge has some discriminating pages on the subject in his *Man and the Universe.*

exhibited in its clearest colours, His wrath was expressed
in the withering of the fig-tree, in the cleansing of the
Temple, and in the ' Woes ' pronounced against the Phari-
sees.   Perhaps, too, the Behmenistic view is too much influenced by the thought of the caprice and passion associated
with human anger, and forgets that there is a great deal to
be said for a righteous wrath even in a good man on earth.
Moral indignation against any sort of oppression or baseness
is in the background of every noble character, and must be
part of the Image of GOD imprinted thereon.   Do not
ethical considerations demand of GOD the upholding of
" the interests of righteousness " ?   The question is a very
difficult one, which neither Boehme's earnestness nor Law's
dialectic clears up quite satisfactorily.

The next of Law's writings which Byrom versified was
the appendix to *An Appeal to Those who Doubt*, entitled
" Animadversions on Dr. Trapp ".   This egregious divine
had written a *Discourse on the Nature, Folly, Sin, and
Danger of being Righteous Overmuch*, and Law, in
dealing faithfully with him, had protested against the unjust
prejudice excited by the use of the word ' enthusiasm '.
In the skilful piece of metrical argumentation entitled *Enthusiasm, A Poetical Essay*, Byrom follows very closely
Law's contention that " No people are so angry at religious
enthusiasts as those that are the deepest in some enthusiasm
of another kind " (instancing enthusiasts for classical anti-
quities, Egyptologists, and other connoisseurs), and that
" Enthusiasm is not blameable in religion when it is true
religion that enkindles it ".   Here are are some of the concluding lines of the poem :—

> Blame not Enthusiasm, if rightly bent ;
> Or blame of Saints the holiest intent,

The strong persuasion, the confirm'd belief,
Of all the comforts of the soul the chief,
That GOD'S continual will and work—to save,
Teach, and inspire—attend us to the grave ;
That they, who in His faith and love abide,
Find in His Spirit an immediate guide.
This is no more a fancy or a whim,
Than that " we live, and move, and are in Him ".

   .     .     .     .     .     .

In this one Fountain of all help to trust,—
What is more easy, natural, and just ?
Talk what we will of morals, and of bliss,
Our safety has no other source but this.
Led by this faith, when man forsakes his sin,
The gate stands open to his GOD within :
There in the temple of his soul is found,
Of inward central life the holy ground ;
The sacred scene of piety and peace,
Where new-born Christians feel the Life's increase ;
Blessing and blest, revive to pristine youth,
And worship GOD in spirit and in truth.
      Had not the soul this origin, this root,
What else were man but a two-handed brute ?
What but a devil, had he not possess'd
The seed of heaven, replanted in his breast ?
The spark of potency, the ray of light,
His call, his help, his fitness to excite
The strength and vigour of celestial air,
Faith and—the breath of living Christians—prayer ?
Not the lip-service, nor the mouthing waste
Of heartless words without an inward taste ;
But the true kindling of desirous love,
That draws the willing graces from above ;
The thirst of good that naturally pants

After that Light and Spirit that it wants ;
In whose blest union quickly coincide
To ask and have, to want and be supplied.
Then does the faithful suppliant discern
More of true good, more of true nature learn,
In one meek intercourse with Truth Itself,
Than from a thousand volumes on the shelf.
　　　All that the Gospel ever could ordain,
All that the Church's daily rites maintain,
Is to keep up, to strengthen, and employ
This lively faith, this principle of joy ;
This hope and this possession of the end,
Which all her pious institutes intend ;
Fram'd to convey, when freed from wordy strife,
The truth and spirit of an inward life ;
Wherein the Eternal Parent of all good
By His own influence is understood,
That man may learn infallibly aright,—
Blest in His Presence, seeing in His Light,—
To gain the habit of a Godlike mind,
To seek His Holy Spirit, and to find.
　　　In this Enthusiasm, advanc'd thus high,
'Tis a true Christian wish, to live and die.

This poem led Byrom into a correspondence with Warburton (later, Bishop of Gloucester), who had been not
obscurely alluded to as an instance of one with an over-
powering passion for " unblest erudition ". The author of
*The Divine Legation*, whom Byrom castigated more than
once in his verse, protested against the poet's definition of
enthusiasm, and also against the insinuation that he spoke of
Christians as " a brainsick, visionary crew," adding, however, a statement that this was the first time he had answered
" the vast numbers who have abused me to the public, and

you are entitled to it, as I think you are the only honest man of that number ".    Byrom, in reply, while claiming that his object in writing was, " not to abuse, but to disabuse," was able to produce some of Warburton's words about the Methodists which justified his insinuation.    A letter in this connexion by Warburton to his crony, Hurd, is worth quoting as giving both a contemporary's view of the poet and also a definition of enthusiasm.    He speaks of Byrom as " a man of genius, plunged deep in the rankest fanaticism. His poetical epistles show him both, which, were it not for some unaccountable negligence in his verse and language, would show us that he has hit upon the right style for familiar didactic epistles in verse.    He is very libellous upon me ; but I forgive him heartily, for he is not malevolent, but mad. . . . I disagree with him in supposing an intense application of the mind to any object is enthusiasm.    If I were to define it, I should say it is such an irregular exercise of it as makes us give a stronger assent to the conclusion than the evidence of the premises will warrant : then reason begins to be betrayed, and then enthusiasm proper begins. . . ."

Manifestly, the objection to enthusiasm centres round its definition.    We have to remember that saints like George Herbert and Henry More before this time, and like Keble and Isaac Williams after it, condemned enthusiasm, the last-named defining it, in *Tract* 80, as " a state of mind when the feelings are strongly moved, but the heart is not adequately purified nor humbled, . . . first of all deceiving itself into a false apprehension, and then, in order to support this, deceiving others ".    This seems rather to beg the question ; and that was precisely what the eighteenth century invariably did in this matter.    The epithet was a missile, a weapon of offence and defence, invaluable to an age lacking in moral intensity, to which religion had become either a calculating selfishness or a matter of cynical indifference. Encomiastic epitaphs of that time claimed for the aristocratic dead that they were "religious without enthusiasm". Even Dr. Johnson could praise the pompous inanities of Blair as admirable sermons, diffusing "warmth without fanaticism, the most rational transport," and Hannah More justified her preference for the lifeless worship of pre-Tractarian Anglicanism by claiming for it a fervour that was "free from enthusiasm". Well might Coleridge insist that "the disease of the age is want of enthusiasm". That careful thinker distinguishes (in *Notes Theological, etc.*) between enthusiasm and, what is often confused with it (as, apparently, by some of the above-mentioned critics), fanaticism : "Enthusiasm is the absorption of the individual in the object contemplated from the vividness or intensity of his conceptions or convictions ; fanaticism is heat, or accumulation and direction of feeling, acquired by contagion, and relying on the sympathy of sect or confederacy ; intense sensation with confused or dim conceptions. . . . Enthusiasts, from ἔνθεος οἷς ὁ θεὸς ἔνεστι,, or possibly from ἐν θυσίαις, those who in sacrifice to, or at, the altar of truth or falsehood, are possessed by a spirit or influence mightier than their own individuality. *Fanatici—qui circum fana favore mutuo contrahunt et afflant*—those who in the same conventicle, or before the same shrine, relic, or image, heat and ferment by co-acervation". In the *Notes on English Divines*, he draws a similar distinction, arguing that "enthusiasm implies an undue (or when used in a good sense, an unusual) vividness of ideas, as opposed to perceptions, or of the obscure inward feelings". There, in the alternative choice between the epithets 'undue' and 'unusual,' centres the whole dispute. But this, at least, seems incontrovertible, that the religious enthusiast is far closer than the religious formalist to the mind and practice of our Lord, and that the neutral zone between the two is not an easy clime in which to breathe.

Dr. Inge (in *Faith and Psychology*) speaks of distrust of Reason as " the only blot on Law's fine and manly religious writings," and gives an illustrative extract from *The Way of Divine Knowledge*. This was yet another of Law's writings which Byrom versified, entitling his paraphrase *A Dialogue between Rusticus, Theophilus, and Academicus on the Nature, Power, and Use of Human Learning in Matters of Religion*. It is unnecessary to give any excerpts from this piece, or from the very similar *Contrast between Human Reason and Divine Illumination exemplified in three different Characters*, viz. : Bolingbroke (who is dismissed as hopelessly rationalizing), William Hay, author of the *Religio Philosophi* (who is commiserated as one groping with his reason), and Behmen (who " all mere reasoners far transcends "). We never find in Byrom any disparagement of Holy Writ ; but we do find, as in the *Letter to Mr. Ponthieu*, a claim, very difficult to resist, that inspiration did not end with the first century of the Christian era, and that Bible-study is worthless without inward illumination.

We have to remember that the eighteenth century was the age of the *Aufclärung*, that cold loveless enlightenment which was the very antithesis of the mystic's illumination. Since the appearance of Locke's *Reasonableness of Christianity* in 1688, Reason had been granted the supreme arbitrament, not in the acceptable sense of rejecting all that is not in accordance with it, but in the extreme sense of rejecting all intuitive perception and every witness of the indwelling Spirit. All this justifies Byrom's protest in his *Thoughts upon Human Reason :*—

> Sense to discern, and reason to compare,
> Are gifts that merit our improving care,
> But want an inward light, when all is done,
> As seeds and plants do that of outward sun :
> Main help rejected, tasteless fruits arise ;
> And wisdom grows insipid in the wise.
>
> Though all these Reason-worshippers profess
> To guard against fanatical excess ;
> Enthusiastic *heat*, their favourite theme,
> Draws their attention to the *cold* extreme ;
> Their fears of torrid fervour freeze a soul ;
> To shun the Zone they send it to the Pole.

There have been remarkable ups and downs in the reputation of Reason, which suffered, in England, an almost entire eclipse in the mid-seventeenth century, but reached its zenith a hundred years later. Then followed Methodism, and the Evangelical revival with its Bibliolatry, its ' simple Gospel,' and its reliance on the inward experience. Again, a generation ago there was " a kind of idolatry of reason," since when we have witnessed a rebound from intellectualism and from the apotheosis of scientific progress. But the misology of Lotze and the pragmatism of William James find their correctives in the teaching of Eucken and of Dr. Inge, whose sympathies with the mystical consciousness have not made them one-sided. The mystic need not dismiss the intellect from his service : he needs it to warn him against subjective delusion, and to preserve him from the self-sufficiency which often lurks beneath faith. No doubt, " knowledge puffeth

up," but the arrogancy has not invariably been on one side
only.   The charity of the mystics, moreover, has not always
" edified " ; nor was St. Paul's prayer likely to return into
his own bosom, when he prayed that his converts' "love
might abound yet more and more in knowledge ".

Of Byrom's other paraphrases from Law, it will be enough
to name, without quoting, the noble *Prayer* from *The
Spirit of Prayer.*   In all these paraphrases it is impossible
to deny his great technical faculty.   He rhymes with skill,
and moves with considerable freedom within his metres ;
but his choice of metre is often lacking in taste and judgment.
Moreover, nearly all the verse referred to above suffers from
being so markedly propagandist ; many of his pieces are
merely metrical essays, in which, instead of transmuting
commonplaces into poetry, Byrom has debased eloquent prose
into prosaic doggerel.   But, characteristically, his contemporaries thought highly of his efforts.   Law himself deeply valued
the work of his paraphrast ; Warburton eulogised his poetical
talents ; while John Wesley, though hostile to Law's teaching,
declared, with a curious inconsistency, that his disciple's verse
contained " some of the noblest truths expressed with the
utmost energy of language and the strongest colours of
poetry ".   A friend, speaking of him as a poet, said that
" he scarce took aim, yet seldom missed the white " ; and
here, perhaps, we have the secret of his failure : he was too
fluent, and might have done better work if versification had
not been so easy to him.

A good deal of his more independent work deals with
the subject of *The Disinterested Love of God,* another
question on which it seems impossible to reach finality.
Dr. Illingworth, in his *Christian Character,* spoke of disinterested love as being " not really Christian : it belongs to

Pantheistic systems, which like those of the Indian mystics or Spinoza, do not conceive of GOD as personal, and therefore capable of returning the affection of a person ". Byrom, probably, would have retorted

> Love of disinterested kind
> The man, who thinks it too refin'd,
> May, by ambiguous language, still
> Persist in metaphysic skill.

But, as a matter of fact, the modern philosopher was nearer Byrom's notion of disinterested love when he added, " but true human love, though it inevitably desires response, is not therefore selfish ". Byrom would simply wish to add —and Dr. Illingworth would have agreed—that true Christian love must be unselfish. He did not adopt the extreme form of 'mystic paradox'. He could never have thought (as R. A. Vaughan asserted some of the Quietists to have taught) " that since GOD is equally glorified in our perdition and in our salvation, we should have no preference, if our love be truly disinterested, for the one mode of glorifying Him above the other ". For Byrom had clearer views on the nature of Heaven and Hell : he knew that

> His love is Heaven ; and want of it is Hell.

But with Tauler, St. Catherine of Siena, and others too numerous to quote, he believed that the GOD-united man works " without any wherefore," and loves for no self-serving ends. On this question he ranged himself definitely beside Fénélon, who has been represented as meaning a great deal that he never said. Of Byrom's several poems on this subject this is perhaps the best :—

I love my GOD, and freely too,
With the same love that He imparts ;
    That He, to Whom all love is due,
Engraves upon pure, loving hearts.

I love, but this celestial fire—
Ye starry powers !   Ye do not raise :
    No wages, no reward's desire,
Is in the purely shining blaze.

Me, nor the hopes of heavenly bliss,
Or Paradisic scenes excite ;
    Nor terrors of the dark abyss
Of death's eternal den affright.

No bought-and-paid-for love be mine ;
I will have no demands to make ;
    Disinterested, and divine
Alone, that fear shall never shake.

Thou, my Redeemer, from above,
Suffering to such immense degree,
    Thy heart hath kindled mine to love,
That burns for nothing but for Thee.

Thy scourge, Thy thorns, Thy Cross, Thy wounds,
Are, every one of them, a source
    From whence the nourishment abounds
Of endless love's unfading force.

These sacred fires, with holy breath,
Raise in my mind the generous strife ;
    While, by the ensigns of Thy death
Known, I adore the Lord of Life.

Extinguish all celestial light,
The fire of love will not go out ;
    The flames of hell extinguish quite,
Love will pursue its wonted route.


Be there no hope if it persist—
Persist it will, nor ever cease ;
    No punishment if 'tis dismiss'd—
What caus'd it not will not decrease.


Shouldst Thou give nothing for its pains,
It claims not anything as due ;
    Shouldst Thou condemn me, it remains
Unchang'd by any selfish view.


Let Heaven be darken'd, if it will,
Let Hell with all its vengeance roar,
    My GOD alone remaining, still
I'll love Him, as I did before.

Here we find a real spark of divine fire ; and we get
still nearer to true soaring in the *Hymn to Jesus*—the following stanzas, at any rate, suggest a genuine afflatus of
religious fervour, and awaken in the reader's breast an
answering glow :—

Lord, let Thy sacred Presence fill
    And set my longing spirit free,
That pants to have no other will
    But day and night to think on Thee.

.    .    .    .    .    .

To Thee my longing heart aspires ;
    To Thee I offer all my vows :
Keep me from false and vain desires,
    My GOD, my Saviour, and my Spouse !

> Henceforth let no profane delight
>   Divide this consecrated soul !
> Possess it Thou, Who hast the right,
>   As Lord and Master of the whole.

>         .   .   .   .   .   .

> Thee one may love, and Thee alone,
>   With inward peace and holy bliss ;
> And when Thou tak'st us for Thine own,
>   Oh ! what a happiness is this !

*The Soul's Tendency towards its True Centre* is an expansion—but a very fine one—of Law's note in *The Spirit of Prayer*, that the " holy spark of the divine nature within man has a natural, strong, and almost infinite tendency, or reaching, after that eternal Light and Spirit of GOD, from whence it came forth ". In part, too, it derives from Eckhart's thought : " Consciously or unconsciously, all creatures seek their proper state ; for, as the stone cannot stop until it touch the earth and the fire rises up to the sky, so a loving soul cannot rest but in GOD ".

> Stones towards the earth descend ;
>   Rivers to the ocean roll ;
> Every motion has some end :
>   What is thine, beloved soul ?

> *Mine is where my Saviour is ;*
>   *There with Him I hope to dwell :*
> *Jesus is the central bliss ;*
>   *Love the force that doth impel.*

> Truly, thou hast answer'd right :
>   Now may Heaven's attractive grace,
> Towards the Source of thy delight,
>   Speed along thy quickening pace !

*Thank thee for thy gracious care !*
*Heaven, that did the wish inspire,*
*Through thy instrumeutal prayer,*
*Plumes the wings of my desire.*

*Now, methinks, aloft I fly :*
*Now with angels bear a part :*
*Glory be to God on high !*
*Peace to every Christian heart !*

Several of the anthologies include Byrom's experiment (and a very successful one, too) in chain-verse, which he called *The Desponding Soul's Wish ;* but *The Answer* is very rarely given.   Here it would not be fair to separate them, more especially as they express respectively the mutual need felt by man for GOD and by GOD for man :—

My spirit longeth for Thee
  Within my troubled breast,
Although I be unworthy
  Of so divine a Guest.

Of so divine a Guest
  Unworthy though I be ;
Yet hath my heart no rest
  Unless it come from Thee.

Unless it come from Thee,
  In vain I look around ;
In all that I can see
  No rest is to be found.

No rest is to be found
  But in Thy blessed love.
Oh ! let my wish be crown'd
  And send it from above !

Cheer up, desponding soul,
  Thy longing, pleas'd, I see ;
'Tis part of that great whole
  Wherewith I long'd for Thee.

Wherewith I long'd for thee ;
  And left My Father's throne,
From death to set thee free,
  To claim thee for My own.

To claim thee for My own
  I suffer'd on the Cross.
Oh ! were My love but known,
  No soul could fear its loss.

No soul could fear its loss,
  But, fill'd with love divine,
Would die on its own cross
  And rise for ever Mine.

Before bringing this notice to an end, a few of Byrom's sacred epigrams may be given. He showed a marked aptitude for this form of composition ; and while he could have echoed Gray's claim that his epigrams " can boast more truth than wit," the witty point is never lacking and is usually led up to quite successfully. Of his secular efforts in this vein, two, at least, are famous : the ambiguous toast " God bless the King," and the lines on the feuds between Handel and Bononcini. Of the sacred epigrams, we may take one which rebukes the deadness of eighteenth-century religion :—

> To own a GOD Who does not speak to men,
> Is first to own and then disown again ;
> Of all idolatries the total sum
> Is having gods that are both deaf and dumb.

And we may contrast with this another that reveals something of the mystic's certitude :—

> Faith, Hope, and Love were question'd what they thought
> Of future glory which religion taught :
> Now Faith believ'd it, firmly, to be true ;
> And Hope expected so to find it too ;
> Love answer'd, smiling with a conscious glow,
> *Believe ?  Expect ?*  I *know* it to be so.

A few pages must be devoted to the writings of another student of Behmenism, as elucidated by Law. HENRY BROOKE (1703-83) seems to have resembled Byrom in the loveableness of his character, but to have lacked the latter's sanity and balance. Born and educated in Ireland, Brooke made three sojourns in London, but returned to his native land, once to attempt practice as a lawyer (a profession for which his nature seems to have been too transparent), and finally to lose his inherited fortune in well-intentioned, but ill-advised schemes of agrarian reform.   He married a child of fourteen years, who bore him three children before she was eighteen, and twenty-two in all.   He did much literary work, journalistic, pamphleteering, and dramatic.   But he is best known as the author of an extraordinary novel, *The Fool of Quality*, which had a considerable success on its appearance in 1766-70.   This was given a new lease of life in 1781, by its re-issue under a fresh title, and in a mutilated form, by John Wesley, who, without naming its real author, commended it warmly " to all who are already, or desire to be, lovers of GOD and man ".   Two subsequent attempts to revive its popularity have not met with much success.   Charles Kingsley, attracted by Brooke's effervescent high spirits, insistence on mucular Christianity, and sympathy with the poor, re-issued the book in full with a not very discriminating preface, in which he speaks of him as " the pupil of Swift and Pope, the friend of Lyttleton and Chatham, the darling of the Prince of Wales, beau, swordsman, wit, poet, courtier, the minion once of fortune, yet unspoilt by all her caresses, long known to Irishmen only as the saintly recluse of Longfield, and latterly as an impoverished old man, fading away by the quiet euthanasia of a second childhood, with one sweet daughter—the only surviving child of twenty-two—clinging to him, and yet supporting him, as ivy the mouldering wall ".   Much more recently, a very carefully prepared edition of *The Fool of Quality* has been issued by Mr. E. A. Baker (Messrs. Routledge & Son), who speaks of it as being, " in spite of numerous defects, a work of art ".   The reader has to bear in mind that when it appeared the novel was still in a very early stage of its development ; but he will, beyond all doubt, find the story hopelessly ill-constructed, exasperatingly prolix, and full of sentimentality, exaggeration, and improbable coincidence. Its theory of education is notable, though manifestly influenced by the study of Rousseau ; and its theology, which is freely introduced with a manly candour and often with a noble eloquence, is as manifestly influenced by the teaching of Boehme. Our quotations must be restricted to those which illustrate his verse, or to those which may be regarded as autobiographical. When, for instance, we recall the bereavements and disappointments of Brooke's life, we can appreciate the long passage in which he maintains that " we are brought to nothing that our all may be in GOD. . . . Since GOD, therefore, cannot communicate happiness to one who refuses to trust in His goodness, or to repose upon His power, where He is peculiarly favourable, He blesses him with all sorts of crosses and disappointments. He breaks under him all the props of worldly confidence. He snatches from him the helps on which his hopes had laid hold ; that in the instant of sinking he may catch at his Creator, and throw himself on the bosom of that infinite benevolence ". A description, by one of the characters, of a vision of Jesus—after a sense of dereliction —in which " sensations of indescribable blessedness " were experienced, is too long to reproduce here, but it seems not unlikely to have been based on personal experience. Apology is made for the appearance of boasting ; but it is claimed that " it boasteth of nought except Christ crucified, or rather arisen in me, whereby all worldly matters are crucified unto me ". Possibly, it is in this connexion that we may seek the true explanation of Brooke's sudden withdrawal from London " in the very hey-day of his success ".

His two mystical poems are entitled *Universal Beauty*

18

(1735) and *Redemption* (1750). The former is idealistic rather than mystical ; but it insists very forcibly on the Immanence of GOD in man and nature, a truth enforced again and again in *The Fool of Quality*. " GOD is Himself," the hero is taught by his guardian, " the beauty and benefit of all His works. As they cannot exist but in Him and by Him, so His impression is upon them, and His impregnation is through them. . . . He is the secret and central light that kindles up the sun, His dazzling representative ; and He lives, enlightens, and comforts in the diffusion of His beams. His spirit inspires and actuates the air, and is in it a breath of life to His creatures. He blooms in the blossom and unfolds in the rose. He is fragrance in flowers and flavour in fruits. He holds infinitude in the hollow of His hand, and opens His world of wonders in the minims of nature. He is the virtue of every heart that is softened by a sense of pity or touch of benevolence. He coos in the turtle and bleats in the lamb ; and through the paps of the stern bear and implacable tigress He yields forth the milk of loving-kindness to their little ones. Even when we hear the delicious enchantment of music, it is but an external sketch and faint echo of those sentimental and rapturous tunings that rise up, throughout the immensity of our GOD, from eternity to eternity. Thus all things are secretly pregnant with their GOD. And the lover of sinners, the universal Redeemer, is a principle of good within them, that contends with the malignity of their lapsed state."

Many glowing passages on Essential Beauty could be extracted from the novel, passages more poetical than the poem itself, which was composed too entirely under the ascendancy of Pope to satisfy twentieth-century canons of taste. It is in six Books, of which the first two give a

general prospectus of the whole scheme ; the Being and
Attributes of GOD, and the use and beauty of the universe.
From the third Book, which contains a survey of the veget-
able world, two extracts, at least, are worth giving :—

> Thus Beauty, mimick'd in our humbler strains,
> Illustrious through the world's great poem reigns!
> The One grows sundry by creative power ;
> The Eternal's found in each revolving hour ;
> The Immense appears in every point of space ;
> The Unchangeable in Nature's varying face ;
> The Invisible conspicuous to our mind ;
> And Deity in every atom shrin'd.
>
> .    .    .    .    .    .    .    .    .
>
> Our transient optic o'er the surface plays,
> And Nature's superficial mien surveys ;
> But rare with deeper inquisition pries
> Where Beauty's wrapt, recluse from vulgar eyes ;
> Essential, sits on Truth's eternal throne,
> And universal, reigns o'er worlds unknown ;
> Displays her sway through unimagin'd scenes,
> Elysian tracts, and philosophic plains :
> These, these are climes of ever-living joy
> Truth ne'er can satiate, Reason ne'er can cloy.

Books IV and V deal with man and the other animals ;
from the latter we may take a characteristic reproof of
rationalistic speculation :—

> Oh, think !  If superficial scenes amaze,
> And e'en the still familiar wonders please,
> These but the sketch, the garb, the veil of things,
> Whence all our depth of shallow science springs ;
> Think, should this curtain of Omniscience rise,
> Think of the sight ! and think of the surprise !

Scenes inconceivable, essential, new,
Whelm'd on our soul, and lightning on our view !—
How would the vain disputing wretches shrink
And, shivering, wish they could no longer think,
Reject each model, each reforming scheme,
No longer dictate to the Grand Supreme,
But waking, wonder whence they dar'd to dream !
    All is phenomenon and type on earth,
Replete with sacred and mysterious birth,
Deep from our search, exalted from our soar :
Proud Reason's task is only to adore.

The sixth Book brings the poem to an end thus (a few
lines being omitted, the value of which modern evolutionary
theories have somewhat depreciated) :—

Thus through the maze of Thy eternal round,
Through yon steep heaven, and nether gulfs profound,
The dusky planet and the lucid sphere,
Earth's ponderous ball, and soft enfolding air,
The fish who glance or tempest through the main,
The beasts who trip or thunder o'er the plain,
The reptile wreathing in the wanton ring,
The bird high wafted on the towering wing,
All, all from Thee, Sole Cause Essential, tend,
Thence flow effusive, thither centering end.

    .    .    .    .    .    .    .

Yet ere material entity begun,
Or from the Vast this universe was won ;
While finitude erewhile was unconfin'd,
Nor space grew relative, to form assign'd,
Thou did'st Thine own Eternal Now sustain,
And space was swallow'd in Thy boundless main ;
Thyself the filler of Thine own abyss,
Thyself the great Eternity of Bliss !

All when, and where, in Thee imbosom'd lay,
The blaze of majesty and self-born day ;
No void was found, where Endless Beauty beam'd ;
No darkness, where Essential Glory flam'd ;
No want, no solitude, where Thou wert bless'd,
And in Thyself the unbounded whole possess'd.

The poem on *The Redemption* is a good deal shorter,
and need not detain us long.   It first celebrates man's
original glory ; and then, after narrating his Fall to "his
God-abandon'd Hell," it represents GOD as promising
Christ's Victory ; but

> This in due time.
Jesus, meanwhile, shall steal, like doubtful morn,
Into the breasts of all of women born ;
There shed His dawn of co-eternal Light,
There struggle with their length and depth of night,—
A solid gloom which He alone can melt,
Which, like Egyptian darkness may be felt.
His seed, in flesh, My Holy One shall sow,
And give it strength to root, and grace to grow ;
Man within man, begotten from above,
Bearing the likeness of the Son of Love ;
Sons of My Son, ordain'd to see My Face,
All embryon heirs of glory and of grace ;
But not mature to win their native skies
Till their New Adam shall from death arise.
Thus to a sensual, to a sinful shrine,
The Saviour shall entrust His Speck Divine ;
In secret animate His chosen seed,
Fill with His love, and with His substance feed ;
Inform it with sensations of His own,
And give it appetites to flesh unknown.
So shall the lusts of man's old worm give place,
His fervour languish, and his force decrease,

Till, spoil'd of every object, gross or vain,
His pride and passions humbled, crush'd, and slain,
From a false world to his First Kingdom won,
His will, and sin, and sense, and self, undone,
His inward man from death shall break away,
And soar and mingle with Eternal Day.

WILLIAM BLAKE (1757-1827) is, strictly speaking, outside the scope of this volume, since, far from being a Churchman, in much of his work he is hardly to be ranged in the ranks even of Christianity. Yet, as one of the greatest of English mystics and, perhaps, the greatest poet among English mystics, he cannot be entirely ignored here. No attempt will be made, however, to treat him exhaustively, and he may be studied, in this connexion, as a warning ; for, despite the purity of his character and the unworldliness of his private life, he illustrates to a most marked degree the faults which have at times brought mysticism into ill-odour. He had, indeed, the excesses of his qualities ; and, beginning with a sound and exquisite mystical consciousness, which was expressed in verse, faulty in technique and syntax, but charming in its lyrical quality and simplicity of diction, his visionary extravagance and strident dogmatism gradually choked his utterance and brought him to the very confines of sanity.

His earliest volume, *The Poetical Sketches*, hardly concerns us ; but a mystical sense of the Divine universality suffuses the well-named *Songs of Innocence* (1789). It is, for the most part, implicit rather than explicit, but comes out very finely in *The Divine Image*, a poem which, in the excellent account of Blake given in the *Cambridge History of English Literature* (vol. xi), is described as " his vision of that Spirit which is at once universal and

particular, GOD and man ". Although well known, it must
here be printed in full :—

> To Mercy, Pity, Peace, and Love
> All pray in their distress;
> And to these virtues of delight
> Return their thankfulness.
>
> For Mercy, Pity, Peace, and Love
> Is GOD our Father dear,
> And Mercy, Pity, Peace, and Love
> Is man, His child and care.
>
> For Mercy has a human heart,
> Pity, a human face,
> And Love, the human form divine,
> And Peace, the human dress.
>
> Then every man of every clime
> That prays in his distress,
> Prays to the human form divine,
> Love, Mercy, Pity, Peace.
>
> And all must love the human form,
> In heathen, Turk, or Jew;
> Where Mercy, Love, and Pity dwell,
> There GOD is dwelling too.

The *Book of Thel* was begun in the same mood and
spirit. It relates how the fretful discontent of " a daughter of
the Seraphim " was reproved, in turn, by a lily of the valley,
a cloud, a worm, and a clod of earth from whom she learns
that

> Everything that lives
> Lives not alone nor for itself.

But in the closing section of the poem Blake abruptly drops out of his first phase into his second, the phase of revolt against the restraints and insincerities of conventional Christianity. This finds its full expression in the prose *Marriage of Heaven and Hell*, which, in Swinburne's judgment, " gives us the high-water mark of his intellect ". The study of it is certainly essential to an understanding of Blake's position. In form, it is a parody of Swedenborg, to whom Blake was never generous enough to own his deep obligation. Its main positive statements are that " all Deities reside in the human breast," and that " if the doors of perception were cleansed, even this world would appear to men, as it is, infinite ". Negatively, it runs amuck of all authority, morality, and reason. Its Christology, subsequently developed in the poem, *The Everlasting Gospel*, is summed up in the decision that " no virtue can exist without breaking these ten commandments : Jesus was all virtue, and acted from impulse, not from rules ". We now reach the Prophetical Books on *The French Revolution, America*, etc., in which we have Blake's reading of history, much distorted by his wrong-headed ethics, and wholly confused by the bewildering mythology under which his prophecy became a ranting mystification. Swinburne's criticism of these is, probably, as fair as any one's : " The confusion, the clamour, the jar of words that half suffice and thoughts that half exist, all these and other more absolutely offensive qualities— audacity, monotony, bombast, obscure play of licence and tortuous growth of fancy—cannot quench or even wholly conceal the living purport and the imperishable beauty which are here latent ".

It was about now (1794) that Blake published the companion-volume to the *Songs of Innocence*. Compared with the latter, these *Songs of Experience* are grim and joyless, wholly destructive in their cheap anti-clericalism and perverse antinomianism. It is easy to applaud the righteous indignation aroused in him by the social injustices of his time (e.g. in the second version of *Holy Thursday*), but not so easy to sympathize with his fury over the swaddling of infants and the educating of truant boys. The best of these *Songs of Experience* is, perhaps, *The Clod and the Pebble*, in which the former voices his own doctrine of self-forgetful love and the latter the world's doctrine of self-interest.

The preposterous *Urizen* trilogy was written, apparently, to prove that " it was not Satan, but the GOD of this world, the author of the moral codes, who fell " (*Cambridge History of English Literature*) ; whilst *The Song of Los* is a eulogy of Mahometanism at the expense of Christianity. There can be no reasonable doubt that by this time Blake's mind was becoming unhinged : a lengthy sojourn in the country was only just in time, if in time, to save his sanity. He himself speaks of having " again emerged into the light of day ". It was this recovery, partial or entire, of balance which made *The Four Zoas* so inconsequent that the author despaired of making it intelligible and tried, in vain, to recast it. And it was during this lucid interval that he wrote the lines in which he best expressed his piercing cosmic consciousness, *The Auguries of Innocence*, described by Mr. G. K. Chesterton as " a string of verses against cruelty to the smallest creature as a sort of mystical insult to the universe ". This may pass as a rough description ; but the distichs are extraordinarily inconsecutive, Mr. Sampson, the editor of the Oxford edition of Blake's poems, finding it advisable to attempt a re-arrangement of them.

Here are a few lines from the beginning, from the middle, and from the end of the poem :—

To see the world in a grain of sand,
And a Heaven in a wild flower,
Hold Infinity in the palm of your hand,
And Eternity in an hour.
A robin redbreast in a cage
Puts all Heaven in a rage.
A dove-house fill'd with doves and pigeons
Shudders Hell through all its regions.
A dog starv'd at his master's gate
Predicts the ruin of the State.
A horse misus'd upon the road
Calls to Heaven for human blood.
Each outcry of the hunted hare
A fibre from the brain does tear.
A skylark wounded in the wing,
A cherubim does cease to sing.

.    .    .    .    .    .    .

A riddle, or the cricket's cry,
Is to Doubt a fit reply.
The emmet's inch and the eagle's mile
Make lame Philosophy to smile.
He who doubts from what he sees
Will ne'er believe, do what you please.
If the sun and moon should doubt,
They'd immediately go out.

.    .    .    .    .    .    .

GOD appears, and GOD is Light,
To those poor souls who dwell in Night ;
But does a human form display
To those who dwell in realms of Day.

While at Felpham, too, Blake indited the lines *To*

*Thomas Butts*, which contain a good deal of his mystical philosophy, and enough of his inconsecutiveness of thought to justify a mutilated extract, more especially as the respective claims of Butts and Hayley on the poet's attention do not concern us :—

> With happiness stretch'd across the hills
> In a cloud that dewy sweetness distils ;
> With a blue sky spread over with wings,
> And a mild sun that mounts and sings ;
> With trees and fields full of fairy elves,
> And little devils who fight for themselves—
> Remembering the verses that Hayley sung
> When my heart knock'd against the roof of my tongue—
> With angels planted in hawthorn bowers,
> And GOD Himself in the passing hours ; . . .
> With a thousand angels upon the wind,
> Pouring disconsolate from behind
> To drive them off, and before my way
> A frowning thistle implores my stay.
> What to others a trifle appears
> Fills me full of smiles or tears ;
> For double the vision my eyes do see,
> And a double vision is always with me.
> With my inward eye 'tis an Old Man grey,
> With my outward, a Thistle across my way.
>
> .   .   .   .   .   .   .
>
> Now I a fourfold vision see,
> And a fourfold vision is given to me ;
> 'Tis fourfold in my supreme delight,
> And threefold in soft Beulah's night,
> And twofold always.—May GOD us keep
> From single vision, and Newton's sleep !

The more important of Blake's latest productions were

*Milton* and *Jerusalem*. Of these he claimed to be no more than the amanuensis, receiving dictation from above ; and, therefore, he did not hesitate to call them " the grandest poems in the world ". *Milton* is a protest against the worst features of Puritanism ; *Jerusalem* purports to describe the great battle between ' Imagination ' and ' Natural Religion '. Both contain noble passages on the supreme duties of self-sacrifice and forgivingness ; but both are marred by over-statement and incoherence, and both, to be at all intelligible, demand a knowledge of Blake's private nomenclature for his personified likes and dislikes. In *Milton* we get the magnificent lines, now well-worn by constant quotation, but still unhackneyed :—

> And did those Feet in ancient time
> > Walk upon England's mountains green ?
> And was the holy Lamb of GOD
> > On England's pleasant pastures seen ?
>
> And did the Countenance Divine
> > Shine forth upon our clouded hills ?
> And was Jerusalem builded here
> > Among these dark Satanic mills ?
>
> Bring me my bow of burning gold !
> > Bring me my arrows of desire !
> Bring me my spear ! O clouds, unfold !
> > Bring me my chariot of fire !
>
> I will not cease from mental fight,
> > Nor shall my sword sleep in my hand,
> Till we have built Jerusalem
> > In England's green and pleasant land.

From *Jerusalem* we may quote two passages.    One
illustrates the misology of Blake :—

O Spirit Divine ! sustain me on Thy wings,
That I may awake Albion from his long and cold repose ;
For Bacon and Newton, sheath'd in dismal steel, their terrors hang
Like iron scourges over Albion.    Reasonings like vast serpents
Enfold around my limbs, bruising my minute articulations.
I turn my eye to the schools and universities of Europe,
And there behold the loom of Locke, whose woof rages dire,
Wash'd by the water-wheels of Newton : black the cloth
In heavy wreaths folds over every nation : cruel works
Of many wheels I view, wheel without wheel, with cogs tyrannic,
Moving by compulsion each other ; not as those in Eden, which,
Wheel within wheel, in freedom revolve, in harmony and peace.

The other passage sets forth his own conception of his
mission in life, with a touching prayer :—

I rest not from my great task
To open the Eternal Worlds, to open the immortal eyes
Of man inwards into the Worlds of Thought, into Eternity
Ever expanding in the bosom of GOD, the human Imagination.
O Saviour, pour upon me Thy Spirit of meekness and love ;
Annihilate the Selfhood in me ; be Thou all my life.

There is, no doubt, a good deal of affectation in the admiration so loudly voiced to-day both for Blake's drawings
and for his verse.    It is a little annoying to find people
wasting time in the elucidation of his mystifying myths,
taking his vagaries so seriously, and mistaking the ridiculous
for the sublime.    But we can be unfeignedly grateful to him
for his protest against materialism and religious convention-
ality, and for his efforts to bring home to us the divinity of
man (or, as Blake preferred to put it, the humanity of GOD),
the reality of Imagination (by which term he meant the

infinite ' world of eternity '), and the tragedy of resting satisfied with " single vision ".   It was no idle boast which suggested to him the lines in *Jerusalem* :—

> I give you the end of a golden string ;
> Only wind it into a ball,
> It will lead you in at Heaven's gate,
> Built in Jerusalem's wall.

At the same time, there seems need to enter a protest—
modestly, because it is easy to misapprehend a genius—
against a twofold defect in Blake's mysticism.   There is, in
the first place, his depreciation of Nature, which he declared
to Crabb Robinson to be " the work of the devil ".   This
perverse attitude does not appear in the *Songs of Innocence*,
which were written with " a rural pen " and overflow with
joy in natural beauty ; but in several of the poems of the
*Pickering MS.* we notice a morbid dread of deriving
pleasure from the beauties of the physical world, which had
become to Blake merely " a shadow of the world of eternity ".   Almost to the last, however, he seems inconsistent
in this respect, as witness the *Auguries of Innocence*,
partially quoted above ; and in conversation he claimed to
find Divine glories in the sunrise and to be moved to tears
of joy by a tree.   And yet he would have agreed, apparently, with the Yogin dictum, that " this world is a delusive
charm of the great magician Maya ".   Doubtless, there are
many to-day to whom mysticism, to be genuine, must be
extra-phenomenal.   But for some of us Nature-mysticism
has fully established its orthodoxy ; and those who still need
to be convinced " not only that man may hold communion
with nature, but that, in and through such communion, he
is in living touch with the Ground of Existence," should

study the fascinating volume on *Nature-Mysticism* written
by Bishop Mercer (George Allen & Co.).

Again, the stress laid by Blake upon visions and auditions
is not a mark of the highest mysticism.   He stands, indeed,
almost alone among the great mystics in the importance which
he attaches to such experiences.   Dr. Inge, in his *Christian
Mysticism*, quotes several warnings, uttered by mystics of
all ages, against the dangers to humility and to bodily and
mental health, to which this sort of spiritual indulgence exposes the Christian.   He might have added the words of
St. John of the Cross (who had himself many such experiences, but resented them as a danger and a hindrance) that
many who hear interior words are simply answering themselves and then persuade themselves that these answers come
from GOD.   "These persons fall into great absurdities,"
he adds ; and one is tempted to apply the words to Blake,
whose spiritualistic vouchsafements induced a painful self-
assertiveness, and extinguished his sense of the ridiculous and
his power of self-criticism.   They led him into many a
spiritual phantasmagoria ; and, under their malign influence,
he advocated a licence with which his own practice did not
in the least accord.   It was a pity that he did not learn from
St. Paul that in genuine visions " unspeakable words " are
heard, and that he did not take to heart the Apostle's words,
in 1 *Corinthians* xiv, on the relative value of the various
spiritual gifts.   On this point the reader should consult, if
he has not done so already, the pages of admirable wisdom
to be found in the 14th chapter of Bishop Chandler's *Ara
Coeli*, in which it is convincingly argued that inward union
with GOD, and not outward visions or messages, is the true
mystical aim.

The vexed question of Blake's mental condition will,

perhaps, never be answered decisively. Paley defined insanity as an incapacity to distinguish between impressions on the mind and impressions on the senses : in that sense Blake would probably have been proud to be written down insane. Ruskin declared that " visions, where most distinctly received, are always—I speak deliberately—always, the sign of some mental limitation or derangement " : this makes short work of St. Paul's claim to be a trustworthy guide in the study of theology. Lionel Johnson, after an heroic study of the commentaries of Messrs. Ellis and Yeats, argued, with considerable cogency, that Blake's conceptions have a rational consistency and that " he lived, wrote, and designed under one inspiration, obedient to one service of the imagination, without extravagance, without absurdity ". Many, however, will withhold assent from the negative portion of that statement. Mr. G. K. Chesterton has, possibly, given insufficient attention to Messrs. Ellis and Yeats ; but he contends, with his customary force, that " a man who could write so well and did write so badly must be mad," and that " something, when all is said and done, had eaten away whole parts of that powerful brain, leaving parts of it standing like great Greek pillars in a desert ". Moreover, he believes himself to have found the key to the mystery in Blake's indulgence in spiritualism : he says that Blake " threw the doors of his mind open to what the late George MacDonald called in a fine phrase ' the *canaille* of the other world '. I think it impossible to look at some of the pictures which Blake drew, under what he considered direct spiritual dictation, without feeling that he was from time to time under influences that were not only evil but even foolishly evil ". Let it be conceded, at least, that in his irrational hatred of reason, Blake allowed, or rather forced, his imagination to

pass beyond the control of his reason, and that, in his revolt
against the materialism and hypocrisy of his times, he said
much for which it would be impossible to find excuses if it
were the calm and considered utterance of a well-balanced
mind. *Tout comprendre, c'est tout pardonner*—the most
valuable, perhaps, of the lessons inculcated by Blake himself.

NOTE.—Mention should be made, in passing, of Cowper's translations from the poems of Madame Guyon.
This was, presumably, a task undertaken to counteract the
diametrically opposite grain in his own religious temperament ; for it was the most pathetic lot of that veritable
saint to live—in the main—and to die (in his own phrase)
in " unutterable despair," believing " hatred and vengeance
to be his eternal portion ". There is, however, in the last
Book of *The Task* a distinct approach to Nature-mysticism. It may, of course, be no more than an echo of
Thomson's *Spring* and *Hymn ;* but the lines are worth
printing here, as Cowper's more serious work is not very
widely read nowadays :—

> From dearth to plenty, and from life to death,
> Is Nature's progress when she lectures man
> In heavenly truth ; evincing, as she makes
> The grand transition, that there lives and works
> A soul in all things, and that soul is GOD.

> .    .    .    .    .    .    .    .

> The Lord of all, Himself through all diffus'd,
> Sustains and is the life of all that lives.
> Nature is but a name for an effect
> Whose cause is GOD. . . .

> .    .    .    .    .    .    .    .

> One Spirit—His
> Who wore the plaited thorns with bleeding brows—
> Rules universal nature.
>
> . . . . . . . . . .
>
> Happy who walks with Him! whom what he finds
> Of flavour or of scent in fruit or flower,
> Or what he views of beautiful or grand
> In nature, from the broad majestic oak
> To the green blade that twinkles in the sun,
> Prompts with remembrance of a present GOD.

# CHAPTER IX.

## WORDSWORTH, COLERIDGE, TENNYSON, MYERS, GEORGE MACDONALD, COVENTRY PATMORE, FRANCIS THOMPSON.

THE limits of this volume make it imperative that our last period should be treated much more cursorily than those with which we have dealt heretofore. This is the less regrettable since, indisputably, the writings of the poets which remain for consideration are more accessible to readers and have received more attention from modern students of mysticism.[1] Thus, WORDSWORTH'S poems, even if (as one suspects) they are seldom read to-day, are being constantly re-issued in inexpensive editions, and have been the subject of careful study by several modern writers on mysticism. Indeed, since Dr. Inge and others have called attention to Wordsworth's philosophy, it has seemed amazing that Viscount Morley could ever have written that " when he says that it is his faith ' that every flower enjoys the air it breathes,' and that when the budding twigs spread out their fan to catch the air, he is compelled to think ' that there was pleasure there,' he expresses a charming poetic fancy and no more, and it is idle to pretend to see in it the fountain of a system of philosophy ". This is not quite as bad as Lord Macaulay's remarks about " flimsy philosophy "

---

[1] In the *Oxford Book of Mystical Verse*, e.g., more than 500 pages are devoted to the nineteenth century, while only 109 pages suffice for the earlier centuries.

and " crasy mystical metaphysics " ; but perhaps Lord
Morley, despite his unquestioned greatness in certain spheres,
is not much better qualified than his predecessor to pass
judgment on the philosophy of a mystic.   Wordsworth was
pre-eminently and consciously the hierophant of Nature-
mysticism ; and in considering his verse here the points
which it seems necessary to indicate as salient are his Panpsychism, his sense of vocation, and his psychological
system.[1]

To Wordsworth the crude mythological faith of early
times seemed far preferable to a materialistic and mechanical
interpretation of Nature.

> Great GOD ! I'd rather be
> A Pagan suckled in a creed outworn ;
> So might I, standing on this pleasant lea,
> Have glimpses that would make me less forlorn ;
> Have sight of Proteus rising from the sea ;
> Or hear old Triton blow his wreathed horn.

Less vehemently, in lines written *At Sea off the Isle of
Man*, he extols

> That age when not by *laws* inanimate,
> As men believ'd, the waters were impell'd,
> The air controll'd, the stars their courses held ;
> But element and orb on *acts* did wait
> Of Powers endued with visible form instinct
> With will, and to their work by passion link'd.

And in *The Excursion* he justifies even superstitious attempts :—

---

[1] For a vindication of Wordsworth from the charge of Pantheism, sometimes
brought against him, the reader may be referred to A. C. Fraser's Gifford Lectures
*The Philosophy of Theism*, 1895, p. 155.

Filling a space else vacant—to exalt
The forms of Nature and enlarge her powers.

Wordsworth unreservedly rejected the notion of ' dead
matter '. Not only was he convinced that " there is a
spirit in the woods " ; he believed wholeheartedly in

The Being that is in the clouds and air,
That is in the green leaves among the groves.

The sight of the sea from Calais beach evoked from him
the cry, " Listen ! The mighty Being is awake ". He tells
us that, at Cambridge,

To every natural form, rock, fruits, or flower,
Even the loose stones that cover the highway,
I gave a moral life : I saw them feel,
Or link'd them to some feeling : the great mass
Lay bedded in a quickening soul.

And in the rôle of the Wanderer—confessedly a self-
portrait—he insisted that

To every form of being is assign'd,
An active principle—howe'er remov'd
From sense and observation, it subsists
In all things, in all natures ; in the stars
Of azure heaven, the unenduring clouds,
In every flower and tree, in every pebbly stone
That paves the brooks, the stationary rocks,
The moving water, and the invisible air.
Whate'er exists has properties that spread
Beyond itself, communicating good,
A simple blessing, or with evil mix'd ;
Spirit that knows no insulated spot,
No chasm, no solitude ; from link to link
It circulates, the Soul of all the worlds.

It is impossible to withhold sympathy from the special form of the doctrine of Immanence known as Panpsychism, which several leading philosophers have, in modern times, expounded with enthusiastic eloquence and insight. Fechner has most winningly disclosed " the soul-life of plants " in *Nanna ;* and in *Zend-Avesta* he describes Nature as a spiritual being, not only pervaded with consciousness, but participating in the Divine Spirit. More recently, Dr. Hans Driesch has applied his outstanding scientific attainments to the elucidation of *The Soul as a Factor in Nature.* Others claim that they have demonstrated that " the Dryad, living and breathing, moving and sensitive, is again within the tree ". And none of these exceed the daring of the most philosophic and not least inspired of the Apostles, who could scarcely have been using a mere figure of speech when he wrote to the Romans of the groans and pains of the whole creation. Decidedly, Wordsworth is in good company when he places the ultimate reality of Nature in spirit, and its purpose in the development of the spiritual life. In a private letter written when seventy-five years of age, he says that what he especially valued in his attempts was " the spirituality with which I have endeavoured to invest the universe, and the moral relations under which I have wished to exhibit its most ordinary appearances ".

These words make it clear that Wordsworth had a clear sense of his high calling as Nature's mystagogue. For his exposition of the deepest mysteries of Nature, general reference may be made to the *Lines composed above Tintern Abbey* and to the 4th Book of *The Excursion.* The Lake District was to him " a solemn temple," in which he had received—too carelessly, he feared—" his earliest visitations," and to which he ultimately retired as " a dedicated

spirit ".   And his conviction was clear that the insight and
uplift which he had himself gained must not be regarded as
a private possession, but as a gift to be ministered to others
" as a good steward of the manifold grace of GOD ".

> Poetic numbers came
> Spontaneously to clothe in priestly robe
> A renovated spirit singled out—
> Such hope was mine—for holy services.

He thought of himself, too, in *The Recluse*, as assistant
at the marriage rites of Man and Nature,—a novel setting
of the symbol so dear to mystics, The Marriage of the
Soul :—

> I, long before the blissful hour arriv'd,
> Would chant, in lonely peace, the spousal verse
> Of this great consummation.

It is especially noteworthy that Wordsworth was not
simply vapouring when he thought of himself in this hieratic
light.   He believed that he could psychologically make
good his claims to have learnt heavenly mysteries and to be
able to initiate others in them.

> I seem'd about this time to gain clear sight
> Of a new world—a world, too, that was fit
> To be transmitted, and to other eyes
> Made visible ; as rul'd by those fixed laws
> Whence spiritual dignity originates,
> Which do both give it being and maintain
> A balance, an ennobling interchange
> Of action from without and from within ;
> The excellence, pure function, and best power
> Both of the objects seen, and eye that sees.

In the next—and last—Book of *The Prelude* he names,
in a few close-packed lines, the faculties which he regards

as essential for the nature-mystic. These are a love which sees the spiritual in all forms of beauty, an imagination very different from fancifulness, and an illuminated reason, the two latter qualities being not easily differentiated.

> This spiritual love acts not, nor can exist
> Without imagination, which, in truth,
> Is but another name for absolute power
> And clearest insight, amplitude of mind,
> And reason in her most exalted mood.

It was to teach others how to love " what we have loved," and to

> Instruct them how the mind of man becomes
> A thousand times more beautiful than the earth
> On which he dwells,

that Wordsworth wrote his spiritual autobiography, " the discipline and consummation of a poet's mind," as a *Prelude* to *The Recluse*. In this priceless product of a retentive memory, penetrating introspection, and sanctified egotism, he traced the gradual sublimation of the inchoate and undisciplined sensations roused in him, as a boy, by the life and beauty of Nature, checked for a time, as the process was, by the dark night into which his soul was plunged by his disappointment over the French Revolution. Rescued from this by the influence of the sister whose memory must be ever fragrant to all Wordsworthians, he resolutely set foot on the first rung of the mystic ladder, striving to purge his soul of all that was mean and sordid, and of " unmanageable thoughts ". The former was the easier task ; for he had never tampered

> With conscience from a private aim ;
> Nor was in any public hope the dupe

> Of selfish passions; nor did ever yield
> Wilfully to meaner cares or low pursuits.

But when Reason bade him

> Be mild, and cleave to gentle things,
> Thy glory and thy happiness be there,

such was the natural turbulence of his disposition that long
he strove in vain " to mitigate the fever of his heart ".
Here too, however, grace triumphed over nature ; and he
who had longed that " winds might rage," and had loved
" tempestuous nights," came rather to expect the " shock of
aweful consciousness in some calm season ". And so he
acquired that " wise passiveness " which students of mysticism have called ' Waiting upon GOD ' ; he reaped that
" harvest of a quiet eye " which, as the second rung in the
mystic ladder, is known as Illumination ; and in *A Poet's
Epitaph* he was able to say of himself :—

> The outward shows of sky and earth,
> Of hill and valley, he has viewed ;
> And impulses of deeper birth
> Have come to him in solitude.

Leaving aside the statements in the *Tintern Abbey* lines,
we know that even in youth he had experienced some sort
of ecstasy, or at least trance,

> When the light of sense
> Goes out, but with a flash that has reveal'd
> The invisible world.

So he tells us in *The Prelude;* while in *The Excursion*
he describes an experience yet more akin to the mystic's
ultimate aim of union with the Absolute :—

> Far and wide the clouds were touch'd,
> And in their silent faces could he read

Unutterable love.   Sound needed none,
Nor any voice of joy ; his spirit drank
The spectacle : sensation, sound, and form,
All melted into him ; they swallow'd up
His animal being ; in them did he live,
And by them did he live ; they were his life.
In such access of mind, in such high hour
Of visitation from the living GOD,
Thought was not ; in enjoyment it expir'd.
No thanks he breath'd ; he proffer'd no request ;
Rapt into still communion that transcends
The imperfect offices of prayer and praise,
His mind was a thanksgiving to the power
That made him ; it was blessedness and love.

And if, as we gather from the famous *Ode* and elsewhere, he found it, with advancing years, more and more difficult to keep these heights, and finally had to admit that " those fervent raptures are for ever flown," yet there was not " utter loss ".   Tranquil age brought

Fresh power to commune with the invisible world,
And hear the mighty stream of tendency
Uttering, for elevation of our thought,
A clear sonorous voice, inaudible
To the vast multitude whose doom it is
To run the giddy round of vain delight,
Or fret and labour on the plain below.

And, on his 63rd birthday, he could address to the Deity immanent in Nature, Whom he had come more and more clearly to identify with the Deity transcendent in Revelation, such a prayer as this :—

Teach me with quick-ear'd spirit to rejoice
In admonitions of Thy softest voice !

Whate'er the path these mortal feet may trace
Breathe through my soul the blessing of Thy grace,
Glad, through a perfect love, a faith sincere
Drawn from the wisdom that begins with fear,
Glad to expand ; and, for a season free
From finite cares, to rest absorb'd in Thee !

A more serious study of Wordsworth's gospel, and of his doctrine of the duty and privilege of cultivating a spiritual relationship to Nature is, perhaps, one of the crying needs of to-day. Even those of us who are quite hopeless of attaining the mystic heights reached by him in his communings with " the mighty Being," can assimilate something of his reverent and receptive spirit. We can go forth, and take with us " a heart that watches and receives". We can learn from him how to train our " inward ear " ; and, if it be vouchsafed to us to catch echoes from afar, we can " listen, ponder, hold them dear," with a full assurance that " of GOD—of GOD they are ". And, even if the " tidings of invisible things " which Nature imparts to us lack this note of authenticity, still we shall be at least in the number of those

Who look
In steadiness, who have among least things
An under-sense of greatness, see the parts
As parts, but with a feeling of the whole.

COLERIDGE'S verse, unlike that of Wordsworth, is almost negligible as a consistent exposition of mysticism. If, as we gather from the volume entitled *Anima Poetae*, Coleridge sometimes protested vigorously against Wordsworth's Nature-worship, the elder poet secured his ' retort courteous ' in *The Prelude :—*

I have thought
Of thee, thy learning, gorgeous eloquence,
And all the strength and plumage of thy youth,
Thy subtle speculations, toils abstruse
Among the schoolmen, and Platonic forms
Of wild ideal pageantry, shaped out
From things well-match'd or ill, and words for things,
The self-created sustenance of a mind
Debarr'd from Nature's living images,
Compell'd to be a life unto herself,
And unrelentingly possess'd by thirst
Of greatness, love, and beauty.

In a classification, which he borrowed without acknow-
ledgement from Schlegel, Coleridge divided mankind into
born-Aristotelians and born-Platonists.  He was himself a
Platonist, and from childhood was a zealous student of
mystical writings.  But it is an open question whether (to
use his own  rather perplexing  terminology) he was so with
the ' reason ' or with the ' understanding '—by intuitive perception or by a chain of reasoning.  Hurrying chronologically through the pieces which are relevant to our subject
—in *Religious Musings* we find him

Strong to believe whate'er of mystic good
The Eternal dooms for His immortal sons :
From Hope and firmer Faith to perfect Love
Attracted and absorb'd : and centred there
GOD only to behold, and know, and feel,
Till by exclusive consciousness of GOD
All self-annihilated it shall make
GOD its identity : GOD all in all !
We and our Father One !

A few lines further on, he asserts the conscious divinity

of man, claiming, as it were, for each, by virtue of his human
nature, the title Immanuel, GOD with us :—

> 'Tis the sublime of man
> Our noontide majesty, to know ourselves
> Parts and proportions of one wondrous whole !

And in the closing lines of the poem, he enunciates the
theory—not an original one, of course—of emanations from
the Absolute with widely differing functions, contemplative
in heaven or plastic in the universe :—

> Contemplant spirits ! ye that hover o'er
> With untir'd gaze the immeasurable fount
> Ebullient with creative Deity !
> And ye of plastic power, that interfus'd
> Roll through the grosser and material mass
> In organizing surge ! Holies of GOD.

To this, in *The Destiny of Nations*, he adds the possibility of other spirits sent forth from the Divine essence to
preside over the destinies of the nations, a suggestion for
which he might have claimed support from the closing section of the Book of *Daniel*.   He demands freedom

> Him first, Him last to view
> Through meaner powers and secondary things
> Effulgent, as through clouds that veil His blaze.
> For all that meets the bodily sense I deem
> Symbolical,[1] one mighty alphabet
> For infant minds ; and we in this low world
> Plac'd with our backs to bright reality,
> That we may learn with young unwounded ken
> The substance from its shadow. . . .

.   .   .   .   .   .   .

---

[1] Cf. his *Statesman's Manual*, p. 84 : " By a symbol I mean, not a metaphor
or allegory or any other figure of speech or form of fancy, but an actual and essential
part of that, the whole of which it represents ".

Others boldier think
That as one body seems the aggregate
Of atoms numberless, each organized ;
So by a strange and dim similitude
Infinite myriads of self-conscious minds
Are one all-conscious Spirit, which informs
With absolute ubiquity of thought
(His one eternal self-affirming act !)
All His involved Monads, that yet seem
With various province and apt agency
Each to pursue its own self-centring end.
Some nurse the infant diamond in the mind ;
Some roll the genial juices through the oak ;
Some drive the mutinous clouds to clash in air.

.    .    .    .    .    .    .

If there be beings of higher class than man,
I deem no nobler province they possess,
Than by disposal of apt circumstance
To rear up kingdoms : and the deeds they prompt,
Distinguishing from mortal agency,
They choose their human ministers from such states
As still the Epic song half fears to name.[1]

.    .    .    .    .    .    .

Glory to Thee, Father of Heaven and Earth !
All-conscious Presence of the Universe !
Nature's vast ever-acting energy !
In will, in deed, impulse of all to all !

In *The Aeolian Harp* we find the first hint of the attitude towards Nature which subsequently developed into the
extreme subjectivism of the *Dejection* Ode :—

---

[1] He instances the voices which inspired the heroism of Joan of Arc.

And what if all of animated nature
Be but organic harps diversely fram'd,
That tremble into thought, as o'er them sweep,
Plastic and vast, one intellectual breeze,
At once the soul of each, and GOD of all ?

That communion with Nature had brought Coleridge ecstatic moments, we can learn from *This Lime-tree Bower my Prison* :—

So my friend,
Struck with deep joy, may stand, as I have stood,
Silent with swimming sense ; yea, gazing round
On the wide landscape, gaz'd till all doth seem
Less gross than bodily ; and of such hues
As veil the Almighty Spirit, when yet he makes
Spirits perceive His Presence.

But, having failed to persevere in the purgative way, Coleridge had no steady sense of illumination such as Wordsworth enjoyed. Moreover, his indulgence in romantic fantasies, beneficial as it decidedly was to his secular verse, was detrimental to his spiritual development ; and when the " shaping spirit of imagination " became " suspended," his unsatisfied longing for intercourse with the Infinite and the Eternal, induced that Dark Night of the Soul which became articulate in *Dejection* :—

A grief without a pang, void, dark, and drear,
A stifled, drowsy, unimpassion'd grief,
Which finds no natural outlet, no relief,
In word, or sigh, or tear—
O Lady ! in this wan and heartless mood
To other thoughts by yonder throstle woo'd,
All this long eve, so balmy and serene,
Have I been gazing on the western sky,
And its peculiar tint of yellow green :

And still I gaze—and with how blank an eye !
And those thin clouds above, in flakes and bars,
That give away their motion to the stars ;
Those stars that glide behind them and between,
Now sparkling, now bedimm'd, but always seen :
Yon cresent moon, as fix'd as if it grew
In its own cloudless, starless lake of blue ;
I see them all so excellently fair,
I see, not feel, how beautiful they are !

        My genial spirits fail ;
        And what can these avail
To lift the smothering weight from off my breast ?
        It were a vain endeavour,
        Though I should gaze for ever
On that green light that lingers in the west ;
I may not hope from outward forms to win
The passion and the life whose fountains are within.

O Lady ! we receive but what we give,
And in our life alone does Nature live :
Ours is her wedding-garment, ours her shroud !
    And would we aught behold, of higher worth,
Than that inanimate cold world allow'd
        To the poor loveless ever-anxious crowd,
        Ah ! from the soul itself must issue forth,
A light, a glory, a fair luminous cloud
        Enveloping the Earth—
And from the soul itself must there be sent
        A sweet and potent voice of its own birth,
Of all sweet sounds the soul and element !

This view, that Nature has but what our transient feelings
project into it, is closely akin to ' The Pathetic Fallacy '
denounced, not altogether fairly perhaps, by Ruskin in

*Modern Painters.* In Coleridge, however, it undoubtedly was " the sign of a morbid state of mind," described by the poet himself, in the poignant lines addressed to Wordsworth, as

> Sense of past youth, and manhood come in vain,
> And genius given, and knowledge won in vain.

Of the " archangel a little damaged " (*vide* Lamb's *Letter*), who settled at Highgate to struggle, not unsuccessfully, against his opiate lethargy, living in Beulah, and teaching a younger generation to keep in reverent touch with the Invisible world and the Eternal Will, and to find in the great Book of Nature " correspondencies and symbols of the spiritual world " (*Lay Sermons*)—of all this we learn nothing from his poems.

Wordsworth's Anglicanism is proclaimed in the *Ecclesiastical Sonnets ;* and Coleridge, having recanted his youthful " aberrations from the Catholic Faith," avowed himself " a self-convinced and disinterested lover of the Church of England " ; but can TENNYSON be claimed as a member of the English Church ? Perhaps an indocile one, out of sympathy with much of her doctrine and discipline ; but as a son of a parsonage, and as having had his children baptized by Anglican rites, he can scarcely be described as anything but an English Churchman. His mysticism came out with clearness only in his old age ; but, as we know from the official *Life*, it was strong in him from the first.

*The Holy Grail* is often cited as an attack upon mysticism ; but it makes no sweeping condemnation. It is a protest, needed when Tennyson wrote and no less needed to-day—one which most mystics would themselves endorse —against a selfish, unpurged craving for spiritual sensationalism at the expense of obvious duty. No blame attached to

Percivale's sister, the dedicated nun, to whom the vision came in the fulfilment of her appointed task of fast and prayer. For Galahad, too, the pure-hearted knight who was willing to lose himself, the quest was GOD's call and was crowned with success. Only those who, acting on unhallowed impulse, forgot earlier vows and nearer duties to seek a spiritual privilege for which they were morally unfit, were condemned to " follow wandering fires lost in the quagmires ". As for Arthur himself, he had his times of mystic attainment, which were not the less real because vouchsafed in the fulfilment of his GOD-given task. He rightly felt that he must

> Not wander from the alloted field
> Before his work be done ; but, being done,
> Let visions of the night or of the day
> Come, as they will ; and many a time they come,
> Until this earth he walks on seems not earth,
> This light that strikes his eyeball is not light,
> This air that smites his forehead is not air
> But vision—yea, his very hand and foot—
> In moments when he feels he cannot die,
> And knows himself no vision to himself,
> Nor the high GOD a vision, nor that One
> Who rose again : ye have seen what ye have seen.

It is most striking how many phases of mysticism are touched upon, more or less intimately, by Tennyson. In the consummate collection of *Poems* issued in 1842, apart even from the *Sir Galahad*, both of the main types of the mystic consciousness are portrayed. The Mystic Quest is authentically described in *The Voyage :* this gives an impression of irresponsible youthfulness, but a similar search is set forth more sedately in the much later *Merlin and the*

*Gleam*, to which the poet referred those who asked of him an autobiography. The erotic mysticism of the Spiritual Nuptials is pictured with sympathetic insight, and with Pre-Raphaelite touch, in *St Agnes' Eve*.

Ten years later came the recognition, if not the discovery, of the ultimate reality hidden beneath such natural phenomena as the *Flower in the Crannied Wall*, and, in *The Higher Pantheism*, a predication, somewhat hypothetical, perhaps, of what has been called ' the illuminated vision of the world,' with no dubious claim for the indwelling and abiding Presence in man's soul.

Then, with the birth of his eldest son, came *De Profundis*, with its conviction (first mooted in *The Two Voices*) of man's pre-existence " in the true world within the world we see," and the sense of life on earth as a mysterious exile. The complementary truth of the home-going, with a hint, possibly, of the doctrine of absorption with loss of identity, like a river or a tide absorbed in the ocean, is most exquisitely given in *Crossing the Bar*.[1]

Meanwhile, in the cxxivth section of *In Memoriam*, we have one of the classical utterances in English of that mystic mood of " mingled certitude and despair," in which a profound certitude of GOD's reality is met by a blank despair of the adequacy of thought to measure it or of language to express it :—

> That which we dare invoke to bless ;
> Our dearest faith ; our ghastliest doubt ;
> He, They, One, All ; within, without ;
> The Power in darkness Whom we guess.

---

[1] On all this, cf. Wordsworth's lines,

> Though inland far we be,
> Our souls have sight of that immortal sea
> Which brought us hither.

> I found Him not in world or sun,
>   Or eagle's wing, or insect's eye ;
>   Nor through the questions men may try,
> The petty cobwebs we have spun.
>
> If e'er when faith had fallen asleep,
>   I heard a voice ' Believe no more '
>   And heard an ever-breaking shore
> That tumbled in the Godless deep ;
>
> A warmth within the breast would melt
>   The freezing reason's colder part,
>   And like a man in wrath the heart
> Stood up and answer'd ' I have felt '.

Nearly all these scattered rays of mysticism, and others too, are brilliantly focussed in *The Ancient Sage*, a piece which gains additional interest from Tennyson's avowal that " the whole poem is very personal ". Resisting the temptation to reproduce it in its entirety, we must, at least, recall the reminiscence of his boyhood's mystical presentiments, and the later more definite experiences of which he wrote,

> More than once when I
> Sat all alone, revolving in myself
> The word that is the symbol of myself,
> The mortal limit of the Self was loos'd,
> And pass'd into the Nameless, as a cloud
> Melts into heaven.

Of the reality and frequency of this trance-condition, induced by silently repeating his own name, the Laureate assured his friends. To some it may suggest a pathological distemper rather than a mystical process. But, in conversation with Professor Faraday, Tennyson insisted, with a vehement asseveration, that " there was no delusion in the matter ; it was no nebulous ecstasy, but a state of transcendent wonder, associated with absolute clearness of mind ". And in a private letter he explained that " out of the intensity of the consciousness of individuality, the individuality itself seemed to resolve and fade away into boundless being, and this not a confused state, but the clearest of the clearest, the surest of the surest, utterly beyond words, where death was an almost laughable impossibility, the loss of personality (if so it were) seeming no extinction, but the only true life ".

In a juvenile poem, called *The Mystic* and printed by Hallam Tennyson in the *Memoir* of his father, the poet described how he had penetrated

> The cloud
> Which droops low-hung on either gate of life,
> Both birth and death ; he, in the centre fix'd,
> Saw far on either side through the grated gates
> Most pale and clear and lovely distances.
> He often lying broad awake, and yet
> Remaining from the body, and apart
> In intellect and power and will, hath heard
> Time flowing in the middle of the night,
> And all things creeping to a day of doom.

A similar enhancement of the consciousness, but this time occurring involuntarily, is indicated in section xcv. of *In Memoriam*, where Tennyson says that, as he communed in thought with his dead friend, his soul was

> Whirl'd
> About empyreal heights of thought,
> And came on That Which Is, and caught
> The deep pulsations of the world.

Any one reading the whole section cannot fail to note how closely his account corresponds with St. Augustine's account (*Confessions*, xvii. 17) of how his consciousness, "with the flash of one terrible glance, arrived at That Which Is ; and then I saw Thy ' invisible things understood by the things which are made,' but I lacked strength to fix my gaze thereon, and, my weakness being struck back, I returned to my accustomed ways ".

There need be named but one more piece, the haunting *Far, Far away*, in which, in his eightieth year, the Laureate recalled once more his earliest intimations of other-worldliness. His son describes how, at this time, lying convalescent after severe illness, and gazing out of his window across a wide expanse of country, the ancient sage would say that he was having " wonderful thoughts about GOD and the universe, and felt as if looking into the other world ". On another occasion he exclaimed, " My most passionate desire is to have a clearer and fuller vision of GOD : the soul seems to me one with GOD, how I cannot tell ". The man who spoke thus, who in the presence of doubt " stood up and answered, ' I have felt,' " and used his talent so consistently for impressing on his generation his " strong feeling as to the reality of the Unseen," even if he did in *The Holy Grail* reprove those who took up psychic investigation as a fashionable toy, may be called, without any fear of contradiction, a mystic of the true succession.

FREDERICK MYERS could have told us a good deal about Tennyson's psychical experiences, if the Laureate's son had not explicitly asked him to suppress that side of their intimacy. And even in his lines *To Tennyson*, he barely hints at it, speaking rather of the " soul that yearned to soar and sing, enamour'd of immortal air ".

This " fusion of a minor poet and an amateur *savant* "

—as Myers styles himself in the autobiographical fragment, from which several passages are borrowed below—was, like Tennyson, a son of a parsonage ; and, although he lost his father when eight years of age, he had in his mother a mentor of " profound religious conviction ". From his earliest years the boy seemed pre-occupied with unseen things—anguished by the thought of a mole dying without hope of resurrection, unspeakably shocked by the suggested possibility of the soul's annihilation at death, and hoping that GOD might give " just once, such a vision of Him as would make us happy all our lives after ".

At the age of sixteen " a kind of conversion " was brought about by the reading of the *Phaedo*, Plato's dialogue on immortality, and for six years his only effectual creed was a fervid Hellenism, which fed the intellect and emotions but, while detaching him from sordid interests, encouraged pride —so he humbly confesses. This phase ended in a species of Dark Night, with a numb loneliness of soul. Meanwhile his Christian faith, though not a living one, had not been repudiated ; and in his twenty-third year it was rekindled and inflamed by a revivalistic conversion. He claimed to have reached Christianity's " heart of fire " by " an inner door," but to have escaped " its encumbring forms and dogmas ". In other words, he luxuriated in its emotional refreshments, but declined its disciplinary restraints.

To this phase belongs the lengthy poem, *St. Paul*, which, in spite of its too conscious art, its studied cadences and insistent alliteration, seems to give evidence of experiential knowledge, as in the following stanzas, placed in the mouth of the Apostle :—

> Oh, could I tell, ye surely would believe it !
> Oh, could I only say what I have seen !

> How could I tell, or how can ye receive it,
>     How, till He bringeth you where I have been?

Then, picturing the disconsolate longing of a Greek bard for inspiration and the sudden fruition of his hopes, he adds—

> So even I athirst for His inspiring,
>     I who have talk'd with Him forget again ;
> Yes, many days with sobs and with desiring,
>     Offer to GOD a patience and a pain.
>
> Then through the mid complaint of my confession,
>     Then through the pang and passion of my prayer,
> Leaps with a start the shock of His possession,
>     Thrills me and touches, and the Lord is there.
>
> Whoso hath felt the Spirit of the Highest
>     Cannot confound, nor doubt Him, nor deny :
> Yea, with one voice, O world, though thou deniest,
>     Stand thou on that side, for on this am I.

This sense of certitude is also expressed very finely in some private letters of this date (1865). In this period, too, presumably, the shorter piece, *The Saint*, was written : here is the last stanza, describing the consummation of a nun's tireless devotion :—

> Yea, when the sense of earth is rapt and gone,—
>     No dream nor vision nor spirit nor any ghost,
> A solemn Presence seems to light upon
>     The wafer of the Host.
> Then surely from her trance she would not fall
>     Were bolts on thunderbolts about her hurl'd,
> Nor in her ecstasy would heed at all
>     The blazing of the world :
> But when the last, the day of days, shall come
>     And by strange hosts the space of air is trod,

And Christ the Lord descends to gather home
    His saints, elect of GOD :
Then shalt Thou find that woman waiting there,
    And with Thine own hands wake her wonderfully,
And lift her from her last most precious prayer
    To Thee, my GOD, to Thee.

But the phase of Christian assurance, with its acknowledgment of " the splendid generosity of GOD," did not last long. Possibly, the growth of the soul was artificially promoted by hot-house methods. He became conscious, in any case, of " an inward make-believe "—perhaps the " hollow mysticism " of which he speaks as traceable in some of the witnesses examined in the course of his later psychical researches. He was, not unnaturally, alienated by supposing—how erroneously ! — that Christianity hindered the soul from gazing onward " beyond the problem of one's own salvation ". With a rare humility, he admitted that his nature was " well fitted to bring out the defects of any form of religion " ; and, perhaps now, with his fuller light, he would admit that he would have done better to have cultivated the institutional element of Christianity as thoroughly as he did the mystical.

He now passed, as he tells us, " through various moods of philosophical or emotional hope, which are reflected in *The Implicit Promise of Immortality*, the *Ode to Nature, Ammergau*, and other poems written 1869-73 ". The first-named of those poems will stand " the hideous test of extracts " : it is notable, from a literary point of view, for its successful handling of the heroic couplet, here made musical as never since Marlowe's *Hero and Leander*.

    I know it, such a one these eyes have seen
    About the world with his unworldly mien,

And often idly hopeless, often bent
On some tumultuous deed and vehement,
Because his spirit he can nowise fit
To the world's ways and settled rule of it,
But through contented thousands travels on
Like a sad heir in disinherison,
And rarely by great thoughts or brave emprise
Comes out about his life's perplexities,
Looks through the rifted cloudland, and sees clear
Fate at his feet and the high GOD anear.
Ah, let him tarry on those heights, nor dream
Of other founts than that Aonian stream !
Since short and fierce, then hated, drown'd, and dim
Shall most men's chosen pleasures come to him,—
Not made for such things, nor for long content
With the poor toys of this imprisonment.
Aye, should he sit one afternoon beguil'd
By some such joy as makes the wise a child,
Yet, if at twilight to his ears shall come
A distant music through the city's hum,
So slight a thing as this shall wake again
The incommunicable hopeless pain,
Until his soul so yearns to reunite
With her Prime Source, her Master and Delight,
As if some loadstone drew her, and brain and limb
Ached with her struggle to get through to Him.
And is this then delusion ?   Can it be
That like the rest high Heaven is phantasy ?
Can GOD'S implicit promise be but one
Among so many visions all undone ?

.     .     .     .     .     .     .     .

For some, methinks, in no less noble wise
Divine prevision kindles in the eyes,
When all base thoughts like frightened harpies flown
In her own beauty leave the soul alone ;

When Love,—not rosy-flush'd as he began,
But love, still Love, the prison'd GOD in man,—
Shows his face glorious, shakes his banner free,
Cries like a captain for Eternity :—
O halcyon air across the storms of youth,
O trust him, he is true, he is one with Truth !
Nay, is he Christ ? I know not, no man knows
The right name of the heavenly Anterôs,—
But here is GOD, whatever GOD may be ;
And whomsoe'er we worship, this is He.

Then followed for Myers a period of blank agnosticism,
" which sometimes was a dull pain borne with joyless
doggedness, sometimes flashed into a horror of reality that
made the world spin before one's eyes ". This may be described, perhaps, in such poems as *Solomon* and *Pallida
Morte Futura.*

Towards the end of 1871, Myers had taken what seems
to many the retrogressive step of seeking knowledge of the
Unseen World from the study of ghosts and similar phenomena. He frankly owns to an initial " repugnance to re-
entering by the scullery-window the heavenly mansion out
of which I had been kicked through the front-door ". But
two years later he had a personal experience which deeply
impressed him, as if a panel had yielded in the walls of his
prison-house. He now " moved through a strange pano-
rama of scenes of solitary exaltation, of bewildering introduction into incommunicable things ". It did not take him
long, however, to become dissatisfied with the ordinary
methods of Spiritualism ; and in 1882 he founded the
Society for Psychical Research, with its much more cautious
and scientific procedure. Henceforth, until his death in
1901, he devoted himself with most laudable patience and

sincerity to the investigation of " the $x$ region in human faculty ".   His final creed—it was scarcely a creed, for he claimed scientific demonstration for it—contained three clauses : the first proclaimed man's survival after death, the second, " the registration in the Universe " of everything ever done or felt or thought, and the third, " a progressive moral evolution towards an infinitely distant goal ".   As to practice, he recognized the importance of purgation, but insisted that its sole end should be " to intensify each his own being, a pulse of the existence of all ".   But throughout this period of psychologism Myers did not lose touch altogether with Christianity.   He was married by the Church's rites, and believed that then he and his bride

> For a moment rose and were alone
> With Him Who was our own.

He declined to contrast his creed with the Christian faith, regarding it rather as " a scientific development of the attitude and teaching of Christ," Whom he looked upon as " a Revealer of immortality absolutely unique, the incomparable pioneer of all wisdom that shall be learnt concerning unseen things ".

Before speaking of his great prose work on human personality, reference may be made to the poem entitled *A Cosmic Outlook*, mystical, no doubt, but hardly Christian ; and two stanzas may be quoted from *Sunrise*, in which words of adoration are followed thus :—

> From above us and from under,
> In the ocean and the thunder,
> Thou preludest to the wonder
>   Of the Paradise to be :
> For a moment we may guess Thee
> From Thy creatures that confess Thee

When the morn and even bless Thee,
And Thy smile is on the sea.

Then from something seen or heard,
Whether forests softly stirred,
Or the speaking of a word,
Or the singing of a bird,
      Cares and sorrows cease :
For a moment on the soul
Falls the rest that maketh whole,
      Falls the endless peace.

*Human Personality and its Survival of Bodily Death* has, from two points of view, an important bearing on mysticism : in the first place, as Myers' final exposition of the theory of the subliminal self, and secondly, as an attempt to hoist the materialist with his own petard.    Setting out, apparently, from Leibnitz's conviction of subconscious perceptions of incalculable number and influence, Myers definitely formulated the theory, now very widely accepted, of the three concentric circles of human personality : the central self, the marginal self, and the subliminal self, the first two differing only in degree, but the last lying beneath the threshold of consciousness.    In Professor William James's brilliant epitome of the theory we read that " it contains such things as all our momentarily inactive memories, and it harbours the springs of all our obscurely motived passions, impulses, likes, dislikes, and prejudices.    Our intuitions, hypotheses, fancies, superstitions, persuasions, convictions, and in general all our non-rational operations come from it. It is the source of our dreams, and apparently they return to it.    In it arise whatever mystical experiences we may have."    In all this, what some are inclined to resent is the treatment of the mystic as a ' subject,' whose ' case ' is psychologically explicable—an interpenetration of the subliminal and supraliminal consciousnesses, or even a mere matter of reminiscence—something, at any rate, which may enable rationalists to admit the genuineness, while rejecting the reality, of the mystic's experiences.  Not that Myers himself desires to do this ; but is it equally certain that all who adopt his general conception are as guileless ?

Myers hoped that he would confute materialists by facts, a task not, perhaps, quite so hopeless as the overthrow of militarism by military means, of which much is being heard at the time when this is being written.  But, apart from Sir Oliver Lodge and a few others, scientists have proved to be " like the deaf adder which refuseth to hear the voice of the charmer, charm he never so wisely ".  Believers, too, are inclined to ignore, if not to despise, a proof of immortality which is based on ghostly apparitions, haunted houses, and mediumistic communications.  Récéjac's measured protest against a superstition for the unknown is entirely to the point : " the mysticism which we have in view has nothing at all in common with mere wonder and curiosity ; it has no impulse towards the Absolute to discover ' the new,' but its impulse is to discover ' the better ' ".  Myers' industry and candour in investigation are beyond all praise, and his purity of motive beyond question.  Very possibly souls have been, and will be helped by the " experimental approaches to spiritual knowledge " to which he attached such great importance ; but for those who " know Christ and the power of His resurrection," no resource to psychical research can make the hope of immortality any brighter or more certain.

Any attempt to sum up GEORGE MacDONALD in a

few pages is foredoomed to failure; for his was an expansive personality and a prolific pen. Despite an interest in ghosts and second-sight, he was in many respects the antithesis of Frederick Myers—with a conviction of immortality that was in no need of scientific support, but with a copiousness of output that did need a less sparing pruning-hook and a more critical revision. His gifts were sown too broadcast and not cultivated intensively enough to secure him that niche in the temple of literary fame which he might have won, had he been less concerned to rouse the hearts of the many, rather than to charm the ears of the few.

During his life-time, MacDonald was best known as a novelist ; but it is not at all certain that his poetry will not live longer than his prose. However that may be, a study of his greatest novels is essential to the understanding of the man. For that purpose *David Elginbrod*, *Robert Falconer*, and *Sir Gibbie* may be unhesitatingly named, in spite of their baffling, but decidedly piquant, Scottish dialect ; and, for the sake of including an English novel, *Thomas Wingfold* may be added. All these help us to understand MacDonald, who could not help making his favourite characters illustrate and express his own feelings and convictions. David and Robert, with their unwavering confidence in GOD's fatherly love and wisdom, accepting every circumstance, and facing every perplexity in life with an attitude too robust to be called resignation—these are MacDonald himself. As also, in spite of superficial differences, is Sir Gibbie, the self-forgetful and love-lavishing mute, with his inborn apprehension of Nature's spirituality and his peasant-taught knowledge and love of GOD. In *Thomas Wingfold*, Polworth is the main mouthpiece of the author's religious philosophy, while the eponymous hero learns the secret that " all about us in earth and air, wherever eye and ear can reach, there is a power ever breathing itself forth in signs, now in a daisy, now in a wind-waft, a cloud, a sunset ; a power that holds constant and sweetest relation with the dark and silent world within us ; that the same GOD Who is in us, and upon Whose tree we are the buds if not yet the flowers, also is all about us—inside, the Spirit, outside, the Word ; and the two are ever trying to meet in us ; and when they meet, then the sign without and the longing within become one in light, and the man no more walketh in darkness, but knoweth whither he goeth ".

In all four of these stories it is impossible to miss the adoring attitude towards GOD's Fatherhood, with its corollary of man's brotherhood. The prayer in *David Elginbrod :* " Come Thou, an' abide in us, and tak' us to bide in Thee ; an' syne gin we be a' in Thee, we canna be that far frae ane anither " ; Robert's search for an earthly parent which was all the while bringing him the knowledge of the heavenly Father ; Gibbie's passionate clinging even to a worthless father, as a type of the blissful knowledge of " a Father of fatherhood, who never slumbers nor sleeps but holds all the sleeping in His ever-waking bosom " ; Polworth's distress that so few seem " able even to entertain the idea of the indwelling in them of the original power of their life " : these are but a few instances of MacDonald's reiteration of his gospel of the Fatherhood. Indeed, his mysticism flows entirely from his conviction of the immanence of the Eternal Father. In one of his *Unspoken Sermons*—they fill three volumes of some of the freshest and deepest exegesis in the English language—speaking of the parental relation, he says that " GOD making human affairs after His own thoughts, they are therefore such as to be the best teachers of love to Him and love to our neighbour ". And he adds that " thousands more would find it easy to love GOD if they had not such miserable types of Him in the self-seeking, impulse-driven, purposeless, faithless beings who are all they have for father and mother ".

He was himself abundantly blessed in his father, a fact which he would wish mentioned in every notice of his life, and to which he has not failed to bear repeated witness in his verse, as in the dedication of his second volume of poems :—

> Yet most I thank thee, not for any deed,
> But for the sense thy living self did breed
> Of Fatherhood still at the great world's core.

The home atmosphere was able to counteract the narrow Calvinism which the boy had to breathe in church ; and it was an unusually broad-minded and wide-hearted Congregational minister who began his ministry at Arundel in 1850. But his ministerial career was a very brief one ; for what could the average churchgoer of Arundel—or of anywhere else—be expected to make of the poet who was evolving from his inner consciousness *Within and Without*, and of the preacher who cared nothing for traditional orthodoxy if contradicted by his deepest convictions ? An Anglican congregation, recognizing its impotence in view of ' the parson's freehold,' would have apathetically acquiesced in the discordance between pulpit and pew, or in the case of individuals, would have dropped the outward observance of religion without any sense of loss. And yet the English Church is entitled to some measure of satisfaction in the recollection that George MacDonald in later life joined her communion.  At the time, however, when requested, kindly but firmly, to resign his pastorate at Arundel, he retired into lay communion, and henceforth sought a livelihood by teaching, journalism, and literary production.  His short sojourn in Manchester, before settling in London, was memorable for bringing him under the stimulating influence of A. J. Scott, Edward Irving's early assistant, and into close touch with the Swedenborgian, Henry Septimus Sutton, whose mystical verse has never received its due recognition.[1]

MacDonald's verse, like his prose, is excessive in quantity and unequal in quality, sometimes sinking to triviality of thought as well as carelessness of form.  The longer poems which especially illustrate his mystical standing are *Within and Without*, *The Hidden Life*, *Somnium Mystici*, and *The Diary of an Old Soul:* to each of these a few lines must be devoted.

*Within and Without* is a dramatic poem, which won the approval of Tennyson and other sound judges, though it could never have succeeded as a drama, for MacDonald is always himself, and the catastrophe is not sufficiently accounted for.  Significant preludes to each of the four acts supply the place of the argument, while the plot reveals the progress of a soul from the recognized need of GOD to the full knowledge of the Father.  In the 1st Act, Julian voices the intolerable emptiness of a soul which feels that it is created for GOD to fill :—

My soul leans towards Him ; stretches out its arms,
And waits expectant.  Speak to me, my GOD ;

---

[1] He lies outside the scheme of this volume, but his mystical publications may be noted : *The Evangel of Love* (prose), 1847 ; *Quinquenergia*, 1854 (subsequently suppressed, except *Rosie's Diary*) ; Collected *Poems* (1886).  Some of his verse, but not very characteristic specimens, may be read in Palgrave's *Treasury of Sacred Song*.

And let me know the living Father cares
For me, even me ; for this one of His children.
Hast Thou no word for me ?   I am Thy thought.
GOD, let Thy mighty heart beat into mine,
And let mine answer as a pulse of Thine.

.     .     .     .     .     .     .     .

I am an emptiness for Thee to fill ;
My soul a cavern for Thy sea.   I lie
Diffus'd, abandoning myself to Thee. . . .
I will look up, if life should fail in looking !
Ah me !   A stream cut from my parent-spring !
Ah me !   A life lost from its father-life !

In the 3rd Act he can make thanksgiving for the answer
to that prayer, far different though it was from what he had
hoped to receive.   Part of that answer was the gift of a
daughter,

Come as a little Christ from heaven to earth,
To call me ' Father,' that my heart may know
What Father means, and turn its eyes to GOD.

Still importunate in his search for GOD, an inner voice
directs him to Christ, and, at first, failing to recognize the
One-ness of Father and Son, he regards this as a rejection ;
but, having learnt that " from out Christ's eyes God
looked," he can address Him thus :—

Lord of Thyself and me, through the sore grief
Which Thou didst bear to bring us back to GOD,
Or rather, bear in being unto us
Thy own pure shining self of love and truth !
When I have learnt to think Thy radiant thoughts,
To love the truth beyond the power to know it,
To bear my light, as Thou Thy heavy cross,
Nor ever feel a martyr for Thy sake,

> But an unprofitable servant still—
> My highest sacrifice my simplest duty
> Imperative and unavoidable,
> Less than which *All*, were nothingness and waste ;
> When I have lost myself in other men,
> And found myself in Thee—the Father then
> Will come with Thee, and will abide with me.

But so intense is his preoccupation with his soul's need that his wife becomes gradually estranged and at last leaves him. This blow, too, he accepts as a necessary step in his unitive way. At first he boldly tells GOD that, without her, his heart can never feel satisfaction ; but soon he recognizes the falsity of this attitude, and withdraws his words :—

> Oh yes ; Thou art enough for me, my GOD ;
> Part of Thyself is she, else never mine :
> My need of her is but Thy thought of me ;
> She is the offspring of Thy beauty, GOD ;
> Yea, of the womanhood that dwells in Thee :
> Thou wilt restore her to my very soul.

Finally, in a higher state of being, where GOD's love is perfectly revealed and perfectly reflected, husband, wife, and child are reunited in " an infinite embrace," and the poem ends with Julian's avowal :—

> O GOD, Thy thoughts, Thy ways are not as ours :
> They fill our longing hearts up to the brim.

*A Hidden Life* is an idyll of a farmer's son, to whom love, unrequited, unavowed, and even unguessed, brings illumination. " GOD," the poet says,

> And not woman, is the heart of all.
> But she, as priestess of the visible earth,
> Holding the key, herself most beautiful,

Had come to him and flung the portals wide.
He enter'd : every beauty was a glass
That gleam'd the woman back upon his view.
Shall I not rather say : each beauty gave
Its own soul up to him who worshipp'd her,
For that his eyes were open now to see ?

. . . . . .

Each morning now was a fresh boon to him ;
Each wind a spiritual power upon his life ;
Each individual animal did share
A common being with him ; every kind
Of flower from every other was distinct,
Uttering that for which alone it was—
Its something human, wrapt in other veil.

Later, he has an attack of hæmorrhage (an autobiographical touch which should not be missed) :—

And GOD, Who speaks to man at door and lattice,
Glorious in stars and winds and flowers and waves,
Not seldom shuts the door and dims the pane,
That, isled in calm, His still small voice may sound
The clearer, by the hearth, in the inner room.

The youth sets himself, not simply to submit to GOD's
will, but to echo *ex animo* St. Chrysostom's " Thanks be to
GOD for everything ".   " Father ! " he cries,

We need Thy winter as Thy spring ;
We need Thy earthquakes as Thy summer showers ;
But through them all Thy strong arms carry us,
Thy strong heart bearing large share in our grief.
Because Thou lovest goodness more than joy
In them Thou lovest, Thou dost let them grieve :
We must not vex Thee with our peevish cries,
But look into Thy face and hold Thee fast,
And say, ' O Father, Father ! ' when the pain

Seems overstrong.   Remember our poor hearts :
We never grasp the zenith of the time !
We have no spring except in winter-prayers !
But we believe—alas, we only hope !—
That one day we shall thank Thee perfectly
For every disappointment, pang, and shame,
That drove us to the bosom of Thy love.

And when death is imminent, he pens a letter to his lady, revealing the secret history of his love, and begging her to justify his faith in womanhood.

The *Somnium Mystici* needs no comment ; its inner significance is sufficiently intimated in its closing lines :—

Lord, I have spoken a poor parable,
    In which I would have said, Thy name alone
    Is the one secret lying in Truth's well,
Thy voice the hidden charm in every tone,
    Thy face the heart of every flower on earth,
    Its vision the one hope ; for every moan
Thy love the cure !   O sharer of the birth
    Of little children seated on Thy knee !
    O human GOD ! I laugh with sacred mirth
To think how all the laden shall go free ;
    For, though the vision tarry, in healing ruth
    One morn the eyes that shone in Galilee
Will dawn upon them, full of grace and truth,
    And Thy own love—the vivifying core
    Of every love in heart of age or youth,
Of every hope that sank 'neath burden sore !

*A Book of Strife in the form of the Diary of an Old Soul* is a more important work than any of the above ; and its importance will be best indicated by recalling some of the judgments passed upon it by others. Ruskin, for instance, pronounced it " one of the three great sacred poems of the nineteenth century " : and, on the issue of a new edition, a reviewer in *The Spectator* declared that " with some it has almost replaced à Kempis as an aid to devotional thought and inspiration ". The poet's son, Greville, speaks of it as " witnessing an evolution from keen sympathy with Nature to ardent oneness with the Godhead ". It provides a seven-lined meditation for each day in the year, and may be described, broadly, as suggesting—in spite of marked dissimilarity in certain details both of form and spirit—a combination of some of the best features of Wordsworth's *Prelude* and St. Augustine's *Confessions*. One line of self-criticism may be quoted : " How oft I say the same thing in these lines ! " True enough, the same points are dwelt upon again and again, but never with mere repetition ; and, although it is best to restrict one's reading to the daily portion, duly pondered, yet a prolonged perusal from cover to cover produces no weariness nor sense of tedium. From first to last, the chief refrain is the longing for closer union with the Father. Almost the first word is this :—

> I breathe, I think, I love, I live but Thee :
> Oh breathe, oh think—O Love, live into me.

But this with no self-centred object ; for these are almost the last words :—

> It must be possible that the soul made
> Should absolutely meet the soul that makes ;
> Then, in that bearing soul, meet every other
> There also born, each sister and each brother :
> Lord, till I meet Thee thus, life is delay'd ;
> I am not I until that morning breaks,
> Not I until my consciousness eternal wakes.

Throughout Christ is thought of as " Great elder Brother of my second birth," the imitation of Whose outward

example is made possible by His inward dwelling.  Here
is a characteristic prayer :—

> O Christ, my Life, possess me utterly.
> Take me and make a little Christ of me.
> If I am anything but Thy Father's son,
> 'Tis something not yet from the darkness won.

Another constantly recurring thought is suggested by the
symbol of the spark from the central flame.  " From the
sun-heart I came, of love a spark " ;  but so did others, too ;
therefore,

> O GOD of man, my heart would worship all
> My fellow-men, the flashes from Thy fire;
> Them in good sooth my lofty kindred call,
> Born of the same one heart, the perfect Sire;
> Love of my kind alone can set me free.

MacDonald is not at all afraid of the truth of GOD's
wrath : the Divine indignation is accepted as " love turn'd
on the evil that would part love's throng " : he sees that
GOD's " anger scathes because it needs must bless ".

He is no stranger to the Dark Night of the Soul, but not
in its most poignant mood : his is

> The Night
> When crumpled daisies shut gold sadness in,
> And some do hang the head for lack of light,
> Sick almost unto death with absence-blight.

He knows times

> When all things common seem,
> When all is dust, and self the centre clod,
> When grandeur is a hopeless, foolish dream,
> And anxious care more reasonable than GOD.

And at another time he has to pray, " Loosen in me the
hold of visible things " ;  but, so far as the will is concerned,

he surrenders all secondary delights and imperfect loves for
the satisfaction which St. Paul knew in " having nothing
and yet possessing all things " in the perfect love.

> Take all Thy outside fair ;
> Draw nearer, taking, and to my sober thinking,
> Thou bringst them nearer all.

He knows, not a continuous, but a continual Presence ;
for, even when immersed in what would be called by some
secular occupations, there comes

> A pause at length—oh, sudden then,
> Back throbs Thy tide with rush exultant rare,
> And for a gentle moment I divine
> Thy dawning Presence flush my tremulous air.

He recalls his youth, when often " windows would open
into Heaven," and deplores a dulling, with age, of " the
heart's swift fluttering beat " ;

> But a quiet hope that keeps its household seat
> Is better than recurrent glories fleet.

Death, of course, is contemplated always as a Home-
going, and the Beatific Vision is desiderated as the time
when " I shall love as Thou, and love in Thee ".

Of MacDonald's shorter pieces, mention may be made
of *Love is Home*, *The World* (thought of as nursery,
playground, and schoolroom, in which we must expect in-
completeness and perplexity), and *A Prayer for the Past*,
with its touching reminiscences of his boyhood, and with this
moral :—

> And are we not at home in Thee,
> And all this world a vision'd show,
> That, knowing what abroad is, we
> What Home is too may know ?

*Blessed are the Meek* develops an attractive interpretation of the earth-inheritance, reminding us of some of John Norris's poems.   It ends thus :—

> Each hue, each harmony divine,
> The holy world about,
> Its soul will send forth into mine,
> My soul to widen out.
>
> And thus the great earth I shall hold,
> A perfect gift of Thine ;
> Richer by these, a thousandfold,
> Than if broad lands were mine.

But MacDonald could not find full satisfaction in Nature ; and in the poem called *God not Gift* he said of the wind and the sea and the cloud :—

> O Father, these are but Thy signs !—
> For Thee I hunger, not for these !

In this connexion, his words in that delightful anthology of sacred verse, *England's Antiphon*, may be recalled : " Some one must yet do what Wordsworth has left almost unattempted, namely—set forth the sympathy of Nature with the aspirations of the spirit that is born of GOD, born again, I mean, in the recognition of the child's relation to the Father ".   It would be interesting, but too big a task to undertake here, to cite the passages in which he himself touched on that aspect of Nature : it is, as already implied, one of the striking points in his prose picture of the development of Thomas Wingfold's soul.

The symbol of *Light* is finely treated in the poem named after that

> Universal something sent
> To shadow forth the Excellent.

" Such symbols," he wrote in *England's Antiphon*,
" are the true bodies of the true ideas. For this service
mainly what we term Nature was called into being, namely
—to furnish forms for truth, for without form truth cannot
be uttered." And he went on to sound a warning note
against the danger of using symbols logically, and narrowing
them down until their glory vanishes and they wither into
' apples of Sodom '.

To name but two more, out of many notable poems, *De
Profundis* deals with the doctrine of the mystical death,
and *Approaches* is the title of a series of quaint distichs
conceived and expressed quite in the vein of Blake.

No adequate impression of George MacDonald as a
mystic could be conveyed without reference to his fairy tales,
which, like his novels, are frequently helped on by verse.
The first of these, *Phantastes*, although outwardly influenced
by Fouqué's *Undine* and by the Arthurian legends, is one
of the most original books in English literature. The hero's
name, Anodos, may be taken, and was perhaps intended
by the author to be taken in two senses : first, a pathless
one, and secondly, one upon an upward way. Anodos
suddenly passed into another, more vivid existence, where
he was haunted by his shadow, the part of his nature which
vulgarised all that it fell upon. His main achievement was
getting rid of that lower self ; but first he had to learn the
truth in the lines :—

> Oh, well for him who breaks his dream
> With the blow that ends the strife ;
> And waking, knows the peace that flows
> Around the noise of life.

Then, from that " trampled self," " another self seemed
to arise, like a white spirit from a dead man " ; and " he

who set out to find his ideal, came back rejoicing that he had lost his shadow ". The book is simply crammed with mystical teaching, and requires more than one reading to extract its full value.

The main lessons of *Phantastes* are repeated, with a surer touch, in *Lilith*, a book in which the *dramatis personæ* of the Talmud, Adam and his two wives, Lilith and Eve, are borrowed. Adam convinces the hero, Vane, that there is a door, " one step through which carries us into a world very much other than this," not, as most suppose, a door out, but " a door in ".

> Ah, the two worlds ! so strangely are they one,
> And yet so measurelessly wide apart !
> Oh, had I liv'd the bodiless alone
> And from defiling sense held safe my heart,
> Then had I scap'd the canker and the smart,
> Scap'd life-in-death, scap'd misery's endless moan !

Vane, having learnt the necessity of " growing the other way," and becoming a Little One, gains the freedom of that inner world, which he thus describes : " Everything showed me, by its shape and colour, its indwelling idea—the informing thought, that is, which was its being and sent it out. My bare feet seemed to love every plant they trod upon. The world and my being, its life and mine, were one. The microcosm and the macrocosm were atoned at length in harmony ! I lived in everything ; everything entered and lived in me. . . . Sense after sense, hitherto asleep, awoke in me—sense after sense indescribable, because no correspondent words, no likenesses' or imaginations exist wherewith to describe them. Full indeed—yet ever expanding, ever making room to receive—was the conscious being where things kept entering by so many open doors ! "

Neither *Phantastes* nor *Lilith* is, strictly speaking, a

book for children ; but *The Day-boy and the Night-girl*,
*The Princess and the Goblin* (both inculcating faith in
the unseen world), and *At the Back of the North Wind*
(where there is the central peace), are genuinely children's
stories, and in each MacDonald strives to initiate the little
ones into eternal mysteries. Indeed, in well-nigh everything
he wrote he was deliberately a mystagogue ; and the mysticism which he taught was pre-eminently practical and unselfish. Of a character in *Salted by Fire*, he says, " He
was what the parson called a mystic, and yet the most
practical man in the neighbourhood, making the best shoes
because the Word of the Lord abode in him ". Elsewhere
he says, " To find GOD in others is better than to grow
solely in the discovery of Him in ourselves, if indeed the
latter were possible ". And here, finally, is his closing
comment on the text, " Father, into Thy hands I commend
my spirit " : " We may commend any brother, any sister
to the common Fatherhood. And there will be moments
when, filled with that spirit which is the Lord, nothing will
ease our hearts of their love but the commending of all men,
all our brothers, all our sisters, to the one Father. Nor
shall we ever know that repose in the Father's hands, that
rest of the Holy Sepulchre, which the Lord knew when
the agony of death was over, . . . till the Fatherhood is
fully revealed to us in the love of the brothers. . . . Never
shall we know Him aright until we rejoice and exult for
our 'race that He is *the* Father." It is because Mac-
Donald's mystical doctrine of the Divine Fatherhood is so
balanced and so practical, and because (as one is inclined
to fear) his writings are beginning to fall into neglect, that
what some may regard as disproportionate space has been
allotted to him in these pages.

This chapter is necessarily imperfect ; for, not to speak of Roden Noel (a Churchman with strong Pantheistic tendencies, as revealed in *Pan* and in *The Modern Faust*) and Edward Dowden (who wrote his exquisite sonnet-sequence, *The Inner Life*, before he broke loose from " the Anglican paddock ")—it would be only at an expense of space quite impossible here that anything like adequate consideration could be given to the work of such living writers of distinction as, *inter alia*, John Rhoades (whose *Out of the Silence* and *City of Five Gates* should be missed by no lover of mystical poetry) and D. H. S. Nicholson (whose modesty has unfairly excluded his own work from *The Oxford Book of Mystical Verse*). But, before passing on to consider a group of parson-poets, it seems necessary to touch on the work of two mystical poets of outstanding merit, who were not, however, members of the Anglican Church—Coventry Patmore and Francis Thompson.

COVENTRY PATMORE was the singer of wedded love as the sacramental symbol—the sure witness, the effectual sign, and the instrument, as our Articles might say—of the love betwixt the soul and GOD. This doctrine, it is needless to remark, was far from original : something very like it has been noticed more than once in these pages already, and the source whence Patmore derived it will shortly be named ; for its philosophic rationale the reader may be referred to Coleridge's *Anima Poetæ* (1895), p. 133.

Patmore's published verse falls pretty sharply into two divisions, of which (as will appear shortly) the first might be called the angelico-domestic, and the second, the incognito-erotic. The water-shed of these two lyric streams was the transference of his ecclesiastical allegiance from Canterbury to Rome. Of his first period the main influence was his first wife, " a ray of GOD," whose devout Anglicanism might have saved the poet from the tasteless rodomontade of describing Popery as the only flag " which gentlemen might doff to ". A friendship with H. S. Sutton (*vide supra*) introduced him to the teaching of Swedenborg, whose *Conjugal Love* he assimilated with enthusiasm. From the literary point of view, Tennyson, in the rustic and idyllic vein of *Dora* and *The Gardener's Daughter*, was the supreme influence of this first phase.

Of the second period, a woman was again, probably, the most potent influence, his second wife,[1] a Roman Catholic, whose wealth secured him leisure, later on, to cultivate with ardour his mystical bent. Like so many neophytes, he became, as a Romanist, an unusually embittered partisan, and frankly adopted the role of a party-poet. His Swedenborgianism was never abandoned, but it was now qualified by devotion to St. Thomas Aquinas and St. John of the Cross ; while Crashaw became his literary model, instead of Tennyson.

To his earlier period belong *The Angel in the House*, and its sequel, *The Victories of Love*. They were held up to scorn by some, extravagantly praised by others. Some, like Swinburne, stigmatized Patmore as the prattling idyllist of the Deanery parlour ; others, like Ruskin, thought it " impossible to read him too often or too carefully ". To-day, not a few would be willing to have a prose précis of the intervening conversations and events, if they could retain in verse the Preludes of *The Angel in the House*.

Great results often flow from small beginnings, and the

---

[1] *Tired Memory* was the *apologia pro nuptiis secundis* ; no apology was offered for the third marriage, however.

process by which Patmore ultimately became the most erotic of mystics began, apparently, in his idealization of the tendency of every ' lady's man ' to scintillate in female society, no matter how dull things may have seemed previously. The reference is to the second Prelude of Canto II, entitled *Love at Large*.   In the Prelude, *Heaven and Earth*, to Canto VII, the poet asks, *apropos* of love, why men should " deny the flower because its roots are in the earth "—a fair question which might, however, provoke some critics to ask if the poet did not manage sometimes to make the flower a trifle earthy.

The crisis induced by the difficulty of finding a suitable occasion on which to make an offer of marriage was marked by a mystical experience, which is partially described in the Prelude, *Life of Life* :—

> What's that, which, ere I spake was gone ?
> So joyful and intense a spark
> That, whilst o'erhead the wonder shone,
> The day, before but dull, grew dark.
> I do not know ; but this I know,
> That, had the splendour liv'd a year,
> The truth that I some heavenly show
> Did see, could not be now more clear.
> This know I too : might mortal breath
> Express the passion then inspir'd,
> Evil would die a natural death,
> And nothing transient be desir'd ;
> And error from the soul would pass,
> And leave the senses pure and strong
> As sunbeams.   But the best, alas,
> Has neither memory nor tongue !

One more Prelude, *The Prototype*, must be given as containing the germ of all his later philosophy :—

Lo, there, whence love, life, light are pour'd,
    Veil'd with impenetrable rays,
Amidst the presence of the Lord
    Co-equal Wisdom laughs and plays.
Female and male GOD made the man ;
    His image is the whole, not half ;
And in our love we dimly scan
    The love which is between Himself.

In *The Victories of Love* we get Patmore's doctrine put from the woman's point of view, as in these lines :—

All that I know of love he taught ;
And love is all I know of aught.
My merit is so small by his,
That my demerit is my bliss.
My life is hid with him in Christ,
Never thenceforth to be entic'd ;
And in his strength have I such rest
As when the baby on my breast
Finds what it knows not how to seek,
And, very happy, very weak,
Lies, only knowing all is well,
Pillow'd on kindness palpable.

Here we are reminded of words written by Patmore in his book of mystical prose, *The Rod, the Root, and the Flower :* " The Babe sucking its mother's breast and the Lover returning, after twenty years' separation, to his home and food in the same bosom, are the types and princes of mysticism ". These words recall the likeness which Suso suggested between his own attraction to the Eternal Wisdom and, not only the lover's joy in his bride, but also the sucking babe's joy in its mother's bosom. The Wedding Sermon in *The Victories of Love* should, also, be carefully read

22

by any one wishing to get to the heart of Patmore's teaching

Of the later poems, found for the most part in the volume to which *The Unknown Eros* gave its name, there are many which one would like to quote, and to which the epithet ' great ' could not well be denied. None of the so-called Pindaric Odes fall far short of the supreme mark, while several reach it with ease. Those especially to be named here are *Eros and Psyche, To the Body*— " Little sequester'd pleasure-house for GOD and for His spouse "—*Sponsa Dei*,[1] and, above all perhaps, *Deliciæ Sapientiæ de Amore*, in which he declares that

> Love makes the life to be
> A fount perpetual of virginity,

and, apostrophizing in turn wedded lovers, betrothed lovers, and penitent lovers of irregular passion, he bids them gaze at the heavenly Marriage-feast, and meditate " the Husband of the Heavens," for

> Who Him love, in potence great or small,
> Are, one and all,
> Heirs of the Palace glad,
> And inly clad
> With the bridal robes of ardour virginal.

Of the verse which he devoted to the elucidation of the mystery of the Blessed Virgin Mary, the most important is *The Child's Purchase*, wherein he imagines a child returning to his mother, for a kiss, the coin given him for the purchase of a toy ; and then, referring to his own gift of " golden speech," granted him (as he holds) by the Ma-

---

[1] Patmore wrote another work under this title, but felt constrained to suppress it.

donna, he resolves to forego such toys as " power, pleasure,
and renown," and to restore it to her who bestowed it.
The poem contains several items of quite surprising information : that, at Mary's petition, "the Heavens themselves
decree that, as it were, they will be weak " ; that there are
" unwashed boors that hail GOD to His face," instead of
paying her the compliment of suing by her ; that she is
" our only saviour from an abstract Christ " ; and that some
souls are " wandering disemparadised," for refusing to bend
the knee to her. But, in spite of such fatuities and some
encomiastic falsetto, there are some fine passages in the
poem. The Blessed Virgin is invoked under many styles,
notably as " Spouse blissful, Daughter, Sister, milk-sweet
Mother ". But the most significant lines are those, at the
close of the piece, in which the poet gives us what is both
a bird's-eye view of his own mystical trend, and a partial
vindication of his earlier, Anglican verse : still addressing
Our Lady, he says,

> Bless thou the work
> Which, done, redeems my many wasted days,
> Makes white the murk,
> And crowns the few which thou wilt not dispraise,
> When clear my Songs of Lady's graces rang,
> And little guess'd I 'twas of thee I sang.

It is much easier for an Anglo-Catholic to revere FRANCIS
THOMPSON than it is to respect his elder co-religionist. This
is partly, no doubt, due to the fact that, having been born
and bred a Romanist, Thompson did not find it necessary
to bear malice or hatred in his heart to the English Church.
Moreover, there is the misgiving which any Christian must

have, that an arrogant mystic is a contradiction in terms : there is no trace of arrogance in the younger poet.

Many good judges are prepared to call Thompson the greatest mystical poet of the English tongue ; and it is certainly no easy task to name any writer of mystical verse who surpasses him in his combination of ardent devotion, splendid imagination, and sumptuous diction. His visions are, perhaps, a little suspect, since he did not take them un-adulterated but blended them with opium. But he is simply steeped in mystical thought and feeling, which show them-selves continually even in those of his poems not strictly mystical.

Highly commendable is his attitude of reverent reserve, evinced, partly in his reluctance to apply to his own writ-ings an epithet which has come to be used very carelessly— he preferred to call his essentially mystical pieces *Poems of Sight and Insight*—and partly, too, in the awed sense of responsibility for high privileges, to which he gave utterance in *The Dread of Height* : " for low they fall whose fall is from the sky ".

Of the vividness of his illuminated vision of the world no clearer proof could be required than the unrevised poem beginning, " O world invisible, we view thee," in which he describes " Jacob's ladder pitch'd between Heaven and Charing Cross," and " Christ walking on the water, not of Gennesareth, but Thames ". Further evidence may be sought in the melodious lines in *The Mistress of Vision*, telling how

> All things by immortal power,
> Near or far,
> Hiddenly
> To each other linked are,

That thou canst not stir a flower
Without troubling of a star.

Or again, there is the account in *Contemplation* of the
poet's cosmic consciousness, who

His mortal house unbars
To the importunate and thronging feet
That round our corporal walls' unheeding beat;
Till, all containing, he exalt
His stature to the stars, or stars
Narrow their heaven to his fleshly vault:
When, like a city under ocean,
To human things he grows a desolation,
And is made a habitation
For the fluctuous universe
To lave with unimpeded motion.

Living in such close proximity to the Eternal World,
Thompson sought and found communion with GOD by
every legitimate channel or medium—Beauty, Nature, Love.
In the famous essay on Shelley, he reminds the " pastors
and pious laics of the Church " that St. Francis d'Assisi
" discerned through the lamp, Beauty, the Light, GOD " ;
and he points out that " with many the religion of beauty
must always be a passion and a power, only evil when
divorced from the worship of the Primal Beauty ".   In *Her
Portrait* and other pieces, he platonizes, quite in the vein
of Donne, about the beauty of woman, whose flesh scarcely
exists for him even as a veil.   Here the artistry is always
delightful, but the intellectuality a trifle too subtle to be
entirely convincing.   This idealization of womanhood finds
its climax in the *Assumpta Maria*, a glowing panegyric
of the Madonna, of whom he says very finely, in prose,

that, like her Son, she is " at once high enough for worship and low enough for love ".

We may heartily congratulate ourselves that Thompson's scruples about his three great Nature Odes were overcome. It is, indeed, a little disappointing that he should ever have entertained them, or should have thought these poems in the least degree inconsistent with the Catholic Faith. Who could possibly scent serious heterodoxy in the *Orient Ode*, quite the most daring of the three ?

> Light out of Light !
> Resplendent and prevailing Word
> Of the Unheard !
> Not unto Thee, great Image, not to thee
> Did the wise heathen bend an idle knee ;
> And in an age of faith grown frore
> If I too shall adore,
> Be it accounted unto me
> A bright sciential idolatry.
>
> .    .    .    .    .    .    .    .
>
> Ay, if men say that on all high heaven's face
> The saintly signs I trace
> Which round my stoled altars hold their solemn place,
> Amen, Amen !   For oh, how could it be—
> When I with winged feet had run
> Through all the windy earth about,
> Quested its secret of the sun,
> And heard what things the stars together shout—
> I should not heed thereout
> Consenting counsel won :—
> ' By this, O Singer, know we if thou see.
> When man shall say to thee : Lo, Christ is here,
> Believe them : yea, and this—then art thou seer,

When all thy crying clear
Is but : Lo here !  Lo there !   Ah me, lo everywhere ! '

The glorious *Anthem of Earth* hardly lends itself to brief quotation ; but the following lines from the *Ode to the Setting Sun* are complete in themselves, and present nobly a valuable thought :—

Thou art of Him a type memorial.
Like Him thou hang'st in dreadful pomp of blood
Upon thy Western rood ;
And His stain'd brow did veil like thine to night,
Yet lift once more its light,
And, risen, again departed from our ball,

But when it set on earth arose in heaven.
Thus hath He unto death His beauty given :
And so of all which form inheriteth
The fall doth pass the rise in worth ;
For birth hath in itself the germ of death,
But death hath in itself the germ of birth.

It would be hardly possible to suggest more devotionally the mystery of Autumn than Thompson does in the lines in that majestic *Corymbus*, which begins " All Nature sacerdotal seems, and thou ".   Nor would it be easy to propound more exquisitely the truth of GOD'S immanence in Nature than he does in the poem on a *Field-Flower*, which

Came up redolent of GOD,
Garrulous of the eyes of GOD
To all the breezes near it ;
Musical of the mouth of GOD
To all had eyes to hear it ;
Mystical with the mirth of GOD,
That glow-like did ensphere it.

Dr. Newman drew out the symbolism of Spring in a well-known sermon : " Once only in the year, yet once, does the world which we see show forth its hidden powers, and in a manner manifest itself.  Then there is a sudden rush and burst outwardly of that hidden life which GOD has lodged in the material world.  Well, that shows you, as by a sample, what it can do at His command, when He gives the word.  This earth which now buds forth in leaves and blossoms, will one day burst forth into a new world of light and glory."  In *The Night of Foreboding*, Thompson condenses this into one striking line : " And all the springs are flash-lights of one Spring ".  His Nature-creed is eloquently affirmed (though almost recanted in a foot-note) in the essay on *Nature's Immortality :* " The Supreme Spirit, creating, reveals His conceptions to man in the material forms of Nature.  There is no necessity here for any intermediate process, because nobody obstructs the free passage of conception into expression.  An ideal wakes in the Omnipotent Painter ; and straightway over the eternal dykes rush forth the flooding tides of night, the blue of heaven ripples into stars ; Nature, from Alp to Alpine flower, rises lovely with the betrayal of the Divine thought. An ideal wakes in the Omnipotent Poet ; and there chimes the rhythm of an ordered universe.  An ideal wakes in the Omnipotent Musician ; and Creation vibrates with the harmony, from the palpitating throat of the bird to the surges of His thunder as they burst in fire along the roaring strand of Heaven."

Another essay that should be studied as a clue to Thompson's mystical standing is the paper on *Health and Holiness.*  Here, comparing the relationship of body and soul to a wick dipped in oil, he says : " But this oil, this soul,

is enriched a hundredfold by the infusion of the Holy
Spirit ; the human will is intensified by union with the
Divine Will ; and for the flame of human love or active
energy is substituted the intenser flame of Divine Love or
Divine Energy : rather it is not a substitution, but the
higher is added to the lower, the lesser augmented by and
contained within the greater ". The whole essay may be
taken as a comment on the poem entitled *Any Saint*, in
which Thompson comes perilously near the tortured ingenuity of analogy which vitiated the poetry of the seven-
teenth-century concettists, though not painfully so in the
lines here extracted :—

> Man ! swinging-wicket set
> > Between
> > The Unseen and Seen,
>
> Lo, GOD'S two worlds immense,
> Of spirit and of sense,
> > Wed
> > In this narrow bed ;
>
> Yea, and the midge's hymn
> Answers the seraphim
> > Athwart
> > Thy body's court !
>
> Great arm-fellow of GOD !
> To the ancestral clod
> > Kin,
> > And to cherubin.

The reading public has decided, not unwisely, that
Thompson's supreme achievement is *The Hound of
Heaven*, the mingled audacity and sublimity of which—

from title to last line—simply silences all criticism that is
sincere.  Its popularity proves it to reflect the mentality of
an age which has veered round from the doubt-haunted
mid-Victorianism reflected by *In Memoriam* to a conviction of the compatibility of religion and science, so that the
sacred poet of to-day is expected, not only to make articulate man's need of GOD, but to give generous expression
also to GOD'S need of man.  Not that this recognition is
original to our own times : the symbol of the Love-chase,
used by the poet here to describe GOD'S need, has, of
course, been constantly used before—amongst others by
Eckhart : " He who will escape Him only runs to His
bosom " ; and again by Ruysbroeck : " The Spirit of GOD
gives chase to our spirit ".  A medieval setting, too, has
been noticed above (p, 15) in the poem, *Quia amore
langueo*.  But it may safely be claimed that this converse
of the Mystic Quest, this tireless pursuit by the Eternal
Lover Who thwarts our every mundane hope and refuses
to grant us satisfaction in material well-being, has never been
described with such soaring imagination or with such majestic music.  It would be sacrilegious to mutilate, by making
extracts, a poem which is a unity to be truly appreciated
only in its entirety.  But the following stanzas from the
Epilogue to *A Narrow Vessel* may be given ; it employs
the same symbolism, but presents the appalling alternative,
in which, instead of the soul's surrender depicted in *The
Hound of Heaven*, we have the great refusal :—

> She, that giving part, not whole,
> Took even the part back, is the Soul :
> And that so disdained Lover—
> Best unthought, since Love is over.

> .    .    .    .    .

Such a Soul, for saddest end,
Finds Love the foe, in Love the friend ;
And—ah, grief incredible !—
Treads the way of Heaven, to Hell.

There is one reservation to be made with regard to
Francis Thompson.   He is, in some respects, not a good
advertisement for mysticism.   Mystics are often taunted
with lack of practical ability and failure in application.   In
the vast majority of cases, the charge fails : often it is not
proven ; still oftener it ends in a clear acquittal.   But in
Thompson's case, the verdict must be a decided ' Guilty '.
The seminarist who, to his intense disappointment, was
rejected as a candidate for the priesthood, not for any
devotional or theological failure, nor for any intellectual or
physical defect, but on the ground, apparently, of invincible
indolence ; the medical student who from his access to
drugs gained nothing better than a slavery to laudanum ;
the errand-boy of adult age, incapable, from sheer feckless-
ness, of keeping the situation which was alone between
himself and degrading poverty—this was one for whom the
mystic mood was an indulgence not altogether unlike that
of drug-taking.   His story gives " occasion to the adversary
for reviling ".

# CHAPTER X.

KEBLE, ISAAC WILLIAMS, R. C. TRENCH, CHARLES KINGS-
LEY, T. E. BROWN, R. W. DIXON, G. S. HOLLINGS, A. S.
CRIPPS.

CHRONOLOGICAL order has been deliberately neglected in
order to treat in a group a number of poets, more or less
mystical in tendency, who were in holy orders. We must
now retrace our steps to the year 1827, when JOHN
KEBLE reluctantly and anonymously published *The Christian Year*.

Keble would never have claimed the style ' mystic,' although every one who came into contact with him very soon
became aware of his nearness and devotion to a Living
Lord. Like all the Tractarians, he observed a reverent
reticence in speaking of personal experiences ; and in the
*Morning* hymn (familiar to our congregations in an abbreviated form) he deprecates the attempt " to wind ourselves too high," and urges that the coming and going of
rapture should be left entirely to the will of Heaven ; all
that we ought to seek is opportunities for self-denial and
such tasks as may " bring us daily nearer GOD ". In a
similar strain he asks (in the poem for the *Fourth Sunday
in Lent*), in view of GOD'S secret working both in Nature
and in Grace,

> Then why should gentle hearts and true
> Bare to the rude world's withering view
> Their treasure of delight !

There are signs that English Churchmen to-day find less

significance and charm than their fathers and grandfathers did in *The Christian Year ;* and it may not be amiss to draw attention to the appreciation of a devout critic of another communion, M. Thureau-Dangin, author of *The English Catholic Revival in the Nineteenth Century :* " Besides being a work of art, these hymns are the expression of personal feelings of the utmost sincerity and depth. One finds in them an exquisite purity of heart, a brooding and tender piety, the love and fear of GOD, and sorrow for sin. Christ is no mere abstraction, but a living Friend. Nature lives in them, as one would expect from a contemporary and admirer of Wordsworth ; but she is the radiant veil behind which the Creator speaks to the soul, and on each page there are, as it were, beatings of wings to lift us by means of all visible things towards infinite beauty."

There is a tendency to suppose that the leaders of the Oxford Movement, because they valued the institutional aspect of religion, were out of sympathy with the mystical aspect. In reality, they afford admirable examples of the characteristic Anglican method, which seeks, by harmonizing the two elements, to avoid their respective excesses and defects. It is hardly necessary to underline the strain of mysticism in Newman's nature, and for Dr. Pusey the reader may be referred to such a sermon as *The Christian's life hid in Christ* (*Parochial Sermons*, Vol. I.). The mystical element in Keble's verse—we have no *data* for his inner life—illustrates R. L. Nettleship's definition of " true mysticism " as " the consciousness that everything that we experience, every ' fact,' is an element and only an element in ' the fact,' i.e. that, in being what it is, it is significant or symbolic of more ".[1]

---

[1] *Philosophical Remains* (1901), p. 32.

No doubt there is a rather slippery descent from this type of mysticism, through symbolism, to mere allegorism—the last-named being a valuable method of teaching (when not unduly forced) but in no sense mystical.   Symbolism may, or may not, be mystical, according as it represents a sign vitally connected with its significance, or a merely invented and arguable analogy.   In the opinion of many mystical writers, it is not even a stage towards mysticism ; others regard it as a stage which involves the whole process. Keble, in *Tract* 89, *On the Mysticism attributed to the Early Fathers*, deals at some length with this question, but was unable to bring his treatise to its contemplated conclusion.   While sometimes distinguishing between what is mystical and what is allegorical, he seems to regard the allegorizing of GOD'S Word and the spiritualizing of GOD'S Works as equally branches of mysticism.   The latter, however, he defines and subdivides, speaking of it as " the way of regarding external things either as fraught with imaginative associations, or as parabolical lessons of conduct, or as a symbolical language in which GOD speaks to us of a world out of sight : which three might, perhaps, be not quite inaptly entitled the Poetical, the Moral, and the Mystical phases or aspects of this visible world ".   Later he anticipates the objection, " How are we to know whether any particular image . . . be properly mystical, or merely moral or poetical ? "   But his answer is not quite convincing, and is based upon a sort of universal consent : " there is a wonderful agreement among the Fathers in the symbolical meanings which they assign to the great objects in Nature ; such an agreement as completely negatives the supposition of the whole having sprung from mere poetical association ".   Omitting certain sentences which a hostile critic could ' wrest' to imply that the very irrelevance of some patristic analogies is a sign of their Divine origin, we may extract the following statement of the ' symbolical or sacramental view of Nature ' : " The works of GOD in creation and providence, besides their immediate uses in this life, appeared to the old writers as so many tokens from the Almighty, to assure us of some spiritual fact or other, which it concerns us in some way to know ; so far, therefore, they fulfilled half at least of the nature of sacraments, according to the strict definition of our Catechism : they were pledges to assure us of some spiritual thing, if they were not means to convey it to us ".

To purists in mysticism, this last admission may seem a fatal disqualification ; but from Keble's verse it is clear that he himself found in Nature sacramental symbols which afforded him channels of communion with GOD. It is not necessary to read many lines before we find manifest indications of this. Presumably, his earliest utterances in this vein are to be found in certain pieces printed in the posthumous volume of *Miscellaneous Poems*. One of these, which was composed when the poet was barely in his nineteenth year, may be given :—

> GOD'S mercy is in the pure beam of Spring :
> The gale of morning is His blessed breath,
> Cheering created things, that, as they drink
> At those low founts of intermitting joy,
> Their souls may bless Him, and with quickened thirst
> Pant for the river of life and light of heaven.
> O sun-bright gleams, and ye unfolding depths
> Of azure space, what are ye but a pledge
> And precious foretaste of that cloudless day,
> Gladdening at intervals the good man's heart

With earnest of infinitude ?   The while
He on his rugged path moves cheerily,
Towards joys that mock the measuring eye of hope,
As yon abyss ethereal mocks our gaze.

Unquestionably, Keble's most striking utterance as a
Nature-mystic is the poem for *Septuagesima Sunday*, in
*The Christian Year*.   Although well-known, it may be
studied in some detail, as illustrating clearly both his strength
and his weakness.   The opening words, " There is a book
who runs may read," versify the thought expressed long ago
by Sir Thomas Browne :   " There are two books from
whence I collect my divinity ; besides that written one of
GOD, another of His servant Nature, that universal and
public manuscript that lies expansed unto the eyes of all ".
Coming to particulars, " the glorious sky embracing all "
may be accepted as a symbol of " the Maker's love," and
the sun as a symbol of our Lord ; but the resemblance of
the moon to the Church on earth, of the stars to the saints in
heaven, and of the trees to the saints on earth, while permissible as allegories, has justly been scouted as " a mere ecclesiastical reading of Nature's symbols " (Professor Shairp).
In his *Tract* Keble has no difficulty in finding patristic support for these analogies, and no objection can be raised to
his calling these natural phenomena " Divine hieroglyphics " ;
but they are not true symbols affording, or even facilitating,
access to GOD.   They evidently had a great charm for
Keble, who uses them again, both in the *Miscellaneous
Poems* and in the *Lyra Innocentium*.   Later in the
Septuagesima hymn we get back to truer symbolism in the
analogies drawn from the dew, fire, and wind ; and in the
penultimate stanza we have an admirable paraphrase of St.
Thomas Aquinas's contention that Nature being symbolic

of GOD, and the human soul being made in the image of
GOD, man can behold GOD in Nature, if pure from sin :—

> Two worlds are ours : 'tis only sin
> Forbids us to descry
> The mystic heaven and earth within,
> Plain as the sea and sky.

This consciousness of the blinding power of sin was constantly with Keble, and gives its characteristic tone of yearning regret to much of his verse. In the poem for the *Fourth
Sunday in Advent*, for instance, he claims that " we see
far in holy ground, if duly purg'd our mental view," but he
deplores that, at present, his " eye unworthy seems to read
one page of Nature's beauteous book " ; he must await the
Beatific Vision, when it " shall behold, and not in trance,
the region ' very far away '". The same thought occurs in
the *All Saints'* hymn ; and in the poem for *Trinity iv.*,
again, he chafes beneath the power of sin to drown GOD's
voice in Nature and to " deafen the ear that fain would
wake to Nature's simple lay ".

Returning to the *Septuagesima* hymn, we find in the
last stanza a petition for grace to see and love natural things
*sub specie æternitatis*, to recognize every visible creature
as a theophany : it may be used by every Nature-lover as
a prayer that he may become, by GOD's grace, a Nature-
mystic :—

> Thou Who hast given me eyes to see
> And love this sight so fair,
> Give me a heart to find out Thee,
> And read Thee everywhere.

Other pieces in *The Christian Year* to which special
attention may be called are those for the *Second, Seventh,*

*Twentieth*, and *Twenty-third Sundays after Trinity*, and also the *St. Matthew's* hymn. In the first of these Keble utters his conviction that Nature is animated and energized by love : the clouds " mantle round the Sun for love " ; and

> Such signs of love old Ocean gives,
> We cannot choose but think he lives.

The poem for *Trinity xx.* is notable for its insistence on the " Eternal Voice " being audible in Nature's sacred tones " :—

> Such sounds as make deep silence in the heart
> For Thought to do her part.

Many critics regard the lines for *Trinity xxiii.* as Keble's finest effort in verse ; it certainly is not the least significant in its treatment of Nature as suggesting " gleams beyond it," and as bringing " bliss " to the heart. The poem for the Festival of *St. Matthew*, in which the lot of the country-dweller is contrasted with that of the town-worker, begins by dwelling on

> The secret lore of rural things,
> The moral of each fleeting cloud and gale,
> The whispers from above that haunt the twilight vale.

It ends by reproaching those who " live in Paradise, as if GOD was not there ".

The *Lyra Innocentium*, although containing a section on ' Lessons from Nature,' is not nearly so full of Nature-teaching as *The Christian Year*. Three extracts may be made, as apposite to our subject. The Dedication re-echoes the regret that loss of innocence has dimmed the mystic consciousness in communing with Nature :—

There are, who gazing on the stars
    Love-tokens read from worlds of light,
Not as dim-seen through prison-bars,
    But as with Angels' welcome bright.
Oh, had we kept entire the vow
    And covenant of our infant eyes,
We too might trace untrembling now
    Glad lessons in the moonlight skies.

In *The Waterfall*, a beautiful thought is gathered from
the analogy of the interconnexion between cloud, raindrops,
river, and ocean :—

    If of the Living Cloud they be
        Baptismal drops, and onward press
        Toward the Living Sea
        By deeds of holiness.

    Then to the Living Waters still
        (Oh, joy with trembling !) they pertain,
        Join'd by some hidden rill,
        Low in earth's darkest vein.

In *Whitsun Eve*, the poet imagines the pity felt by " the
attendant spirits who float unseen on wave or wind " at
man's failure to heed " the tunes for holy times " made by
" wild Nature's chords ".

One of the poems of *The Christian Year*, the *Evening*
hymn, has been left unnoticed hitherto, as it introduces a
thought unconnected with Nature-mysticism. It has, indeed, these notable lines on Nature :—

    When round Thy wondrous works below
    My searching rapturous glance I throw,
    Tracing out Wisdom, Power, and Love,
    In earth or sky, in stream or grove—

> Let not my heart within me burn,
> Except in all I Thee discern.

But the thought referred to above is found in the closing
lines :—

> Till in the ocean of Thy love
> We lose ourselves in Heaven above.

No doubt, these words, on the lips of many members of
an average evening congregation, are a mere *façon de parler*,
meaning little more than that they hope to be on the right
side of whatever happens after death.   But of Keble, it
was known that in his verse " never for a moment is the
very truth sacrificed to effect.   I will venture to say with
confidence [the words are Bishop Moberley's] that there is
not a sentiment to be found elevated or amplified beyond
what he really felt ; nor, I would add, even an epithet that
goes beyond his actual and true thought."   Keble was quoting here—perhaps unconsciously—almost *verbatim* from
Molinos, who was thinking—as apparently Keble was not
—of this as a present possibility.   The lines hardly suggest
that Keble agreed with Tauler that a man can, here and
now, " lose himself in the Divine substance as a drop of water
is lost in a cask of strong wine " ; or that he would have
altogether approved Ruysbroeck's highest experience of
feeling " that our spirits are stripped of all things and bathed,
beyond thought of rising, in the pure and infinite Ocean of
Love".   In the *Tract* already quoted, he asks if it may
not be " that our Blessed Lord, in union and communion
with all His members, is represented to us as constituting,
in a certain sense, one great and manifold Person, into which,
by degrees, all souls of men, who do not cast themselves
away, are to be absorbed ".   Evidently then, without ad-
vocating a present negativism, he did hope for ultimate

absorption ; the metaphor used in the poem seems to imply the loss of personal identity and of conscious harmony with the Eternal.   Such a thought, attractive as it is to many natures, is abhorrent to the minds of those to whom love suggests the completion of one being by another being, but not the absorption of one personality by another.

It will be no difficult task to adduce a passage to illustrate the similarity of thought between Keble and his disciple, ISAAC WILLIAMS.   Here is one from *The Baptistery :—*

> All things speak of Thee—every sun that shines
> Sets forth Thy image, and each day's return
> Is herald of the Morn that ne'er declines :—
> The bright recovering year, at every turn
> Speaks of the great New Year, where all things burn
> In glorious beauty round the Source of Light ;
> All are Thy teachers—grant us to discern
> Their heavenly lessons—cleanse our mortal sight,
> We have enough to preach, did we but hear aright.
>
> Show me the way that leadeth unto Thee,
> Though it be difficult Thou art all might,
> Though low Thou art of love a boundless sea,
> Though dark Thou art Thyself the living Light,
> Though toilsome Thou art goodness infinite,
> And wilt refresh the heavy-laden soul
> That comes to Thee ; guide me to Thee aright,
> I cannot come unless Thou dost control ;
> Lead Thou, enlighten, draw, and fill my being whole.
>
> May I be lost in Thy great Majesty,
> Myself no more, to have no cherish'd thing,
> No choice, no hope, no sorrow, but in Thee,
> My Shepherd, my Father, and my King :

Nothing is good but what in Thee doth spring,
Nothing is good but what in Thee doth end ;
Oh, let me hear Thy voice, let all things bring
Thy voice to me ; whatever Thou dost send
Shall be my welcome guest, shall be my honour'd friend.

.　　.　　.　　.　　.　　.　　.　　.　　.　　.　　.

Thrice happy they, who as they draw more near
More clearly can discern their being's end,
Gird up their loins with hope, and year by year
Unto their stable home still steadier wend ;
And from the sinuous road will still ascend
Unto the straiter path, while the calm ray
Lightens them step by step, nor even bend
Their firm resolve from that their steadfast way,
Until they are absorb'd in the Eternal Day.

It was Isaac Williams' misfortune—he himself would have
said ' privilege '—to be overshadowed by Keble.   Antholo-
gists have done him scant justice, and his publications are
rarely seen except on the dustiest shelves of second-hand
booksellers.   And yet, although his verse was palpably inspired by *The Christian Year*, it bears strong marks of
originality, and is the product of a mind which was, perhaps, more poetical than Keble's.   Dean Church has told
us how, under John Keble's influence, Isaac Williams was
converted from a proud, ambitious scholar to one who put
faithfulness to conscience far above intellect and came to regard with horror anything like display or aiming at effect.
From Thomas Keble, with whom he worked for two years
as assistant-curate, he acquired a still deeper severity of tone
and sobriety of statement.   He returned to Oxford, as
Fellow of Trinity, with " a character of great sweetness,
tenderness, and lowly unselfishness, pure, free from all

worldliness, and deeply resigned to the will of GOD ". All these traits are easily discernible in the *Autobiography* which he wrote for his children, without view to publication, but which his friends most wisely decided to give to the world. Needless to say, he makes no claim to the title ' mystic,' but his nature was unmistakably mystical, finding a devout and reverent joy in the cultivation of the inner life. His *Tract* on *Reserve in Communicating Religious Knowledge* (so often maligned by those who have not read it and distorted by those who give mutilated extracts from it) is—to quote Dean Church again—" a beautiful and suggestive essay, full of deep and original thought, though composed in that spirit of the recluse which was characteristic of the writer ".

Such a nature as Isaac Williams', to which noisiness and partisanship were abhorrent, would instinctively shrink from the vulgarizing of sacred words and the shallow repetition of party shibboleths which were, at the time, the foibles of certain Evangelical circles. To these abuses he definitely refers in his *Tract*, while explaining that the main object of his inquiry is " to ascertain whether there is not, in GOD'S dealings with mankind, a very remarkable holding back of sacred and important truth, as if the knowledge of them were injurious to persons unworthy of them ". He draws attention to our Lord's habit of shrouding truth in parabolic form, and His anxiety that the report of His miracles should not be noised abroad. He instances George Herbert, Thomas à Kempis, and others, as solitary spirits, self-effacing in disposition and reserved in utterance. An interesting paragraph deprecates the " tendency to feel after sensible signs . . . a craving after palpably felt evidences . . . a looking out for miracles ". This, however, is differentiated from " a readiness to receive miracles which is observable in the best men, when they come upon them in the line of duty ". A poetical version of this paragraph is found in the poem on *St. Thomas* in *The Cathedral*:—

Blessed are they who needing no loud sign
Of reason, or felt proof, or voice divine,
Believing, love ; and loving, ask not sight !
They on the bosom of the Infinite
Have been, and there in faith for ever lie :
Believe because they love, and ask not why ;
But on His bosom lie they all day long,
And drink His words, and are refresh'd and strong ;
Through all Thy works, Thee, Lord, at every turn,
Through all Thy Word, Thee and Thy Cross discern ;
Shrine within shrine, and hall encircling hall,
Pass unto Thee, to Thee, the All in All.
    Thine too are they, of ruder sense, who deem
Such thoughts but fancies of the mystic's dream ;
Then to their questioning and ruder sense,
In palpable and solemn evidence
Thy Presence breaks, in providential change
Defying thought, or visitation strange :
They see and feel Thy hands and pierced side,
Worship, and their adoring heads would hide.
Such dwell in Thy blest courts and see Thy face,
But not most near Thine altar have their place.

The regular system adopted especially by the Alexandrine Fathers, and subsequently called the *Disciplina Arcani*, is barely mentioned in *Tract* 80, but it is dwelt upon more fully in a later *Tract* (87), in which Isaac Williams discusses how it may have arisen and quotes in illustration from early writers. " The one great practical consideration " with which he brings *Tract* 80 to a conclusion, " is one

which is full of awe, indeed, but also full of consolation, as
tending to keep the mind quiet in times of universal movement and excitement : that Jesus Christ is now, and has
been at all times, hiding Himself from us, and at the same
time exceedingly desirous to communicate Himself, and that
exactly in proportion as we show ourselves worthy, He will
disclose Himself to us ; that if we constrain Him, He will
come and abide with us ; that unsatisfying as human knowledge is, and the increase of which is the increase of care, a
knowledge which puffeth up, yet that there is a knowledge
which humbleth, which is infinite in its nature and is nothing
else than deeper and higher and broader views of the mystery
which is hid in Christ ; that although Scripture does not set
before us any sensible joy or satisfaction to be sought for,
as the end of holiness, yet it does this knowledge, which is
obtainable by nothing else but by making the study of
divinity to consist in a divine life. . . ." How strongly he
felt about all this may be recognized by any one who will
read such pieces as the sonnets on *Christian Reserve* (in
*Thoughts in Past Years*), the poem entitled *Disciplina
Arcani* (in *The Cathedral*), and *The Treasures of the
King's Palace* (in *The Baptistery*), where the soul is
bidden, " Pass the things of GOD in holy silence by ".

An important section of *Tract* 87 deals with the so-
called mystical interpretation of Holy Scripture and may be,
in part, quoted here as illustrating Isaac Williams' type of
mind. He speaks of our Lord as " hiding and concealing
Himself throughout the inspired writings, and going about
(if I may so speak reverently) seeking to whom He may disclose Himself ". And later he asks, " Besides that knowledge and practical wisdom, information and warning which
is more in the letter of Holy Scripture as a lantern unto our

feet—why may there not be also concealed and laid up something of the vastness and infinity of His counsels, things divine and spiritual, which He may also open and reveal to men to carry on the purposes of His wisdom, and of their probation ? " In this connexion his own *Devotional Commentaries* and sermons on Biblical characters may be recalled as pre-eminently helpful, even if at times a trifle forced in typical application. His lines in *The Cathedral* on *Holy Scripture* are too many to be printed here in full, but some of them ought to be given, more especially as they paraphrase other sections of his *Tract :*—

Who shall descry
His steps of light, Who, in His boundless Word,
The wilderness of waters walks unseen ?
In this Thy visible house, mankind's abode,
Thy hand withdraws from search of human ken ;
Whene'er the depths we trace, there opes beyond
An inner world, where Science lifts her torch,
And wonder leads through dim enchanted halls.
And glorious links we see of heavenly mould,
But cannot track the chain ; Thyself, unseen,
Sittest behind the mighty wheel of things,
Which move harmonious, tho' unheard below,
Save when Thine order'd ways, at interval,
Break forth, as falling on some traveller's ear
Musical notes, which make the landscape smile.
The Hand that kindles up the rolling moon,
Lifts up the worm's blue lamp beside our path ;
And haply in Thy Word there hidden lies
Infinity, coil'd up in narrowest bound ;
We on the surface walk, and know it not.

.    .    .    .    .    .    .    .    .

O perfect energy of Thy deep Word,

With varied ends combining all in one,
Like Nature's works, all one, all manifold!
Each has its single lesson, each is part
Of one great whole, where earth and sea and skies
Are mirror'd ; now at random thrown a part,
In thousand scintillations far and wide,
Each fragment bears the earth and sea and skies,
Each on the other throws its pictur'd form,
And all combine in one mysterious whole.

. . . . . . . . .

    Through that blest realm
Scarce doth a sacred track unharm'd remain,
At Nazareth's lone hillside, or silent lake,
(Dear lake, dear hills, where Thy blest eyes repos'd!)
But in the living page Thy steps abide,
Fresh as of yesterday.   Faith lights her lamp,
And rising thence she sees Thee all around ;
She walks the earth, in amice of the morn,
And wheresoe'er the need of human woe
Varies its shape, she finds Thee standing nigh,
And burns to follow.   Oft Thy Presence lies
Hidden in busy scenes ; but, as they pass,
The parting step reveals Thy form divine,
And gentle dealings : as we backward bear
The thoughtful eye, we see in vision clear,
And lost occasions mourn.   Oh, that we thence
Might gain the enduring sense of Thy deep love,
How in that light would things terrestrial wear
Celestial colourings, that we no more
Should droop, or in Thy Presence feel alone!

It is, perhaps, unnecessary to explain that in the collection of poems which he entitled *The Cathedral*, Isaac
Williams draws analogies from the material structure of
such a building, rising from visible emblems to invisible

truths. The scheme is extraordinarily intricate and gives good scope for moral and religious instruction ; but it is not, on the whole, especially mystical. Here and there, however, lines occur which reveal the Nature-mystic, as, for instance, in the poem on *St. Bartholomew*, who is introduced as one of ' The Pillars of the Church ' :—

> Thine is the art of artless souls, true seer !
> To know thy GOD in all things standing near,
> Divine prerogative !   The blameless soul,
> Its own simplicity, its sweet control,
> Leads on, and, like a guardian spirit, brings
> Into the palace of the King of kings,
> The Mount of GOD.   To Him all Nature stirs,
> Ranging herself in glowing characters ;
> Seen through Faith's lightning mirror ; blooming skies
> Come down on earth and sea, like vernal dyes,
> Speaking of Resurrection ; all are rife
> And animate with forms of beauteous life,
> Unseen before ; 'mid busiest scenes below
> The messengers of mercy come and go.

The volume called *Thoughts of the Past* (composed long before, but published only in 1838, very soon after the last-named collection) has much about the need of purgation and voices many aspirations after illumination. It contains many lines, too, on the mystical aspects of Nature, of which it may be enough to name *Heavenly Signs, A November Scene*, and *Wroxton Abbey*, extracting these lines from the last as its quintessence :—

> What if the meanest things of earthly ruth
> Shadow the kingdoms of the Paraclete,
> And be reflections of eternal truth,
> Ere it be seen to rise in its unfailing youth ?

Again, in *The Baptistery*, clogged though the Muse is by the rather disconcerting Dutch emblems, a true mystical longing for purgation, contemplative calm, and illumination finds frequent utterance. A sense, too, of the Presence is constantly revealed, the main lesson being that

> To them that watch, this world becomes a shrine,
> And every sight they see a messenger divine.

The initial poem, explanatory of the title, insists upon the essential duality of things :—

> From parable, or type, or living scene,
> Come speaking forms to people our blest well ;
> GOD'S words and works are here responsive seen
> As in a twofold mirror, both to tell
> And speak the language of the Invisible :
> When Wisdom to the soul gives ears to hear,
> Nature becomes one living oracle,
> Whose Sybil leaves need no interpreter
> But the understanding heart and the obedient ear.
>
> Hour after hour, like some melodious chime,
> Creation speaks Thee ; when Thou giv'st to see
> And read Thy lessons, things of flying time
> Range themselves in their order while they flee
> To form Thy language and to speak of Thee.
> Thou call'st them by their names, when through our night
> Like stars on watch they answer ' Here we be,'
> And at Thy bidding give their cheerful light
> To speak unto Thy sons of things beyond the sight.

One further quotation may be permitted, as illustrating Isaac Williams' conviction that Christ's parabolic teaching is a clear proof that GOD designed the visible universe to be for man a means of intercourse with Himself :—

> For if Christ is within, enshrin'd in light,
> From all without, from like or opposite,
> From scenes we meet, or by the way behold,
> He forms his parable, as erst of old,
> Giving the seeing eye and hearing ear,
> And heart to understand His Presence near;
> Till all about our life shall find a tongue,
> And witnesses of GOD our pathway throng.
> Then Nature all becomes a living book,
> Wherein the eyes of faith for ever look,
> And see a Father's love, a Father's care,
> And the eternal kingdom rising there.

Pastoral scenes, he goes on to say, may recall the mind to the Presence of the Good Shepherd, others to that of the True Vine, a parent's love to that of the Divine Father, and so on.  The poem ends with lines which afford some justification to those critics who complain that Isaac Williams was little more than a feeble reflexion of John Keble :—

> Soul-lifting Wisdom, unto whom is given,
> To find on earth a shadow of Thy Heaven,
> Purge from the dross of sin my feeble sight,
> That I Thy blessed lore may read aright,

RICHARD CHEVENIX TRENCH, successively Dean of Westminster and Archbishop of Dublin, carried on the line of Tractarian poets who recognized the sacramental character of material phenomena.  In his famous work on *The Parables of Our Lord*, quoting Milton's "What if earth be but the shadow of heaven," he points out that "the world of Nature is throughout a witness for the world of spirit, proceeding from the same hand, growing out of the same root, and constituted for that very end".  But so far as the written word carries us, there is nothing to show

that he found direct access to GOD by communing with
Nature. In such poems as *The Descent of the Rhine* and
*A Century of Couplets*, he simply draws reflective anal-
ogies from Nature, which "solemnize our souls". "All
Nature has a voice," he says again ; but to be reminded of
GOD, or even to receive a message from Him, is to fall
very short of the mystic's goal.

It is interesting to learn from Trench's *Letters* that, as
a young man, he had to pass through a prolonged Dark
Night, which is clearly reflected in *Despondency* and two
or three other pieces. From this he was extracted by the
discovery of Henry Vaughan, Boehme, and the great
Spanish mystics, whose writings brought him some degree
of illumination. The lines *To a Friend* describe this recovery of spiritual hope and insight, ending with the question,
which supplies its own answer,

> Have we left
> Our love of Nature, now to love her less,
> Since we have learnt that all we so admire
> Is only as her soil'd and weekday dress,
> And nothing to the glory she shall wear,
> When for the coming sabbath of the world
> She shall put on her festival attire—
> Or clos'd our eyes to what of beautiful
> Man by strong spell and earnest toil has won
> To take intelligible forms of art,
> Now that all these are recogniz'd to be
> Desires and yearnings, feeling after Him,
> And by Him only to be satisfied,
> Who is Himself the Eternal Loveliness?

For months he had abandoned the writing of verse. Of
this, and of his return to the practice, he speaks in the lines

*To Poetry*, from which his ideal of the poet's function must be extracted :—

> Though now there seems one only aim
> For poet—that my strength were as my will!—
> And which renounce he cannot without blame—
> To make men feel the Presence by his skill
> Of an Eternal Loveliness, until
> All souls are faint with longing for their home,
> Yet all the while are strengthen'd to fulfil
> Their task on earth, that they may surely come
> Unto the land of life, who here as exiles roam.

Would that these words might be dinned effectually into the ears of the Puritan, with his alternate fear and contempt of beauty as either a snare or a vanity, and of the sensualist, with his perversion of it to self-gratification, and into the ears, too, of those to-day whose profession of faith is summed up in the motto, " Art for Art's sake " !

One short poem by Trench is especially notable, not only as giving an autobiographical clue, but also as supplying another version, marked by a terseness and restraint characteristic of his school, of the Divine Chase, treated so copiously and exuberantly by Francis Thompson in *The Hound of Heaven* :—

> If there had anywhere appeared in space
>     Another place of refuge, where to flee,
> Our hearts had taken refuge in that place,
>     And not with Thee.
>
> For we against creation's bars had beat
>     Like prison'd eagles, through great walls had sought
> Though but a foot of ground to plant our feet,
>     Where Thou wert not.

And only when we found in earth and air,
In heaven or hell, that such might nowhere be—
That we could not flee from Thee anywhere,
We fled to Thee.

As one who theoretically maintained the desirability of an immediacy between the soul and ultimate reality, CHARLES KINGSLEY may be classed among the mystics, although *Hypatia* reveals an anti-mystical bias, and in his Introduction to Miss Winkworth's translation of Tauler's Sermons (published after *Hypatia*) he stated that he had never had mystical experiences himself. Besides the advocacy—a little cautious and apologetic—of mysticism in that Introduction, he also introduced and recommended to the British public the *Theologia Germanica* and Brooke's *Fool of Quality* (see p. 272 above) ; while in an important review of Vaughan's *Hours with the Mystics*, he ranged himself definitely with the mystics rather than with their flippant and cocksure critic.

As a young man, Kingsley had seriously studied mysticism both in its active and passive aspects, with the intention of writing Lives of St. Elizabeth and of St. Theresa. We get an interesting intimation of these studies in the dialogue between Elizabeth and Guta in *The Saint's Tragedy* :—

> *Eliz.* I do not love that contemplative life :
> No ! I must headlong into seas of toil,
> Leap forth from self, and spend my soul on others.
> Oh ! contemplation palls upon the spirit,
> Like the chill silence of an autumn sun :
> While action, like the roaring south-west wind,
> Sweeps laden with elixirs, with rich draughts
> Quickening the wombed earth.

*Guta.*                           And yet what bliss,
When dying in the darkness of God's light,
The soul can pierce these blinding webs of nature,
And float up to The Nothing which is all things—
The ground of being, where self-forgetful silence
Is emptiness—emptiness fulness—fulness GOD—
Till we touch him, and like a snow-flake melt
Upon His light-sphere's keen circumference !

Before the publication of this drama, Kingsley had, in a letter to his betrothed, unburdened his mind as to " the great mysticism," which he defined as " the belief which is every day stronger with me that all symmetrical natural objects, aye, and perhaps all forms, colours, and scents which show organization or arrangement, are types of some spiritual truth or existence, of a grade between the symbolic type and the mystical type.   When I walk the fields," he added, " I am oppressed every now and then with an innate feeling that everything I see has a meaning, if I could but understand it.   And this feeling of being surrounded with truths which I cannot grasp amounts to an indescribable awe sometimes !   Everything seems to be full of GOD's reflex, if we could but see it. . . . When I feel that sense of the mystery that is around me, I feel a gush of enthusiasm towards GOD, which seems its inseparable effect."

It is surprising to find that, although such convictions found expression in his sermons, there are very few traces of them in his verse.   In the *Palinodia*, written shortly before the letter just quoted, he recalls the emotions of joy and exultation roused in him, as a boy, by natural phenomena—mountains, winds, and waves.   And he deplores, as he does in some of his private letters, that a period had intervened during which his soul had not responded to these influences.   But now he bids

Mountains, and winds and waves, take back your child :
Upon thy balmy bosom, Mother Nature,
Where my young spirit dreamt its years away,
Give me once more to nestle : I have strayed
Far through another world, which is not thine.
Through sunless cities, and the weary haunts
Of smoke-grimed labour, and foul revelry
My flagging wing has swept.   A mateless bird's
My pilgrimage has been ; through sin, and doubt,
And darkness, seeking love.   Oh, hear me, Nature !
Receive me once again, but not alone ;
No more alone, Great Mother !  I have brought
One who has wandered, yet not sinned like me.
Upon thy lap, twin children, let us lie ;
And in the light of thine immortal eyes
Let our souls mingle, till the Father calls
To some eternal home the charge He gives.

It was eight years later that he wrote *Dartside*, the only
other poem bearing on the subject.   He sent it to his wife
with a covering letter, in which he described it as produced,
" with many happy tears," by " scenery more lovely than
tongue can tell," on " the most charming solitary day I ever
spent in my life " :—

> I cannot tell what ye say, green leaves,
>     I cannot tell what ye say ;
> But I know that there is a spirit in you,
>     And a word in you this day.

> I cannot tell what ye say, rosy rocks,
>     I cannot tell what ye say ;
> But I know that there is a spirit in you,
>     And a word in you this day.

I cannot tell what ye say, brown streams,
   I cannot tell what ye say ;
But I know in you, too, a spirit doth live,
   And a word doth speak this day.

'  Oh, green is the colour of faith and truth,
   And rose the colour of love and youth,
     And brown of the fruitful clay.
Sweet Earth is faithful, and fruitful, and young,
   And her bridal day shall come ere long,
And you shall know what the rocks and the stream
    And the whispering woodlands say.'

It would be difficult to say what is not mystical in the
verse of THOMAS EDWARD BROWN, the schoolmaster-
deacon, whose unconventional creed and practice did not
prevent his being offered—in vain, of course—the office of
Archdeacon in his beloved Manxland. He had in full the
reserve which we have had to notice in other mystics ; and
in *Credo* he scouts the notion of revealing to the casual
reader his " faith as strong as steel," the " hope that streaks
my night with bars of heavenly blue," or the " love that
fills my heart, a love that's known to few ". But he tells
us a good deal, in his own enigmatical fashion, in such
pieces as *Pain*, with these final stanzas :—

For there is threefold oneness with the One ;
   And he is one, who keeps
   The homely laws of life ; who, if he sleeps
Or wakes, in his true flesh GOD'S will is done.

And he is one, who takes the deathless forms,
   Who schools himself to think
   With the All-thinking, holding fast the link,
GOD-rivetted, that bridges casual storms.

> But tenfold one is he, who feels all pains
>   Not partial, knowing them
>   As ripples parted from the gold-beak'd stem,
> Wherewith GOD'S galley onward ever strains.
>
> To him the sorrows are the tension-thrills
>   Of that serene endeavour,
>   Which yields to GOD for ever and for ever,
> The joy that is more ancient than the hills.

It is hardly possible that any one can have been more aware than Brown was of the Divine Immanence. GOD is in *My Garden* (no matter what " the fool contends "), in the bird whose song dissipated the sorrow of *A Morning Walk*, in the salmon of *Per Omnia Deus*, and in various other *Disguises ;* while every pure laugh is a *Risus Dei.*

A striking characteristic of his Nature-mysticism is his way of describing his own experiences in terms of Nature, as in *The Dhoon*, the stream which " leapt into his mother's arms," and, " wrapt in that dear embrace," found " everywhere what stillness "; or, again, as in *Wastwater to Scawfell*, a meaningless poem unless we read GOD for Scawfell and, for Wastwater, T. E. Brown. But perhaps the best of the pieces in this vein is *The Well*, in which he makes his protest against all that restricts and deadens in him the flow of the Divine Life :—

> I am a spring—
> Why square me with a kerb ?
>
> . . . . . . .
>
> O cruel force,
> That gives me not a chance
> To fill my natural course,
> With mathematic rod
> Economising GOD ;
>
> . . . . . . .

One faith remains—
That through what ducts soe'er,
What metamorphic strains,
What chymic filterings I shall pass
To where, O GOD, Thou lov'st to mass
Thy rains upon the crags, and dim the sphere.
So when night's heart with keenest silence thrills,
Take me, and weep me on the desolate hills!

In *Dartmoor*, perhaps the most original of his poems, we find Brown in a mood of cynical interrogation. But that he had his moments of certitude we know from the apostrophe of Bradda in the *Epistola ad Dakyns* :—

I charge you by the tears
And by the passion that I took
From you, and flung them to the vale,
And had the ultimate vision, do not fail!

And as regards the Presence, although in *Specula* he can offer only an hypothesis—

Belike thou then shalt know
He hath been with thee all the time,

in *Praesto* he can say,

How enter'd, by what secret stair,
I know not, knowing only he was there.

But he had his times of dreariest dereliction :—

Oh, I cannot bear
This empty cup :
If it must be with gall,
Fill it up! fill it up!
Fill my soul, fill my soul!
And I will bless
The hand that filleth
Mine emptiness.

This sense of loss is the more poignant when it is felt
that the emptiness in oneself is due to the careless reception
of " Him that filleth all in all ". This is Brown's conviction
in the poem wherein he pictures himself as *The Pitcher*,
placed beneath GOD'S fountain, " expectant of the everlasting flow " :—

> So He fill'd me—then I lost Him,
> Lost Him in His own excess;
> For He could not but transcend me
> In my very nothingness.
>
> Wretched soul, that could'st not hold Him!
> Soul incapable and base!
> Hardly 'ware that He doth bathe thee
> Steep'd in largess of His grace!

The piece entitled *Indwelling* reveals the poet imagining
the soul a shell, and reproaching it because, being not yet
dead to self, it cannot receive the Ocean :—

> But thou art all replete with very *thou*;
> And hast such shrewd activity,
> That when He comes, He says: 'This is enow
> Unto itself—'Twere better let it be:
> It is so small and full, there is no room for me'.

The longing for union finds expression in the poem on
*Dreams*, which are denounced as " a waste of time " :—

> Oh, but if GOD would make a deep suspense,
> And draw me perfect from the adhesive sheath;
> If all the veils and swathings of pretence,
> Dropt from me, sunk beneath,
> Then would I get me very far from hence.
>
> I'd come to Him with one swift arrow-dart,
> Aim'd at the zenith of the o'erbrooding blue;

> Straight to the centre of His aweful heart
> The flight long-wing'd and true
> Should bear me rapt through all the spheres that part.

A goodly number of Brown's pieces describe, by different metaphors, the Mystic Quest, notably *Climbing*, *Land ho!* and *The Schooner* (surely the inspiring source of the Masefield plainness of speech) ; while *In a Fair Garden* gives a delightful version of the Ludus Amoris, the mystic game of love which GOD plays with the soul : the poet recalls a game of hide-and-seek played by a mother and child, with its perturbations and " half-acknowledged fears," its " joyous sallies " and " sweet irrational blisses," and he draws the moral—

> Blest child! blest mother! blest the truth ye taught—
> GOD seeketh us, and yet He would be sought.

Tracing his artistic descent from Keats and Pre-Raphaelitism, RICHARD WATSON DIXON is, in style, the antipodes of T. E. Brown. A member of the bright and ardent group of undergraduates who gathered round William Morris and Burne Jones at Oxford in the ' fifties,' Dixon's ministerial career was undistinguished ; but his fame is secure as the writer of a history of the English Reformation, in which the literary excellence of the picturesque school is admirably combined with the critical erudition of the scientific historians ; while his poetry, in spite of occasional obscurity and faultiness of technique, is now winning its way to a wider and truer appreciation.

An autobiographical interest attaches to the poem which he entitled *A Lenten Mystery:* it reflects his dismal experiences as an assistant-curate in Lambeth. Appalled and sickened though he was by the sights and circumstances of

slumdom, his soul caught the accents of an inner voice which
enheartened him with this message :—

> GOD His eternity on time,
> GOD His infinity on space,
> Casts : GOD proceeds in all earth's ways,
> In all that He hath made GOD lurks,
> He waiteth man in all His works :
> Dost thou in any wise observe
> His Presence as the living nerve
> Of life, and dost thou reverence
> For His sake every form of sense,
> And strive to take each for thine own ?
>
> .    .    .    .    .    .    .
>
> How mightily heav'n overflows,
> How countlessly doth GOD indite
> Himself in darkness and in light,
> And all that grows between these two—
> Star-form'd, and written on the blue
> Void of the all-embracing shade—
> Shade-form'd, and solemnly inlaid
> Between bright forms of life that crawl
> In and out the mother-womb of all
> The solemn all-embracing shade.

This piece comes from *Christ's Company* (1861), his
earliest and, to some tastes, his best volume of verse, from
which also some passages of the *St. Paul* must be extracted. This poem takes the form of a letter addressed to
Seneca by Gallio, who, after depicturing the Apostle's
person, passes to his message :—

> The sum of all was hope in things to come,
> And faith that gives hope substance in our pain,
> And love that perfects faith ; yes, love the sum
> Of sums : the sweetness in the thing

Seem'd here, that love was nam'd the ring
Which linketh man to GOD, the wing
Which strikes the eternal shadowing
With one firm shadow ; the great category
(Rest here, rest here) from which the truth doth sing,
Through every other form with brightest glory.

The proud but high-minded proconsul describes to his
philosopher-brother how unaccountably his scepticism had
been shaken, until at last he had

Felt such a gush of joy about
My heart-roots, as if in and out
'Twas life-blood billow'd ; and as stout
As once we sent the battle-shout,
Pitching clear notes against barbaric din—
O brother, my soul's voice against the rout
Of unbeliefs a man doth nurse within,
Arising and protesting wild,
Spake, speaking out untruth defil'd ;
Spake, speaking in the truth exil'd ;
Spake, Little head and weary child,
Come home, GOD loves, GOD loves through sin and shame ;
Come home, GOD loves His world ; and thy so-styl'd
Instincts, which whisper'd this even in the name
Of doubts and of carnalities,
Were true conclusions, nature-wise ;
In thy old scorn'd formalities
And creeds, GOD looks thee in thine eyes.
Wherefore believe again thine ancient lore,
For whatsoever Reason doth devise,
Her fiery wings and fire-cloud car to soar,
They truly gain the living height,
Because as their most proper freight
They carry love, the infinite

> Of man, up to the rapturous site
> Of love, the infinite in nature spread.

He ends by recounting a dream, in which the Apostle's face had appeared to him and had mysteriously changed, becoming in part Another's, in part his own ; and this is the disturbing truth impressed upon his mind and heart—

> Paul spake of One : what man is He,
> We ask ; what other could He be
> Save Whom I saw, Whom all may see
> Of us—Another and the Me ?
> Thou wouldst inquire concerning Him, of Whom
> Spake Paul—the Christ ?   My dream I tell to thee :
> I saw Another striving to become
> Myself in self ; this was the Christ.
> I think, be sure I have not miss'd
> Paul's meaning, that GOD'S Word uprist
> Doth grant to all who list.

Soon after *Christ's Company* came a prize poem on the subject of *St. John in Patmos*.   From it we must have the central stanzas, in which the beloved disciple says :—

> And I am happy now, so manifold
>     The past is, and the present so serene :
> Thought I my soul was ready for the gold
>     Of visions ? but they come not ; therefore e'en
> As ever, let me think to keep my soul
>     Fix'd on the whole circumference, which weds
>     The centre ever to itself and spreads
>
> In light like waves for ever ; on the whole
>     Of love in love divinely multiplied ;
> Not generated in the onward roll
>     Of ages, though to men 'tis centuried ;

But rather in all points of time perfected,
    As in the bosom of the mind divine,
    So in the thoughts of life which thence outshine;

And thirdly, in the sparkles thence deflected
    Into the bosom of this world of man;
In oracles and laws of grace connected
    Through the six ages; GOD alone, Who can
Know how the stream of time doth measure round
    Into a breathing circle held within—
    The eternal circle which doth both begin

And end it; He alone can know the sound
    Which that glad circle in its rounding makes
In both my ears: for say, was I not found
    In the blest bosom of that Love, which slakes
Our human thirst, when all the rest at gaze
    With distant eyes were murmuring, Is it I?
    Lord, is it I?   And think ye no reply

Did make me nearer to the hidden ways
    Of love, no response beat into my ear
From that deep heart which puls'd the aweful rays
    To the eyes beneath whose curve I did upsteer
My reverent gaze, whilst holding solemn state
    In the upper room;—no benediction press'd
    Like a spear's head of bliss into my breast?

Yes, truly, as I then beheld elate
    The very form itself of Love indeed;
And comprehended in a moment's fate
    That which all comprehending doth exceed,
By science all incomprehensible;
    Incomprehensible things comprehending,
    So ever since that saintly ray's first sending

The bliss renews itself in visions still,
    And urges me for ever to aspire
To that great knowledge which drew out my will
    To ecstasy, as fire to flame draws fire;
And thus last night the triple period
    Saw I of love; beheld I love in man,
    In angels, and in GOD; that love began

In agony, liv'd in service, but in GOD
    Existed in a wise no tongue can tell;
That, as flowers issue from the underclod,
    Man's anguish gives angelic love its shell
Of service; whence the angels owe to man
    Much bliss; of love and anguish GOD doth mix
    Peace, which He gives His world in golden pyx.

But for considerations of space, *The Ode to Rapture*, from *Historical Odes and Other Poems*, would be given in full; for, like the pieces already quoted, it was strangely rejected by the present Laureate when he assisted in the issue of the *Selected Poems*. Opening with a closely observed picture of clouds and blossom and streamlet, the poet asks :—

Ah, what is this, that now with sated eyes
And humming ears the soul no more descries?
Drawn back upon the spirit all the sense
Becomes intelligence;
And to be doubly now unfolded feels
That which itself reveals;
Double the world of all that may appear
To eye or hand or ear;
Double the soul of that which apprehends
By that which sense transcends.

He passes on to speak of " a soul occult in Nature," the shadow of which floats into man's soul.   And

Then are we lifted up erect and whole
In vast confession to that universe
Perceiv'd by us: our soul itself transfers
Thither by instinct sure ; it swiftly hails
The mighty spirit similar ; it sails
In the divine expansion ; it perceives
Tendencies glorious, distant ; it enweaves
Itself with excitations more than thought
Unto that soul unveil'd and yet unsought.

Ye winds and clouds of light,
Ye lead the soul to GOD ;
The newborn soul that height
With rapturous foot hath trod,
And is receiv'd of GOD :
GOD doth the soul receive
Which mounts towards Him, and alone would dwell
With Him ; though finite with the Infinite,
Though finite, rising with a might
Like to infinitude.
Gently receiving such he doth dispel
All solitary horror with delight,
Honouring the higher mood.

For though the soul pants with fierce ecstasy
The unattainable to grasp, to be
For ever mingled with infinity ;
And this in vain, since GOD Himself withdraws
From human knowledge, e'en as its own laws
Seclude the soul from sense ;
Yet not from love He hies ;
From love GOD never flies.

Love is the soul's best sense, which GOD descries,
Which bares the covert of intelligence :
And, honouring in love the higher mood,
With lovely joys He fills the solitude
Of His own Presence, whither trusting Him
The soul hath mounted : lo, it might have found
Utter destruction on this higher ground,
Tenuity of air and swooning dim
For lack of breath ; but now it finds hereby
A lovely vesture of infinity,
And ecstasies that nourish ecstasy.
GOD giveth love to love, and ministers
Substance to substance ; life to life he bears.

Finally the poet apostrophizes winds and cloud, river and sea, bush and flower, as " portions of entity supreme," and as giving access to that " kingdom known to the spirit only ".

Dr. Dixon's later volumes of verse contain very much less that is to our purpose here. He seems to have passed through something like Wordsworth's experience of " seeing no more the things which he had seen ". Among the *Lyrical Poems* of 1887, there are several which suggest the " fruitless deploring " of the fled " visionary gleam ". One of these is the beautiful Ode, *The Spirit Wooed*, which ends on a note of hopeless interrogation :—

Can the weeping eye
Always feel light through mists that never dry ?
Can empty arms alone for ever fill
Enough the breast ? Can echo answer still,
When the voice has ceased to cry ?

The *Ode on Advancing Age*, which some have called his best piece of work, seems also to reflect this mood of

Dark Night.   But here, after comparing the middle years
to the dreariness of a beach at low tide with " the inarticu-
late cries of the waves, of the shore, of the bird," and again
to a dog's neglect of that which " roused his rapture once,"
in the closing lines he succeeds in throwing off his dejection :—

> But no!   Resume thy pride,
> O man, that musest thus.
> Be to the end what thou hast been before :
> The ancient joy shall wrap thee still—the tide
> Return upon the shore.

As a poet, GEORGE SEYMOUR HOLLINGS is scarcely of
the same calibre as Dr. Dixon, but his mystical standing cannot
be impugned.   It is now many years since English Churchmen
began to look to the Society of St. John the Evangelist of
Cowley for a leadership in which the claims of institutional
discipline and of mystical spontaneity are rightly adjusted—
in particular, to the prose of Father Congreve and to the
verse of Father Hollings.   The latter, indeed, gave us, in
such books as *Porta Regalis* and *Paradoxes of the Love
of God*, prose treatises of practical mysticism of the very
highest value, interspersed or ending with verse.   From the
former volume we may take some lines from *The Arrow*,
in which an angel is represented as carrying to the Throne
an arrow of prayer shot upwards by an archer faint and
chilled by a sense of dereliction ; it is received by the
Master with these words :—

> Came, then, this arrow from chill'd hand and bow?
> Nay, that is strange; it's kindling point's aglow !
> See how with but a gentle breath I blow—
> It flames on high !—Cold, did you say, below?
>
> .    .    .    .    .    .    .    .    .    .

Say, ' I will hold thee, loyal heart, from sin.
Thy dart came hither burning nigh to flame,
So is the source from whence the arrow came.
Cast dart on dart, speed all thy soul in prayer !—
Worms draw from out their life what kings may wear,
So lift thy heart !   It is lift up above,
Since Jesus is the object of thy love! '

Much the same message is found in *The Wayfarer*, one
of the pieces included in *The Paradoxes of the Love of
God* :—

> Though I see not for the dark,
> Yet I stoop to feel the mark
> Where Thy sacred feet once trod :
> Is it here, my Lord, my GOD ?
> Draw me ; we will run to Thee,
> Leading thus mysteriously !
>
> .     .     .     .     .     .
>
> From His lips sweet accents flow,
> ' Not as yet My Face to show
> Come I, but to make thee know
> Nigh thy Jesus when most low
> Stoops My child, and lowlily
> Only seeks to follow Me '.

But perhaps the best poem in the last-named volume is
one called *The Gardener*, which was inspired by the words
in the *Song of Solomon* (v. 1), " I am come into My
Garden " :—

> Why bows the lily's lustrous head ?
> Why burns the rose with deeper glow ?
> What lightens every flower-bed ?
> He cometh, Whom my heart doth know !

25

He cometh! Dews of herbs arise,
Sweet veils of wreathed fragrance float,
The lark, high hid in melting skies,
Wakes welcome from a blitheful throat.

He cometh! wondrous brightness lies
About His path on either hand,
Whilst every chilling shadow flies
From Light that glads a Heavenly Land.

Beams from their gentle Gardener's sight
Search all those glowing roses through :
And light yon lily's lustrous white
With opal gleams of rainbow hue.

Therefore, yon lily bows her head ;
Therefore, the rose's deeper hue ;
His sunshine o'er each flow'ret spread, ·
He cometh Whom my soul doth know !

It may not be fanciful to be reminded by this poem of
the poet's early ambition to be an artist—an ambition re-
linquished for reasons quite other than those prompted by
failure. Possibly he was recalling here the sermon in which
Tauler speaks of the red roses of sacrifice and the lilies of
chastity. Father Hollings himself, in the prose text, speaks
of " the white lily of detachment " ; and he has a striking
comment on whiteness, which he declines to think of as
a negation of colour : " this whiteness needs only to be
analysed by a heavenly science, that it may be seen to be
composed of every colour, . . . colourless to the world,
because only to be seen and analysed by that discerning
power which belongs to GOD Himself ".

The most notable of Father Hollings' books consisting
entirely of verse are those entitled *In Via* and *The Divine*

*Lover*. The former has an interesting preface, in which he urges, as John Keble used to do, that " only in verse can we even partially express what stirs within us : as the Psalmist has it, ' I will declare my dark speech upon the harp ' ". Of the poems included in that volume, the most important from a mystical point of view is *One Born of the Spirit*. It is, however, too long to be given here in its entirety, and it does not lend itself to abbreviation. But we can take a few lines from *The Morning Cometh*, without any injustice to the poet ; it carries us back to a favourite thought of Henry Vaughan's : the poem describes a dawn and closes with this prayer :—

> Lord, Who this heavenly pageant doth display,
> A parable of mysteries to come,
> Teach me to read this rare illumin'd page,
> From which, at Prime, Thine angel-cantors sing
> Such songs as mingle praise with pensive notes
> Of longing for *that* Dawn *these* dawns rehearse.

*The Divine Lover* is a long poem on a subject sufficiently indicated by the title. The opening lines show the speaker in a mood of Dark Night ; but relief comes at last :—

> A rainbow arches round my head
> As on the stair I hear His tread,
> And, e'er my swooning senses flee,
> I know One bending over me.
>
> Half-risen, I saw one Face and gaz'd,
> Drunken with love and all amazed.
> Pain'd, yet not blinded, by that sight,
> And ravish'd with a keen delight,
> And strengthen'd by the very gaze,

I saw in ecstasy of praise
The heavenly wonder clearer shown,
His gracious countenance made known.

As the present writer has protested against Crashaw's fondness for the metaphor of intoxication, it seems necessary to state here that, out of consideration for those who shrink from the implications of the word ' drunken,' Father Hollings gives, in a note, Scriptural authority for its use : " The spouse in the Canticles exclaims, ' Drink and be drunken with love, O beloved ' (*Cant.* v. margin).   The love of GOD ' shed abroad in our hearts by the Holy Ghost ' inebriates, that is to say, transports the soul beyond itself. . . . As the Scripture has it, ' Thy love is better than wine ' (*Cant.* i. 2) and it awakens a response which carries the soul out of itself and lifts it beyond the power of sorrows, cares, and pain ; cf. *Ephes.* v. 18."

In the closing lines of the poem, the taunt of ' Dreamer ! ' is retorted :—

No, I have learnt what stands for aye,
Have seen the light of fadeless Day.
Within, a well of waters clear
Yields me refreshment ever near ;
Such knowledge of my loving Lord
Shall on my weary way afford
Strength to press onward in the quest.
Have I not Jesus in my breast ?

And the objection that Christ seems capriciously to "hide, then show His Face again," is met by the conviction that it is

In love He hides Himself from sight
And bids us seek a clearer light ;
In other form, yet still the same,
Calls us the fuller Gift to claim.

That clearer light and fuller Gift came to Father Hollings quite suddenly, in Holy Week, 1914, while ministering at GOD's altar, *felix nimis opportunitate mortis*.

One living writer, at least, must be named, to prove that the line of mystical poets has not come to an end in the ranks of the Anglican clergy ; and it will be readily conceded that, in that connexion, the most distinguished name is that of ARTHUR SHEARLY CRIPPS, who has for many years been working as a missionary in Rhodesia. The easiest way to gain an insight into his verse is to read some of his tales in prose. There is one on *The Scales of Passion*— " the everlasting dissatisfaction of some souls with their own satisfaction," exemplified in the hero's craving for Oxford when in South Africa, and when at Oxford for South Africa, with " the thatched villages, the country people who might have stepped out of Theocritus if their skins were fairer. . . . He had watched English country life in those Upper River villages, and planned to deliver his own rustics from European violence, fraud, and contempt. He had worshipped before the All Souls' reredos and seen the vision of the souls of Africa. He had watched that inscrutable Christ of all times and all races in the Keble picture, and yearned towards the rejected Black Christ with new glows of devotion."

His verse, Theocritean in form and Franciscan in spirit, reverts again and again to the thought of the Black Christ— the Divine immanent in the African native. Eastertide finds him longing to mitigate the wrongs done, still as of old, by Church and State, to " a Christ the Father gave " :—

> By strait starlit ways I creep,
> Caring while the careless sleep,
> Bearing palms, and flowers to crown
> That poor Head the stone holds down ;

> Through some crack or crevice dim
> I would reach my sweets to Him.

The union of South Africa, achieved at the cost of a colour-bar, suggests the thought of a *Peace-offering* made upon Table Mountain as altar :—

> He that hath vision, let his eyes descry
> Huge mystic forms to that same altar tied.
> There England's honour bleeds, how proudly slow !
> There from Five Wounds in Feet and Hands and Side,
> Five dusky Wounds, how fast the runnels flow !

This note of courageous protest against the seamy side of Imperialism is often struck, both in his prose and in his verse, and not least bravely in his latest book of verse, *Lake and Water*. But he does not spare himself : the sense of his own neglectfulness wrings out such lines as these :—

> O Christ, I did it *not* to You, and why ?
> That year is gone. Its Wounds remain. Oh, set
> To wrongs that linger—Love's allotted term !
> Cover my fault, dark Patience, with a sigh,
> Accept, dark Wounded Hands, balms that may not amend !

The *Envoi* to the collection named above ends thus :—

> O happy eyes
> Are mine that pierce the black disguise
> And see my Lord ! O woe of woe
> That I should see, that I should know
> Whom 'tis they use that use Him so.

The Quest is another phase of mysticism which constantly recurs—sometimes with striking originality—in Mr. Cripps' books, where such terms as ' Pilgrimage ' and ' The Way ' are repeatedly used as titles. And here, again, we are greatly helped by one of his prose tales. It is called *The Open Way*, and tells of a visit paid to South Africa by an artist, who after a disappointing round of sight-seeing, was persuaded to accompany a priest on one of his missionary journeys, and showed his gratitude for the experience by painting a picture for a new Church. The legend beneath the painting was, " I am the Way," and it depicted " a hugely wide Mashonaland hill-side with a white way running up it ". . . . The story ends with the adverse criticism of " one of the Chosen British People," who thought that the artist would have been better employed in painting the bridge over the Victoria Falls, or the tomb of Cecil Rhodes, or a Government House, or " something with some human interest in it " ; and the missionary who tells the story adds, " But then he did not know what Ward and I know about the secrets of the Way".

Some inkling of these secrets may be gathered from such a poem as the *Ascension Day* meditation, the *Way-Song*, *The Lost Way*, and others, of which the lines *Ad Viam Viator* may be given as a sample :—

> GOD of the road, I hail Thee, I that hold
> My roofless nights so august and so dear.
> Men count their travellings trouble, toil, and fear ;
> But I unwilling, when my home is near,
> Leave the scorch'd plains, the darkling thickets cold—
> Loth as one haled from shrine he sought to pray—
> Roads are Thy shrines, Thou saidst, " I am the Way".

The above-named are all from the volume entitled *Lyra Evangelistica*. From another collection, *Pilgrimage of Grace*, an entire section might be instanced, with special mention of *Pilgrim's Progress*. And from the latest volume a whole short piece, *Via Mystica*, must be borrowed :—

> Wear sandal-wings of Venture's charm
> What time you flout the stings of Harm :

Your head hold high amid the stars
What time your feet wage footsore wars :
'Tis the long miles you parch and burn
That water-pools to nectar turn :
'Tis being scant and burnt in haste
Gives bread the true ambrosia's taste.

Fire's glow and sky's roof-silver rare
Pay a day's debts, and leave to spare :
O' weary nightfalls—veld-grass dry
For limbs' rest may with rose-leaves vie :
When the dusk's deep, your way unknown,
Hold the High Feast of the Alone :
Wrapt in His own rich livery
Of loneliness, trust Him to be
Both Way, and lone Wayfarer's Glee !

Some readers may remember that the earliest poem noticed in this volume (see above, p. 7) was one dealing with the seafarer's quest ; and now this last published poem to be noticed is on the same phase of mysticism. Men in these days—perhaps in all days—dislike to think of themselves as wayfarers with " no continuing city " here ; and they are in constant danger of lapsing, almost unconsciously, into the conception of Christ as a merely historical figure, Who, by truth-teaching and pattern-life, made plain the way in which GOD would have us walk. The mystics do us an incalculable benefit by insisting that He is something infinitely greater : the Way Itself, the Truth Itself, the Life Itself. After all, we have travelled no great distance from Judaism, or even from the highest Paganism, until we know ourselves to be " strangers and pilgrims on earth," and know Christ as the Living Personal Way by Which we can pass freely from the finite world to the Infinite.

# CHAPTER XI.

## EMILY BRONTË, CHRISTINA ROSSETTI, EVELYN UNDERHILL.

IT is not from any lack of chivalry that the treatment of mystical verse produced by women has been left to the last, and that it occupies so small a space. The position has been decided on chronological grounds, and the amount of space settled by the factor of supply, not that of demand. Doubtless, English women did express mystical feelings and aspirations in verse before the nineteenth century ; but they seemed to have lacked either the desire or the opportunity to give their poems to the world. The Lady Julian left mystical writings of supreme value, but not in verse, although full of poetry. The Countess of Pembroke, on the other hand, wrote sacred verse, but not of a mystical character. Mention should be made, perhaps, of Elizabeth Rowe and her *Devout Exercises of the Heart*, edited by Isaac Watts early in the eighteenth century. They are not distinguished, however, as poetry, and hardly required the editor's apology for being " too near akin to the language of the mystical writers " ; moreover, Mrs. Rowe was not a Churchwoman.

When we note—as we can scarcely avoid doing—that much of the best mystical verse and most of the best mystical prose is now being produced by women, we can account for the silence of earlier ages only by recalling the wide-spread persuasion that authorship was an unladylike proceeding. It was, we know, from dread of the charge of

(393)

impropriety that EMILY BRONTË, the first of the women poets to be considered here, issued the few poems which she did herself issue, under the pseudonym of " Ellis Bell ".

It is extremely difficult to ' place ' Emily Brontë. Both her personal character and her literary methods have defied the curiosity of Brontë-students, in spite of their untiring zeal in the pursuit of gossip and side-lights. Her powerful novel, *Wuthering Heights*, is one of the most impersonal —some have said, inhuman—books ever written ; and her poems seem designed to conceal, rather than to reveal, feeling. " My sister Emily," says Charlotte (who had " accidently lighted on a MS. volume of verse " in her sister's handwriting), " was not a person of demonstrative character, nor one on the recesses of whose mind and feelings even those nearest and dearest to her could, with impunity, intrude unlicensed ; it took hours to reconcile her to the discovery I had made." The only remark that any one could recall Emily to have made on the subject of religion was an almost monosyllabic approval of the opinion that a person's religion should be entirely a matter between that person and GOD. This is hardly the highest or truest conception of religion ; but we have to bear in mind that, in this case, it was probably formed, partly as a result of, and partly as a protest against, the Ulster type of Protestantism with which the Reverend Patrick Brunty (to give him his original name) had familiarized his daughters.

Mrs. Gaskell, whose impartiality there is no reason to call in question, failed to gain " a pleasant impression of " Emily Brontë. It was said that " she never showed regard to any human creature ; all her love was reserved for animals," and what often recommended an animal to her was " the fierce, wild intractibility of its nature ". She was reserved with a reserve which was "indifferent whether it pleased or not". She was "impervious to influence". "She appeared egotistical and exacting compared to Charlotte, who . . . allowed her to exercise an unconscious tyranny over her." A cynic might gleefully assert that this is precisely what might have been expected of one to whom "Liberty was the breath of her nostrils".

We may agree with Swinburne that

Holier
Name of the soul's there are none

than that of Liberty and Freedom, if by them we mean emancipation from all that is alien to the highest life. There is a service which is perfect freedom, while the claim for liberty may simply cloke a demand for a false independence in a life of selfish isolation. St. Paul could speak of a deliverance "from the bondage of corruption into the glorious liberty of the children of GOD," meaning by 'liberty' freedom to develop to the utmost every Godlike faculty of our nature. He could speak, too, of the liberty to be found "where the Spirit of GOD is"—liberty, that is, to "behold with open face as in a glass, the glory of the Lord". Liberty, in this Pauline sense, every mystic must claim. Was it this that Emily Brontë contemplated when, in the character of *The Old Stoic*, she demanded for herself "in life and death a chainless soul"? Quite probably it was; for, against the impression we get of one whose "sufficiency" was of self rather than "of GOD," and against the rhetorical note of defiance in her verse which may have been no more than a protective device, we must set the daily life of well-fulfilled duty in a particularly dreary home and in a most unattractive parish.

There are several of Emily Brontë's poems which suggest very strongly that she enjoyed something akin to that Cosmic Consciousness of which a good deal has been said already in these pages. It is, no doubt, arguable that her words refer, not to an illuminated apprehension of Reality, but to an ordinary, though extraordinarily developed imagination. The lines *To Imagination* seem more applicable to the lower gift, but are not incapable of covering a higher faculty —that to which Blake gave the name ' Imagination '. *The Visionary*, too, is susceptible of either interpretation : and the same may be said of several other pieces, like that beginning, "*Aye—there it is ! it wakes to-night*". But the last of the well-known *Stanzas* manifestly reveals the longing, which Richard Jefferies expressed in *The Story of my Heart*, to learn the partially divined esoteric meaning of the Cosmos :—

> What have those lonely mountains worth revealing ?
> More glory and more grief than I can tell :
> The earth that wakes one human heart to feeling
> Can centre both the worlds of Heaven and Hell.

The poem entitled *Stars* might conceivably have been composed simply to relieve an overwrought imagination, as indisputably were the many lines about ' Rosina ' and ' Julius ' which have been recently resurrected by too enthusiastic admirers :—

> Thought follow'd thought, star follow'd star,
> Through boundless regions on ;
> While one sweet influence, near and far,
> Thrill'd through, and prov'd us one.

But it is more natural to take them as early intimations of the Cosmic Consciousness. If they were so, Emily Brontë (unlike William Watson) was not " content if whispers from

the stars . . . come blown at midnight through our prison
bars ". The claim for freedom to soar above surface-ex-
periences, and to break through corporeal barriers and
material limitations, is expressed most vividly in the poem
called *The Prisoner*. Anxious as ever to veil her inmost
feelings, she here describes, rather melodramatically in the
opening stanzas, such a captive as Joan of Arc might have
been, "confined in triple walls," who yet can say :—

A messenger of Hope comes every night to me,
And offers for short life, eternal liberty.

He comes with western winds, with evening's wandering airs,
With that clear dusk of heaven that brings the thickest stars.
Winds take a pensive tone, and stars a tender fire,
And visions rise, and change, that kill me with desire.

Desire for nothing known in my maturer years,
When Joy grew mad with awe, at counting future tears.
When, if my spirit's sky was full of flashes warm,
I knew not whence they came, from sun or thunderstorm.

But, first, a hush of peace, a soundless calm descends:
The struggle of distress, and fierce impatience ends ;
Mute music soothes my breast—unutter'd harmony,
That I could never dream, till earth was lost to me.

Then dawns the Invisible ; the Unseen its truth reveals ;
My outward sense is gone, my inward essence feels :
Its wings are almost free—its home, its harbour found ;
Measuring the gulf, it stoops and dares the final bound.

Oh! dreadful is the check—intense the agony—
When the ear begins to hear, and the eye begins to see ;
When the pulse begins to throb, the brain to think again ;
The soul to feel the flesh, and the flesh to feel the chain.

Experts assure us that these lines bear the authentic marks of a genuine rapture, with the agonizing drop back to the corporeal plane after the ecstatic flight.

Reference must be made to *The Philosopher*, a poem which, by means of a somewhat obscure dialogue, reveals an intense yearning to reach up to the Absolute. Nor must those *Last Lines* (which "stirred like a clarion-blast the soul" of Matthew Arnold) be left unnoticed. They illustrate very finely Professor Seth Pringle-Pattison's statement that "the thought most intensely present to the mystic is that of a supreme, all-pervading and indwelling Power, in Whom all things are One".[1] A poem can hardly be omitted here, which Lord Haldane reproduced in full in his Gifford Lectures as philsophically sound and as transferring philosophy "from the abstract to the concrete" :—

> No coward soul is mine,
> No trembler in the world's storm-troubled sphere :
> I see Heaven's glories shine,
> And faith shines equal, arming me from fear.
>
> O GOD within my breast,
> Almighty, ever-present Deity !
> Life—that in me has rest,
> As I—undying Life—have power in Thee !
>
> Vain are the thousand creeds
> That move men's hearts : unutterably vain ;
> Worthless as wither'd weeds,
> Or idle froth amid the boundless main,
>
> To waken doubt in one
> Holding so fast by Thine infinity ;

[1] Quoted from the twenty-six Definitions of Mysticism, given by Dr. Inge in an Appendix to his Bampton Lectures.

So surely anchor'd on
The steadfast rock of immortality.

With wide-embracing love
Thy spirit animates eternal years,
Pervades and broods above,
Changes, sustains, dissolves, creates, and rears.

Though earth and man were gone,
And suns and universes ceas'd to be,
And Thou wert left alone,
Every existence would exist in Thee.

There is not room for Death,
Nor atom that his might could render void:
Thou—Thou art Being and Breath,
And what Thou art can never be destroy'd.

But if this were all that could be quoted, no more could be claimed for Emily Brontë than a certain degree of cosmic emotion and insight, with far less religious devotion than many a non-Christian mystic has displayed. But in the collection of poems which were last given to the public, there are some which testify to the writer's Christianity, and one, at least, in which we get what we have missed hitherto —some suggestion of the motive underlying the Psalmist's desire for Liberty : " Bring my soul out of prison, that I may praise Thy Name ". This poem is entitled *In Memory of a Happy Day in February*, and it is given here as the work of Emily Brontë on the authority of the great Brontë-student, Mr. C. K. Shorter, although it has been usually attributed to her sister Anne, an attribution which internal evidence would seem to support. After an opening thanksgiving, and a rejection of various possible explanations of a rapturous experience, the correct solution is given, and the resultant convictions are described :—

It was a glimpse of truths divine
Unto my spirit given,
Illumin'd by a ray of light
That shone direct from Heaven !

I knew there was a GOD on high,
By Whom all things were made ;
I saw His wisdom and His power
In all His works display'd.

And while I wonder'd and ador'd
His wisdom so divine,
I did not tremble at His power—
I felt that GOD was mine.

I felt that my Redeemer lived ;
I did not fear to die ;
I felt that I should rise again
To immortality.

I long'd to view that bliss divine
Which eye hath never seen,
To see the glories of His face
Without the veil between.

A mere critic might object that these lines exemplify the
blight of metrical commonplace which so often settles on
sacred verse ; but, at least, the poet rises here above paganism, and, besides the claim to have attained insight into the
spiritual cause of material effects, we find the gratitude of a
redeemed soul for a living Savour.

There could hardly be a stronger contrast than that presented by Emily Brontë's attitude of bravado, expressing
itself in immature (though occasionally quite successful)

metrical exercises, and CHRISTINA ROSSETTI'S shrinking
diffidence and unusual mastery of metrical forms. "The
high-priestess of Pre-Raphælitism" was born of a father
whose poem, *T'amo e fra dolci affani*, reveals, in the
daughter's English version, a genuinely mystical consciousness.
Christina's mystical standing, however, is not above challenge. It does not rest upon her allegorical poems, such as
*The Prince's Progress* and *A Ballad of Boding*—noble
as they are in the warning they utter against earthly allurements—but upon the wistful adoration of her divinely-
enamoured soul. Dr. Bigg, in his volume on *Unity in
Diversity*, singled out her lines, "We are of those who
tremble at Thy Word," as expressing the typical attitude of
an unmystical nature ; yet in the same work he insists on
the mysticism of the *Epistle to the Hebrews*, which lays
no slight stress on Fear.

Christina Rossetti's attitude was precisely that of the
Psalmist : "I refrain my soul and keep it low" ; and it
was a sure instinct that led her brother, William, to choose
for the inscription on her grave the short poem commencing,
"Give me the lowest place," a poem which carries more
conviction than Sir Thomas Browne's vaunted ambition "to
be but the last man and bring up the rear in Heaven".
But with another Psalmist she learnt also to "rejoice with
trembling" ; she discovered, too, that "the secret (*R.V.* margin, 'friendship') of the Lord is with them that fear Him".
This fear is, of course, that Holy Fear which forms the
climax of the Sevenfold Gifts of the Spirit (*Isaiah*, xi. 2),
and it would be an endless task to quote from the great
mystics who have dwelt upon "the awe and delicious
trouble," which (according to Plotinus) must fall on those
who stand before the Authentic Beauty—St. Augustine,

26

St. Bernard, Tauler, St. Francis de Sales, and many others
who, in Christina Rossetti's words,

> Pent passions in a house of clay,
> Fear and desire, and pangs and ecstasy.

Every mystic must know something of the Bride's experience in the *Canticles:* " My soul failed when He
spake " ; and it is the absence of Holy Fear in our own
times which makes the average Christian's attitude towards
GOD so deplorable—a shallow, easy-going patronage of
One thought of as a weakly good-natured Father. Very
rightly does our Prayer-Book couple the fear and love of
GOD's Name as graces to be sought in prayer ; for, if it is
true that fear without love means servility, it is equally true
that love without fear means familiarity. " They love Thee
little, if at all," says the mystically-minded hymnodist,
Faber, " who do not fear Thee much " ; and there are
very few mystics who would not agree with Hermann (one
of the keenest detractors of mysticism) when he declares
that " the communion of the Christian with GOD never succeeds in overcoming the inner opposition between fear and
love ".

Most readers will recall Mr. Fearing in the second part of
*Pilgrim's Progress*—" one of the most troublesome pilgrim's that ever " old Honest met with, who could " scarce
believe " when he was over the Slough of Despond, who
hardly dared knock at the Gate from a sense of unworthiness, but fairly revelled in the Valley of Humiliation,
" made no stick at the Hill Difficulty, nor did he fear the
lions," while " he would have fought with the men in Vanity
Fair, so hot was he against their fooleries ". Christina
Rossetti could have said, with Christiana, " I see there was
some resemblance 'twixt this good man and I, only . . . his

troubles made him that he could not knock at the houses provided for entertainment ; but my trouble was always such as made me knock the louder ".

Her fear lay at the root of her mysticism, for it proceeded from her intimate knowledge of spiritual mysteries. It contained a deep mistrust of self, but no misgiving about GOD'S goodness. It spurred her to flee, not from GOD, but from self to GOD. It was compounded of a humility which was abjectly aware of its own imperfection, and of a reverence profoundly aware of the Divine Perfection. " When I consider, I am afraid of Him," said Job ; she could have made the words her own ; but she would have meant afraid, not of finding Him, but of losing Him. She loved GOD so intensely that she realized with peculiar vividness what an awful calamity it would be to forfeit His love.

It is time, however, to see more fully what she has to say for herself ; and to understand her aright it is essential to read some of her prose as well as her verse, especially, perhaps, *Time Flies* and *The Face of the Deep*. The latter is " A Devotional Commentary on the Apocalypse," a Book of which she characteristically says that the " study of it should promote holy fear, unflinching obedience, patient progress and patient waiting, unhesitating trust, conformity to the Perfect Will ; . . . so long as these are aimed at, to sit down ignorant and even to rise up equally ignorant, may along with these virtues help forward humility ". Elsewhere in the volume, in connexion with " the mystery of GOD " (x. 7), she speaks of Faith, Hope, and Love, " holy fear likewise ; but never such fear as paralyzes those other graces. . . . Faith discerns, embraces. Hope anticipates, aspires. Fear curbs, spurs. Love curbs, spurs, anticipates, aspires, discerns, embraces, cleaves unto, unites."

Again and again, she underlines the importance of Fear :
" holy fear incites to humility, hope to prudence, love to
obedience ; faith without humility presumes ". This particular passage is introductory to one of the many poems
interspersed in her prose ; it opens thus :—

> Faith, Fear, and Hope have sent their hearts above :
>> Prudence, Obedience, and Humility
> Climb at their call, all scaling Heaven towards Love.
>> Fear hath least grace but great expediency.

She is especially fond in her verse of coupling Fear and
Hope, finding that

>> Fear ballasts Hope, Hope buoys up Fear ;
>> And both befit us here.

In her nature " Hope toils yoked in Fear's copartnery,"
and she has to admit that often

>>> Hope itself is Fear
>>> Viewed on the sunny side.

And yet what clear witness such a sonnet as the following bears to the mystic's aim and certitude !

> Experience bows a sweet, contented face,
>> Still setting to her seal that GOD is true :
>> Beneath the sun, she knows, is nothing new ;
> All things that go return with measur'd pace,
> Winds, rivers, man's still recommencing race :—
>> While Hope beyond earth's circle strains her view,
>> Past sun and moon, and rain and rainbow too,
> Enamour'd of unseen eternal grace.
> Experience saith, ' My GOD doth all things well ' :
>> And for the morrow taketh little care,
>>> Such peace and patience garrison her soul :—
>>> While Hope, who never yet hath eyed the goal,
>> With arms flung forth, and backward floating hair,
> Touches, embraces, hugs the Invisible.

It is easy, too, to trace the connexion of her Fear with Love. Sometimes a person shrinks from loving another for fear of what it may involve—how far it may disorganize the daily life with its settled habits ; what demands the loved one may make. It was not so with Christina Rossetti : fear conditioned her love only by the sense of unworthiness which it brought. No lover ever cried more sincerely, or felt more acutely, " I am not worthy of Him ". But, at the same time, none felt more deeply the thrill of exultation at the thought of having her love returned. Something of all this we can trace in the beautiful sonnet which she wrote *After Communion* :—

> Why should I call Thee Lord, Who art my GOD ?
> > Why should I call Thee Friend, Who art my Love ?
> > Or King, Who art my very Spouse above ?
> Or call Thy Sceptre on my heart Thy Rod ?
> > Lo, now Thy banner over me is love,
> All Heaven flies open to me at Thy nod :
> For Thou hast lit Thy flame in me a clod,
> > Made me a nest for dwelling of Thy Dove.
> > What wilt Thou call me in our home above,
> Who now dost call me friend ? How will it be
> > When Thou for good wine settest forth the best ?
> Now dost Thou bid me come and sup with Thee,
> > Now dost Thou make me lean upon Thy breast :
> > How will it be with me in time of love ?

In the collection of *Verses*, reprinted from *Called to be Saints* and other volumes, we find much faltering and stammering, as is to be expected from so tremulous a lover, but never any reluctance to risk anything, or to surrender everything, for Him Whom (in *Till To-morrow*) she calls " My Heavenly Lover ". In this connexion, it should be recalled that William Rossetti has lifted for us the curtain which veiled the personal bearing of certain poems. When eighteen years of age, Christina's love was sought by a Roman Catholic, whom temporarily she converted to the English Church ; but when he felt it right to return to his former allegiance, she withdrew from the engagement—with an uncommendable scrupulosity, some would say. Some years later again, she was loved by one whom her brother described as a much better man, and he tells us that " she loved him deeply and permanently, . . . but she must have probed his faith and found it either strictly wrong or woe-fully defective ; . . . so she declined his suit . . . but she loved him to the last day of his life and his memory to the last day of her own ". He tells us, further, that traces of this sorrow can be readily found in certain pieces which he names. There is, for example, *From House to Home*, in which resignation is won by a vision of " one who lost her love in pain," but in Heaven

> Drank love, and bathed in love, and mirror'd it,
> And knew no end thereof.

We find in this poem a splendid passage descriptive of Heaven—one of the many passages which justify her words, " Golden Jerusalem floats full in view ".

And then there are two sets of Sonnet-sequences, *Monna Innominata* and *Later Life*, which reveal something of what her surrender meant to her. To the former she sup-plies this key : " In that land and period which gave simul-taneous birth to Catholics, to Albigenses, and to Troubadors, one can imagine many a lady as sharing her lover's poetic aptitude, while the barrier between them might be one held sacred by both, yet not such as to render mutual love incompatible with mutual honour ". The central passage of the sequence is where she speaks of her

> Love that foregoes you but to claim anew
> Beyond this passage of the gate of death.

In *Later Life* she speaks less openly, but is even more self-revealing ; for we get the suggestion of a soul benumbed by a piercing sorrow but yet striving to make its self-surrender a wholehearted one, as in the Sonnet which contains these lines :—

> O Love accept, according my request ;
> O Love exhaust, fulfilling my desire :
> Uphold me with the strength that cannot tire,
> Nerve me to labour till Thou bid me rest,
> Kindle my fire from Thy unkindled fire
> And charm the willing heart from out my breast.

This bitter experience, ending in the triumph of resignation, is reflected, too, in the vision of *An Old-World Thicket*, seen by one overwhelmed with grief, and fiercely rebellious against her fate, in which the outward beauty and joy of shape and colour and sound gradually give place to the opposite extreme of gloom and lamentation. The seer's mood changes, through

> Rage to despair ; and now despair had turn'd
> Back to self-pity and mere weariness,
> With yearnings like a smouldering fire that burn'd,
> And might grow more or less,
> And might die out or wax to white excess.

And then the wood is flooded with a sunset which gilds every object—water-drop, twig, and bird, and the sufferer sees, " filing peacefully between the trees,"

> A homeward flock, at peace
> With one another and with every one.

She has no need to say, in so many words, that she has found the comfort for which her heart was craving :—

> Patient, sun-brightened too,
> Still journeying towards the sunset and their rest,

the sheep have taught the needed lesson.

We can find many another trace of these earthly disappointments. Thus, in *Time Flies*, commenting on the commemoration of St. Agatha (Feb. 5), she says, " The love of Christ, like a touchstone, has tested much human affection, and over and over again has proved it dross. Yet, now and then, two who have differed—and two who differ cannot both hold the entire truth—have loved on faithfully, believing and hoping the best of each other, one (perhaps each) praying for the other, both alike exercising themselves to have always a conscience void of offence. In such a case, where both have loved the Truth and have accounted it ' great and mighty above all things,' there surely remains a strong consolation of hope to flee unto. For can an utter alien from GOD love Truth and make sacrifices for Truth's sake ? "  And here is a passage from *The Face of the Deep* which shows that her self-surrender brought to her (and, let us hope, to her rejected lover) something much more positive and satisfying than the previous extracts might suggest : " Many women attain their heart's desire ; many attain it not.  Yet are these latter no losers if they exchange desire for aspiration, the corruptible for the incorruptible : ' Thou shalt no more be termed Forsaken, neither shalt thy land any more be termed Desolate ; for thou shalt be called Hepzibah, and thy land Beulah ; for the Lord delighteth in thee, and thy land shall be married '." These words introduce a poem, beginning :—

O Lord, when Thou didst call me, didst Thou know
My heart dishearten'd, through and through,
Still hankering after Egypt full in view
Where cucumbers and melons grow ?
                                        *Yea, I knew.*

It is clear that she could make the humble yet confident appeal of St. Peter : " Lord, Thou knowest all things, Thou knowest that I love Thee ".

In the collected *Verses*, there are a goodly number in which the symbol of the Bride is adopted ; and, although it is nearly always applied impersonally, we find in *The Face of the Deep* a comment on " The New Jerusalem . . . prepared as a Bride," in which the application is extended from the Church to the individual : " Behold her in tenderness His dove, in likeness His sister, in union His spouse. Behold her ! yea, also behold thyself, O thou called to be a saint. Her perfections are thy birthright ; thou art what she was, what she is thou mayest become. That Goodness which is her fountain of good overflows to thee likewise. Covet earnestly gifts such as hers ; practise self-adornment for love of Him Who loveth thee." In the same volume, after praying, " O Lord Jesus, Who hast called Thy Church Thy sister, love, dove, spouse, abide close to us our Brother, our Friend, and prepare us "—speaking so far as if the soul's betrothal must be postponed until death—she ventures in verse to speak of herself as

Thy fainting spouse, yet still Thy spouse ;
Thy trembling dove, yet still Thy dove ;
Thine own by mutual vows,
By mutual love.

One stanza from a poem which Christina herself suppressed, but her brother published after her death under the

title *Now they Desire*, must be given as having the authentic
accent of a mystical soul :—

> There is a Love which fills desire
> And can our love requite :
> Like fire it draws our lesser fire,
> Like greater light our light :
> For it we agonize in strife,
> We yearn, we famish thus—
> Lo, in the far-off land of life
> Doth it not yearn for us ?

This erotic type of the mystical consciousness has its
temptations to become merely self-regarding ; but this danger
Christina Rossetti recognized in more than one of her pieces,
notably in that which she entitled *Take Care of Him*,
some stanzas of which will be a fitting close to this notice
of one aptly styled by Swinburne, " A shrine of holiest-
hearted song " :—

> *Thou whom I love, for whom I died,*
> *Lovest thou Me, My bride ?—*
> Low on my knees I love Thee, Lord,
> Believ'd in and ador'd.

> *In Me thou lovest Me : I call*
> *Thee to love Me in all.—*
> Brimful my heart, dear Lord, that so
> My love may overflow.

> *Love Me in sinners and in saints,*
> *In each who needs or faints.—*
> Lord, I will love Thee as I can
> In every brother man.

It was not originally designed that this volume should
deal with living writers ; but one such has already been

included, and, of the many women writing mystical verse
to-day, it would be base ingratitude to leave unnoticed her
who has done more, probably, than any other modern writer
to spread among English readers the knowledge and appreciation of mystical thought—the lady who still writes
under her maiden name of UNDERHILL. Nor could this
essay on English Mystical Verse end more appropriately
than with a short review of her efforts in this direction.

Miss Evelyn Underhill came to the front with a lengthy
treatise on *Mysticism*, which was well described by its
sub-title, " A Study in the Nature and Development of
Man's Spiritual Consciousness ". Manifestly the work of
a sound historian, with a philosophical training and a first-
hand knowledge of mystical experience, it was an almost
ideal introduction to the subject, and its readers awaited the
author's next work with eager expectation. This, when it
came, in the shape of a volume entitled *The Mystic Way*,
proved less acceptable to many minds. It certainly lacked
none of the qualities which marked its predecessor, and in
some respects showed an even surer touch. But it was
more abstruse and wordy, and inevitably disappointed the
more orthodox, as revealing a drift from historic Christianity
and from the institutional element of religion. Some of the
criticism which it aroused was, no doubt, unfair ; but it did,
perhaps, lie open to some slight stricture on its fog of technical terms and its inconsiderate handling of theological
problems. Again, the sub-title placed it well : it was
" A Psychological Study in Christian Origins " ; and even
those who disagreed most violently with the author's
Modernism could not deny the value of her two main con-
tentions :—

(*a*) That our Lord (Whose Divinity received reverent

recognition) perfectly fulfilled in His human nature the various stages of the Mystic Way ; and

(*b*) That the Sacraments (which there is no attempt to depreciate) are dramatic symbols of the mystic process.

But it is Miss Underhill's third mystical treatise, *Practical Mysticism*, that demands the fullest notice here. It is a complete manual, systematic in arrangement, yet carrying the reader along with an almost breathless swing, simple yet forceful in diction, full of humour and common-sense. It is proposed to give here the briefest possible abstract of its teaching, with illustrative extracts from Miss Underhill's verse, contained so far in two volumes entitled *Immanence* and *Theophanies*.

The book is quite definitely designed for " normal people," everyone being regarded as a potential mystic. The author knows (witness her poem, *Lux in Tenebris*) that there is danger in exposing " an untaught vision " to the glare ; and in her first book on *Mysticism*, she admitted that a " mystical education, of course, presumes a something that can be educated : the ' New Birth,' the awakening of the deeper self, must have taken place before it can begin ". But she rightly feels that the old esoteric attitude, " My secret to myself," is an unworthy one ; and she has a deep pity for " the practical man " with his shut-in, unillumined life in a " stuffy world ". Like *Celestial Beauty*, who speaks in a poem of hers so named, she finds it sad to

> Watch mankind go walking in its sleep
> About the bit of heaven it calls the earth.

In a more recent poem, she divided mankind into two great classes, *Bond and Free*, the latter being in yet another piece described as *The Secret People*, who, being

Yet mortal, are immortal made :
They are aware of sudden intimations, quickening streams
Of energy untainted by the flesh,
And in their deeds attain
New splendour of fulfilment.  Through the mesh
Of baffling sense, sometimes upon the hair
They know a hand in benediction laid,
And feel a Presence there.

Defining mysticism as "the art of union with Reality,"
Miss Underhill declares that "the essence of mystical contemplation is summed up in these two experiences—union
with the flux of life, and union with the Whole in which
all lesser realities are resumed".  This may be illustrated
by a short piece called *Theophany* :—

Deep cradled in the fringed mow to lie
And feel the rhythmic flux of life sweep by,
This is to know the easy heaven that waits
Before our timidly-embattled gates :
To show the exultant leap and thrust of things
Outward toward perfection, in the heart
Of every bud to see the folded wings,
Discern the patient Whole in every part.

Her scheme of mystical development is fivefold, with two
stages of preparation, and three of attainment.  As regards
the first stage of preparation, that disciplining of the attention which is called Recollection, she suggests subjects on
which to meditate by way of gaining "a starry view of
life" : one with "a philosophic twist may try to meditate
on Time, Succession, even Being itself ; or again on human
intercourse, birth, growth, and death, on a flower, a river,
the various tapestries of the sky" ; one with a religious turn
has a wide choice, "from the plaster image to the mysteries

of Faith ".  As examples of such meditations to be found
in her own verse, the poems entitled *The Tree* and *Prima-
vera* may be instanced.

The second stage of preparation is Purgation in its double
sense of Detachment from material things and the Mortification of turbulent passions.  The supreme importance of this
stage is urgently insisted upon, since the mystical character,
compounded of " courage, singleness of heart, and self-
control," is " far more important than the mystical temperament or mystical vision ".

After perseverance in these preparatory stages, the true
contemplative life—a life, not of dreaming, but of strenuous
tension—can begin.  Man has correspondence with three
levels of existence, the Natural, the Spiritual, and the
Divine ; accordingly, by three forms of contemplation, he
should seek union with each of these manifestations of
Reality : the Natural World of Becoming, the Metaphysical World of Being, and the Absolute, GOD Himself,
" within Whom these opposites are found as one ".

The first form of contemplation is " the discovery of
GOD in His creatures ".  The reader is advised by Miss
Underhill to " stretch out by a distinct act of loving will
towards one of the myriad manifestations of life that surround you. . . . As to the object of contemplation, it
matters little.  From Alp to insect, anything will do, provided that your attitude is right ; for all things in this world
towards which you are stretching out are linked together,
and one truly apprehended will be the gateway to the rest."
The result should be a sensitiveness to the Divine Reality
and Beauty of all things, not excluding what the uninitiated
would find mean and despicable.  In this context, reference
may be made to a large number of poems : besides some

already named, there are *Immanence, Uxbridge Road,
Heaven or Hell,* and *Planting Time,* all to be found in
the volume named after the first of these poems ; and, in
the volume entitled *Theophanies,* there are *Dynamic Love,
The Likeness,* and *Forest Epiphany,* all well-nigh irre-
sistibly calling for quotation.

Before passing on to the next stage of contemplation,
Miss Underhill bids her readers beware " the blasphemous
other-worldliness of the false mystic," a warning which is
finely echoed in the poem, *Memento Homo,* with these as
its first and last stanzas :—

> Remember, man, that dust thou art—
> Dust, by the spirit stung to life ;
> Yea, recollect thyself a part
>     Of the eternal strife.

> .    .    .    .    .    .

> Remember, then, with healing pain
> Thy graceless other-worldly mood ;
> Turn to the living earth again,
>     And thou shalt find her good.

On the other hand, a *caveat* is entered against " the
cardinal error of the nature-mystic ". This, too, has a
verse-parallel in the piece entitled *Nature ;* while *The
Summit* and *Beyond the Garden* both repeat the warning
note struck in the prose manual against the " limited desire "
that

> Cannot dare
> To risk the upper air,
> The hard ascent
> And stony summits, but would ever go
> Just high enough for beauty and too low
> For desolation. You shall never know,

> Thus shelter'd by the ring
> Of noble dreams and mounting thoughts, the sting
> Of truth, the wide horizons of the real.

The soul, then, must aim, in a second stage of Contemplation, at "a more perfect and unmediated union with the Substance of All That Is, on a plane of existence with which the bodily senses have no attachment". Here the contemplative enters into a silence in which he is promised a satisfaction and certitude, ineffable and unanalyzable. "It calls for the utmost adoration of which you are capable, and, mysteriously, gives love for love." In this connexion, resting satisfied with a mere reference to the poem called *Introversion*, we must reproduce, in its entirety, that entitled *Supersensual* :—

> When first the busy, clumsy tongue is still'd,
> Save that some childish, stammering words of love
> The coming birth of man's true language prove :
> When, one and all,
> The wistful, seeking senses are fulfill'd
> With strange, austere delight :
> When eye and ear
> Are inward turn'd to meet the flooding light,
> The cadence of Thy coming quick to hear :
> When on Thy mystic flight,
> Thou Swift yet Changeless, herald breezes bring
> To scent the heart's swept cell
> With incense from the thurible of spring,
> The fragrance which the lily seeks in vain :
> When touch no more may tell
> The verities of contact unexpress'd,
> And, deeply press'd,
> To that surrender which is holiest pain,
> We taste Thy very rest—

Ah, then we find,
Folded about by kindly-nurturing night,
Instinct with silence sweetly musical,
The rapt communion of the mind with Mind.
Then may the senses fall
Vanquish'd indeed, nor dread
That this their dear defeat be counted sin :
For every door of flesh shall lift its head,
Because the King of Life is enter'd in.

But this is, " of necessity, a fleeting experience," and it
will be counter-balanced by " periods of darkness and
boredom ". (Her poem, *The Dark Night*, tells of this,
as may be guessed from the title). The remedy is to
acquiesce wholeheartedly in the deprivation ; and a true
disinterested resignation to the Divine Will may prove the
ante-chamber to the third form of contemplation, involving
" mysterious contacts," with a " clear certitude of intercourse and possession," which may, or may not, be accompanied with ecstasy. The poems *Icthus* and *White
Magic* are apparently reminiscent of such moments of
patience rewarded.

In the closing section of her treatise, Miss Underhill insists upon the practical utility of Mysticism in promoting
enlargement and vigour of soul. The true mystic, not only
leads a life which is a veritable theophany, but also (as
history so plainly shows) serves the Supreme Artist as " a
living ardent tool," employing, as we may gather from
her *Stigmata*,

Busy hands
That labour to fulfill
Industrious love's demands.

In this very inadequate abstract of a book packed with

vitalizing thought and expert guidance, the reader may miss the more distinctively Christian aspects of mysticism. The omission is deliberate, however, for, in this particular volume, Miss Underhill, wishing to spread her net as widely as possible, refrains from urging "the special claim of any one theological system". But in her verse the Christian note is clearly struck. Several pieces reveal what she has elsewhere termed "Nature's Christliness". "In the rapturous vitality of the birds," she says in *Mysticism*, " and in their splendid gleaming flight : in the swelling of buds and the sacrificial beauty of the flowers : in the great and solemn rhythms of the sea—there is somewhat of Bethlehem in these things, somewhat too of Calvary in their self-giving pains". Three poems may be named in this connexion : *Quam Dilecta Tabernacula Tua, Corpus Christi*, and *The Voice from the Cross*, the last-named, especially, bringing out most felicitously the synthesis of all the suffering pangs of Nature in the Passion of Christ.

We need not agree with Miss Underhill that the mystical consciousness is latent in every one, or that the Christian who falls short of it is, necessarily, a rather sorry creature. But, on the other hand, it is quite time that the members of our Church should throw off the distrust of mysticism which is driving not a few out of her communion. There is a growing disgust with the compromises and materialistic stagnation which satisfy too many of those in her ministerial ranks, and, still more, with the arid antiquarianism without conviction of the supernatural, and the merely notional assent to truths not apprehended, of too many of her professional theologians. (Self-knowledge prompts the words.) There is, perhaps, no lesson that modern Anglicanism needs more to learn than that taught in the volume mentioned on page 4 above, *The Mystical Element in Religion,* in which Baron von Hügel shows so convincingly that a religion, to be complete, must be an amalgam of institutionalism, rationalism, and mysticism in due proportions.

The mystic of to-day has to bear in mind our Lord's reproof, recorded by the most mystical of the Evangelists : " Except ye see signs and wonders, ye will not believe " ; and he may well recall, too, St Paul's warning, " not to think of himself more highly than he ought to think, but so to think as to think soberly, according as GOD has dealt to each man a measure of faith ". No one, in fact, must outrun his own convictions, or claim any degree of illumination which is not really his own. But, on the other hand, the Marthas of this age can hardly afford to sneer at the Maries, as though, after all, the latter had chosen the useless rather than the " good part ". Even if we cannot reach ecstasy —if, indeed, we are not at all sure that we should enjoy the experience—we can, at least, appreciate the wider vision, the more vital religion, and the deeper spirituality, to be found in the writings of the mystics. The present writer, at any rate, feels it right to end his task by thanking GOD that there are such possibilities in our human nature as mysticism reveals, and by echoing the wistful regret voiced in William Watson's lines :—

> My mind, half-envying what it cannot share,
> Reveres the reverence which it cannot feel.

# A BIBLIOGRAPHY.

## GENERAL.

Augustine, Saint. *Confessions*, with an English translation by Watts, W. (1631). (Loeb Classical Library), 1912.

Bucke, R. M. *Cosmic Consciousness.* A Study in the Evolution of the Human Mind. Philadelphia, 1905.

Chandler, Arthur. *Ara Coeli.* An Essay in Mystical Theology. 1908.

*Faith and Experience.* An Analysis of the Factors of Religious Knowledge. 1911.

*The Cult of the Passing Moment.* 1914.

Dionysius the Areopagite. (See under Sharpe.)

Hepher, Cyril. *The Fellowship of Silence :* Being experiences in the common use of prayer without words. 1915.

Hügel, Fr. von. *The Mystical Element in Religion. . . .* 2 vols. 1908.

*Eternal Life.* 1912.

Inge, W. R. *Christian Mysticism* (Bampton Lectures). 1899. Cheaper Edn., 1912.

*Light, Life, and Love.* Selections from the German Mystics, with Introduction. (Methuen's Library of Devotion.) 1904.

*Studies of English Mystics* (St. Margaret's Lectures). 1906.

*Personal Idealism and Mysticism* (Paddock Lectures). 1907.

*Faith and its Psychology.* 1909.

James, William. *The Varieties of Religious Experience* (Gifford Lectures). 1902.

Mercer, J. E. *Nature Mysticism.* 1913.

Plato. *Dialogues.* Translated and edited by Jowett, B. 5 vols. 1892.
>  *Five Dialogues.* Translated by various hands. Introduction by Lindsay, A. D. (Everyman's Library.) 1910.

Plotinus. *Select Works.* Translated by Taylor, Thomas. 1817. Reprinted, with Introduction by Mead, G. R. S. (Bohn's Popular Library.) 1914.

Récéjac, E. *The Bases of the Mystic Knowledge.* Translated from the French by Upton, S. C. 1899.

Sharpe, A. B. *Mysticism :* Its True Nature and Value (with a translation of Dionysius the Areopagite's *Mystical Theology*).

Underhill, Evelyn. (See under Chapter XI).

Vaughan, R. A. *Hours with the Mystics.* 2 vols. Third Edition, 1880.

## CHAPTER I.

Morley, Henry. *English Writers.* (Second Volume.) 1887 ff.

Hales, Thomas. *An Old English Miscellany.* Ed. Morris, R. (Early English Text Society.) 1872.

Rolle, Richard. *Works.* Ed. Horstmann, C. 2 vols. (Library of Early English Writers.) 1895.

Benson, R. H. *A Book of the Love of Jesus.* A Collection of Ancient English Devotions. 1905.

Furnival, F. J. *Political, Religious, and Love Poems.* (E. E. T. S.). 1866. New Edition, 1903.

## CHAPTER II.

Spenser, Edmund. *Fowre Hymnes.* 1596.
>  *Poetical Works.* Ed. Smith, J. C., and de Selincourt, E. (The Oxford Poets.) 1912.

Fletcher, Giles. *Christ's Victorie*, and Triumph in Heaven, and Earth, over, and after Death. Cambridge, 1610.

Fletcher, Phineas. *The Purple Island*, or the Isle of Man : together with Piscatorie Eclogs and other Poeticall Miscellanies. Cambridge, 1633.

  *A Father's Testament.* . . . 1670.

Fletcher, Giles and Phineas. *Poetical Works.* Ed. Boas, F. S. 2 vols. (Cambridge English Classics.) 1908.

## CHAPTER III.

Davies, Sir John. *Nosce teipsum.* . . . 1599.

  *Works.* Ed. Grosart, A. B. 3 vols. (Fuller Worthies' Library.) 1869 ff.

Donne, John. *Poems.* 1633. Reprinted, with additions, 1650.

  *Poems.* Ed. Chambers, E. K. 2 vols. (The Muses' Library.) n.d.

  *Works.* Ed. Alford, H. 6 vols. 1839.

  *Devotions*, to which is prefixed his *Life* by Isaak Walton. (Pickering's Edition.) 1840.

  *Life and Letters*, by Gosse, E. 2 vols. 1899.

Heywood, Thomas. *Hierarchie of Blessed Angels.* . . . 1635.

## CHAPTER IV.

Herbert, George. *The Temple.* Sacred Poems and Private Ejaculations. Cambridge, 1633. Often reprinted, e.g. Pickering's Edition, 1838, or in Methuen's Library of Devotion, ed. Gibson, E. S. C.

  *A Priest to the Temple*, or The Country Parson. . . . Included in *Remains*, 1652, and reprinted, ed. Beeching, H. C. Oxford, 1898.

  *English Works.* Ed. Palmer, G. H. 3 vols. 1905.

*Life,* by Isaak Walton. 1670. Reprinted, with other Lives, in the Temple Classics. 2 vols. 1898.

*Life,* by Daniell, J. J. 1902.

*The Hundred and Ten Considerations of John Valdesso.* Translated from the Italian by Nicholas Ferrar, with letter and notes by G. H. 1638. Reprinted, ed. Chapman, F., 1905.

Harvey, Christopher. *The Synagogue,* or The Shadow of the Temple. Published anonymously at the end of 1640 edition of *The Temple.*

*The School of the Heart.* 1647. Published anonymously, and often reprinted as *Emblems* by Quarles.

*Poems.* Ed. Grosart, A. B. (Fuller Worthies' Library.) 1874.

Quarles, Francis. *Divine Poems.* 1630.

*Emblemes.* 1635.

*Enchyridion.* 1640.

*Judgement and Mercy for Afflicted Souls.* 2 Parts. 1646.

*Works.* Ed. Grosart, A. B. 3 vols. (Chertsey Worthies' Library.) 1878 ff.

## CHAPTER V.

Crashaw, Richard. *Steps to the Temple.* . . . 1646. Second Edition, 1648.

*Carmen Deo Nostro.* . . . Paris, 1652.

*Poems.* Ed. Waller, A. R. (Cambridge English Classics.) 1904; or ed. Tutin, J. R. (Muses' Library), 1905.

Beaumont, Joseph. *Psyche,* or Love's Mystery. 1648. With additions, 1702.

*Poems.* Ed. Grosart, A. B. 2 vols. (Chertsey Worthies' Library.) 1878 ff.

*Minor Poems.* Ed. Robinson, Eloise. 1914.

Benlowes, Edward. *Theophila.* 1652.
> *Minor Poets of the Caroline Period.* (1st. vol.) Ed.
> Saintsbury, George. Oxford, 1905.

## CHAPTER VI.

Vaughan, Henry. *Silex Scintillans.* Pt. I, 1650. Pt. II, 1655.
> *Olor Iscanus.* 1651.
> *Thalia Rediviva.* 1678.
> *Poems.* Ed. Chambers, E. K. 2 vols. (Muses' Library.) 1905.
> *Works.* Ed. Martin, L. C. 2 vols. Oxford, 1917.

Vaughan, Thomas. *Anthroposophia Theomagica.* 1650.
> *Lumen de Lumine.* 1651. Reprinted, ed. Waite, A. E. 1910.
> *Aula Lucis.* 1652.
> *Verse Remains.* At end of Grosart's edition of Henry Vaughan's Works. (Fuller Worthies' Library, 4 vols.) 1868 ff. Also in Pembroke Booklets (No. 2). Ed. Tutin, J. R. Hull, 1905.

Pordage, John. *Theologia Mystica.* 1683.

Pordage, Samuel. *Mundorum Explicatio.* . . . [By S. P.]. 1663.

Behmen, Jacob. *Works.* Englished by John Sparrow and others. 1645-1662.

## CHAPTER VII.

More, Henry. *Psychozoia.* . . . 1642.
> *Philosophical Poems* [including the above]. 1647.
> *Observations upon Anthroposophia Theomagica.* [Under the pseudonym, Alazonamastix.] 1650.
> *The Second Lash of Alazonamastix.* 1651.
> *An Explanation of the Grand Mystery of Godliness.* 1660.

*Philosophical Writings.* 1662.

*Divine Dialogues.* 1668.

*Poems.* Ed. Grosart, A. B. (Chertsey Worthies' Library.) 1878 ff.

*Life*, by Ward, Richard. 1710. Reprinted, ed. Howard, M. F., 1911.

*Rational Theology and Christian Philosophy in England in the Seventeenth Century*, by Tulloch, John. 2 vols. 1872.

Norris, John. *Poems and Discourses.* 1684. With corrections and additions, 1687.

*Reason and Faith. . . .* 1689.

*Reflections upon the Conduct of Human Life.* [A letter to Lady Masham.] 1690.

*The Theory and Regulation of Love.* [Letters between J. N. and Henry More.] 1694.

*Letters concerning the Love of God.* [A Correspondence with Mary Astell.] 1695.

*An Essay towards the Theory of an Ideal World.* 1701-4.

*Poems.* Ed. Grosart, A. B., in 3rd vol. of Miscellanies. (Fuller Worthies' Library.) 1868 ff.

*Selected Poems.* Ed. Tutin, J. R. (Pembroke Booklets, No. 2.) Hull, 1905.

Traherne, Thomas. *Christian Ethics.* [With poems included.] 1675.

*A Serious and Pathetical Contemplation of the Mercies of God.* [With poems.] Published anonymously, ed. Hickes, G. 1699.

*Poetical Works.* Ed. Dobell, B. 1903. 2nd ed., 1906.

*Poems of Felicity.* Ed. Bell, H. I. Oxford, 1910.

*Centuries of Meditations.* Ed. Dobell, B. 1908.

## CHAPTER VIII.

Byrom, John. *Poems.* Manchester, 1773. Reprinted, with additions, 2 vols., Leeds, 1814. Reprinted, in 4 vols., by the Chetham Society, 1853 ff.

*Diary.* Ed. Ward, A. R. 4 vols. (Chetham Society.) 1854 ff.

*Works of William Law.* 9 vols. 1753-76. Privately reprinted, ed. Morgan, G. B., 1893 ff.

*The Liberal and Mystical Writings of William Law.* Ed. Scott Palmer, W. 1908.

Brooke, Henry. *Poetical Works.* 4 vols. 1792.

*The Fool of Quality.* 5 vols. 1766-70. Reprinted in condensed form by Wesley, John. 1781. Also ed. Kingsley, Charles. 2 vols. 1859. Also ed. Baker, E. A. 1906.

Blake, William. *Works.* Ed. Ellis, E. J., and Yeats, W. B. 3 vols. 1893.

*Poetical Works.* Ed. Sampson, J. (The Oxford Poets.) 1905.

*Poetical Works,* with the unpublished *French Revolution,* the *Minor Prophetic Books* and *Selections* from the others. Ed. Sampson, J. Oxford, 1913.

*Life,* by Gilchrist, A. 1880. Reprinted, ed. Robertson, W. G., 1906.

## CHAPTER IX.

Wordsworth, William. *Poetical Works.* With Introduction by Morley, John. 1888.

*Works.* [Prose and Verse.] Ed. Knight, W. 16 vols. 1896 f.

*Life,* by Harper, G. M. 2 vols. 1916.

Coleridge, Samuel Taylor. *Poetical Works.* Ed. Coleridge, E. H. (Oxford Poets.)

*The Statesman's Manual.* 1816.

*Aids to Reflection.* 1825. Reprinted, with *The Confessions of an Inquiring Spirit,* etc. (Bohn's Popular Library), 1913.

    *Table Talk.* 2 vols. 1835. Reprinted in 1 vol., 1836. Best edition, 1884.

    *Notes on English Divines.* 2 vols. 1853.

    *Letters.* 2 vols. 1895.

    *Anima Poetæ.* From his unpublished Note-books. 1895.

    *Narrative of Life,* by Campbell, J. D. Second edition, 1896.

Tennyson, Alfred. *Works.* 1894.

    *Memoir,* by his son, Hallam. 1897.

Myers, Frederick W. H. *St. Paul.* 1867.

    *Poems.* 1870.

    *The Renewal of Youth and other Poems.* 1882.

    *Human Personality and its Survival of Bodily Death.* 2 vols. 1903. Abridged by Myers, L. H., 1907.

    *Fragments of Prose and Poetry.* Ed. Myers, Eveleen. 1904.

MacDonald, George. *Within and Without.* 1855.

    *Poems.* 1857.

    *The Disciples and other Poems.* 1867.

    *Poetical Works.* 2 vols. 1893. [Do not include the work following.]

    *The Diary of an Old Soul,* A Book of Strife in the form of. 1880. Reprinted, with Translations, 1905.

    *Phantastes.* 1858. Reprinted in the Everyman's Library, 1915.

    *David Elginbrod.* 1863.

    *Robert Falconer.* 1868.

    *Thomas Wingfold, Curate.* 1876.

*Sir Gibbie.* 1879.   Reprinted in the Everyman's Library, 1914.

*Lilith.* 1895.

*Unspoken Sermons.* 3 vols. 1867, 1885, 1889.

*Fairy Tales.* 5 vols. 1904.

*Biographical Appreciation* by Johnson, J. 1906.

Patmore, Coventry K. D. *The Angel in the House.* 1860.

*The Victories of Love.* 1862.

*The Unknown Eros and other Odes.* 1877.

*Collected Poems.* 1906.

*The Rod, the Root and the Flower.* 1895.

*Memoirs*, by Champneys, B. 1900.

Thompson, Francis. *Poems.* 1893.

*Sister Songs.* 1895.

*New Poems.* 1897.

*Works.* [Vols. I and II, Verse; Vol. III, Prose.] 1913.

*Life*, by Meynell, Everard. 1913.


## CHAPTER X.

Keble, John. *The Christian Year.* 1827.   Often reprinted, e.g. in Methuen's Library of Devotion, ed. Lock, W., 1898.

*Lyra Innocentium.* 1846.   Often reprinted, e.g. in Methuen's Library of Devotion, ed. Lock, W., 1899.

*Miscellaneous Poems.* Ed. Moberley, G., 1869.

*Tracts for the Times.* No. 89. 1841.   Reprinted 1868.

*Life*, by Lock, W. 1892.

Williams, Isaac. *The Cathedral.* 1838.   Reprinted, ed. Benham, W., 1889.

*Thoughts in Past Years.* 1838.

*The Baptistery.* 1842.   Sixth edition, enlarged, 1852.

*Tracts for the Times.* Nos. 80 and 87. 1839, 1840.

*A Devotional Commentary on the Gospel Narrative.*
1843 ff.
*Sermons on the Characters of the Old Testament.*
1856.
*Autobiography.* Ed. Prevost, G. 1892.
Trench, Richard Chevenix. *Poems.* 1865. New edition, in
2 vols., 1886.
*Letters.* Ed. Author of *Charles Lowder.* 2 vols.
1888.
Kingsley, Charles. *Poems,* Collected Edition. 1872.
*Theologia Germanica,* with Introduction by C. K.
1854. Reprinted in the Golden Treasury Series, 1874.
*History and Life of Tauler,* with 25 Sermons trans-
lated by Winkworth, S. Introduction by C. K. 1857.
*Literary and General Essays.* 1880.
*Life,* by his wife. 1876.
Brown, Thomas Edward. *Collected Poems.* 1901.
*Selected Poems.* (Golden Treasury Series.) 1908.
*Letters.* Ed. Irwin, S. T. 1900.
Dixon, Richard Watson. *Christ's Company and other Poems.*
1861.
*St. John in Patmos.* A Prize Poem. 1863.
*Historical Odes and other Poems.* 1864.
*Mano.* 1883.
*Odes and Eclogues.* 1884.
*Lyrical Poems.* 1887.
*The Story of Eudocia and her Brothers.* 1888.
*Last Poems.* Selected by Bridges, Robert. 1905.
*Selected Poems,* with Memoir by Bridges, Robert.
1909.
Hollings, George Seymour. *Porta Regalis.* 1894.
*Paradoxes of the Love of God.* 1897.
*In Via.* 1906.
*The Divine Lover.* 1908.

Cripps, Arthur Shearley. *Lyra Evangelista.* Oxford, 1909.

> *Pilgrimage of Grace.* Oxford, 1912.
> *Pilgrim's Joy.* Oxford, 1916.
> *Lake and War.* Oxford, 1917.
> *Faerylands Forlorn.* African Tales. Oxford, 1910.

## CHAPTER XI.

Brontë, Emily. *Poems*, by Currer, Ellis, and Acton Bell. 1846. [22 poems by E. B.]

> *Wuthering Heights*, by Ellis Bell. 1847. Reprinted, with Selections from the *Literary Remains* of Ellis and Acton Bell, 1850. [17 unpublished poems by E. B.]
> *Poems.* Privately printed [67]. New York, 1902.
> *Complete Works.* 2 vols. [The volume of Poetry contains 71 unpublished poems.] 1914.
> *Life of Charlotte Brontë*, by Gaskell, E. C. 1857. Reprinted, ed. Sinclair, May. (Everyman's Library), 1908.
> *The Brontës and their Circle*, by Shorter, C. K. 1896. Reprinted in the Wayfarer's Library, 1914.

Rossetti, Christina. *Poems.* 1890.

> *Verses.* Reprinted from *Called to be Saints, Time Flies*, and *The Face of the Deep*, 1893.
> *New Poems.* Ed. Rossetti, W. M. 1896.
> *Poetical Works*, with Memoir by Rossetti, W. M. 1904.
> *Called to be Saints.* The Minor Festivals devotionally studied. 1881.
> *Time Flies.* A Reading Diary. 1885.
> *The Face of the Deep.* A Devotional Commentary on the Apocalypse. 1892.